Eighth Edition

Basic Camp Management
An Introduction to Camp Administration

Armand and Beverly Ball

An American Camp Association Book

enriching lives, building tomorrows

Copyright 1979, 1987, 1990, 1995, 2000, 2004, 2009, 2012 by American Camping Association, Inc. Available in Russian from the Union of Children Associations of St. Petersburg, in Japanese from the National Camping Association of Japan, and in Portuguese from Christian Camping International/Brazil.

ISBN: 978-1-60679-208-7
Library of Congress Control Number: 2012931764
Book layout: Studio J Art & Design
Front cover design: Studio J Art & Design
Front cover photo: Cheley Colorado Camps, Estes Park, CO

Healthy Learning
P.O. Box 1828
Monterey, CA 93942
www.healthylearning.com

American Camping Association, Inc.
5000 State Road 67, North
Martinsville, Indiana 46151-7902
www.ACAcamps.org

Dedicated to Kathy and Robin, who found a love of people
and of the outdoors while growing up at camp.

And to the staff of YMCA Camp Widjiwagan, St. Paul, Minnesota,
1963–1974, who will always be a part of our lives.

Dedication

Acknowledgments

We wish to express our thanks to the staff of the American Camp Association, Ed Schirick of Schirick and Associates Insurance Brokers, Inc., (a division of Bollinger, Inc.), Linda Ecerg, RN, of Concordia Language Camps and the Association of Camp Nurses, Dr. Dwight Jewson of Strategic Frameworking, Inc., and Dr. Paul Schlag of Western Illinois University for their assistance reviewing and contributing relevant materials. We also express our appreciation to Connie Coutellier and the training teams of the Basic Camp Director's Courses for their leadership in revising the Basic Camp Director Course curriculum, which, to a large degree, we are trying to parallel in the outline of this edition.

Contents

Contents

Contents

Contents

The idea of the first edition of *Basic Camp Management* in the mid-1970s was to provide a manual for the very new camp director and to keep the volume short and simple. With each revision, additional information and topics have been added, changing it from the rather elementary volume we had originally visualized. The major factor in that change has been the growing complexity of the management of camps and conference centers. The other has been the continued use of the book as a text in college courses, the American Camp Association's Basic Camp Director Courses, and the International Camp Director's Courses, all requiring additional information.

The quotations at the beginning of the chapters come from a variety of publications dating back some years and further illustrate the ongoing efforts of many directors toward professionalism, lest we come to think that all of our concepts are new to this century.

We hope this book will be a practical help to persons entering our field as well as to the experienced director and will inspire better camping for all.

Armand and Beverly Ball
Sanibel Island, Florida
January 2012

Preface

Terminology

Throughout this book, terms have been used that should be thought of in the broadest sense. Following are some brief explanations.

The term *camp* has been used throughout as the comprehensive term describing all types of operations; it can also be interpreted as a camp, a camp that also rents its facilities for conference/retreat/environmental education use, a conference/retreat center, or an environmental education center. It may be a program using a rented site, a site that rents facilities, or a site that encompasses its own program.

The term *director* is used to refer to the administrator of the camp, conference/retreat center, or program who is responsible for the site the majority of the time. (Although some organizations operate multiple camps and may have an administrator in the central office who supervises several directors, this pattern is not the most common.)

The term *operator or owner* is used to designate the entity (whether an individual, a partnership, an organization or corporation) that owns the operation. In some cases, the ownership involves the property and site and/or the program operated on the site. In other cases, it involves only the program operated in a rented facility.

The term *independent* camp refers to a camp ordinarily organized for profit, sometimes identified as a private-independent camp or for-profit camp. The term *not-for-profit* is used to identify camps that operated under a 501(c)(3) Internal Revenue Service classification or by a government body.

This classification would include agency, organizational, public, and religiously affiliated camps, as well as number of camps that were at on time for profit camps and now operate under a board of directors in compliance with 501(c)(3) regulations. The term *core areas* refers to the 14 topics that make up the body of knowledge for the camping profession, as defined by the American Camp Association. All the core areas are addressed in the book. Since this book provides an introduction to camp administration, you will want to pursue a more in-depth study of each as you gain experience. The core competencies are:

- Youth/Adult Growth and Development
- Learning Environment and Curricula
- Program Planning
- Observation, Assessment, Evaluation

- Professional Development and Leadership
- Health and Wellness
- Risk Management
- Cultural Competence
- Families and Community Connection
- Nature and Environment
- Business Management and Practices
- Human Resources Management
- Site/Facilities Management

Listed at the end of each chapter are references to the *American Camp Association's Accreditation Standards for Camp Programs and Services* (2012 edition) and the self-assessment tool, Foundational Practices, which is a part of that volume. Though these are modern documents, they have been developed through a professional review process over 50-plus years. These tools are updated regularly, so it behooves the reader to check current editions for updates, and the website of the American Camp Association: www.ACAcamps.org.

Readers will note a variance in the use of American Camping Association and American Camp Association. The former is used in historical references and in citing publications since the corporate name remains American Camping Association, Inc. The American Camp Association is used in reference to activities and work after 2003.

Terminology

Disclaimer

The purpose of this book is to provide an overview of issues with which camp directors should be familiar. It should be recognized that camp directors and others who run camp operations will require further education and experience in each of the areas covered herein. Neither the publisher nor the authors of this book undertake to verify that individuals who use this book are trained appropriately. Nor do the publisher or authors assume any responsibility for liability for any consequences of the use of information in this book. Further, the American Camping Association, Inc., and the authors hereby expressly disclaim any responsibility, liability, or duty to camp administrators, operators, personnel, any program participants or their families, for any such liability arising out of injury, illness, or loss to any person or organization, by the failure of such administrators or camp personnel to seek further training.

THE TRADITION OF CAMPING

Chapter One

Camp Echo (Burlingham, NY)

Camping needs the imaginative, the picturesque, the romantic; needs it for its own attractiveness and for the sake of young America, for whom the imaginative will be the only enduring type of play … [I]f it is worthy, [the camp] is one of the greatest socializing, humanizing, civilizing factors which can enter the life of a boy or girl.[1]

—Bernard S. Mason

Organized camping began in North America in the mid-19th century. No accurate record exists of the exact location of the first actual camp. To gain a better understanding of the growth of the organized camp movement during its first hundred years, *History of Organized Camping: The First 100 Years* by Eleanor Eells and *Blue Lake & Rocky Shore* by the Ontario Camping Association provide historical context. However, it may be helpful to offer a brief summary of that history as a background for readers new to the field.

Historical Overview

The Beginnings

The Ontario Camping Association Committee reports that, in 1840, a church camp group met for summer camping under canvas at Hogg's Hollow (since renamed York Mills), just north of Toronto's present city limits. It appears that other camps did not come into existence in Canada until the late 1800s. The first recorded organized camp experience in the United States occurred in 1861, when Frederick William Gunn, the headmaster of the Gunnery School for Boys in Washington, Connecticut, led a group of students on a 40-mile trek to Milford on Long Island Sound. After the two-day hike, the boys camped out for 10 days and then hiked back to the school. This experience was stimulated by the interest of youth at that time in the Civil War, and the encampments and campfires common to the soldiers of that day. A plaque commemorates that camp at Welch's Point near Milford. Mr. Gunn continued to offer such camp experiences until 1879.

In 1876, the first private independent camp was organized by Dr. Joseph Rothrock, a practicing physician in Wilkes-Barre, Pennsylvania. The camp was designed to improve the health of children and emphasized physical fitness and health; the camp was short lived. In 1880, Camp Chocorua for boys aged 12 to 16 was organized on Asquam Lake, New Hampshire, by Ernest Balch. This camp continued for eight years and centered around sports activities as well as the actual daily living chores of cooking, cleaning, and dishwashing. A decidedly spiritual emphasis was given to the camp. In both of these camps, fees were charged to cover the costs. These fees were, however, not very realistic because both camps closed with deficits.

The first camp run by an organization was founded in 1874 by the Philadelphia YWCA as a vacation camp named Sea Rest at Asbury Park, New Jersey. In 1885, Sumner F. Dudley founded a YMCA camp near Newburg, New York. The camp, which still bears his name, later moved to Lake Champlain near Westport, New York, and is the oldest continuously operating camp in the United States. The oldest camp continuously operating on the same site is Keewaydin Camps, Salisbury, Vermont, which was founded as an independent camp in 1894 and is operated by the Keewaydin Foundation.

In Canada, the first organizational camp and first independent camp were both organized in the same year: 1894—YMCA Kamp Kanawana in Quebec and Camp Keewaydin (formerly Kamp Kah Kiou) in Ontario.

All of these camps were exclusively for boys. In 1876, the French Recreation Class for Girls was opened on Lake Placid, New York, as a summer experience for girls. In 1900, Camp Redcroft was opened in Hebron, New Hampshire by Mrs. Oscar Holt. In 1892, an independent camp, called Camp Arey, reserved a summer session for girls. By 1902, three camps for girls began: Kehonka in New Hampshire, and Wyonegonic Camps and Pinelands Camps in Maine.

It was not until 1922 that the first independent girls' camp was organized in Canada: Camp Glen Bernard in Ontario. This delay in providing organized camping for girls was due in some degree to the Victorian attitudes toward young women's dress, decorum, movement, careers, and education.

During this same period, organizational camping was growing rapidly, with the development of Fresh Air Camps, designed to serve inner-city youth. These camps sprang up in Connecticut (1886), Wisconsin (1887), and New York City (1892), as did Life Camps (1887) in Connecticut and New Jersey. Settlement houses sprang up during this period and established camps in such urban centers as Boston, Pittsburgh, New York City, and Chicago (1898 to 1908). A camp for children with disabilities began in Chicago circa 1900. National youth organizations came into being in the early 1900s with their own camping programs: Boy Scouts of America (1910), Camp Fire Girls [now Camp Fire Boys and Girls] (1911), and Girl Scouts of the U.S.A. (1912).

Camps throughout this period primarily focused on getting young people out of the city and into a healthy, rural environment with wholesome recreational activities. However, much of the experience dealt with activities necessary to daily living (e.g., cooking, cleaning). Boys' camps tended to place value on rugged outdoor living. Girls' camps also included hiking and aquatics, with an emphasis on the creative arts. Most of the camps of this era had a strong spiritual component, often in conjunction with Bible study. Moral or character development was a key element. Camps were often small in size during this period, quite rustic, and placed a great deal of emphasis on small group living.

The emergence of national youth organizations and local social-service organizations and the continued growth and success of independent camps stimulated growth of camps in a number of areas. Camps began to spread westward, springing up in Pennsylvania, West Virginia, Illinois, Missouri, and California. Local governments started camps in Los Angeles in 1914, Detroit in 1915, and Kansas City in 1920.

Camps began an expansion from around 1910 onward. Abigail A. Van Slyck attributes World War I as a factor related to "intensifying the military practices at boys' camps, while also providing a powerful rationale for extending the summer camp experiences to girls." She also ascribes World War I with "encouraging newly formed groups such as Camp Fire Girls and the Girl Scouts to enter the camping field in a big way."[2] The more militaristic alignment of tents/cabins in rows with a flagpole at one end and a central building at the other end lived on for many years beyond the time of such a strong military emphasis in some camps.

A new type of camp appeared on the scene when the Pierce family opened Pierce Country Day Camp in 1918 in Deal, New Jersey. Began by Forester Pierce, a physical education teacher and coach, with a strong emphasis on health and fitness, the camp moved over the years from New Jersey to Long Island, New York, and in the 1930s settled in Roslyn, New York. The idea spread, and in 1921, the Des Moines Playground Association operated a day camp, and the first Girl Scout day camp was started in Chicago as an idea inspired by Mrs. Herbert Hoover.[3]

After the war years, a more open emphasis on the educational values of the camp experience surfaced. Activities such as arts and crafts, music, and dancing were added to the curriculum. The progressive education movement began to make its philosophy felt during this period. The training of camp staff gained acceptance as a necessary part of camp planning. By the 1920s, many camps were more deliberately structured with greater emphasis on competition, awards, and scheduled activity. Good character, spiritual attainment, and a companionable personality were stressed. Natural sciences also became part of the instructional activities in many camps.

International Expansion

The greatest expansion of camps into other countries occurred through the efforts of several youth organizations in the United States and Canada that were international in scope, as well as through missionary efforts by various Christian denominations. The world headquarters of various international youth organizations such as Boy Scouts, Girl Scouts (Girl Guides in most other parts of the world), YMCA, and YWCA provided some guidance to develop camp programs in their movements in other countries.

Missionaries from various Christian denominations simply replicated the camp model utilized in the United States, as they were prone to do with church, church school, and educational programs. These camps were not always successful in meeting the needs of the people indigenous to other countries, but gradually models adapted to the needs and culture of the people emerged.

At least three countries developed models that were utilized by their respective governments to provide services to youth in their countries: France, where camps began in the late 19th century, and Russia, where camps began in the early 1900s. In Russia, camps were primarily operated in canvas tents prior to World War II. After that war, camps began to spread and to upgrade their facilities, and by the 1980s, Russia had the largest camping movement in the world. The Greek government also lent its support to the camping movement in its country.

In Japan, camps began in the early 1900s. In Australia, camps began in the 1940s and developed primarily as facilities for schools to conduct outdoor education. Camps began in Venezuela in the mid-1900s.

Professional Associations

As camps grew in numbers early in the 20th century, camp directors began to meet together to discuss common problems and to learn from each other. A professional association for directors of boys' camps, the Camp Directors Association of America, was begun in 1912. By 1916, an association of directors of girls' camps, the National Association of Girls' Private Camps, emerged. These organizations merged in 1924 into the Camp Directors Association that published a new journal, *Camping*, in 1926. Concerns about health and safety were emerging, and directing a camp began to be taken more seriously as a profession. Conventions or training conferences began for camp directors during this period. Camp directors in Ontario and Quebec also attended many of the professional meetings in the United States. In 1933, the Ontario Camping Association was formed, and for a period of time it was a part of the American Camping Association.

The emphasis on structured or regimented education in camp began to lessen in the 1930s as the White House Conference on Child Health and Protection, coming at the beginning of the Great Depression, focused camps' attention on youth and health: "One of the significant findings of that conference was the demand for an inclusive national organization to … articulate the needs and interests of the growing camping movement in the United States."

The next several years led to the reorganization in 1935 of the Camp Directors Association (CDA) into the American Camping Association (ACA), with local offices based upon geographical boundaries. This organization began to evolve a set of health and safety standards, which eventually became the set of accreditation standards accepted throughout the United States. The association's name was changed to American Camp Association in 2004, and it remains the only professional organization for directors of all types of camps and the nationally recognized accrediting body.

The Canadian Camping Association (CCA) was formed in 1947, and included the Ontario and Quebec Camping Associations, as they withdrew from the American Camping Association. Gradually, each Canadian province formed associations as part of CCA.

Camps Increase

Following World War II, a rapid expansion of camp paralleled the increased population of youth in the country. The period heralded a wide acceptance of camp as the appropriate summer experience for youth. The numbers of camps and campers expanded rapidly. As Nelson Wieters—then of George Williams College—pointed out, many camps with generally global objectives began because of that broad acceptance and a ready marketplace, while other camps began for very specific purposes, either philosophical or instructional in nature. The latter objective led to a specialty camp boom in the 1960s. More and more questions were raised by parents and educators about the specific impact of the camp experience on character development, improvement of physical skills, or spiritual growth, with parents requesting growth in one or more specific skill areas.

School camping or outdoor education began to flourish in the early 1940s. Large programs were begun in Michigan, under the auspices of the Kellogg Foundation, and in Tyler, Texas, and San Diego. Though initial efforts began in the early 1930s, it was not until the 1950s that rapid growth came about. Colleges and universities began teacher education programs in this field. The Outdoor Education Council of the American Association of Health, Physical Education, Recreation, and Dance (AAHPERD) began during this period and provided leadership for much of the professional development in this field.

Camps for very specific spiritual objectives grew beyond church-sponsored camps to interdenominational and nondenominational camps and conference settings—many privately operated. Out of this growing segment of camps emerged Christian Camping International (CCI) in 1963, which initially required the signing of a statement of personal Christian faith for membership. The organization changed its name to Christian Camp and Conference Association (CCCA), and moved its national offices to Colorado Springs, Colorado.

The past 40 years has seen a growth of experientially based outdoor programs, primarily involving adventure and stress/challenge activities. The growth of this type of program accelerated greatly with the establishment of Outward Bound, an adventure program that began in England and spread to the United States and other countries. Variations of the Outward Bound methods have spread to many settings, including work with at-risk youth, adjudicated youth, and even business executives. In 1972, the Association for Experiential Education (AEE) began as a professional organization to bring together persons interested in this discipline. During the same period, the camping movement saw a significant increase in the number of specialty camps offering a primary focus on a single activity or skill. The variety of camps continues to expand.

Camps and camping associations are now operating around the world. National camping associations can be found in at least 17 countries: Australia, Canada, China (Hong Kong), Colombia, Georgia, Greece, Japan, Liberia, Malaysia, Mexico, Mongolia, Russia, Taiwan, Turkey, Ukraine, United States, and Venezuela. With the help of the Canadian Camping Association and the American Camp Association, three international conferences have been held: in Toronto (1983), in Washington, D.C. (1987), and again in Toronto (1994). In 1987, the International Camping Fellowship was organized to provide information sharing among individuals interested in international education and exchange. This group publishes a newsletter, maintains a website at www.campingfellowship.org, and promotes international events. Since its formation, the International Camping Congress has held international camping conferences in St. Petersburg, Russia (1997), Tokyo, Japan (2000), Melbourne, Australia (2003), Mexico City (2005), Quebec City, Canada (2008), and Hong Kong, China (2011). Within many of these countries are regional and provincial associations. The Asia-Oceania Camping Fellowship was founded in 2004 at a Congress in Mongolia, and holds regional congresses every two years. Camps in Europe have formed the European Camping Fellowship.

Types of Camps

Camps are almost as varied as people, but they can be divided into basically two types: day and resident. Day camps operate only during a portion of the day, typically morning and afternoon, and usually for five successive days of the week, Monday through Friday. However, some day camps operate only three days a week, others operate in the evening hours, and many camps include at least one overnight experience as part of their camp period. Resident camps bring participants to a setting in which housing is provided for a period of days. The typical resident camp provides lodging and meals. However, the resident camp experience may also take the form of travel or trip camping, in which housing may be tents, shelters, or hotels and motels, and the campers move every day. Camp sessions vary in length from 3 to 60 days.

The camp program is operated and staffed by the camp, and supervision of individual campers is a camp responsibility. Camps may be operated with paid or volunteer staff, or a combination thereof. Many camps operate 12 months a year, providing a more typical summer-camp experience, as well as outdoor education programs, conference groups, retreat groups, and adult-education groups. A camp may also be operated by a given group for only one or two weeks a year on property owned by an individual, public park, or other camp. Camps may serve youth, adults, senior adults, or families.

Camps are generally designated as for-profit (commercial) or not-for-profit. The for-profit camp or entrepreneurial camp may be operated by an individual, partners, or a corporation to return a profit to the owner, including some return on the capital investment made in property and facilities. While for-profit camps are commonly known also as independent camps, some not-for-profit camps also use the term "independent" because they are not connected to any national organization.

The not-for-profit camp may be operated by an organization such as the YMCA, Girl Scouts, Boy Scouts, a settlement house, a health-related association, a religious entity, or a government body. Public camps are operated by a government body, such as parks-and-recreation departments, school systems, 4-H groups, and the like. Funding comes from fees and tax dollars. In all of these cases, the camp has a tax exemption under article 501(c)(3) of the federal tax code or is operated by a governmental body. In the last two decades, a number of independent camp owners have moved from for-profit to not for-profit corporations and secured 501(c)(3) status from the federal government in order to continue their ability to serve youth and maintain their tradition. The camp is owned by a not-for-profit corporation and is provided the related tax benefits, and the camp is preserved for the future. This situation is especially true when second or third generations of the family are no longer interested in running the camp.

The goals of many not-for-profit camps and for-profit camps are similar. The facilities in some not-for-profit camps may, in fact, be more expensive than in some for-profit camps, because they have the advantage of securing tax deductible contributions for facility improvements. The for-profit camp generally charges higher fees for many reasons, including the need to recover income from the capital investment made by private parties, as well as being subject to many taxes not-for-profit camps do not have to pay. Therefore, the for-profit camp's clientele tends to come from a socioeconomic level that can pay such fees. Both types of camps may give financial assistance to those who cannot afford the fee and thus accommodate a more diverse camper group. The for-profit camp has most often offered longer sessions (three to eight weeks) than the not-for-profit camp, though many have changed to shorter sessions in recent years. Not-for-profit camps have tended to offer shorter sessions (one or two weeks) than for-profit camps, though some camps offer four- or eight-week sessions.

Few generalizations can be made about one type of camp or another concerning wages, clientele, program, goals and objectives, and facilities. Peter Drucker, noted management guru, suggests, "The task of the not-for-profit manager is to try to convert the organization's mission statement into specifics." The task of any camp director is to try to bring the camp's purpose or mission into practical accomplishments, and that purpose or mission may be very similar for a for-profit camp and a not-for-profit camp.

In both cases, it is essential that the camp operates in a fiscally sound fashion and that the director earns a decent living. In the not-for-profit camp and in some independent for-profit camps, where the owner is the director, the director receives a set salary. In other independent, for-profit camps, the director receives a bonus or a portion of the profit (if any) as salary. A not-for-profit camp may have a hard time offering a competitive salary; however, it will be difficult to retain a good director if the compensation is not consistent across comparable professions. The camp will probably not continue to operate in today's competitive climate (however lofty the stated purpose or mission) if it does not have as a parallel purpose to be financially accountable.

One of the growing complexities of the camp world is the increase in camps providing a variety of services and serving a variety of audiences. Many camps operate 12 months a year, a portion of which is devoted to the more traditional camp experience, and the other portion to short-term programs run by the camp or by rental or user groups. Such short-term programs often include weekend retreats, environmental education classes, parent-child programs, and the like. When a camp is accredited, the public assumes that all programs on the site are accredited. Many of the principles in the management of camps, short-term and year-round programs, and conference centers are the same. This text identifies the differences wherever possible.

What Is Camp?

Early camps were primarily directed toward getting youth out of the city and into a healthy and moral environment, and little energy went into defining a camp.

By 1929, a special committee of the New York Section of the Camp Directors Association reported the essential functions of the camp as "education for: physical health, emotional integration, an understanding of primitive processes, enlightened social participation, the acquisition of tastes and appreciations, and spiritual growth."

The "primitive processes" referred to outdoor experiences. By the late 1940s, Hedley S. Dimock, author and former professor at George Williams College, identified that the "characteristic elements, blended together in the right proportion, of an organized camp included: 1) persons, 2) outdoor life, 3) living in groups, 4) a camp community, and 5) leadership and conditions designed to satisfy personal needs and interests, and to stimulate wholesome personal, social and spiritual development."[4]

Dimock goes on to underline the importance of experiences that are "indigenous to group living in the out-of-door setting." For many years, the American Camp Association offered as its definition: "A sustained experience that provides a creative, recreational, and educational opportunity in group living, often in the outdoors. Camp programming uses trained leadership and the resources of the natural surroundings to contribute to each camper's mental, physical, social, and spiritual growth."[5]

In the 2012 edition of the *Accreditation Process Guide* and the *Accreditation Standards for Camp Programs and Services* book, ACA has changed their statement. The new language places a more detailed emphasis on outcomes.

> *The ACA community of camps promotes active participation, caring relationships, and focus on the emotional, social, spiritual, and physical growth of the individual. Camps vary in their purpose and desired outcomes, but each encourages risk taking, valuing the resources of the natural world, maintaining healthy lifestyles, and learning through a variety of fun and life-changing experiences."[6]*

With all of the words that have flowed from experts, it is still difficult to draw narrow lines around what a camp is and what a camp is not. Substantial support can be found for the basis that a camp provides a group living experience, with trained leaders who facilitate that group and community experience and utilize the outdoor surroundings to accomplish the mental, physical, emotional, social, and spiritual goals of the sponsoring body or owner.

In recent years, many programs have discovered the word "camp" for marketing purposes. Such programs may provide one or two of the elements essential to a traditional camp definition, but may be providing *some* of the same youth development outcomes. Others are often a purely a teaching or recreational program. The increasing numbers of such programs, however good they may be, can confuse parents who are searching for a more integrated living experience.

As Bernard Mason suggests in the opening of this chapter, camps must be imaginative to interest individuals in the outdoor experience. Camp owners and directors have not always been at their best in interpreting the value and meaning of the camp to the general public, but have more often relied upon the voice of previous campers to propagate the camp. There is no question that "word of mouth" is a highly effective means to sell the camp experience, but the myriad programs available today demand a varied and stronger interpretation of the uniqueness of the camp experience in the marketplace.

The commonalties among all types of camps—resident or day, for-profit or not-for-profit—are far greater than the differences. The basic similarities are easily discovered when the directors of camps take the opportunity to sit down together, get to know each other, and get beyond labels, terminology, and preconceptions. Regardless of the type of camp and program, similarities bind camps together because they all work for an ultimate developmental experience for each camper.

Generic Values of Camping

A review of the literature in the camp field concerning how others perceive the value of the camp experience will find the lists to be varied and idealistic, as camp directors tend to be idealistic individuals. However, several values would be found on almost any list:

- *Understanding the outdoor environment*: The environment of camp should be a key factor in determining program and objectives. Being outdoors is one of the distinctive features of the camp experience as youngsters have few other opportunities to learn about the natural world and recognize their responsibility as stewards of its resources.
- *A group living experience*: The learning experience of living in a group of one's peers provides opportunities for teachable moments not easily encountered elsewhere.
- *Fun*: Camp should be fun. Play is a natural process that enables children to grow and is a lifelong need of adults. Gaining leisure skills and attitudes that can be used throughout life is a valuable experience.

To these values, Betty Lyle would add:

- *Experience in democracy*: "With campers from various backgrounds, children may for the first time have an opportunity to live in a really democratic community."
- *Participation in program*: Programs should be "related to the interests and needs of the camper" and "campers must have an active share in planning what the camp life and program shall be."
- *Understanding and guidance*: "The relationship with a counselor is a new kind of relationship with an adult for most campers . . . a good counselor (is) one who likes his campers, understands them as individuals, helps, suggests, listens, guides."[7]

Reynold E. Carlson would add the following to that list:

- *Experiencing individual growth and development*: "Camp should offer children a chance to discover their own potentialities, to exercise their personal initiative, and to earn respect for what they do as individuals."

- *Practicing health and safety*: In camp, children should be "practicing … good personal health habits … [and] practicing rather than talking about health and safety."
- *Developing new skills and interests and perfecting old ones*: "Many of the camp activities have a high carryover value into later years."
- *Developing spiritual meanings and values*: "Many of these insights are caught as well as taught."[8]

James C. Stone, in a 1986 study, found that "campers made a statistically significant gain overall, and increases in the following characteristics:

- *Responsibility*: Skill in being accountable for one's own behavior.
- *Decision-making*: Skill in thinking for one's self.
- *Self-concept*: Skill in getting along with others.
- *Interpersonal relations*: Skill in making friends and being accepted.
- *Citizenship*: Skill in respecting the rights of others.
- *Environmental concern*: Skill in appreciating one's natural surroundings."[9]

A study conducted by Philliber Research Associates and the American Camp Association from 2002 to 2004 suggests that a stay at summer camp typically benefits children in the following ways:

- Children become more confident and experience increased self-esteem.
- Children develop more social skills that help them make new friends.
- Children grow more independent and show more leadership qualities.
- Children become more adventurous and willing to try new things.
- Especially at camps that emphasize spirituality, children realize spiritual growth.[10]

What Are Conference/Retreat Centers?

As camps have moved to year-round operations and facilities designed and improved for multi-season use, many have had to reevaluate their purpose. Most operations that desire to provide programs or lease facilities to other groups for camp-style programs focus primarily on outdoor and recreation activities, but the improved facility allows the operation to provide year-round services. Some camps design multipurpose facilities and may operate a conference/retreat center along with other camp-style programs. Designing one facility that serves both a camp-style group and an adult-conference group and that focuses primarily on indoor meetings, utilizing the outdoors for release from the thought process, is a challenge. Many operations that desire to serve both groups have both kinds of facilities on one piece of property. As a camp moves into more year-round use and develops its statement of purpose, and subsequent goals and objectives, these client and usage differences should be kept in mind.

One definition of a conference/retreat center is:

> *A residential facility designed for adults and other groups who come together for meetings, training sessions, and educational*

or inspirational programs. Such a facility generally operates at least three seasons of the year and is designed to minimize outside distractions. It provides dedicated meeting space, food service, hospitality and support services, access to facilities and natural environments for release and diversion, and housing styles appropriate to the target clientele.[11]

Kathleen M. Trotter illustrates these conceptual differences in an article for *Camping Magazine* and through her camp consultancy firm, Kaleidoscope, Inc. The myriad of camp and conference center programs for persons of all ages takes place in a variety of natural settings and styles of accommodations. Notice in Figure 1-1 that the spectrum from rustic camps to refined centers is, indeed, wide, and it is sometimes difficult to see common ground among these diverse facilities and programs.

Both camps and conference/retreat centers offer opportunities for holistic growth for youth and adults. However, they differ in their relationship to the outdoors and the role played by facilities and services. *(Used by permission)*

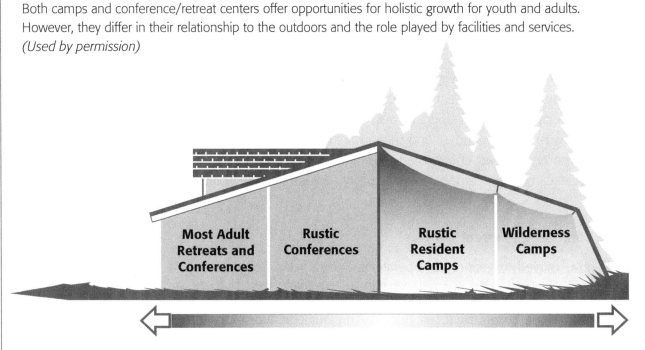

Indoor Focus/Outdoor Release

- "Home-like" comfort and convenience prevent distraction of learning.
- Personal, private space helps facilitate comfort, study, and reflection.
- Learning usually begins conceptually and then is applied "experientially."

Outdoor Focus/Indoor Release

- Rustic accommodations help teach simplicity and creativity.
- The outdoors becomes a focal point of the curriculum.
- Facilities and activities are designed to foster community participation and group independence.
- Learning usually begins experientially, then is conceptualized.

Figure 1-1. Diversified camp settings

One common denominator has to be human growth and development. Facilities and program styles differ because of what the interested parties want to accomplish. Camps increase their effectiveness with their clients and with other camp professionals when they focus on shared values and understand that different camps offer different environments in order to implement diverse missions. According to Trotter:

> *All of us as camp and conference center leaders strive to positively influence our clients in holistic ways so that they leave camp healthier, stronger, more skilled, and mature. Some of us facilitate this process by designing educational activities for our campers or guests.*
>
> *Others among us provide the context for the experience by creating comfortable, caring residential environments that free campers or guests to fully engage in learning and growth. Regardless of the focus, the very nature of our enterprise calls for two essential ingredients: some kind of structured experience, usually called a program, and the group living accommodations, which can be referred to as hospitality services. Neither of these is dispensable if we are to truly accomplish our mission.*[12]

Specific goals and objectives may deal separately with each type of operation, but both operations should contribute to the overall mission of the camp and/or conference center. As long as the decision concerning facilities and program styles is a conscious part of the planning process and is consistent with the mission, there should be few problems that are insurmountable. However, to slip into one style or the other for expediency in meeting number, dollar, or other goals without being a part of that mission can only lead to severe problems in setting priorities and serving clientele. Additional considerations about budgeting for a year-round operation can be found in Chapter 16.

Checkpoints

- Compare the history of the subject's camp to the historical overview of camp.
- What are the overall generic values of camps, and how do the subject's camp values compare?
- What determines whether a camp is for-profit or not-for-profit?
- What are some of the differences between camps and conference/retreat centers?

Related Standards

Listed at the end of most chapters are references to specific standards from the *American Camp Association's Accreditation Standards for Camp Programs and Services*. These are the accepted industry standards. References are also made to the "Additional Professional Practices," a section in the *American Camp Association's Accreditation Standards for Camp Programs and Services*.

Endnotes

1. Bernard S. Mason. 1930. *Camping and Education*. New York: McCall.
2. Abigail A. Van Slyck. 2006. *A Manufactured Wilderness*. Minneapolis, MN (London): University of Minnesota Press. p. xxiv.
3. Connie Coutellier. 2011. "Years of Adventures and Challenges: The History of Day Camp", *Camping*. Vol. 84, No. 1, January/February, p. 41.
4. Hedley S. Dimock. 1948. *Administration of the Modern Camp*. New York: Association Press (YMCA of the USA).
5. American Camping Association. 2012. *Accreditation Standards for Camp Programs and Services*. Monterey, CA: Healthy Learning. p. 286.
6. American Camp Association. 2012. *Accreditation Process Guide*. Monterey, CA: Healthy Learning. p. 11.
7. Betty Lyle. 1947. *Camping: What Is It?* Martinsville, IN: American Camping Association. pp. 4–5.
8. Reynold Carlson. 1975. *The Values of Camping*. Martinsville, IN: American Camping Association. p. 4.
9. James C. Stone. 1986. "Kids Learn Responsibility." *Camping Magazine*. Vol. 59, No.1, September/October, p. 21.
10. American Camp Association. 2005. *Directions: Youth Development Outcomes of the Camp Experience*. Martinsville, IN: American Camping Association.
11. American Camping Association. 1993. *Standards for Conference and Retreat Centers*. Martinsville, IN: American Camping Association. p. 5.
12. Kathleen M. Trotter. 1989. "Getting Out of the 90-Day Mentality." *Camping Magazine*. Vol. 61, No. 7, May, pp. 28–29.

WHAT IS THE CAMP DIRECTOR'S JOB?

Chapter Two

Camp Laurel South (Casco, ME)

The philosophy under which a camp functions, the morale of staff and counselors, the contributions the camp makes to the lives of youngsters, the adequacy of physical equipment—all are reflections of the insight, character, and competency of the camp director. His/her executive ability, together with a sense and appreciation of justice, needs to be at a high level. He/she needs insight, a world of patience, physical stamina, and ability to command the respect as well as the friendship of those associated with him/her in the camping enterprise.[1]

—John A. Ledlie

If you were to line up 10 experienced camp directors and ask them what the job of a camp director is, you would probably get 10 different answers. To survive, a camp director must possess a smattering of many skills and must combine many roles: cook, bookkeeper, plumber, minister, teacher, nurse, electrician, mechanic, risk manager, salesperson, lawyer, politician, corporate executive, naturalist, and eternal optimist. Every camp director discovers new dimensions to the job each summer.

Job Description

A new camp director's first task, if a thorough job description is not supplied, should be to develop such a description, in consultation with various individuals at the particular camp. Each camp owner will have different expectations. For example, in one camp, the bookkeeping may be handled entirely by a centralized organization office, while, in another camp, the bookkeeping may be part of the director's job. A summer day-camp director's duties and concerns will differ from those of a year-round residential camp director. Therefore, it is difficult to outline one model job description for a camp director.

However, the aspects of the job in any camp are somewhat uniform and require specific duties, depending upon the administrative situation. A camp director's job might include all of the following responsibilities:

- Develop and implement the mission/purpose, desired outcomes, and indicators of the camp and/or year-round operation.
- Determine the constituencies or target populations to be served by the camp.
- Design a program based upon the mission, desired outcomes, and various constituencies to be served.
- Develop and implement a risk management system to protect the participants, the camp, and the staff.
- Develop and implement a marketing plan for the camp. Recruit participants.
- Design and implement a staff organization based upon the program and target population; develop job descriptions and personnel policies.
- Design and implement a plan for the development and maintenance of the camp site and facilities.

- Develop and implement a health care plan that provides for the health and safety of the campers and staff, and a security plan that protects the camp from intruders.
- Develop and implement a nutritious and sanitary food service program.
- Develop and implement a safe transportation system to meet the needs of program, maintenance, and safety.
- Design a financial development program that includes not only fund-raising, but also a sound business plan and budget that is monitored regularly.
- Recruit, screen, and train staff.
- Develop and implement an evaluation system that allows campers, parents, staff, etc., to assess program facilities, operations, the staff structure, and youth development outcomes.
- Develop a plan for supervision of staff including training for supervisors, staff structure, expectations for behavior, job responsibilities, and addressing performance issues.
- Maintain relationships with the local community near the camp and the broader community served by the camp.
- Maintain the director's own professional growth through study, peer relationships, and conferences.
- *For not-for-profit camps only*: Serve as the principal staff member to the governing board or committee, working to ensure the strongest, most effective board or committee possible, and providing the staff with support to help that board define the philosophy and policies governing the operation.

Once a job description is created, it is vital for a new director to have a clear understanding with his supervisor about the priorities of the job. Meeting all of these expectations is not possible immediately, so the supervisor's expectations need to be clarified. The plan of work for the upcoming months should reflect the priorities of both the supervisor or camp owner and those of the camp director.

Administrative Roles

The camp director is an administrator and needs a clear understanding of the principles of administration that shape the day-to-day camp operations. Following are some of those principles.

Developing Desired Outcomes and Indicators Statements

This topic will be discussed in detail in Chapter 3.

Planning

Planning is a matter of securing facts about the present operation, looking ahead to what is predictable based on those facts, and examining the unusual or unpredictable events that could occur. With this information, a short-term and/or a long-range or strategic plan for action should be developed. In the not-for-profit camp or conference center, the long-range or strategic plan may be incorporated into the organizational plan and approved through the board of directors.

Organizing

A director cannot do everything simultaneously, even if he has the time. The plan should be broken into units of work and delegated to individuals who are given clear tasks and timetables with adequate physical support and supervision.

Developing and Managing Resources

Developing and planning resources means pulling together anything that is needed to accomplish the organized plan: people, materials, and finances. It also involves maintaining those resources for the future, whether it is technology, land, buildings, staff, campers, or contributors. This aspect will probably be the most time-consuming of the administrative roles.

Directing

Once the plan is in place and delegated to individuals with adequate resources, the administrator must become the overall resource for implementation and keeping the plan on course. This involves consultation, supervision, communication, coordination, and decision-making. An aspect of directing is the control of the overall plan, making sure the desired outcomes and indicators are being met. This is where the day-to-day supervision comes into play.

Evaluating

Evaluation is actually the first step in starting over, for here a director examines whether mission and desired outcomes were met, whether adjustments need to be made in the desired outcomes and indicators another time, and where to begin again.

Reporting

In the not-for-profit camp, one aspect of evaluation is reporting to the board or committee and the constituency of the organization. The camp director must gain skills in each of these administrative areas. It is far more important that these skills be mastered than that the director become certified in aquatic skills, learn medical information, or be an expert in building repair. The director is a manager, and management is complex and demanding. Success in camp management is built upon being a generalist in a community of specialists and generalists.

Leadership Styles

Beyond asking what the job is, it may be more important for the new director to determine what kind of director he/she wishes to be. The attitude with which a director begins work may well affect the ultimate job performance. Only careful thought can prevent a new director from being cast in stereotypic roles such as the following:

- *Tony Doer*: He is the only one who knows how a thing is to be done, and, consequently, he does everything. Others may assist him, but ultimately, he must be in the forefront and do it.
- *Indra Delegator*: She delegates everything. Everyone else does the work; she simply makes assignments and gives out gold stars.
- *Happy Mary*: She wants to make everyone happy and cannot operate if anyone is unhappy with her or does not like her decisions.
- *Juan Fix-It*: He loves to fix anything that goes wrong: plumbing, locks, computers, motors, or cars. He leaves the program and other areas of camp to the rest of the staff.
- *Kyla Waterfront*: She was always a great swimmer and directed waterfront when she was a camp staff member. You will always find her at the waterfront. She personally plans the water carnival.
- *Uncle Henry*: He is the father figure of camp. Everyone calls him "Uncle." He loves to sit by the fireplace and spin tales.
- *Office Sam*: He spends all day in the camp office, signing checks and letters, updating the website, and e-mailing parents. He lets the program directors walk over camp and check on activities, the kitchen, or the health service. You know where to find him anytime you need him: behind his desk.
- *Easy Jennifer*: What do you want to do? The decision is yours. Do it in whatever way you would like. Any way suits her, and she seldom expresses an opinion.
- *Bossy Jose*: He will tell you how to do it. He makes the ultimate decision on anything in camp—from where the hiking trip is going, to when camp is having roast beef. Who is boss is not in question.

It is hoped that no one will become one of these directors, but they do exist.

Select Your Own Style

Three areas of skill, in combination, make a leader effective. To select an individual leadership style as a camp director, it is necessary to take a look at the three areas: technical skills, interpersonal skills, and conceptual skills.

- *Technical skills*: A camp director plans, implements, and evaluates programs and services, and is also responsible for logistics, safety, legal issues, and office routines.
- *Interpersonal skills*: These techniques involve working with people. A camp director must understand the dynamics of a group and be able to resolve conflicts. To accomplish this end, a director also needs to value and respect every individual and be able to communicate with infinite varieties of people.
- *Conceptual skills*: These skills are probably the most difficult to develop, but they are the key for a successful director. They involve evaluative

thinking, problem solving, and an ability to see the whole picture. Central to the leadership role of a camp director is the conceptual ability to relate a camp's philosophy to program and to see its impact upon the style of leadership.

In an article in *Camping Magazine*, Debra Jordan describes six styles of leadership: democratic, benevolent autocratic, consultative, participative, laissez-faire, and coaching (Figure 2-1). In the article, she also points out the importance of understanding the appropriate style of leadership necessary for different situations.[2]

Style	Leader	Group	Situation
Democratic	Good knowledge of group and task	Some confidence, skills, and knowledge	Task and people orientation; no time constraints
Benevolent, autocratic	Skilled, experienced; explains actions; maintains control	Low skills; gives up control to leader; needs much guidance	Safety-hazard crisis; people and task orientation
Consultive	High in skills and knowledge; some trust in group	Moderate skills and knowledge; trusts leader; wants to learn	No crisis or time constraints; people orientation
Participative	Trusts group; confident in own and group's abilities	High skills and knowledge; involved, cohesive; utilizes synergy	Consensus approach; no time constraints; relaxed, comfortable; people orientation
Laissez-faire	Serves as resource; trusts group's ability; gives up control	Trusts leader; group dynamics; takes initiative	Focus on process; group development; task orientation
Coaching	High skills and knowledge; group-focused	Lacks confidence; needs assistance using skills	People orientation with concern for teaching

Figure 2-1. Six styles of leadership

Being a Leader or a Manager?

When examining leadership styles, the differences between being a leader and a manager begin to appear. A director is employed to be a manager and is consciously evaluated on the results of managing. On the other hand, a camp director is also expected to be a leader, and many times is unconsciously evaluated on the ability to lead staff or volunteers. The administrative roles identified earlier in this chapter align with managerial responsibilities in that they lead a director to consider the following:

- Confine discussion to current problems and options.
- Focus on outcomes and accountability.
- Control change and evolution.
- Monitor staff uniformity according to known procedures.
- Determine actions and decisions based on rules and policies.
- Plan for the future.

A leader will also:
- Investigate and discuss diverse ideas openly.
- Focus on people to obtain outcomes.
- Strive to make change happen.
- Empower others and encourage decision making.
- Build actions and decisions around values.
- See the future, and make plans to attain it.

Being a good manager can be learned through study and evaluation. Being a leader comes with self-examination and observation of others in leadership roles, and is more natural for some people than for others. The two are not mutually exclusive, and the most successful directors are able to blend the two.

Camp as a Community

One of the unique insights into administration in the camp setting is that the camp is a community. Hedley S. Dimock points out:

> *The camp community possesses most of the elements of a normal community, but in a simplified form. Here may be found the functions of government, home, health, employment, recreation and religion. Because of the relative simplicity and immediacy of the camp community, these basic functions can be concretely visualized, participated in, and shared by the camper. Here, further, may be found in concrete, visible, and manageable form the inner and informal aspects of community life common purposes and aspirations, traditions, customs, cohesiveness, and control.[3]*

Although many businesses or institutions develop a sense of family among their employees, the opportunity for developing a community relationship does not exist. Therefore, the ability to create a community can be a distinct advantage of the camp setting and experience. However, it can also create problems and tensions for the camp administrator that would not ordinarily arise in other situations. The camp community is interdependent and, to some degree, isolated from the outside. Little opportunity is available for relief from the 24-hour-a-day, intense environment in a resident camp. Building a sense of community can have great educational benefits, as well as developing the sort of relationships and loyalty that endures for many years.

In this context, one of the primary tasks of the camp director is to be an enabler. In her book, *Social Group Work: A Helping Process*, Gisela Konopka characterizes the leadership role as one of enabling, trying to discover the way in which others can be motivated to achieve their best performance.[4] To be an enabler, a person has to consciously outline the goals an individual wishes to attain and to analyze that individual's abilities and capacity to reach those goals. Where a person's abilities are inadequate for the task, an enabler must consider what can be done to help that person accomplish that task.

To be an enabler requires confidence in what the person can do or become. Often, that person must look beyond an individual's immediate abilities or failures to see the potential for future accomplishments. The effective enabler sees potential and seeks to provide opportunities for the individual to grow and fulfill that potential. Such an approach to leadership will inevitably cause some disappointments, but may also provide many moments of shared pleasure.

Ultimate Responsibilities

For some aspects of camp life, the director cannot escape responsibility. These are ultimate responsibilities that belong only to the director and cannot be totally delegated to anyone else. However, in some situations, the owner, executive, or camp administrator may keep the responsibility and not delegate it to the on-site camp director. The director's ultimate responsibilities include the following:

- Adhering to the mission
- Maintaining the desired outcomes, and camp policies
- Setting the standards for operation and health and safety
- Relating to the governing committee or board, if applicable
- Handling legal obligations
- Protecting the investment in property, reputation, and assets
- Managing the bottom line financially
- Supervising personnel administration
- Assuring that the public voice to media, parents, and constituency is honest, accurate, and consistent

To make sure that these ultimate responsibilities are met, the camp director must understand the basics of every area of camp life. A director must observe these areas first hand at regular intervals and use checkpoints to help evaluate performance. The supervision of areas in which the director has expertise can easily be delegated and checked informally. Areas in which the director has little experience require the employment of individuals with skills and experience in those areas and close supervision from the director until he/she understands the essential functions of a given area and is sure that they are being covered.

Certainly the camp director should enjoy and be fulfilled by the job. If a director is skilled in a particular area, there is no reason why those skills should not be utilized as long as the director's ultimate responsibilities are not neglected. On the other hand, if staff and campers are to feel that all parts of the camp program are equally valid, the director must exhibit an understanding and appreciation of all areas of camp life.

Directors are faced with situations that often place stress on them as well as require sensitivity and common sense. The ability to handle the cumulative stress throughout the camp season is a challenge to a director, requiring healthy outlets to relieve the stress and provide a positive daily demeanor and is critical to a happy and positive camp community.

A camp director, by the very nature of the responsibilities, cannot readily avoid being the key person in camp. However, many tasks may be delegated or responsibility shared, and the director's role will change as the comfort level and experience increases. For the camp director to be such a dominant figure is not necessarily undesirable, but the ultimate effect of such dominance will depend on the role the director takes on and the individual's ability to enable other staff to reach their greatest potential.

Checkpoints

- What are the administrative roles of the camp director?
- What are the ultimate responsibilities of the camp director?

Related Standards

American Camp Association's Accreditation Standards for Camp Programs and Services: HR.1, HR.6

Endnotes

1. John A. Ledlie [ed.]. 1961. *Managing the YMCA Camp*. New York: Association Press (YMCA of the USA).
2. Debra Jordan. 1996. "Leadership Styles, Which One Is Right for You?" *Camping Magazine*. Vol. 68, No. 4, March/April, pp. 19–21.
3. Hedley S. Dimock. 1948. *Administration of the Modern Camp*. New York: Association Press (YMCA of the USA). p. 29.
4. Gisela Konopka. 1983. *Social Group Work: A Helping Hand*. Englewood Cliffs, NJ: Prentice-Hall.

WHERE DOES THE PROGRAM BEGIN?

Camp Laurel South (Casco, ME)

Chapter Three

In no other educational enterprise can the child have such continuous exposure to approved leadership, experience living closely with a small group of people where qualities of cooperation and consideration for others are the type of behavior that pays off, and be exposed to young adults who serve as models for the development of positive ideas and attitudes.[1]

—Alice Van Krevelen

After gaining a clear understanding of the requirements of his new job, a director's next step should be to learn as much about the current operation of the camp as possible, and, particularly, about the camp's philosophy, mission, and outcomes. Though not necessarily recent or accurate, older camp literature may provide clues as to the expectations of the parents of previous campers and the intentions of previous administrators.

Vision, philosophy, purpose, mission, goals, objectives, outcomes, outputs, targets, indicators, and/or values are common terms used in camp organizations. Strategic or long-range planning adds another set of terms (including strategic goals, operational plan, checkpoints, benchmarks, action plans, etc.) that are or should be integrated with the first set. However, the definitions of these terms and their uses vary greatly, depending on the organization, trends in youth development, funding sources, and the like. The process of reaching consensus on mission and outcomes is more important than how they are defined. To help sort through these aspects, the following terms and definitions will be used in this book:

- *Vision*: A mental image of what the organization will look like in the future.
- *Philosophy/Values*: The critical examination of fundamental principles on which the camp desires to operate and an analysis of the basic concepts in the expression of those principles.
- *Mission/Purpose*: A statement of the essential reason for the existence of an organization and/or camp.
- *Outcomes*: The desired results or benefits that contribute to the achievement of the mission (sometimes called goals).
- *Indicators*: More precise statements that define the specific elements that achieve the accomplishment of the outcomes and broader mission of the camp (sometimes called objectives or targets).
- *Outputs*: The direct products of the camp's program activities, often expressed in numbers.
- *Evaluation*: The measure of success in reaching outcomes based upon the previously defined indicators can then be used to adjust targets, goals, and outcomes for the remainder or next period of time. Indicators and outputs provide tools for that evaluation process.
- *Strategic Planning*: A process to periodically evaluate the camp's philosophy and mission, and to design a comprehensive or long-range plan outlining desired outcomes for that future period of time.

Developing a Philosophy

A camp must determine for itself its core values. This determination is identified as the *philosophy* of a camp. *Webster's Dictionary* defines philosophy as "the critical examination of the grounds for fundamental beliefs and an analysis of the basic concepts in the expression of such beliefs."

By its nature, philosophy is theoretical and difficult to measure. Despite its abstract nature, the philosophy is the overall operational grounding of how one works with people in the camp setting. In the context of this book, the term philosophy is used to encompass the stated mission and desired outcomes of a camp. It is a question of the basic values that will always hold true, regardless of how the camp or conference/retreat center facility, program, or services may change. It is more than a physical setting. That philosophy should be determined by the camp's owners, if owned by an individual or group of individuals, and by the camp's board or governing committee. In some not-for-profit operations, the camp may be one programmatic segment of an overall corporation, having an overall mission that influences the philosophy of the camp operation.

A camp director may have his own philosophy or values about working with people in a camp environment. This philosophy is likely to be evident in the leadership style, and is likely to evolve over a period of time. If a major philosophical difference arises between the camp director's philosophy and that of the owner/operator, it is a good idea to discuss it with the supervisor and, ultimately, with the operating committee/board. The owner/operator should not be expected to change the underlying philosophy or values with the arrival of each new camp director. Such changes should really come only after experiences in the operation or in the marketplace can be used to document a need for change. For a camp's philosophy to be meaningful in its operation, the philosophies of the camp owner and the camp director must be compatible and symbiotic.

Mission

Before a new camp director can begin to program, a first step must be to find a way to put the basic philosophy and underlying reason for the existence of the organization or camp into definitive terms. The camp should have a general overriding purpose or mission statement that can be broken down into several specific outcomes that express how the mission will be accomplished.

If the camp is owned by a larger organization—such as a youth agency, school, or religious organization—the basic values and mission may be that of the organization and the camp is a way to accomplish the mission in a unique outdoor setting. The outcomes will be specific to the camp and describe the contribution the camp makes to the organization's mission. For example, the mission of Camp Fire USA is "to build caring, confident youth and future leaders."[2] The YMCA's mission is "to put Christian principles into practice through programs that build healthy spirit, mind, and body for all."[3] Their camps may provide a variety of programs that contribute to the achievement of the organization's mission. Some services the camp chooses to provide may not directly contribute to the mission. For example, rental services, in some cases, may only contribute financially and enable the camp to continue providing their primary services.

The basic philosophy or values of a camp rarely change. Most often, if a mission statement changes drastically, it is because the mission or purpose has been accomplished or the language needs to be changed to make it clearer to the current generation. However, the essence of a mission statement rarely changes. The changes most often take place in outcomes that are more responsive to current trends, emerging youth-development needs, and demographics. To simply change the program activities and staff of a camp without carefully tying the changes to the mission, outcomes, and indicators can lead to considerable confusion on the part of staff and families of campers.

The approval of the camp's mission and outcomes in organizational-type camps may involve a time-consuming process of working with their governing boards and committees, but it is an essential part of a board's educational and ownership experience. Though the owner/director of an independent camp has greater latitude to change its philosophy and stated mission and outcomes more readily than organizational-type camps, no less careful thought should be given to developing such statements.

The new camp director may need to research a variety of sources to discover a camp's purpose or mission statement. If not found in the camp's brochure or on the camp's website, examination of other camp documents will be necessary. In some cases, the mission of the sponsoring organization becomes the mission of the camp. Perhaps an overriding purpose or some specific outcomes have been defined by previous directors. If these goals are not included in specific documents, they may be discovered in a number of different places:

- On the camp website
- In camp brochures
- In previous minutes, if the camp is operated by a governing board or committee
- In the articles of incorporation, if the camp is incorporated
- In conversation with a previous director or staff or with the executive of the organization or long-time board members
- In reports from previous summers
- In staff manuals

When the director has collected statements of purpose and various outcomes (whether verbal or written), it may be useful to write them out as clearly as possible and then to examine them carefully. The director should examine them for clarity, appropriateness to current community patterns and attitudes, and for consistency with the operator's expectations. The director should examine these statements with a supervisor or peer to see if that person interprets the purpose in a similar fashion. If possible, the director should also examine them with an operating committee or board, the executive committee, or a small, responsible group of camp alumni.

With a clearly stated purpose as it was defined in the past and as it is now perceived by the operator (committee, board, or executive), the camp director should determine if any parts of the purpose are in conflict with his own personal philosophy. Regardless of such discrepancies, it is wise for the new camp director to operate under the stated purpose for at least one summer before making or suggesting any significant changes. Operation is a test of the validity and relevance of a camp's mission and outcomes. A director should never hesitate, however, to seek clarification of the meaning of the mission.

Developing Statements of Purpose or Mission

The *purpose* or *mission* states the essential reason for the camp's existence and may not necessarily be easily measured. The purpose, along with its clarifying outcomes, brings the more intangible philosophy or values of the camp into more concrete terms. Some examples are shown in Figure 3-1.

Camp A: The principal purpose is to help young people of all backgrounds grow into responsible maturity in an outdoor setting through the application of Christian principles.

Camp B: The mission of the camp is to provide an outdoor setting for group living, where people can design programs to meet their group's needs and to provide a regular opportunity for youth to gain a deeper understanding of their relationships to their fellow man and their natural environment.

Camp C: The purpose of this camp is to help each individual camper gain skills that help him achieve a strong self-concept, self-responsibility, and an ability to get along with his peers.

Camp D: The [name of organization]'s mission is to provide quality developmental programs to help disadvantaged youth become productive adults and citizens.

Figure 3-1. Mission and purpose statements

The focus of each of the mission statements shown is quite different. Camps A, C, and D focus on the individual camper. Camp B focuses both on the facility and provision of program, (i.e., where a camp or conference center rents facilities as well as operates camp sessions). Camp A is directed more toward application of Christian principles and outdoor living; whereas Camps C and D focus on interpersonal and skill development Camp D's mission is the same as that of the larger organization that owns the camp.

If a camp serves a narrow age group or a specialized clientele, the developmental needs of that group should be considered in designing a mission statement. A camp may not be able to address all the developmental needs, but certainly many of them will be the foundation for the mission and outcomes. Refer to Chapter 4 for more details on human growth and development.

Peter Drucker states that "a mission statement has to be operational, otherwise it's just good intentions. A mission statement has to focus on what the institution really tries to do and then do it so that everybody in the organization can say: This is *my* contribution to the goal."[4] Therefore, the statement should be simple, clear, and concise—something others can remember and to which they can relate. A starting point is to write a statement, cut it to 15 or 20 words, and then test it on others.

At this point, a director should pause and ask if this mission statement identifies the essence of the camp. What is the essential purpose of existence or identity of the camp? Does one word or one phase clearly identify what the camp is about? For the moment, the director must shed the multiple words that identify the good things the camp wishes to accomplish in the lives of people and focus on the camp's clear identity. For one camp, it may be "wilderness adventure," another might be "fun outdoors," another "personal growth," and another "aquatic skills."

Next, go back and evaluate that essence phase with the mission statement. Are the two compatible? For example, Camp B's mission is lengthy and includes multiple phrases actually identifying two elements of its mission (serving groups and individuals) that are actually outcomes rather than a description of the essential qualities. A clearer statement might be: "The mission of the camp is to provide an outdoor setting for a quality experience in group living."

Desired Outcomes

Outcomes are the desired change. The dictionary defines an outcome as "the result or consequence" of an action. In other words, outcome statements are an effort to define the result to be achieved in a given period of time.

Outcome statements may be developed for a variety of purposes:
- *Operation*: These outcomes could cover such administrative areas such as completing facility construction, improving quality of food, lowering food costs, balancing the budget, and utilizing technology. These outcomes are primarily measured in quantities, deadlines, and quality.
- *Hospitality*: These outcomes come into play when a camp rents its facilities to other groups and becomes the host. They might deal with providing resources for the groups, developing facilities specifically for such groups, or adding services.
- *Training*: These outcomes would be achieved in the precamp staff training week, ongoing in-service training, and, in cases where there is a year-round staff, for each person annually. Online training will also be an option in some cases.
- *Personnel performance*: These outcome statements could be developed with a staff person in conjunction with the individual's supervisor for a given time period and relate to the successful performance of job functions.

The camp director may find it useful in the planning process to examine each of these elements and determine if the development of outcome statements in one of these areas will be helpful. Some of these areas may require outcomes that take more than one calendar period to achieve, and are therefore renewed or continued.

Camps, like most human service organizations, are in business to provide programs and services to people. Therefore, outcomes in any of the aforementioned areas must ultimately help to accomplish such benefits. For example, if an operational outcome is a new building, the need should be based on how the design and use contributes to the accomplishment of the mission and provide benefits to the participants. Is it the best use of resources to accomplish the mission and achieve desired participant outcomes? Training outcomes should include knowledge and achievement of benefits to participants. Personnel performance outcomes can be evaluated on the success of the staff in helping participants benefit from the program.

In the context of this chapter's focus on the development of camp program, outcome statements are concentrated on *programmatic and/or youth development.* These outcomes are the desired benefits to the participant during or after the experience at camp, with hopes of identifying measurable attainments for the participant.

Desired outcomes in the youth development context should be the starting point for camp directors given that is the principal business of the camps. It is well to examine research that has been done in the field, both in youth development literature as well as expectation of parents. Of particular note is the study conducted on "Youth Development Outcomes of the Camp Experience" by the American Camp Association that examined responses of more than 5,000 families between 2001 and 2004. Significant growth in the following areas was reported:

- Independence
- Adventure and exploration
- Leadership
- Self-esteem
- Environmental awareness
- Peer relationships
- Friendship skills
- Values and decisions
- Spirituality
- Social comfort

Examination of benefits observed in this study may provide examples in the choice and development of desired outcome statements for the camp.[5]

Some examples of youth development outcomes relating to each of the previous mission statements are shown in Figure 3-2. A number of the outcomes identified in all four camps tie into some of the benefits noted in ACA's study. However, Camp B, as a rental facility, focuses on providing a facility that enables the rental groups to accomplish their desired outcomes. The four camps have individual missions from which related outcome statements have grown.

Camp A: The principal purpose is to help young people of all backgrounds to grow into responsible maturity in an outdoor setting through the application of Christian principles.
- Outcome #1: Increased interpersonal and social skills
- Outcome #2: Increased knowledge of man's impact on the natural environment
- Outcome #3: Increased ability to apply Christian principles to daily life experiences

Camp B: The mission of the camp is to provide an outdoor setting for a quality experience in group living. The camp shall provide appropriate facilities and equipment for rental groups:
- Outcome #1: To accommodate small living groups
- Outcome #2: To utilize the natural environment for appreciation and education
- Outcome #3: To teach certain outdoor skills

Camp C: The purpose of this camp is to help each individual camper gain skills that help him achieve a strong self-concept, become responsible, and get along well with his peers.
- Outcome #1: Improvement in skill level
- Outcome #2: Increased social skills
- Outcome #3: Increased self-reliance

Camp D: The [organization's] mission is to provide quality developmental programs to help disadvantaged youth become productive adults and citizens.
- Outcome #1: Demonstrated progression in knowledge and personal skills
- Outcome #2: Increased interpersonal skills
- Outcome #3: Increased sense of belonging

Figure 3-2. Youth development outcomes

Indicators

Indicators are more precise than mission statements or outcomes. They more clearly define specific measureable processes or actions that will accomplish the outcomes in a given time period. Indicators should be realistic and achievable. Examples of indicators relating to the mission and desired youth development outcomes of the camp examples are shown in Figure 3-3.

Some of the preceding indicator statements further define the stated purpose and directions for a given period of time, but others leave room to define the specifics in measurable statements in the future. Review the outcomes and one will note:

- An indicator needs to be identified with pre- and post-targets to make it measurable.
- The focus of an indicator should be on the change that will occur or benefit to the participants, regardless of the program or service.

Camp A: The principal purpose is to help young people of all backgrounds to grow into responsible maturity in an outdoor setting through the application of Christian principles.

- Outcome #1: Increased interpersonal and social skills
  - ✓ Indicator: By the end of camp session, the camper will have participated in planning and performance of a cabin skit for a campfire.
- Outcome #2: Increased knowledge of man's impact on the natural environment
  - ✓ Indicator: By the end of the camp session, the camper will have used at least one low-impact skill being taught in the environmental education program.
- Outcome #3: Increased ability to apply certain Christian principles to daily life experiences
  - ✓ Indicator: A staff member has observed the camper applying at least one Christian principle discussed during camp.

Camp B: The mission of the camp is to provide an outdoor setting for a quality experience in small-group living. The camp shall provide facilities and equipment for rental groups:

- Outcome #1: To accommodate small living groups
  - ✓ Indicator: Change living cabins to accommodate no more than six or seven camper beds.
- Outcome #2: To utilize the natural environment for appreciation and education
  - ✓ Indicator: Provide a nature trail with a leader's guide.
- Outcome #3: To teach certain outdoor skills
  - ✓ Indicator: Provide a new archery range.

Camp C: The purpose of this camp is to help each individual camper gain skills that help the camper achieve a strong self-concept, become responsible, and get along well with peers.

- Outcome #1: Improvement in a skill level
  - ✓ Indicator: Progression in one skill area of the camper's choice before the end of camp will be documented.
- Outcome #2: Increased social skills
  - ✓ Indicator: Two new friends made by the camper will be identified during the session.
- Outcome #3: Increased self-reliance
  - ✓ Indicator: The camper shall be observed choosing an activity he/she wishes to undertake during a free-time period.

Camp D: The [organization]'s mission is to provide quality developmental programs to help disadvantaged youth become productive adults and citizens.

- Outcome #1: Progression in knowledge and skill
  - ✓ Indicator: The camper shall demonstrate progression in one skill area of the camper's choice, which shall be documented before the end of camp.
- Outcome #2: Increased interpersonal skills
  - ✓ Indicator: The camper shall be observed being able to identify alternatives to fighting when disagreeing by end of camp session.
- Outcome #3: Increased sense of belonging
  - ✓ Indicator: The camper shall be observed having an increased ability to contribute to the living group and to the larger camp community by the end of camp session.

Figure 3-3. Outcomes indicators

- Each outcome relates to the overall mission and philosophy of the camp and to time-sensitive indicators.
- Some indicators help accomplish more than one outcome.

Though any type of outcome will remain somewhat vague or idealized, they require measurable indicators with identified methods or action plans and evaluation tools for staff to be able to determine success.

Evaluation

After detailing the mission, outcome, and indicator statements of a camp, a director must have some process for evaluating or determining the degree of their success. Based on the evaluation of successful achievements, the camp can make adjustments to its operation and set new expectations in terms of outcomes. A variety of methods can be used to measure successful achievement, including camper, staff, and parent evaluations (written or verbal). Figure 3-4 shows a type of chart that helps plan and evaluate two specific desired outcomes.

This chart takes an outcome and its goal and projects the time frame for evaluation of achievement of the outcome/goal over a time period (three years). This time frame assumes it is unrealistic to expect to achieve the same outcome/goal with the entire camp community in the first year of setting such a goal. *Mission:* The purpose of this camp is to help each individual camper gain skills that help the camper achieve a strong self-concept, self-responsibility, and an ability to get along with peers.

Outcomes	Resources Needed or Inputs	Methods or Action	Indicators	Evaluation Method(s)
Improvement in skill level.	Program equipment appropriate to age and skill. Staff trained in helping campers to improve skills.	Provide activities where campers have time to progress and gain competency in specific skills. Design a system for recognition camper's progress.	85% of the campers progress at least one skill level in two of the three activities during the session.	Pre- and post-skill tests. Parent evaluations.
Increase social skills.	Staff trained in group development and conflict resolution. Equipment for four different team sports.	Design a team sports program where campers can participate on two or more different teams. Assign members to teams rather than use cabin groupings.	80% of the campers demonstrate an increase in respect for others. 75% have friends outside their cabin group by end of session.	Staff observation Camper evaluation

Figure 3-4. Evaluation models

In terms of training and measuring staff progress, it is helpful to align specific methods to accomplish the outcome. When staff members understand the desired youth development outcomes and the changes they should be able to see, they can be much more intentional in their work with the campers and are more likely to be successful.

A checklist for each activity can be developed as an evaluation tool that can be marked for each individual—both at the beginning and end of the camp session. This tool can provide a checkpoint for any report to parents and for evaluating the achievement of the camp's outcomes and indicators for participant outcomes at the end of the season.

At that point, the director and staff can then use the degree of success in reaching these measures to determine adjustments or alterations, if necessary, to the outcomes and indicators for the future. Once the process is in place, it becomes relatively easy to make adjustments in the indicators and methods from year to year.

The American Camp Association's website (www.ACAcamps.org/research) has additional information on both past and current research that includes youth development outcome research. ACA's bookstore (www.acabookstore.org) provides a number of printed and digital volumes, outlining how outcomes can be achieved in the camp setting.

Other methods for evaluation are discussed in Chapter 18. Some of these methods are measuring aspects other than the developmental outcomes of a successful camp and include such operational outcomes (sometimes called outputs) as participants served, budget met, facility vacancies, and the like.

Checkpoints

- Is there a written statement of the camp's mission?
- Has the camp developed written outcome statements and indicators goals specific to the camp's program?
- Has the camp administration tested the purpose, desired outcomes, and indicators with the operator (supervisor, committee, or board)?

Related Standards

American Camp Association's Accreditation Standards for Camp Programs and Services: PD.1, PD.3, PD.5, PD.7; HR.12

Endnotes

1. Alice Van Krevelen. 1979. "Camp as a Fresh Start." *Camping Magazine*. Vol. 51, No. 3, February, p. 9.
2. Camp Fire USA. All About Us Mission Statement (online). Kansas City, MO (cited 8 October 2003); available from: www.campfire.org/all_about_us/mission.asp.
3. YMCA of the USA. About the YMCA (online). Chicago (cited 8 October 2003); available from: www.ymca.net/index.jsp.
4. Peter F. Drucker. 1990. *Managing the Nonprofit Organization: Practices and Principles*. New York: Harper Collins. p. 4.
5. Philliber Research Associates. 2005. *Youth Development Outcomes of the Camp Experience*. Martinsville, IN: American Camping Association.

THE PARTICIPANT

Camp Laurel South (Casco, ME)

Chapter Four

The center of the camp is the camper. He is the only reason for operating the ... camp. As the center about which all life revolves, we need to give our immediate attention to knowing him, to helping him learn to do things for himself, and to helping him learn to do things with others. The staff is in camp for that ... purpose.[1]

—Elmer Ott

Exchange the word *camper* for the broader *participant*, and Elmer Ott's words from 50 years ago still underline the essence of what camp is about. Lofty statements of purpose, desired outcomes, and definitive indicators alone do not ensure the camp will endure or succeed in accomplishing those statements. No matter how elaborately the program is designed to support those goals, success is unlikely unless the persons to be served are matched with that program.

From the very beginning, the focus of the director and owner must include defining the participant or target population, the needs of that population generally and individually, and finally, the program design that will meet those needs and accomplish the goals of the camp. As you will see in Chapter 5, "program" encompasses everything that happens in camp, from activities to group living to the design of the food service.

Determining Your Target Population

Initially, it is helpful to describe the market areas for the participants the camp wishes to serve. This information may relate to the camp's mission, purpose, and outcomes statements. Some camps by their sponsorship will draw campers primarily from the sponsor's sources (Girl Scout membership, a church or synagogue, a neighborhood, a group of individuals with a specific disability), and that sponsor's mission will give direction to the purpose and outcomes statements. Other camps may choose to look nationally and internationally for campers, or may target families at a specific income level or age group.

Year round it is not unusual for camps to serve a range of populations, often resulting from alternating the timing of sessions: summer for children and youth, weekends for family groups, weekdays for school groups or senior adult groups or adult conferences. In these instances, camps will need to identify target populations for each different program. Similarly, the desired outcomes and indicators may differ from each of these target population groups.

Assumptions should not be made about the population a camp chooses to serve. For example, a sufficient camper population may not be available in the geographic area chosen or more groups may be trying to serve a given population than is economically feasible. This situation is particularly true for day camps, where daily transportation is an issue. So the analysis begins.

Camp Market

Once the camp's market area is clearly defined (a county, a state, several states), a demographic analysis is essential. Gather demographic information about the population or area to be served, and include age, gender, geographical area, and economic and ethnic characteristics. The Census Bureau's American FactFinder (factfinder.census.gov) and other websites can be helpful in gathering this information. If the camp's market is the membership of the sponsoring organization, it is important to secure the demographic breakdown of that membership. Whether the camp serves a specific membership or the entire country and international markets, it may be helpful to compare the actual composition of the camp's existing participants with the broader demographics of the country. Some indications of the limitations of the potential market can be gained from this comparison, especially for long-range planning.

Analysis of the camp's potential market should include answers to the following questions: What is the population by age, gender, socioeconomic group, and ethnic group broken down by geographic areas (ZIP codes, communities, counties) within the target market area? What have been the trends over the past five years? What is the projection for the next five years? Where is the largest concentration of prospective campers or groups? What are the economic ranges of the population in given areas? Again, the U.S. Census Bureau's website also provides regularly updated projections to its 10-year enumeration of the country's population giving age, gender, and ethnicity information by census tracts. The federal government also offers more statistics at an interagency website for The Forum on Child and Family Statistics.[2] If the participant population is narrowed to include only persons with certain physical or mental challenges, additional information may have to be secured through public or private organizations which provide services to those groups. The combined data provides a way to examine the various components of potential participants in the chosen geographic area.

Even if the market is limited to the membership of the camp's sponsoring organization, a breakdown of the membership by age, gender, geographic, economic, and ethnic characteristics should be secured. That breakdown should be compared to the similar population statistics of the geographical area covered by the membership and the organization's plans for membership expansion. Some indications of the limitations of the potential market can be gained from this comparison, especially for long-range planning. This comparison may also help the director determine if they are reaching their maximum market share.

Camp Enrollment

Review the statistics from the camp's enrollment over the past five years; break out the statistics by geographic areas, age groups, socioeconomic groups, and ethnic groups for which demographic information has been chosen. Has the camp's previous enrollment followed the trends in the general population for the same period? How does the camp's enrollment match the demographics of the geographic areas designated to be served? How does it match the demographics projected for the next five years?

It may be beneficial for the camp staff to reflect the diversity of the camper population. Review the composition of the camp staff over that five-year period. Overlay that with the camper composition and determine how the two differ.

Camp Diversity

If diversity of the participant population was not considered in the initial development of the mission statement, it is important and appropriate to consider that at this stage. How diverse of a population does the camp wish to serve? How diverse is the population of the market area, and what are the projected changes over the next five years? How will reaching out to new populations affect the current population and staff of the camp? If such changes might develop conflicts, how does the camp take this factor into consideration as it plans? Do the goals and outcome statements illustrate a need to diversify the makeup of the participant population?

Areas of diversity are shown in Figure 4-1. Each basic area of diversity should be considered first, followed by secondary ones. Basic areas are ones that are difficult to change and are most visible to others. Secondary areas are ones that are generally chosen or learned, and can often be changed.

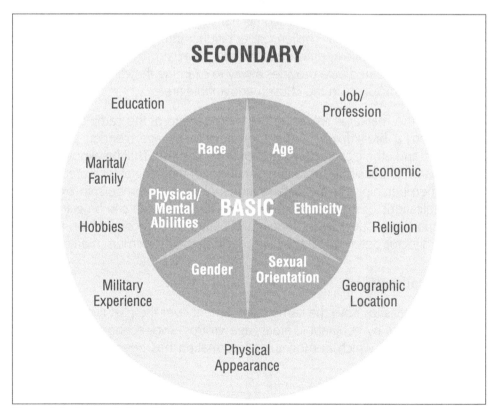

Figure 4-1. Areas of diversity

"Camps ought to be outdoor environments where differences and diversity are not merely tolerated, but appreciated and celebrated. Not all camps will address diversity issues in the same way, but the goal of all camp programs can be to strive toward developing multicultural organization where social oppression does not exist," states Karla Henderson.[3] In today's society, a camp that ignores the issue of diversity in its target market is also ignoring the growing diversity of the country's population and the importance of individuals learning to recognize and consciously deal with prejudice and stereotyping.

Camp Competition

Identify the camp's competition and whom they are serving. Competition may come from other types of programs, other camps, schools, sports, and other types of activities that involve the entire family or segments of it. At this point, the goal should be to see if more programs with similar goals are serving the same population. Is the target population saturated with existing programs?

Comparison of Data

Once a director has compiled and thoroughly analyzed all of this data, it should be compared with the population the camp wishes to serve. Where is overlap found? Where are the groups not being served by the camp or others? Where is their diversity?

Consultation

The information should then be shared with others. Key staff with a great deal of experience at the camp may have insights that will help. If the camp operates with a board or committee, that group should have a presentation of the information and an opportunity to react to it. Another camp director or mentor may be able to offer some observations. Often, outside consultants from the camping field can provide a clearer analysis of this data from a broader perspective, and guide the director, board, and committee in developing an overall market analysis and marketing plan.

Reevaluation

At this point, the camp should reevaluate and consider narrowing or broadening its targeted population.

Understanding the Participants: Growth and Development

Determining a target population is not enough. It is equally important that the director and staff be cognizant of the basic concepts of human growth and development and any special needs of the age groups being served. Without understanding the developmental characteristics of target groups, it is difficult to develop realistic desired outcomes and indicators.

Bob Ditter, a therapist specializing in child and adolescent treatment, states in his book *In the Trenches*:

> *Today, as never before, camping is in a position to be a pivotal player in the growth and development of children. To realize this potential, camping professionals must become more aware of the social and emotional needs of both children and parents. We must be clear, articulate, and specific about exactly how the camp experience makes a positive impact on children and then practice the profession in a more conscious, consistent, and deliberate way.*[4]

Parents have high expectations of camp, and it is important for directors to create a partnership with parents in the development of their child. This strategy helps the camp deal with both the developmental needs and problems of a specific child. It also reduces the exposure to risk when taking on the responsibility of children with behavioral problems or medical, physical, or psychological conditions.

Additionally, it would be ideal if the director and full-time program staff had completed courses in human growth and development during their college curriculum. However, this cannot always be the case, and it is not likely that many of the seasonal staff will have had exposure to such courses. A careful review of current literature in the field should be made once the target population is determined, and an overview of developmental needs is best included in staff training. A helpful resource for staff and for training is *Camp is for the Camper: A Counselor's Guide to Youth Development.*[5]

Developmental Needs

It is difficult to plan an effective developmentally appropriate program unless you have an understanding of the particular characteristics and needs of the age group being served. Since, ideally, camp goals and outcomes are based upon meeting certain developmental needs, developing this understanding is a starting point for creating a program.

An overview of varying age groups is shown in Figure 4-2 as a stimulant to learning more about different age groups. This material was originally developed by Jean E. Folkerth for ACA's Project REACH Camp Staff Training Series and has been updated with information from the University of Connecticut, Steve Wagoner of the University of Illinois Extension Service the Mayo Foundation for Medical Education and Research, and the Child Development Institute.[6]

3- to 4-Year-Olds

Physical
- Kicks, climbs, runs, pedals a tricycle
- Throws ball overhand
- Catches bounced ball sometimes
- Dresses and undresses
- Manipulates small objects
- Begins to uses scissors
- Builds tower with blocks
- Develops physically—girls about a year ahead of boys
- Develops high motor drive

Social
- Begins to cooperate with playmates
- Imitates parents and playmates
- Takes turns
- Tries to solve problems
- Expresses affection openly
- Separates more easily from parents
- Becomes more independent

Emotional
- Expresses affection openly
- Centers emotionally to home
- Defies at points
- Begins to be adventuresome
- Feels much more secure

Intellectual
- Asks "why" questions
- Understands concepts such as morning, afternoon, night
- Begins to understand concepts of same and different (such as colors, etc.)
- Gets involved in more complex imaginary play

Special Considerations for Activities Involving This Age Group
- Cooperates in play activities
- Is ready for physical play
- Likes simple table games
- Begins to be willing to follow rules

5- to 7-Year-Olds

Physical
- Masters physical skills (physical activities)
- Controls large muscles better than small muscles
- Has high activity level (restless and fidgety)
- Works on eye-hand coordination
- Learns best if physically active

Social
- Learns to be friends and have "best" friends
- Becomes more aware of peers and their opinions
- Begins to experience empathy for others from being self-centered
- Begins to relate to nonfamily adults, still family-oriented

Figure 4-2. Child and youth development characteristics

- Gains awareness of sexual differences
- Wants to structure his environment as his home is structured and needs structure in activities
- Wants assurance of an adult's presence

Emotional
- Sees fairness as being nice to others so they will be nice in return
- Seeks parent and adult approval, strong desire for affection and attention of adults
- Behaves in ways to avoid punishment
- Develops modesty
- Expresses feelings and emotions, upsets are usually short-term
- Does not accept failure well and is sensitive to criticism

Intellectual
- Increases attention span (activities best limited to 15 to 30 minutes)
- Likes to explore; more interested in process than product
- Learns to sort things into categories and arrange in a series
- Learns concepts of right and wrong, and cause and effect
- Handles only one mental operation at a time well
- Sees difference between reality and fantasy, but may be afraid of scary figures
- Becomes easily motivated

Special Considerations for Activities Involving This Age Group
Provide opportunities for:
- Experimentation, using bodies, ideas, and material in different ways
- Active, boisterous games, climbing and balance, rhythmic activities
- Practicing skills in eye-hand coordination, such as cutting, pasting, and drawing
- Practicing group cooperation, sharing, and good work habits
- Freedom to do things for themselves (no longer babies) and use and develop their own abilities
- Using all five senses (i.e., use of ears, eyes, nose, mouth, and skin)
- Reenacting routines and events of their known world
- Developing friendship skills of sharing, helping, taking turns, and working with others
- Finding appropriate ways of channeling emotions and behaviors
- Being read to

8- to 10-Year-Olds

Physical
- Experiences steady increases in large-muscle development
- Increases strength, balance, and coordination
- Displays boundless energy, often restless and fidgety
- Matures at differing rates (boys are slower to mature)
- Increases manual dexterity, eye-hand, and small muscle coordination

Social
- Sees adults as authority
- Follows rules out of respect for authority; guidance from parents/adults is important to the child
- Displays noisy and argumentative behavior at times
- Feels loyalty to friendship group, often with "secret" words
- Expands use of reasoning skills to solve problems, negotiation, and compromise
- Displays humorous behavior

Emotional
- Views correct behavior as "obeying" rules set by those in power
- Accepts parent/family beliefs
- Admires and imitates older boys and girls
- Develops decision-making skills

Figure 4-2. Child and youth development characteristics (cont.)

- Begins to take responsibility for his own actions
- Needs acceptance from peer groups
- Emphasizes similarities between self and friends
- Learns about self through relationships
- Looks to adults for guidance and approval
- Needs recognition/praise for good work
- Finds it hard to accept the success of others; erodes self-confidence
- Is self-conscious, afraid to fail, sensitive to criticism
- Is quick to correct others and feels can do no wrong
- Responds to being upset by name-calling and teasing others
- Feels too "cool" for emotions

Intellectual
- Becomes quick, eager, and enthusiastic
- Varies greatly in academic abilities, interests, and reasoning skills
- Increases attention span, but interests changing rapidly
- Begins to think logically and symbolically
- Learning to use good judgment; uses concrete thinking
- Beginning to learn about moral judgments, applying principles of right and wrong
- Wants to know the how, what, and why of things; extremely curious
- Sees things as "black and white" and "yes or no," and has difficulty with opinions different than his

Special Considerations for Activities Involving This Age Group
Provide opportunities for:
- Using large and small muscles in activities
- Organized team games and sports where everyone can be successful
- Working in groups in cooperative activities
- Using skills to explore and investigate the world
- Assuming responsibility
- Discussing other people's viewpoints
- Exploring interests in collections and hobbies
- Expressing feelings and imagination through creative writing or acting
- Discussing reasonable explanations for rules and decisions
- Making and doing "real" things and using "real" tools, equipment, and materials
- Hands-on activities
- Doing work that is laid out in small pieces

11- to 13-Year-Olds

Physical
- Exhibits a wide range of sexual maturity and growth patterns between genders and within gender groups (girls are about two years ahead of boys)
- Changes rapidly in physical appearance: growth of hands and feet, nose, and ears may be faster than arms, legs, and face; causing concern for appearance
- Experiments with behavior to enhance sensory stimulation (e.g., drug and alcohol use)
- Loves food

Social
- Shifts from emphasis on same sex to opposite sex (girls develop interest in boys earlier than boys in girls)
- Looks more toward peers than parents, seek peer recognition
- Seeks acceptance and trust; lacks self-confidence
- Tends to regard sex in a depersonalized way
- Searches for adult role models, and often identify with admired adult hairdos and dress and the mannerisms of popular sports and music stars

Figure 4-2. Child and youth development characteristics (cont.)

- Questions authority
- Questions family values
- Submerges self for benefit of group
- Accepts spirit of group, which sometimes causes disciplinary problems
- Joins friendship groups or cliques that are often small but intense
- Gains more realistic understanding of who they are and what they can do
- Becomes more interested in social activities

Emotional
- Compares themselves to others
- Shows concern about development and emerging sexuality
- Sees themselves as always on center stage
- Becomes more conscious about bodily changes
- Is uneasy about being liked by friends, social graces, grooming
- Strives for independence, yet want and need parent help
- Seeks privacy from parents/adults
- Wants to be a part of something important
- Seeks to find the right words to describe feelings and degrees of emotion
- Exaggerates and uses sarcasm to describe subtle meanings

Intellectual
- Needs information for making decisions
- Finds justice and equality to be important issues
- Thinks abstractly and hypothetically
- Solves problems that have more than one variable
- Imagines consequences of acts
- Is ready for in-depth, long-term experiences
- Moves from fantasy to realistic focus on his life's goals

Special Considerations for Activities Involving This Age Group
Provide opportunities for:
- More structured and adult-like activities
- Exploring other cultures, foods, languages, and customs
- Completing projects (emphasis on precision and perfecting)
- Discussing issues and opposite sex with friends
- Making decisions
- Fun, learning experiences
- Activities involving the opposite sex, and learning to deal with opposite sex

14- to 17-Year-Olds

Physical
- Matures sexually, with accompanying physical and emotional changes
- Is concerned about body image, may have complexion problems
- Discovers various ranges in size and maturity among peers, some smaller, some larger
- Tends to have realistic view of limits to which body can be tested
- Desires to do things that give an adrenaline rush, or the extraordinary
- Has varying appetite and weight issues; girls tend to watch weight while boys have enormous appetites

Social
- Has high degree of social needs and desires
- Shows interest in coed activities
- Beginning to achieve independence from family
- Tends to romanticize sexuality, but moving toward more realistic understanding

Figure 4-2. Child and youth development characteristics (cont.)

- Searches for intimacy
- Prefers to set his own goals rather than accept those set by others
- Accepting of differences more readily
- Makes and keeps commitments
- Sees adults as fallible
- Renegotiates relationships
- Wants adult leadership roles
- Confides in friends more than family
- Developing community consciousness
- Is more secretive

Emotional
- Has strong identification with admired adult
- Desires respect
- Begins to accept and enjoy own individuality, but still seek status and approval of peer group
- Takes on multiple roles
- Is introspective
- Is able to see self from the viewpoint of others
- Is able to initiate and carry out own tasks without supervision of others
- Desires a role in determining what happens in his world

Intellectual
- Begins to think of occupational choices
- Wants his point of view heard and to participate in planning
- Enjoys demonstrating acquired knowledge
- Develops theories to explain how things happen
- Thinks abstractly
- Has gained better understanding of risks and consequences
- Develops goals and values
- Will lose patience with meaningless activity
- Solves problems, but finds frustration when not consulted
- Shows a better understanding of moral principles
- Possesses an idealistic view of adult life
- Begins to think of leaving home for college, employment, marriage

Special Considerations for Activities Involving This Age Group
Provide opportunities to:
- Be a part of the decision-making process
- Be empowered to make a difference in what's happening
- Show and value their individual differences
- Take on responsibility for others
- Be a part of coeducational activities
- Apply leadership skills
- Demonstrate self-expression
- Discuss issues and values

Adults and Senior Citizens

Young Adult Characteristics (18 to 26)
- Becomes independent and making it on own terms
- Focuses on developing marketable skills and knowledge to earn a living
- Displays a rather idealistic view of adult life
- Formulates values and develops a philosophy of life
- Begins to focus on choosing a mate
- Has an interest in expanding base of experiences (travel, vocational experiences, etc.)

Figure 4-2. Child and youth development characteristics (cont.)

Adult Characteristics
- Achieves satisfaction in vocation
- Assumes social and civic responsibilities
- Develops skills that are family-centered
- Chooses to become a parent with goal of raising children to become responsible and well adjusted
- Learns to relate to (or care for) parents and older adults
- Tests and refines values
- Learns to cope with anxiety and frustration
- Learns to handle more financial pressures
- Learns to handle increased family and work-related stress
- Expects housing that will provide some privacy and comfort

Senior Citizen Characteristics
- Adjusts to declining energy and physical changes of aging (e.g., decreased flexibility, balance, auditory and visual problems, less strength and endurance, slower reaction time)
- Builds new relationships with grown children and grandchildren
- Learns to relate again to their spouse
- Comes to terms with their life goals and aspirations
- Reveals principled moral reasoning
- May have less financial pressure
- May have a more conservative outlook on life than younger adults
- Expects housing that will provide privacy and accessibility

These conditions may enhance or detract from certain elements of physical growth or behavior.

Figure 4-2. Child and youth development characteristics (cont.)

In examining the developmental characteristics in Figure 4-2, staff should be conscious of the varying conditions that could alter certain of those characteristics:

- Cultural differences
- Economic situations
- Environmental conditions (home, school, peers, etc.)
- Physical conditions (diet, disabilities, genetics)
- Current societal trends or issues that put children at risk (violence, drug use, sexual activity, technological changes, etc.)

However narrow the age range served by a camp, the director and staff members need a general understanding of all age groups, since they may have ongoing relationships with other staff, parents of participants, board/committee members and such, who may go beyond the age range of participants.

An addition to this list of characteristics is that the advent of technological devices, whether cell phones, MP3 players, smart phones, games, computers, e-books, and so on, that have influenced the social and intellectual aspects of persons of all ages. Continuous contact with parents and friends, instant responses, instant social and intellectual information, and entertainment without physical activity (other than with the digits) or face-to-face relationships has had a tremendous impact on the social behavior, expanded knowledge, and the expectations of the users of various technological devices.

How the possession and use of these devices in the camp setting occurs is an issue that should be examined based on the philosophy and desired outcomes of the camp. Since most of the camp staff members have also been affected by this exposure and related experiences, an examination of this cultural change as it affects the age group with whom they will work needs to be part of staff training.

In examining the characteristics and developmental needs of various age groups, staff should also understand the basic competencies needed by a given age group. All of these competencies should be clearly addressed in the previously developed stated outcomes and indicators. In Figure 4-3, several youth development experts have identified these competencies for children and youth. Although the terminology may be different, general agreement can be found among these experts about what competencies or attributes are essential to the healthy development of young people at certain times in their lives.[7]

Competencies or Attributes Essential to the Healthy Development of Young People

Center for Early Adolescence—Peter Scales, 1991
- Positive social interactions with adults and peers
- Meaningful participation in families, school, and communities
- Competence and achievement
- Structure and clear limits
- Physical activity
- Creative expression
- Self-definition

Character Counts—Michael Josephson, 1996–98
- Trustworthiness
- Fairness
- Respect
- Citizenship
- Responsibility
- Caring

Reweaving the Tattered Web—Basil Whiting for Kauffman Foundation, 1993
- Interpersonal and social skills
- Emotional and psychological maturity and stability
- Basic academic skills and knowledge
- Commitment to higher values
- Cognitive, creative, and mental skills
- Vocational skills

40 Developmental Assets (in these eight categories)—Peter Benson, Search Institute, 1997
- Social competencies
- Empowerment
- Commitment to learning
- Positive values
- Boundaries and expectations
- Support
- Constructive use of time
- Positive identity

Desirable Youth Outcomes—Karen Pitman, International Youth Foundation, 1996
- Social competence
- Civic competence
- Intellectual competence
- Physical and emotional health
- Character (responsibility, spirituality)
- Confidence (self-worth, mastery)
- Connection (safety, structure)
- Cultural competence
- Membership and belonging
- Employability

A Matter of Time—Carnegie Council on Adolescent Development, 1992
- Social
- Civic
- Cognitive or intellectual
- Physical
- Emotional
- Vocational
- Cultural

Figure 4-3. Competencies for growth of youth

In these examples, each relates to the way in which outcomes and indicators are developed for children and youth in a camp setting. Second, these competencies materially affect the way in which program tools are used to accomplish outcomes. As you examine the basic concepts of human growth and development for a target population, you also need to examine the viability of the stated outcomes and indicators for that population.

Persons With Physical, Mental, or Emotional Disabilities

When participants have physical, mental, or emotional disabilities, an understanding of those specific disabilities is critical in helping participants gain the identified competencies. In some situations, a special camp or session is held for participants with a given disability or similar disabilities. This session may provide some common starting points for these participants, but does not eliminate the varying developmental needs of individuals. As Figure 4-1 outlines, disabilities are considered one of the physical/mental abilities of persons, in the basic areas of diversity.

Camp directors need to consider the implications in the Americans with Disabilities Act of 1990 (ADA) in making programs available to all persons, regardless of disability or limitation. The ADA requires that all camps, except those operated by religious groups and private clubs, make their programs and facilities accessible to individuals with disabilities. Religious groups and private clubs are exempted only when serving their own members, and then only if they are not receiving any federal funding or food or milk commodities from the U.S. Department of Agriculture. Further detail on these implications is provided in Chapter 11.

When integrating a camper with a disability into a living group, it should be clear that the goal is to provide a camp experience as close as possible to that provided to other campers. Helping the members of a living group to appreciate and understand each other is one goal of every camp living group, with or without members who have a disability. Counselors and activity specialists should be given as much information as is applicable about the disability of a camper who is being placed in a living group or program activity, including limitations, danger signals, medications, previous camp or outdoor experiences, and parental expectations. The more education and information given the staff will enable them to better work toward achieving the goals of the camp. One potential means of disseminating this information is through disability specific online training.

Behavior Management and Discipline

In camp, behavior management sets a tone or an atmosphere in which a desired behavior is achieved without damaging relationships or hurting people. It is the director's responsibility to outline appropriate and inappropriate camper behavior clearly, as well as appropriate and inappropriate consequences and staff responses to such behavior. These behaviors and responses should be clearly outlined during staff training. Again, the American Camp Association offers an online course for counselors that addresses behavior management.

Camp leadership can encourage acceptable behavior in a number of positive ways, including establishing a caring relationship with campers by opening lines of communication and encouraging a camper to come to a supervisor or the director when a problem arises. Praise is another effective way to encourage positive behavior. When counselors praise positive acts and ignore negative ones, the message is sent that campers must behave in a positive way to gain attention. Another means of encouraging good behavior is to create an atmosphere at camp that is full of cooperation and fun. Children are prone to imitate the behavior of those who are important to them, without judging whether the behavior is positive or negative. Staff members need to be sure that their individual behavior is worth being copied.

When dealing with a large number of youth from a variety of backgrounds and family patterns, in a setting where they can try new and different behaviors, there will be instances when those behaviors will be unacceptable and require discipline. "In every … camp, one of the major demands placed on directors and counselors is discipline. The key to handling this issue well is being prepared, which starts with having a plan and understanding different techniques that work."[8] The camp that enumerates a lengthy list of rules immediately upon arrival at camp invites the violation of those rules. Yet, some rules are necessary in any community and the method of educating youth about those rules and gaining their participation in setting and agreeing to those rules is critical to the educational purposes of the organized camp. Clear limits do need to be outlined with an explanation of the reasons for such limits.

Staff training is a time to set guidelines for discipline and prepare counselors to deal with problem behaviors. The camp's policy on, methods of, and circumstances requiring discipline should be clearly outlined during this training. Time should be devoted to conflict-resolution techniques, modeling behavior by staff, and the use of praise, time-outs, and other behavior management techniques. Role-playing a set of situations which require disciplinary action or group analysis may help staff gain a better understanding of the variable situations as well as appropriate disciplinary measures. Often, time for training is limited, and these important principles receive less-than adequate attention. One solution for increasing training time is to provide some form of online training before staff members come to camp. Such training could cover the nuts, bolts, and rules of the camp and principles of behavior management, while freeing up time for more interactive, hands-on, face-to-face training. It will not eliminate the necessity of covering much of that material in face-to-face sessions, but it may lessen the amount of time needed to cover the material.

Discipline is sometimes regarded as an old-fashioned word; it is also a principle that helps subordinate selfish interests to the welfare of the whole group. Before discipline becomes an issue, some considerations need to be understood and accepted by anyone working with children:
- A child has the occasional need to test the limits.
- A child cannot always manage self-control.
- A child has a strong tendency to the values of his peer group.

- A child has the right to make mistakes.
- A child has a right to be respected as an individual, regardless of unattractive attributes.

When discipline is required, some guidelines can be of help. Discipline should always be used sparingly to be effective—if discipline constantly, it becomes the accepted norm. Discipline should never be used vindictively or emotionally—counselors and administrators should never let a problem being dealt with affect them adversely. Punishment, if given, should follow the deed as quickly as is possible. Using work as a punishment usually creates a poor attitude toward work; the exception might be when the punishable deed created work for others. Physical punishment is not acceptable, nor is verbal abuse, which can be as destructive as physical force. (It should be noted that physical punishment or verbal abuse of a camper by a counselor or another staff member may be symptoms of stress on the part of the staff member.) During those times when punishment is needed, it should be imposed in a calm, respectful manner. The intent of the punishment should be to help the camper change their behavior and understand why such change is necessary.

If initial attempts to control or change an unacceptable behavior have failed, these processes may help:

- Maintain the initiative and try to persuade the camper that it is better to conform.
- Avoid specific threats by using a broad warning of a possible course of action. Rather than saying, "If you do that again, you will be sent home," try "There are consequences for breaking camp rules or for not cooperating." A child may imagine far more fearsome punishments than you can suggest. A specific threat commits the disciplinarian to carry it out or back down and may even dare the child to be confrontational, whereas a general warning reinforces the idea that compliance will be better than defiance.
- Involve other campers in the process. An indication that peers may not like the behavior brings in a different aspect. For example, in a situation where a group of boys were bullying a younger group, the camp director got the two groups together and, by asking questions, forced the older boys to face up to their actions. No threats or punishment were invoked, but the behavior changed.
- Check age characteristics to assess the level of comprehension or the motivation for obeying authority.
- Review any punishment before setting it. Does it fit the offense? For example, if one camper has peppered another's dessert, is it fair that the culprit goes without his dessert? Is punishment necessary to deter a repetition of the behavior? Any persistently antisocial behavior should not be allowed to pass without some appropriate action. Some children respond better to negative consequences, while others respond better to rewards or positive reinforcement.
- Look for causes. Avoiding difficult situations is much better than having to deal with them once they arise. Campers with too much energy can get into trouble; overtired campers are prone to react poorly to provocation. If a camper is more prone to negative behavior, try to start each day in

a manner that will encourage positive behavior. Try to identify campers who might cause problems and have strategies in mind to deal with them. Having a plan will keep the problems from seeming overwhelming.

Medical or Psychological Conditions and Inappropriate Behaviors

However well one understands human growth and development, there are special types of problems and situations that require some advance planning by the camp director. In an informal survey of camp directors conducted by Bob Ditter, the four major concerns most often mentioned were eating disorders, ADHD, increased aggressiveness and conflict among campers, and a surge in rudeness toward adults. The staff should be prepared to deal with these and other problems or conditions based upon training and information, rather than intuition. In addition to training on general behavior management, staff should be given practical guidance in dealing with special behavior concerns such as the following.

Abuse

Camp is often a place where abusive behavior (i.e., physical, sexual, psychological) that has occurred in the home environment comes to the surface, as youngsters find adults they trust and admire. Abuse by staff or other campers may also occur in the camp setting (see Chapter 7 for information on references and background checks). Counselors can pick up signs of abuse in the living situation if they have been given appropriate training. For example, the observation of unusual bruises or scars as the counselor supervises youngsters changing clothes or in the shower should cause the counselor to discuss the potential of physical abuse with the camp nurse and director.

Symptoms of psychological abuse may be obvious but dismissed as other types of behavior: depression or withdrawal, lack of self-esteem, seeking approval endlessly, hostility, rigidity, an inordinate attention to details or constantly self-denigrating behavior.

Symptoms of sexual abuse may also be dismissed or may be difficult to confirm. Some symptoms include abuse of animals, persistent or inappropriate sex play with toys or peers, and inappropriate understanding of sex for the child's age. Other symptoms have been identified by the National Center for Missing or Exploited Children:

- *Changes in behavior, extreme mood swings, withdrawal, fearfulness, and excessive crying*
- *Bed-wetting, nightmares, fear of going to bed, or wearing lots of clothes to bed*
- *Acting out inappropriate sexual activity or showing unusual interest in sexual matters*
- *Regression to infantile behavior*
- *A sudden acting out of feelings or aggressive or rebellious behavior*

- *A fear of certain places, people, or activities, especially of being alone with certain people*
- *Pain, itching, bleeding, fluid, or rawness in the private areas[9]*

Staff should be given a clear understanding of the steps to be taken should they have any suspicion of abuse before or during camp. Camp staff have a legal obligation to report child abuse to the authorities.

Some of the sexual behavior identified as a normal aspect of human growth and development may become abuse when a camper exhibits that behavior with a younger camper or by force on a peer. Camper-to-camper abuse has been a growing concern at camp, and what may have been considered a prank or hazing in the past is today considered abuse.

ADD/ADHD

Attention deficit disorder/attention deficit hyperactive disorder (ADD/ADHD) entails a combination of symptoms that include inattention, distractibility, impulsiveness, and other difficulties associated with attention. Three to five percent of children in the U.S. have ADD/ADHD. Affected boys outnumber girls three to one.

Though most youngsters can be overactive at times, a child with ADD/ADHD may act impulsively and inattentively, race ahead, take chances, and will seldom persist in any activity or goal. Such behavior requires considerable supervision. The role of the counselor is to protect the child from his own actions and to try to get the child to participate in the normal activities. Some children will be on medication such as Ritalin™ for this condition; some parents take their children off the medication for the time away from home. In such cases, it is important that the healthcare manager and related counselor be alerted.

Chris Thurber suggests three strategies relating to working with children with ADD/ADHD:

- *Design activities for all of the campers that provide small successes early on, give them a measure of control, and are intrinsically motivating.*
- *Collaborate with a child's treatment providers by ensuring that the young people ... take prescription medications as directed.*
- *Rather than focusing on diagnoses, focus on the children—all children—and have your repertoire of supportive strategies ready to go.[10]*

Aggression, Violence, and Bullying

Incidents of violence in schools and elsewhere, weapons possession, and threats against others have brought a heightened concern for these problems in camp. (See Chapter 11 for preventative plans.) It is important that staff be trained to recognize warning signs that may precede acts of violence, both in themselves and in others. Although no system for identifying potentially dangerous youngsters is foolproof, the National School Safety Center identified some behaviors that could indicate a youth's potential for harming himself or others: engaging in tantrums and serious disciplinary problems, uncontrollable angry outbursts, name-calling, cursing, abusive language, violent threats, having few or no close friends, being preoccupied with weapons, being bullied or bullying peers or younger children, preferring movies and reading materials dealing with violent themes or rituals, participating in a gang or an antisocial group on the fringe of peer acceptance, demonstrating significant mood swings, and threatening suicide.

Bullying is not new, but in recent years it has become a major societal concern wherever youth are gathered. The emotional, physical, or social distress created by the individual being bullied can have long-term effects. Kim Storey states that bullying has three defining characteristics:

- *Deliberate—a bully's intention is to hurt someone*
- *Repeated—a bully often targets the same victim again and again*
- *Power imbalanced—a bully chooses victims he or she perceives as vulnerable*[11]

Since staff members may have performed the bullying role as youth, the concern for the creation of a bullying-free environment at camp needs to be broad based. Staff training can prepare staff members to recognize bullying and provide tips on skills of intervening. Supervisors need clear guidelines in recognizing and responding to any form of bullying observed or reported.

HIV/AIDS

HIV/AIDS is not a behavior, but awareness by others of persons having either condition can lead to behavior patterns or concerns. Persons with HIV or AIDS should be treated as normally as possible. Counselors should be prepared to deal with situations that might cause bleeding or where bleeding might occur. They should have rubber gloves available in the living quarters (or in first-aid kits when out of camp) and be trained in universal precautions. Persons with HIV or AIDS ordinarily will understand the dangers to others. If the issue arises in the living group, counselors should be prepared to educate the group to the ways in which HIV and AIDS can and cannot be spread to alleviate the fears that some campers may have.

Autism

Autism spectrum disorders (ASDs) are a group of developmental disabilities that can cause significant social, communication, and behavioral challenges. People with ASDs handle information in their brain differently than other people.

ASDs are spectrum disorders. That means ASDs affect each person in different ways, and can range from very mild to severe. People with ASDs share some similar symptoms, such as problems with social interaction. But there are differences in when the symptoms start, how severe they are, and the exact nature of the symptoms.[12]

Autism is often accompanied by mild or profound ritualized or repetitive behavior. This could mean simply that the child needs to talk about the same subject over and over. The severity of this disorder in a child and whether the child has been acclimated to other social settings will determine the ability of nonspecialized camps to provide a positive camp experience.

Linda Ebner Erceg states that "in the interest of being inclusive, especially when the child's camp participation would be possible if someone could be with the child one-on-one, some camps suggest that parents consider having their child attend camp with a personal care attendant (PCA) … . This person is trained … to read the child's behavior, provide coaching at critical points, remove the child from potential trigger situations, and work with the child when frustration erupts."[13]

Eating Disorders

Anorexia nervosa, bulimia, and binge eating (BED) are the three eating disorders that are most familiar to the general public. These conditions tend to be more a problem for girls, although such disorders are on the rise for boys, and are closely associated with depression, low self-esteem, and stress. Adolescent girls who are concerned about weight gain often limit their food intake to a degree that can be problematic, or they may go on eating binges, followed by inducing vomiting to rid themselves of the food. These problems cannot be solved at camp unless you have a staff person with understanding of and training in treating these disorders. Of all the behavioral difficulties a child might have, this group is one that parents are extremely likely to deny, even if confronted with the facts. Because of parent denial and the secretive aspect of these disorders, children often arrive at camp without the director being informed of the condition.

Any counselor should be aware of what to do if he believes a camper has an eating disorder. The camper may react with embarrassment or become defensive or angry. Counselors should assure the camper that they will not discuss it with other campers or counselors, but because they really care about the camper and want the camper to be happy, they will report their concern to the director or camp healthcare manager. The camper should be able to sense acceptance from the counselor, not shock or disappointment. The counselor should encourage the camper to share feelings at any time the camper is disturbed or upset. Directors should also be prepared to address the problem of a staff member suffering from an eating disorder.

Encopresis

It is not unusual for younger campers to "soil" themselves in the process of play or excitement. The key to the situation is to avoid embarrassment or humiliation. The counselor may also help the situation by encouraging a regular time for a bowel movement or reminding the youngster about going to the toilet.

Enuresis

Neither is it unusual for younger campers to be faced with the embarrassing situation of bed-wetting in the resident camp setting. Bed-wetting is not a behavioral problem. No child wants to wake up in a wet bed. Camp is not the place to try to remedy the problem. The role of the counselor is to avoid embarrassment or humiliation of the camper before his peers. A procedure for handling the clothes and bedding should be developed so that counselors can deal with this situation quietly and sensitively without any punishment or additional embarrassment to the camper. Counselors can also help children by encouraging them to limit fluid intake after dinner and by reminding all campers to go to the bathroom before going to bed. Counselors can also wake children in the night and walk them to the bathroom.

Homesickness

Nearly 95 percent of campers have some feeling of homesickness—the distress or impairment caused by an actual or anticipated separation from home. It is characterized by acute longing and preoccupying thoughts of home and attachments to objects, sometimes with symptoms of sadness, crying, lack of interest in activities, isolation, and nonresponsiveness. More and more parents are in constant contact with their children through electronic devices, and a sense of interdependence grows in both the parent and the child. For many children, this may cause homesickness and a sense of separation anxiety.

One of the best preventive measures is to raise the campers' comfort levels right from the start. Campers often enter camp with apprehension because of the unknown. This problem can be lessened to some degree by providing a space on the camp website that helps campers to know what to expect at camp. The website might include an interactive map (virtual tour), pictures of program areas and residence areas, and a description of a typical day at camp. When the campers first arrive at camp, make sure they feel welcome and know what will be happening on the first day. Energetic, fun group activity on the first day of camp can often help set the tone of fun and community for campers who may be prone to homesickness.

Many youngsters miss parents, friends, home, or pets and become despondent and tearful. Involving the youngster in an activity that helps the camper gain friends and forget home is one solution, many times it is not as easy as it sounds. Counselors need guidance during staff training about how to deal with this problem, how it may affect the living group, and when it would become necessary to consult with the supervisor or director.

Sexual Behavior

Young people often find camp an opportunity to explore or "act out" sexual behavior, given that they are in regular contact with peers and out of their home environment. This behavior may be aggressively heterosexual or homosexual in nature, and may be somewhat open in the group or secretive in nature. It is important to deal with sex honestly and openly without great moralizing and to help youth understand the normality of sex. However, they also need to understand the accepted behavior patterns of camp and learn to respect others' rights.

Sleeping Problems

Sleepwalking or nightmares may occur, and if any campers have a history of either, the counselor will need to be particularly watchful of the camper.

Stealing

This problem may be best handled by discussing it with the group and exerting positive peer pressure. When it is discovered that a youngster has stolen something, that camper should be confronted and given the responsibility of returning the item and apologizing. Some discussion with the affected group is important, but ostracizing the individual should be avoided.

Stress

Though stress is a causal factor rather than a behavior, enough stress is imposed upon youth in today's society that it is important to underline its consideration in staff training and supervision. David Elkind has probably been the most articulate voice about the stress on children in his book *The Hurried Child*. He states:

> Children and teenagers are being hurried today as never before. Clock hurrying, [or] being asked to do or achieve too much in too little time, stresses children directly and gives rise to many stress symptoms such as eating, sleeping, and learning disturbances. Calendar hurrying, [or] being asked to do the wrong things at the wrong time, stresses young people indirectly by lowering self-esteem and thus rendering them more vulnerable to stress. The result is a dramatic rise in stress-related behaviors in all age groups.[14]

The role of camp should be to relieve the stress of children rather than to create it. Helping staff understand their role in this endeavor is another step toward preventing problems or acting-out behaviors.

Substance Abuse

Camp is not isolated from alcohol, tobacco, or nonprescription substance abuse, consumption, or sharing among campers or staff. Certainly, there is a high consciousness of substance abuse, and ample materials are available for the education of the director and staff. Legal implications need to be understood by the staff and director, as well as campers. Most important, the camp director must emphasize that it can happen at camp and provide adequate training before campers arrive. Clear statements should be available in the literature distributed to campers, parents, and staff concerning the camp's position in this area, the consequences if violated, and the camp's policy on searching a camper's belongings.

Suicidal Behavior

Society has become much more aware of the seriousness of suicide among youth. Suicide is the third-leading cause of death for young people 15 to 24 years of age. Counselors need to understand the signs of depression and the types of symptoms that often precede suicidal behavior. The warning signs that staff may notice at camp include a camper (or staff member) who:

- Has sudden changes in behavior
- Gives away prized possessions
- Threatens suicide or talks about previous suicide attempts or suicide methods
- Exhibits extreme or extended boredom
- Demonstrates reckless behavior, carelessness, or self-destructive acts
- Withdraws from friends and family and loses interest in activities
- Is unusually sad, discouraged, and lonely, then suddenly calm and happy
- Expresses feelings of hopelessness and/or worthlessness
- Is preoccupied with death (perhaps evident in written expressions or artwork)
- Makes statements about not being missed if he/she were gone
- Has family or relationship disruptions, divorce trauma, ending of a romance
- Demonstrates an unusually long grief reaction from death of a friend, loved one, or even a pet
- Shows physical symptoms such as eating disturbances, sleeplessness, or excessive sleeping
- Experiences chronic headaches or stomachaches, menstrual irregularities, apathetic appearance

Any such behavior should be considered serious, not only by the counselor but by administrative staff as well. Make it clear that talking about thoughts and feelings is okay, express concern, listen attentively, be empathetic and not judgmental, don't promise confidentiality, stress that suicide is a permanent solution to a temporary problem, and remind them that help is available and things will get better. Most importantly, individuals should not assume that they can help them alone. Know where professional help is available in the area (i.e., mental health professional, crisis hot line, intervention team, minister, peer counselors, etc.). A number of organizations offer websites that carry information about suicide statistics and prevention, such as: Patrick Dennehy Foundation's www.thekeltyfoundation.org/depression-resources.htm; the Center for Disease Control's www.cdc.gov/ncipc/dvp/Suicide; and the American Academy of Pediatrics' www.aap.org/advocacy/childhealthmonth/prevteensuicide.htm.

Vandalism

When personal or camp property is vandalized by campers, it may be a symptom of deeper problems. However, vandals should be dealt with directly and in a fashion that not only helps them gain an understanding of the seriousness of this behavior, but also requires them to have a role in restoring or replacing the vandalized property.

Preparation of Participants

Individuals

Determining and understanding a camper or group population are only the first steps in building a positive growth experience that meets the camp objectives. Participants should be made aware of the camp's philosophy and expectations. Thorough preparation can eliminate or, at least, lessen some of the concerns identified earlier.

A camp director who begins or concludes enrollment of a camper with a personal interview with the camper's family will already have begun this preparatory process. In addition, after an interview, the camp director will have a better idea of who that camper is and his expectations as well as how that young person will fit into the camp setting or even if the camp is the best fit for a particular child.

Many camps have found increasing numbers of international campers enrolling. Since expectations vary from culture to culture, a special effort should be made to help such campers and their parents understand not only the mission of the camp, but also the specific activities and foods that are available. It is better to deal with differences in expectations before arrival at camp, in order to make adjustments to meet the needs of certain international participants.

However, many camp directors are not able to interview every new camper, and thus it is most important to carefully prepare a plan for the orientation of campers. The first step is to send confirmation of enrollment and receipt of the deposit with a welcome message by mail or e-mail, indicating pleasure that the camper is coming to camp and providing details about when the camper might expect further information. It should also direct the camper and the family to the camp website, where they should find an opportunity for a family member to e-mail the camp with specific questions or concerns.

An information packet is usually sent to the camper and the camper's parents at least two months before the camper arrives at camp. First, and foremost, a clear interpretation of the type of program the camper and the camper's parents may expect at camp, with very specific references to out-of-camp trips, unusual activities, and the like. Charles R. "Reb" Gregg, an attorney specializing in risk-management matters, states:

> *A participant in your program deserves, fairly, to know what to expect. Perhaps more significantly, a person or family affected by an event or condition cannot be assumed to have*

consented to participation in that situation if they don't know of it beforehand. Failure to disclose the prospect of a remote field trip, or the absence of radios, for example, may allow a family to make a claim that would not otherwise be available to it."[15]

In today's culture, the camp's position on the use of cell phones, MP3 players, computers, and the like should be clearly stated in advance information. On the same note, it is important that a clear statement accompanying promotional information outlines the essential functions the camper will be expected to perform in order to participate in program activities. Informing families allows parents and their medical consultants to make an informed decision about the physical and mental ability of the child to participate. The health-history and physical-examination forms should mirror this essential function information.

Additionally, the following items should be included in this packet:

- A sample clothing list indicating the type and amounts of clothing needed. If special equipment—such as boots, riding gear, or a sleeping bag—is needed, specifications or details should be given about the type needed and potential sources for purchase.

- Information about the appropriate marking of all possessions with the camper's name to assist in lost-and-found problems

- Any restrictions about personal items such as radios, cell phones, MP3 players, knives, pets, personal sporting equipment, or guns

- Information about laundry including whether the camp will arrange for service, whether campers wash their own clothes, or whether quantities of apparel suggested are usually ample for the length of the camp session

- Health examination information, including a form requesting information the parent needs to provide for a health history. If an examination is required, the form should specify information the physician needs to furnish, maximum length of time allowed between examination and camp opening, inoculations required, and health care available at camp. See Figures 12-2 and 12-3 for samples of health forms. Special attention should be paid to ensure the health examination form is mailed early enough for parents to arrange for an appointment with the physician. The form should be explicit about the information needed in addition to the health examination, such as:

  - ✓ Health-history information: allergies, operations, previous illnesses, inoculations, disabilities, and/or psychological concerns

  - ✓ Medications that the camper is taking currently or was taking immediately prior to coming to camp, along with written instructions from the doctor

  - ✓ A release signed by parents or guardians enabling the camp to provide a minor with routine health care and prescribed medications and to seek emergency medical treatment. Some hospitals require notarized signatures.

  - ✓ Health-insurance information (does the camp cover, or is the parent's insurance expected to cover any incidents at camp)

  - ✓ Emergency addresses and phone numbers of parents or guardians

  - ✓ Any limitations on activity participation or living situation and any necessary medical attention

✓ An indication to the parent that if the child has any psychological concerns and/or related medications an interview with a representative of the camp should be requested to ensure that the camp is a proper match for the child and appropriate care can be given at camp

- Information regarding transportation to camp. Will parents be expected to transport the camper to camp? If so, arrival times and directions to the camp should be provided. If group transportation is provided, list the times, fares, and any other related information. If arriving campers can be met at air, train, or bus terminals, explain the procedure and any charges for such service. For day camps, a schedule and times of the pickup and drop points for campers should be provided, as well as a plan for emergency arrangements.

- Visiting days, or times, if any

- The camp's mailing address and e-mail address

- Information about the use of fax, e-mail, blogs, cell phones, or telephone for making or receiving communications; and information about the handling of mail and whether packages containing food items for campers are encouraged or accepted

- Information concerning religious services at camp and availability of services out of camp, especially if the family wishes child to attend special services

- For day camps, an explanation of the plan for daily lunch, including what is to be brought by the camper and what is to be furnished by the camp

- For day camps, the plan and preparation for overnight activities offered during the period (if any)

- For day camps, a clear statement on the camp's policy of contacting the parent/guardian on any unexplained absence of said camper in a timely fashion

When the majority of campers come from the same population center, a camp may have an orientation session or open house during the months preceding camp to answer any questions from campers and parents and to prepare new campers for their first year at camp. This session may include introduction of staff, videos about or from camp, and comments on what to bring to camp. It would also provide a chance for campers of the same age groups to get acquainted and for families to gain a better understanding of the camp organization and policies. Directors should take special note of the questions posed by parents during this meeting in order to determine how these questions could be answered on the camp website.

Groups

Preparing for individuals who are coming as part of rental or program groups is no less important, but it does not require the same direct contact with the individuals since the group leader or organization has that responsibility. Since the information goes through that second party, it is even more important that the information be thoroughly and clearly written, posted on the camp website, and mailed early with the confirmation of the reservation. Such information on the web and in the packet could include the following items:

- A map of the camp property, as well as directions on how to get there
- A description of the sleeping accommodations and what bedding is furnished
- Rules and regulations that affect the activities, safety, and behavior of the group (e.g., alcohol, radios, firearms, drugs, skateboards)
- What health care, if any, will be available and what health-care planning is advised for the group leader in terms of first aid, emergency care, and transportation
- The camp telephone number for emergency purposes
- If the camp is providing any specialized programs, information about clothing or equipment that participants are expected to bring
- The type of leadership the group is responsible for providing persons to supervise participants and their behavior, as well persons with certain certifications (lifeguard, nurse, etc.)
- Advice for the group leader as to the type of information that should be collected in advance (name, address, emergency contact information, health conditions, waivers)
- Any safety procedures requiring orientation by camp staff upon arrival at camp
- Any insurance coverage required by the camp, and the type of documentation needed
- The written use agreement and terms to be signed by the legal representative of the group

When preparing the information indicated, the director should assume that the persons reading it may know nothing about camp. The words and information should be checked for clarity. Every opportunity should be taken in the material to emphasize the potential fun, excitement, and value of the experience.

Checkpoints

- Identify the camp's participant population, and describe efforts made to provide diversity in that population.
- Review the developmental characteristics of the age group(s) served by the camp, and devise a method of sharing this information with the camp staff during precamp training.
- In the precamp training schedule, outline how and where appropriate growth and development, as well as problematic behaviors, of campers is covered.
- Examine the camp program and schedule in light of preventing unnecessary stress in the lives of campers, as well as alleviating the stress felt in daily life during the previous school year.
- Identify everything a new camper and parent needs to know about camp before arrival, and devise a plan for disseminating this information.
- Organize, in chronological order, the steps parents of campers need to take before camp.
- Identify what a group leader would need to know and do prior to bringing a first-time group to camp.
- Check pertinent written materials to make sure they reflect the information in the previous three checkpoints.

Related Standards

American Camp Association's Accreditation Standards for Camp Programs and Services: HR.12, HR.16; OM.9–15; PD.3–5; HW.6, HW.8–9

Endnotes

1. Elmer Ott. 1949. *So You Want To Be a Camp Counselor.* New York: Association Press (YMCA of the USA). p. 21.
2. www.childstats.gov/americaschildren.
3. Karla A. Henderson. 1994. "Unlearning the Isms." *Camping Magazine.* Vol. 67, No.1, September/October, p. 19.
4. Robert Ditter. 1997. *In the Trenches*. Martinsville, IN: American Camping Association.
5. Connie Coutellier. 2007. *Camp Is for the Camper: A Counselor's Guide to Youth Development* (2nd Ed.). Monterey, CA: Healthy Learning.
6. Connecticut Department of Human Resources and the University of Connecticut Cooperative Extension System. "Beyond Opening Day: Building Excellence in School-age Child Care Programs." Jean E. Folkerth. 1981. "Developmental Characteristics." *Perspectives on Camp Administration*. Elizabeth Farley (Ed.). Martinsville, IN: American Camping Association. pp. 26–28. Mayo Foundation for Medical Education and Research, Rochester, MN www.mayoclinic.com/health/child-development. Orange, CA: Child Development Institute, LLC. www.childdevelopmentinfo.com/development/devsequence.shtml.

7. Peter C. Scales. 1991. "The Developmental Needs of Young Adolescents Today and Tomorrow." *Proceedings of a Symposium on Year-Round School*. Martinsville, IN: American Camping Association; and Basil J. Whiting. 1993. *Reweaving the Tattered Web, Socializing and Enculturating Our Children*. Kansas City, MO: Ewing Kauffman Foundation.

8. Donnie Jackson. 1997. "Disciplining Campers." *Camping Magazine*. Vol. 70, No. 4, July/August.

9. National Center for Missing and Exploited Children. 1988. *Camp Director's Guide: Preventing Sexual Exploitation of Children*. Washington, D.C.: Office of Juvenile Justice and Delinquency Programs, U.S. Department of Justice. Rhulen Agency in cooperation with the American Camping Association. p. 19.

10. Christopher Thurber. 2011. "Strategies for Working with Children Who Have Attention Deficits." *Camping Magazine*. Vol. 84, No. 3, May/June, pp. 40-45.

11. Kim Storey. 2010. "Eyes on Bullying: What You Can Do to Prevent and Stop Bullying at Camp." *Camping Magazine*. Vol. 83, No.3, May/June, pp. 48-52.

12. Center for Disease Control and Prevention. 2011. "Facts About ASDs." www.cdc.gov/ncbddd/autism.html.

13. Linda Ebner Erceg. 2011. "Assessing Youth with Autism Spectrum Disorders for Their 'Fit' at Camp." *Camping Magazine*. Vol. 84, No. 2, March/April, pp. 52-55.

14. David Elkind. 1985. "The Hurried Child." *Camping Magazine*. Vol. 58, No. 1, September/October, pp. 25–26.

15. Charles R. "Reb" Gregg. 2002. "Staying in Camp and Out of the Courthouse." *The CampLine*. Vol. X, No. 3, February.

DESIGNING THE PROGRAM

Camp Echo (Burlingham, NY)

Chapter Five

And at each day's end a child should surely have experience with a small fire—sit close to it, tend it, feel its warmth and the warmth and security of her or his close-knit small family group gathered round; and in the wonder and magic of firelight be able to talk, in the semidarkness, of the problems that bother—begin to form attitudes, think out values, grapple for the ends for which he or she might live—begin to put together the fragmented pieces of learning toward becoming a whole person.[1]

—Lois Goodrich

Program is, as was already suggested, only a tool that grows out of the camp's philosophy, mission/purpose, and outcomes. To develop program activities without a mission and youth development outcomes in mind is simply to provide a potpourri of activities, many of which may be just as easily available in the camper's home setting. Program is not just the activities, it is:

All activities, conditions, and relationships that affect the camper: the planned activities as well as the unplanned; the subtle conditions that surround him as well as the more obvious conditions; the relationships that he has with other campers and with counselors; the counselor's attitudes toward him as well as the methods the counselor uses.[2]

If program is everything that happens at camp, it cannot be covered in one chapter. However, it is touched upon in many aspects of the living experience that are discussed from chapter to chapter: eating, sleeping, health care, staff, transportation, the camp setting, and of course, activities.

In smaller camps, the director may give immediate supervision to the coordination of program activities, but as the number of campers and the complexities of camp operations grow, the director will have to secure assistance or delegate this primary responsibility to a program director or coordinator. It is important that this ongoing responsibility be assumed by one individual so that the evaluation of the entire program rests with a single individual. That person needs a clear understanding of the camp's mission and desired outcomes, of the background of the target population, and of the developmental needs of the age groups in camp. This person also needs the ability to maintain a working relationship with the staff. Regardless of the size of the camp, the director can never completely delegate supervision of the program.

The camp director and the program director must share a cohesive and collaborative approach to all of the elements of camp life to make the experience fruitful and to monitor the camp's progress toward meeting its goals and outcome statements.

With the expansion of a summer youth camp into a year-round operation, the program may be different, depending on the purpose of the expansion and on the new target population. Therefore, this chapter has been subdivided to discuss not only the summer-camp approach, but some of the other types of programs and groups that may use a site in other seasons.

Steps in Program Development

There is a temptation to begin program development by simply determining the activities the camp might wish to offer. However, much more is involved, given the 11 steps in program development (Figure 5-1). The first step in the development of program is to go back to the camp's philosophy, mission/purpose, desired outcomes, and identity to determine one or more target populations or customer groups. Only with these elements clearly in mind is it wise to proceed in the planning process. Information gained in the program planning process may lead to the revision of the camp's philosophy or mission statement. When this change happens, it will be a conscious revision or change in direction, and it may influence the actual identity of the camp.

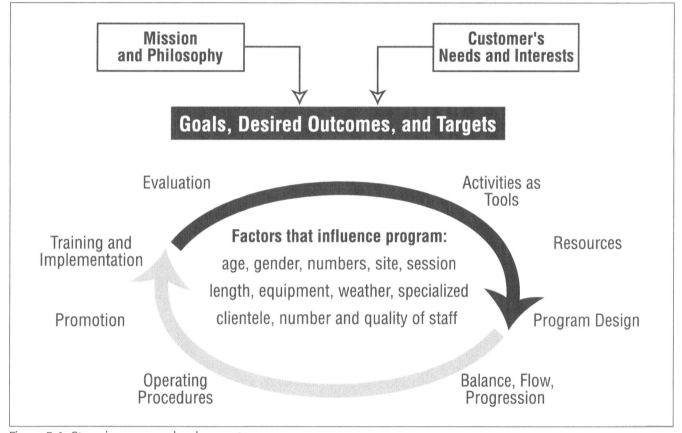

Figure 5-1. Steps in program development

The second step in planning a program is to assess the customers' interests and developmental needs. This assessment is multifaceted since, even if the camp serves solely youth, the parent and the camper are both customers, often with differing viewpoints. Many camps serve not only youth, but also adults, rental groups, schools, and special populations within age groups. Steps in program development necessitate an examination of each group's expectations and needs. Such assessments may take the form of questionnaires, individual interviews, or focus-group interviews. In camps for children, where the parents become the primary customer and the child is the consumer, the expectations and needs of both parties require research. Questions should be formulated carefully to avoid bias on the part of the author or interviewer and be aimed at soliciting the type of information desired.

The third step, once the assessments are compiled, is to review the camp's desired outcomes to see if these are compatible with the needs and interests of the customers. In other words, can a program really be developed that will meet the interests and needs of potential customers and also meet the camp's goals and outcomes? If not, it necessitates a reassessment of the audience served or the mission, outcomes, and identity of the camp. Some alignment of these factors is necessary to expect the camp to be financially viable, to have community support, and fulfill the camp's very reason for existence.

The fourth step is to identify potential program activities that will attract customers, pique their interest, contribute to their developmental needs, and help accomplish the desired outcomes. This step will keep campers and parents engaged and committed to the program.

The fifth step is an appraisal of the camp's resources, including the environment in which the program is to take place. A careful look not only at facilities, but also the natural environment, will be useful in appraising whether the type of program planned will fit in the environment. Will the program be inappropriate or counter-productive in the natural environment? Does the program take advantage of the natural resources at hand? What about staff? Can persons with the expertise and leadership skills required for this particular program be found? What about fiscal resources to initiate the program? What are the start-up costs? What is the cost effectiveness of the program? All of these questions can help the director determine if the camp's resources are situated to meet the needs and wants of its constituents.

The sixth step relates to program design and includes how the total camp experience is organized to fit together and communicate the camp's identity. See the following section for a discussion of overall program design.

Once the resources are appraised and activities identified, the director and key staff should begin the seventh step, the refinement of the specific program, outcomes, and activities. An effort should be made to create a balance between small-group and total-group activities, active and quiet times, and structured and informal times. In addition, the program should be age appropriate and provide progression during the session and from year to year. Progression will add to a camper's opportunity for challenge and foster a sense of accomplishment, as well as aid in filling camp.

Operating procedures need to be determined for each program activity in the eighth step. Such procedures include eligibility requirements for participants, camper-staff ratios, appropriate equipment, safety regulations, emergency procedures, and the qualification of the staff supervising the activity. Further emphasis is given to this process later in this chapter.

Only when the program is clearly defined and outlined consistent with the camp's mission and identity, and fiscal resources committed to its accomplishment, is the ninth step viable: promoting the program to prospective customers. A dry run with a small group of prospective customers is a good idea prior to broadly promoting the program. This information should not only excite the potential participant, but also inform families and/or organizations of the nature of the anticipated activities.

Having secured the customers and determined the necessary personnel, the next step is training the staff in the delivery of the program to accomplish the desired outcomes. Implementation of the program follows. Generally, participant training is integrated into the program design and implementation.

Both during and at the conclusion of the program, the final step should be implemented—that of evaluation. This process will lead to setting new goals, targets, and desired outcomes to improve the program before it is implemented again in the future. Evaluation is discussed more in-depth in Chapter 18.

Program Design

After completing the initial five steps, the director must begin designing the program to meet predetermined outcomes. The first part of this process is to make decisions about what portion of program activities will be planned by individuals, by living groups, by staff, or by the central administration. Decisions should next be made about which activities will be carried out by or within the living group, or if individuals will move into other groups for some activities.

Historically, two different philosophies—centralized and decentralized—evolved in camp programs. Under a centralized program philosophy, activities are carried out so that each individual camper may participate in activities with a variety of campers. These activities may be scheduled by one or more staff persons or by staff in collaboration with a camper council. By taking part in activity selection and scheduling, a camper learns to take responsibility for his/her decisions. The living group is usually a focus only for special events, sleeping, cabin clean-up, bedtime, and sometimes eating. The emphasis in this type of camp tends to be on developing individual skills, as well as participating in occasional all-camp activities or unit activities.

When registering for or upon arriving at a camp with a centralized program, individual campers (or their parents) may sign up for specialized instruction sessions. Depending on the length of the sessions, it may be possible to change to other activities at various points in the camp session. Campers generally move from one level of instruction to another as the camper gains skills.

On the other hand, under a decentralized program philosophy, campers help plan and participate in activities with their living group, using a group work process. The group work process is a social work method that places emphasis on "helping individuals to enhance their social functioning through purposeful group experiences and to cope more effectively with their personal, group or community problems."[3] The group work process began in the early part of the 20th century as the basis of program in clubs, troops, and in settlement houses throughout the United States and found a natural home in many camps.

In a decentralized program, the group performs the planning function for their program. The group joins the larger camp community only for special events, common meals, and/or primary services such as health or acquisition of supplies. The emphasis tends to be on the group relationships and on developing independence from the larger camp community, including the separate preparation of certain meals. In this design, most scheduling is done within the living group. The central program personnel are consulted particularly as scheduling affects the use of central facilities or staff, or as the plan of one living group impinges on another.

In the original format as developed by L.B. Sharpe of Life Camp in New Jersey, a decentralized experience would consist of a living group that constructs its own campsite, complete with cooking areas, toilet areas, and shelters. The group would plan its own daily activities and prepare its own meals.

In reality, most camps do not operate a purely centralized or decentralized program, and find it more realistic to combine the two philosophies. In many camps, the camper's day is a combination of centralized and decentralized activities. This pattern can move along a continuum between centralized and decentralized. Where a camp's program design fits along this continuum should grow out of an analysis of the first five steps of program development: the philosophy and goals of the camp, interest of campers, desired outcomes, program activities, and the facilities and staff of the camp. Figure 5-2 identifies a variety of organizational designs, ranging from the pure centralized to pure decentralized.

Finding the camp's position along this philosophical continuum takes thought and experience. The place to begin is with the camp's stated goals and outcomes, the camp director's leadership style, the facility, and type of staff the camp employs. In looking at these elements together, it is possible to examine several different ways of using these philosophies and to see which one can possibly meet the goals in the most effective manner. With experimentation from summer to summer, a director can soon reach the philosophy that seems to be most effective for your particular camp.

The program philosophy will naturally affect staff recruitment, organization, and design. Consider the following:

- Program specialists are most often the primary focus of the day's activities in a centralized program, while counselors are the primary focus in a decentralized program.
- Authority for program scheduling and supervision lies with program and administrative staff in a more centralized philosophy, whereas it resides with the living-group counselor and unit leader in a decentralized approach.
- The program specialists are more likely to determine program content and the schedule in a centralized design. Campers are often assigned program activity times by age or skill level, or program counselors may assist campers in selecting their activities and determining their individual schedule.
- When the living group is used as the basis of programming, program specialists may need to be prepared to have campers with a variety of skill levels and ages participating at the same time.

Organizational Design	Pure Centralized	Modified Centralized	Combination	Modified Decentralized	Pure Decentralized Camper/Staff
Organization	As a whole camp	As a whole camp	Half day as a whole camp and half day by unit or living groups	As units or cabin groups	As units or cabin groups
Program	Designed and scheduled for individuals	Individual choice by age or skill level	Half day by individual choice and half day by living groups	Planned and scheduled by staff for groups	Planned and scheduled by small groups
Activities	Specialized, standardized, familiar, skill development	Specialized, individual skill development and options	Specialized skill development half day and group activities half day	Specialized, standardized, skill development as small groups	General guidelines, creative, group interaction
Motivation	Individual competition, awards, and rewards	Competition is individual's choice; individual awards and rewards	Individual skill improvement and group decision making and involvement	Group competition or teambuilding, awards, and rewards	Group decision making, involvement, awards, and rewards
Leadership	Primarily specialists with counselors assisting	Primarily specialists with counselors assisting	Half day with specialists and half day with generalists	Primarily generalists with some certified specialists	Primarily generalists with some certified specialists
Evaluation	Individual skill progress measured	Individual popularity and quality of program areas measured	Individual skill progress and quality of group interaction measured	Quality of group interaction and some skill progress measured	Quality of group interaction and some skill progress measured

Figure 5-2. Organizational designs

Thus, the more a camp program leans toward a centralized structure, the more important it is to employ individuals with competence in specific skill areas and with good instructional abilities. Obviously, each instructor must know how to teach children and should have enough child-psychology training to understand the tasks suitable for the various developmental stages of children. Having experience and skill in a program does not necessarily guarantee the ability to teach that skill or apply it at the appropriate age-readiness level.

In a centralized model, program specialists often reside in a camper living unit as secondary counselors, but usually do not assume the chief responsibilities of a counselor. On the other hand, the counselor in a living unit usually also assumes responsibility for assisting in a specific program area, since only a few hours of the day are spent in direct living-group activities.

A decentralized program requires counselors to possess more general skills in a variety of program areas, since the primary authority for daily planning and scheduling lies within their group. Depending upon the degree of decentralization, counselors will need greater maturity and experience since they will be supervising campers nearly 24 hours a day. A decentralized program usually has fewer program specialists. They may be available to lead activities for individual living groups at a group's request.

The location of living areas and physical facilities will influence a camp's ability to operate fully on either a centralized or decentralized basis. Though it is possible to make certain adjustments, the physical layout of the camp does have to be considered early in program planning. For example, a dormitory arrangement that has several camper groups occupying the same building makes it somewhat difficult to operate a truly decentralized program.

Elements of Program Organization

Program organization is essential whether the camp is decentralized, centralized, or some combination thereof. The schedule is one means of organizing the program, and it enables the camp to use a variety of elements in its development. Scheduling and organization relate directly to the camp's program design. Many new directors and staff are more comfortable with a structured centralized program. They know the schedule and where everyone is at all times. The same comfort level also can be achieved with an unstructured decentralized program. In the process of developing the schedule, the director should look at many elements. The sample schedule in Figure 5-3 shows three different program schedules.

The Living Group

In a decentralized program, the living group is the principal structure for the accomplishment of program. The only interaction with the total camp may occur during meals and special activities or all-camp events. Even the all-camp events can be designed for participation by living groups. Many new directors and staff are more comfortable with a structured program. They know the schedule and where everyone is at all times. The same comfort level can be achieved with an unstructured program. Campers, as individuals (centralized) or groups (decentralized), may sign up for activities at the beginning of a session, week or day and then a schedule is made so staff and campers know what activities they are participating in and how many will be there for that period. Figure 5-3. Sample schedule of centralized, decentralized, and combination programs

In a decentralized design, a living group and their counselor may tour camp, identify program areas, discuss program possibilities, and then plan a schedule for their group. This schedule can be negotiated with other staff so that the activities or areas that require a specialist or a given number of campers at a time can be scheduled. A master schedule is created for coordination purposes. In some camps, groups may change their schedule based on "being considerate of others." For example, if a group tells the kitchen staff they are cooking out on

Centralized		Decentralized	Combination	
7:30 a.m.	Arise	8:00 a.m. Breakfast	7:30 a.m.	Arise
8:00 a.m.	Flag raising		8:00 a.m.	Breakfast
8:15 a.m.	Breakfast	Activities that have been planned		Cabin cleanup
	Cabin cleanup	by living groups, which may include	9:00 a.m.	Individual choice
9:30 a.m.	Activity period 1	cabin cleanup, some program	10:00 a.m.	of activities for three
10:45 a.m.	Activity period 2	activity, and lunch as a group or	11:00 a.m.	one-hour periods
12:30 p.m.	Lunch	in central dining hall; some restful	12:30 p.m.	Lunch
	Rest period	activity and time		Rest period
2:15 p.m.	Activity period 3	12:30 p.m. Lunch	2:15 p.m.	Activities planned by
3:30 p.m.	Activity period 4	Rest period		living groups
4:45 p.m.	Open swim		6:00 p.m.	Dinner
	Other activities	Activities planned by living groups	7:00 p.m.	Free time
6:00 p.m.	Dinner		8:00 p.m.	All-camp planned
7:00 p.m.	Free time	6:00 p.m. Dinner		evening program or l
8:00 p.m.	Evening program			iving group activity
9:30 p.m.	Taps	Activities in living groups or units;	9:30 p.m.	Taps
		occasional all-camp activity		

Many new directors and staff are more comfortable with a structured program. They know the schedule and where everyone is at all times. The same comfort level can be achieved with an unstructured program. Campers, as individuals (centralized) or groups (decentralized), may sign up for activities at the beginning of a session, week or day and then a schedule is made so staff and campers know what activities they are participating in and how many will be there for that period.

Figure 5-3. Sample schedule of centralized, decentralized, and combination programs

Tuesday night, it would be hard for the cook to count on having enough food in the dining room if they changed their mind at the last minute.

If they decide to work quietly on a craft in their cabin during rest hour, it probably won't affect another group, unless they are using all the scissors in camp. A unit or living group may have a basic supply of tools and supplies so they are able to be more self-sufficient.

If the group doesn't plan their program until the morning or afternoon they expect to participate, then they may take their chances on getting a space. For example, only two groups can be at archery at a time since only 20 bows are available. A good comparison for this situation is considering a family on vacation: they may reserve a space at a popular tourist attraction before they leave home to make sure they have the space they wish.

In a centralized program, a place is provided for the living group to have time to do things together, whether it is simply meals, cabin cleanup, bedtime chats, or specific activity periods designated daily. Some camps use the living group in competitions with other living groups in sports and other contests. However, too much competition at this level can be counterproductive to the real goals of group living.

The Individual

In centralized camps, the individual is given a choice of activities in set periods both morning and afternoon, and the program is tailored to that person's interests, skill level, and expressed needs. Choices are usually limited by eligibility requirements for certain activities, including a requirement that the camper stick with the activity for a minimum number of days. The camper is assigned a set of activities and given a schedule. In most cases, these camps are very skill-oriented, and they have an expectation of some degree of mastery in the skill or subject area (e.g., some sports camps, science camps, performing arts camps, weight-loss camps, scuba camps).

Even in a camp where the camper has chosen specific activities in which to participate, there is an anticipation of improvement in the skill(s). In some less structured situations, older campers may be allowed to decide what they want to do in each time period and just show up. These campers may be limited by other factors. For example, if all the horses are taken for the 10 o'clock trail ride for beginners, these campers will need to go to another activity and come back at another time.

Any program design should provide opportunities for individuals to have some free time and to be able to do some things on their own. Care should be given to provide a variety of appropriate activities when undirected time is scheduled. A camper may wish to spend time on a specific craft project, fish off the bank of the lake, simply lie on the hillside and watch the clouds, or visit with friends. It is just as valuable to provide free play time to be used for reflection or relaxation as it is to provide physical activities.

Michael Thompson reports that "researchers tell us that over the past two decades, children in the United States have lost nine to twelve hours of free play per week." He goes on to contend that "you can't *teach* children to play alone: you have to *let* them play alone. Many parents are too frightened to do so, and schools cannot find the time to do so. It may be that camp is the place where grown-ups recognize the value of nonscheduled time … . Our children's imagination, spontaneity, leadership skills, and happiness depend in large part on free, undirected play."[4]

Free time is, however, the time when the greatest number of accidents or incidents occurs and should not mean unsupervised time. Campers should know where they can and cannot go. Staff should be stationed in program areas to assist and be available where campers gather in case of a problem. Such a period should be followed by a meal or enrolled activity so counselors can check their groups for the wanderer or lost child.

Interest Groups

Having several living groups join together in a program activity of common interest for a given period has its advantages. In some camps, participation in a joint activity is based upon skill as well as interest. For example, campers who have achieved a given skill level in canoeing can choose to go on a canoe trip. In other situations, it may be interest in a given project, such as an archaeological dig, or the building of a footbridge across a small creek that draws groups together. In another example, a camper council with representatives from various age or living groups may be formed for planning an evening program, recommending changes in the camp, or evaluating a project. The camp's ability to be flexible and provide staff support where needed can make interest groups an exciting dimension of camp life. It may also be an opportunity to combine centralized and decentralized structures for a period of the day, the length of a project, or for a special trip.

Some camps organize sessions by interest groups or by special theme. For example, the third session may be a "Western" theme and feature more activities and instruction time within the equestrian program. The camp may have an "international week" where activities or all-camp programs feature cultural experiences from the countries represented by their international staff. Session themes are promoted in camp brochures or website offerings so that campers who are really interested in a theme may choose to attend a particular session.

Instruction

It is very common for camps to offer skill classes and for campers to move in and out of those classes as they achieve a certain level. For instance, swimming instruction is typically organized in this fashion. In a decentralized program, individuals from a living group may all attend swimming at one time, but once at the site, divide up by skill levels. In this design, the plan and convenience of the group is more important to meeting the outcomes than having the schedule revolve around the activity specialists. In a centralized program, campers are normally assigned or sign up by the level of skill revealed in a test or an evaluation of their previous experience (e.g., a swimming test).

The Unit or Section

Several living groups usually form a unit or section in a camp. Often, evening programs are planned by the unit for all the living groups included, or one meal is cooked out daily within the unit. This approach works best where the living groups in a unit consist of campers of the same age range and general maturity level.

All-Camp Activities

The enthusiasm generated by a well-planned all-camp event is not easily matched by any other type of activity. This type of event can be more spectacular or exciting than a small-group activity, and it often gives campers an opportunity to perform before others, as with a drama group presentation or a carnival where each living group designs a booth and takes turns leading the activity in their booth. All-camp activities often involve decorations or dressing up for the event.

Some long-term camps operate two or three days of all-camp activities around a theme near the end of the season. Some events may involve individual participation, while others involve living groups or units.

The wealth of program ideas usually generated by staff and campers may well replace a manual of operation. However, the perusal by staff members of various program resource books during staff training and throughout the summer can often provide the stimulus needed for staff and campers to generate variations or new ideas. Involving staff and campers in the process of building a program can create buy-in and excitement about that program.

Program as Part of Transportation

In day camps, campers are often transported daily by bus or van to the camp location. Resident camps, trip camps, and special field trips often involve transportation by bus, van, train, or boat. The time on the vehicle should be used as part of the program structure. Staff, other than the driver, should be aboard to provide leadership and supervision. During this period, new campers' anxiety can build or boisterousness can get out of hand. Some activities on the vehicle may be individual in nature, while others may be grouped by sections. Singing can provide an outlet as well as a group spirit-building exercise. The balance of maintaining enthusiasm and variety without distracting the driver will prove a challenge.

Pacing/Flow

The pacing of the day's activities is as important as the activities and structure. Plenty of physical activity should be scheduled to meet the energy and exertion needs of most children. On the other hand, time should also be set aside for quiet, relaxation, rest, and individual initiative. A midday break should be planned, during which participants and staff can catch their breath by lying down, sitting on their bunks or under a tree, reading, or writing letters. The camper's age will dictate the logical approach for this break and its level of supervision. Younger children may need more regimentation or routine to get them to bed for rest; but once there, their bodies generally take over if the morning has been an active one. Teenagers will benefit from a more flexible approach; and of course, adults need this sort of flextime, too.

Varying the scheduled activities with those in which the camper has some choice, as well as varying living-group activities with instructional activities, provides more interest for the camper. In a resident camp, evening also affords an opportunity for activities paced differently from those during the day. Evening activities are often broadened to include the unit or other portions of camp if the day's activities have been in small groups. In camps where daily activities take place outside the living group, a more specialized evening can provide an opportunity for living-unit activities. Such activities should be paced so that the more physical or boisterous activity takes place earlier in the evening. Then, a general slowdown in activity and noise level close to bedtime will help the counselor to quiet the living group for sleep in the resident camp.

Program Emphases in the Summer Camp

A growing trend has been for some camps to focus their entire program or certain sessions on a narrow range of activities, which is then used as a marketing tool. This emphasis has ranged from overall sports to specific sports, such as basketball, golf, tennis, gymnastics, and from foreign languages to music, scuba, and canoeing. The appeal has often been to the consumer's interests as stimulated by schools or commercial sports and/or the customer's concern for the development of certain skills.

On the other hand, the majority of camps continue to offer a general program with a variety of program activities as well as a number of all-camp or all-unit activities. Many general program camps do provide more expertise and experience in certain activities than in others (e.g., providing a general program for younger campers and specialties for older campers). Often, the geographic setting of the camp lends itself to certain specialties (e.g., mountain climbing, sea kayaking, lake sailing, and river canoeing). To argue that specialized or general programs are better or worse is a dubious exercise, since the value of any camp experience is far more dependent upon the camp leadership and upon the rationale for the program design than it is on the specific activities.

Staff in the specialized camp or unit should be careful not to overemphasize skills in one sport or area at too early an age, or the child's experience will be too narrow. Even a camp specializing in one area should offer opportunities for other activities and experiences. More general program camps must recognize that to attract older campers, a greater challenge in skill development and/ or adventurous activity is needed. Similarly, in specialized programs, a staff member striving for greater experience and expertise should not be allowed to overshadow the overall counseling role. Although every staff member need not be a living-unit counselor in every camp, they should have concern for the camper and be willing to deal with the needs and welfare of each individual.

Progression in Programming

Any camp program needs to examine the age groupings served to determine their human development and readiness level for certain experiences. The same program design and activities may not meet the needs of an eight-year old and a 17-year-old. Without age-appropriate program design, camps may have fewer returning campers at one end of the age spectrum or the other. The key is to match the difficulty of the activity to participants' skill levels.

The number of camps, especially day camps, which serve younger and younger campers has grown. Almost simultaneously, as a marketing tool, those camps have tended to expand their variety of program-activity offerings. Without careful program planning, this expansion can lead to campers perceiving that, by age 11 or 12, they have experienced everything that camp has to offer.

Developing outcome statements for different age ranges based upon developmental needs and readiness can provide youth with a different experience at camp each year of their lives right on through high school. This process requires enough study of human development to understand the social and coordination readiness of each age group. The camp manual should include a plan outlining developmental characteristics and needs for each age group. Identified for each age group should be each program activity and the emphasis corresponding with those age characteristics and needs (i.e., what five-year-olds do in swimming instruction should be very different than what 15-year-olds do, even if neither knows how to swim). Not recognizing the importance of providing an age-appropriate program could mean the challenge and excitement of participation could turn into embarrassment and an unwillingness to try. Staff training should emphasize those differences and the philosophy of age-appropriate program progression.

Group Living

The day-to-day living experience should be as carefully considered as the scheduled activities. The interaction between campers, as well as between camper and staff in the living setting, is influenced directly by age-specific developmental characteristics and needs, as is participation in activity skills. Especially in the resident camp setting, more actual hours of the day will be spent in living activities, such as eating, sleeping, and congregating in the living area, than in planned activities. In the day camp, certainly a significant part of the day is spent being transported to and from camp, moving from activity to activity, and gathering during lunch and rest periods.

It is critical that the personnel assigned to supervision of the living group during these times be as sensitive and mature as the personnel in charge of activity periods. Day-to-day activities present some of the most important teachable moments—when the right words, the tone of voice, the intervention or the nonintervention, or a heartfelt smile can make all the difference to an individual or group. These moments cannot be programmed, but staff can be educated and sensitized in the process of staff training and supervision to watch for and take advantage of such opportunities.

Mealtimes should be designed to reinforce camp goals and desired outcomes and to offer a learning and social experience. Providing this opportunity requires thought concerning the shape and size of dining tables, how table groups are formed, the way food is served, the role staff should play at the table, whether everyone comes and goes from the dining hall at the same time, and the agenda before and after meal service. Mealtimes, even breakfast, can easily become the high points of the day for campers and staff alike. Many camps use them as a time for singing, with program staff or counselors alternating as song leaders. During this time, tables and food can be cleared before campers are excused. This activity offers a wonderful opportunity to promote camp spirit with the singing of current and traditional camp songs.

Mealtime programming is as important in a day-camp setting with sack lunches as it is in the largest resident camp with multiple dining halls. The principles and opportunities are the same. To a large degree, it is also as true for the youngest child and the oldest adult participant.

For children, the use of the toilet/bath facility may be one of their first exposures to group use of such facilities. In any case, it is another area in which the living-group leader provides not only supervision, but also leadership in attitudes, language, sensitivity, and privacy. Responsibility for one's surroundings—including the care of facilities such as the toilet/bathhouse and the sleeping areas in a resident camp—is yet another of those teachable moments.

Program Design Beyond Summer

More and more camps are offering short-term program events beyond summer. Such events for youth, by the nature of the school week, tend to be on weekends or during holiday periods. A survey by the American Camp Association (2005) showed that 40 percent of the responding camps offered either a retreat center, family camp programs, or outdoor/environmental education programs, and an equal percentage appeared to operate eight months a year. The number of camps offering programs for all but four months a year jumped to 50 percent.[5] A study in 2008 by ACA's Committee for Advancement of Research indicated that 50 percent of camps continue to operate only in the summer.[6]

Being short term in nature does not lessen the attention that needs to be given to programming, planning, and staffing. In some ways, they are more important, for the camp has less time to reach its goals. The same steps in program development need to be applied in the planning process. Certainly, the basic outcomes for a short-term experience need to be within reach for the time allotted. Therefore, outcomes need to be succinct and also clearly communicated to participants and staff. The experience provided by peer relationships, mealtimes, and nonscheduled activity is as important here as it is in the longer-term experience in the summer.

During the week, a camp might work with one or more school systems to provide outdoor education opportunities for students. Before offering this type program, a camp director should gain an understanding of the school's goals and desired outcomes for bringing a class to the camp setting. A school operates under certain state-mandated standards and curriculum and must align outdoor education experiences with addressing certain elements of an established curriculum. Jim O'Donnell points out that "camps talk about activities, while schools speak of curriculum. … teachers often look on 'activities' as something less than what they themselves offer. Similarly, camps may tend to talk about 'fun' experiences and building self-esteem, while schools are more concerned with developing academic skills and outcomes."[7] Therefore, finding programmatic language consistent with or acceptable to the field of education is critical.

Providing outdoor or environmental education programs for schools allows the camp to share responsibilities with the classroom teachers involved. The development of the program will require teamwork and cooperative planning and should use the strongest elements of the staff and camp resources for maximum benefit. Many camps have personnel with education credentials and experience in environmental education beyond that of classroom teachers. Working to make those personnel available to classroom groups is an opportunity to expand the camp's services and impact more children.

In conjunction, many camps have developed adventure and challenge courses, which have added an exciting new educational dimension to the camp setting. However, these courses require careful construction after consultation with outside experts and need carefully trained leadership who can demonstrate both the skills and requisite safety practices. Directors should not assume that a low-ropes course will need any less capable leadership and safety precautions than a high-course or a rappelling program. In a number of camps, these courses have opened the door to serving at-risk youth and adjudicated youth. This exciting expansion provides service to a population that can greatly benefit from the camp experience. However, it requires careful planning and demands a mature and experienced staff to make it effective. In some locales, year-round school schedules have caused camps to offer regular camp sessions at various times throughout the year. School vacations in some areas are no longer "summer" vacations. Camps should take this aspect into account when developing a program schedule.

Nonsummer events for adults vary from weekend programs to week-long programs. The care and attention given to adult programming should be no less than that given to youth. Though it may require less staff, adult programs require no less development of goals and outcomes, and no less planning based upon the needs, interests, and human development characteristics of the particular age group being served. In fact, since many camp directors and staff are more experienced in working with children than with adults in a group, it may require more time in the initial preparation and planning.

Many camps provide facilities and/or program activities for rental groups as their principal clientele in the nonsummer weeks. These camps are designed to be used by an organization's local group(s) year-round, or by other groups during the non-summer months. If this use is one of the camp's principal goals, then its desired outcomes should be developed accordingly, following the program development steps delineated earlier in the chapter. In this process, the camp becomes an enabling device to help others accomplish their goals. It requires a service-oriented staff and program philosophy and should not be viewed as simply another source of income.

In this type of program, facilities become the primary focus and should be developed to meet the needs of the user groups. The assessment process is critical before expending considerable sums in facility improvement or development.

Specialized Clientele

Many camps have been designed specifically to meet the needs of special populations, while other camps use only part of their season to serve a special needs population or include special-needs populations into regular program groups. Such clientele often have special physical or programmatic needs, and grouping with others who have similar challenges may provide a more comfortable environment for their first camp experience. Such groups include senior adults and at-risk youth, as well as individuals with similar physical conditions or disabilities (e.g., asthma, diabetes, cancer) or those with restricted mobility (e.g., persons who use wheelchairs or are sight-impaired). Some camps work in partnership with a hospital or organization that serves a particular special-needs population and is willing to send medical personnel to camp with their clients. Other camps make the effort to secure employed or volunteer staff who share the same challenges of the special needs group being served, thus providing another level of comfort to the participants.

For some years, a growing effort has been made by many camps to include individuals with special needs into the rest of the camp community wherever the particular difference does not prevent participation in the camp's activities or where adaptive facilities or staff are not necessary. The passage of the Americans with Disabilities Act (1990) underlines the greater obligation on the part of camps to accommodate individuals with disabilities. It dictates that any camp, except a religious camp that serves religious groups, may not exclude such individuals from a camp program on the basis of a disability alone. Note: religious camps that serve the public—such as public schools, scouts, or other organizations—are not exempt from the ADA. See www.ADA.gov for more information about ADA's requirements.

The entire camp community can gain greater sensitivity and learning from special-needs integration if there is a readiness on the part of all participants and careful planning by camp administrators. On the other hand, unless there is careful preparation as well as a clear understanding of any special needs of such a population, the experience can be less than positive for all participants. To become inclusive just for the idea is not enough: careful thought and preparation is essential.

Two varying and valid viewpoints are stated in the following *Camping Magazine* articles:

> *People with disabilities often are overprotected by society, separated from others and given few participation options. Camp is a place where they could become fully functioning members of a community . ... By integrating camp programs, camps will gain the opportunity to celebrate diversity and show how each individual, regardless of ability or disability, has something to contribute to the group's outdoor living experience.*[8]

> *[M]any camp directors try to serve campers who are not appropriate for their particular camp setting. Our personal experience ... has led us to believe that inclusion is not always the best solution for children with differences. Every child deserves a camp where he feels like he's a vital member of the community and truly accepted for who he is—an environment where he is comfortable.*[9]

To include a camper with a disability does not demand the elimination of any overall set of camp activities; this principle has been demonstrated repeatedly by creative and determined individuals who have adapted almost all possible activities and made them accessible in the camp setting. The Internet provides an abundance of examples of adaptive activities.

The critical element in serving a special population is that the camp administration has researched any special needs and characteristics before agreeing to serve that special-needs population. The *Camp Director's Primer* acknowledges: "In a resident or day camp, the issue of program accessibility is of equal or greater importance as the issue of site accessibility. For a camper with a disability to be successful in an integrated program, careful planning is critical to every aspect of the camp operation."[10]

Staff will need additional training and understanding of any particular special population served. Camps may need to have additional medical staff, special menu considerations, or facility modifications. The director of a camp seeking to serve a special-needs population must be careful not to assume that certain things cannot be done, but rather must approach program with an enabling attitude and seek possible alternatives where the traditional approach might not work.

The *Camp Director's Primer* suggests that, in planning for the participation of a camper with a disability in the camp program, several guidelines can be readily followed. The first guideline is to adapt only on an individual basis. The program goal is to keep the camper's experience as realistic as possible, so it is best to not automatically assume that a particular condition means special needs campers cannot participate in an activity. Consultation with the camper and/or his parents will highlight specific difficulties that need to be overcome in order to get the individual involved. Second, the activity should only be adapted as much as is necessary. If unnecessary changes in the activity are made to accommodate the camper with a disability, the camper may feel singled out from peers.[11]

In considering what form these adjustments or accommodations should take, three specific areas should be considered:

- *Materials or equipment adaptation*: Some campers with disabilities may need special devices to fully function in a particular activity and temporary modifications may be necessary. A camper with little upper-body strength may have difficulty with swinging a bat in a softball game (a good substitute is a whiffle ball and bat). Or, a child with paralysis in the lower body may want to wear socks in the pool to prevent foot abrasions from the rough surface of the bottom.

- *Procedural and rule adaptations*: Through making minor changes in rules for the individual with a disability, success in participation for all can be achieved. For instance, if the general rule in archery is that participants retrieve their own arrows, a fellow camper may be asked to pick up the arrows for a friend who uses a wheelchair.
- *Skill sequence adaptations*: If a particular skill is being taught, it may be easier to adapt the process by breaking the skill down into smaller stages and working on each individual part.

Many of the adjustments to be made are minor and easily accomplished with understanding, kindness, and a little ingenuity. Since, in the camp community, the accepted goal is to meet the individual needs of each camper, stretching to meet the needs of special-needs children adds to the challenge. Because each child and each situation may be unique, it is wise to consult available resources regarding the Americans with Disabilities Act.[12]

Specific Program Activities

Camps continue to broaden the variety of activities that can be used in the camp setting. That variety virtually has no limit, except in the camp's program philosophy and consideration of what can be done in the camp setting that cannot be done easily in the camper's normal environment. Obviously, the fact that most camps are located in a setting with natural environmental resources would indicate that they have an advantage in using those resources wherever possible and in building on them as the core of the program emphasis. On the other hand, many camp directors conclude that certain activities are significant enough that they locate other sites with appropriate facilities and/or staff to accommodate those activities.

It is not practical to deal with individual activities in detail in this book, and a wide variety of resources for those activities can be found in the resource list in Appendix C. However, following are the general areas of activities that most often occur in camps.

Land Sports and Games

- *Team sports*: Baseball, basketball, football, hockey, lacrosse, paintball, soccer, softball, volleyball, human foosball
- *Individual sports*: Archery, badminton, horseback riding, horseshoes, in-line skating, pony rides, riflery, snowboarding, table tennis, tennis, trapeze, tightrope, wrestling
- *Informal games*: Tetherball, all sorts of chase and hunt games that have developed in various camps

Water Sports and Games

- *Swimming activities*: Competitive, instructional, recreational, synchronized, water ballet
- *Water activities*: Fishing, scuba diving, tubing, water polo, water slides
- *Watercraft activities*: Canoeing, kayaking, rowing, sailing, sailboarding, waterskiing

Arts

- *Performing arts*: Creative writing, dance, drama, music
- *Arts and crafts*: Ceramics, jewelry, leatherwork, metal crafts, nature crafts, painting, photography, weaving, woodwork

Outdoor-Oriented Activities

- *Outdoor living skills*: Overnight camping, fire building, knot tying, orienteering, outdoor cooking, shelter building, tent pitching
- *Physical skills*: Backpacking, climbing, canoe tripping, cross-country skiing, hiking, mountaineering, mastering ropes courses, snowshoeing, snow skiing
- *Nature-oriented activities*: Animal lore or care, astronomy, birdwatching, butterfly catching and releasing, conservation activities, gardening, marine life study, nature hikes, rock collecting and painting, weather predicting
- *Vehicular activities*: ATVing, biking, go-karting, flying

Special Events

All-camp events that use a theme are common in camp settings: Christmas in July, regattas, Paul Bunyan Days, Color Wars, Circus or Carnival Days, Olympics of all sorts, and pageants. In general, these sorts of events involve campers and staff in planning, preparation, costumes, and performance. Sometimes, the event is tied into a presentation on a visitors' day, a parents' weekend, or a holiday celebration. International counselors and campers can often be encouraged to do presentations about their countries, adding a wider dimension to the world of camp. (Communicating such requests to international staff prior to their arrival will allow them to come prepared with a program, as well as with items representative of their culture.) Preplanned short skits put on by staff often contribute to the sense of fun and provide opportunities for sharing.

Social Recreation

These events range from quiet games in the living area to all-camp cookouts or banquets. Games such as charades and skits that require no equipment are a staple of campfires and evening social programs. Singing is an important ingredient of many of these events, and is often a part of campfires and evening programs. Some camps have dances and other coeducational events.

Spiritually-Oriented Activities

These activities range from nonsectarian vespers, chapel services, or bedtime chats to camps where the religious emphasis is central to the program. In the latter, there may be study groups and religious services daily, as well as a strong emphasis upon religious philosophy in all aspects of the living-group experience. Almost all camps develop certain devices that are used to assist participants in character building and the recognition of the spiritual aspect of life and its integration into the physical, mental, emotional, and social elements. Clarice M. Bowman said it well:

> *Spiritual values are not just another group of desired outcomes; rather they comprise the core of the constellation of all other values, the pulsating heart of the camping program. Very little may be said about spiritual values in words, but they will be communicated if they are present in the spirit of the leaders, in their motives for being at camp, in their vision of the goals, and in their sensitivity for helping campers have worthy goals of their own that may be achieved by engaging in delightful activities.*[13]

Program Operating Procedures

Whatever the activity or program event, some specific standards should be applied in preparation for that event. Part of these standards relate to the concern for risk management (see Chapter 11), and all of them grow out of the camp's concern for quality in its operation. The camp's operating procedure for each activity should include the following information:

- Supervisor and activity leaders' qualifications and skill-verification procedures
- Means for controlled access to activity and ancillary areas
- Availability of equipment appropriate to age, skill level, and size of participant
- Eligibility requirements for participation
- Camper-staff supervision ratios
- Identification and use of appropriate protective equipment
- Knowledge of appropriate safety regulations governing the activity
- Emergency procedures
- Procedures for regular maintenance of equipment
- Identification of safety concerns related to the use area

Leadership

Leadership is the key to any program activity, and the availability and qualifications of staff for an activity are the first considerations. What skills are essential to making it a quality experience for campers? Is the activity such that it requires some type of documented training (e.g., ropes course certification) or completion of a given course? If the activity involves teaching a skill, does the person have the ability to teach? (A considerable difference exists between being skilled at an activity and being able to teach that skill to others.) What is the best camper:staff ratio?

A camper:staff supervision ratio should be established for each activity since the degree of supervision needed and the risk involved will vary for each activity as well as with the age of the participant. In addition to the skills related to the activity, the staff member who is to lead the activity must be trained in the safety regulations established by the camp for the activity. This staff member should have the maturity to be able to identify, prevent, or intervene regarding hazards that may be present in the activity area or any situation that might arise. It should be clear to the staff person what safety procedures should be observed in the conduct of the activity, what emergencies could occur, and what procedures should be followed to deal with them. The staff member leading the activity (or another who is present) should be trained in first aid/ CPR/AED and trained for related situations that might arise from an accident or health situation during the activity.

Appropriate Equipment

Appropriate equipment, including protective equipment for the activity, stocked in adequate numbers, is essential so that no lengthy waiting periods or safety hazards are created for campers. "Appropriate" indicates that, in some cases, the equipment needs to be sized for the age and size of the camper. To use an adult-sized PFD (personal flotation device) for a nine-year-old during a boating activity is dangerous, inappropriate, and negligent. In some cases, such as for riflery and archery, the equipment will need to be stored in a manner that restricts access to everyone but the activity-area leader. In the case of firearms, all should be stored in locked areas (or with gun locks) within a locked room. Ammunition should be stored in a separate locked location. In all cases, such equipment must be checked regularly and be well maintained.

Appropriate Level of Activity

The age and skill level of the participants dictates the level at which an activity should be conducted. The eligibility requirements for age and skill should be established from the outset. If a limited number of persons have the competency to supervise and instruct the activity, then the number who can participate should be limited. The latter element will require the establishment of camper:staff ratios that will ensure quality time with safety for each camper.

In many cases, the resource materials and certification programs developed by various national organizations will provide guidance and an outline of skill levels and appropriate age for participation at those levels. However, many activities have no national certification programs. Resource material exists on most activities that the director or program director can study, and various experts can assist in the development of a written curriculum for instruction and supervision identifying appropriate age and skill levels for all activities.

Use of Off-Site or Public Providers of Program Elements

Many camps choose to use program facilities off the main campsite or use public providers of a particular activity rather than incur the cost of having the same activity on-site. When a camp chooses this approach to a given activity, clear written procedures for the supervisory roles and responsibilities of accompanying staff should be in place. Such procedures may range from behavior management to differentiation between camp staff roles and the roles of staff at the public facility.

In addition, the camp director should visit the facility and/or provider when the program is in operation. Such a visit will give the camp an understanding of the safeguards the provider undertakes as well as the type and skill of staff instructing and supervising the activity. A clear understanding should be developed between the provider and the camp regarding the various roles of staff provided by the provider and staff provided by the camp.

Safety and Emergency Procedures

Obviously, when one reviews the variety of program activities available, differing levels of risks and skill are involved. These factors should be thoroughly considered for each program and become part of the risk-management program of the camp as outlined in Chapter 11.

Safety regulations for each program area need to be established. A more detailed approach would obviously be required for rappelling than for an all camp campfire. Safety concerns about a given program area should be reviewed at the same time. These regulations and concerns should be put into writing, addressed during staff training, and posted where appropriate.

Emergency procedures relating to certain program areas (such as the waterfront) need to be clearly defined in writing and training given to staff and in many cases reviewed with campers.

Program design involves all of these areas with the goal of developing the type of program that not only will appeal to the participant and create a fun and safe experience, but will also accomplish the desired outcomes growing out of the camp's mission.

Checkpoints

- List all the program activities utilized in a designated camp last summer.
- Test the program development guidelines against those activities, and see if other program directions arise.
- Using the modified list of program activities, test each activity against each of the following elements:
  ✓ Goals and outcomes
  ✓ Experienced and qualified staff
  ✓ Adequate and appropriate equipment
  ✓ Safety and emergency procedures
  ✓ Eligibility and numbers of participants
- Review the flow of a typical day at camp; consider where there are times for:
  ✓ Strenuous physical activity
  ✓ Quiet, reflective, relaxed time
  ✓ Choosing an activity
  ✓ Learning new skills
  ✓ Meeting campers from other living groups
- If the camp uses outside providers of facilities or activities, are roles and responsibilities of the camp's staff clearly outlined?
- What special populations does the camp serve, and what are their special needs?

Related Standards

American Camp Association's Accreditation Standards for Camp Programs and Services: PD.1–40; PA.1–36; PT.1–19; OM.14, OM.15

Additional Professional Practices: Program Design and Activities Additional Professional Practices; Program—Trip and Travel Additional Professional Practices

Endnotes

1. Lois Goodrich. 1979. "A Time for Discovery." *Camping Magazine*. Vol. 52, No.1, September, p. 16.

2. Hedley S. Dimock. 1948. *Administration of the Modern Camp*. New York: Association Press (Y.M.C.A. of the U.S.A.). p. 123.

3. Giesla Konopka. 1963. *Social Group Work: A Helping Process*. Englewood Cliffs, NJ: Prentice-Hall. p. 20.

4. Michael Thompson. 2008. "The Impact of the Loss of Free, Undirected Play in Childhood (And What Camps Can Do About It)." *Camping Magazine*. Vol. 82, No. 3, May/June.

5. Jon Malinowski. 2006. "The Words of the Profits: Highlights from ACA's 2005 Business Operations." *Camping Magazine*. Vol. 79, No.5, September/October, p. 17ff.

6. Jon Malinowski. 2008. "Site-Seeing: Selected Findings from the Site, Facilities, and Program Survey." *Camping Magazine*. Vol. 81, No.5, September/October, p. 48ff.

7. Jim O'Donnell. 2002. "The Changing Role of Camps." *Camping Magazine*. Vol. 75, No. 1, January/February.

8. Leandra A. Bedini, M. Deborah Bialeschki, and Karla A. Henderson. 1992. "The Americans with Disabilities Act: Implications for Camp Programming." *Camping Magazine*. Vol. 60, No. 4, March/April, p. 53.

9. Devvie Sasson and Eric Sesson. 2011. "Striving for More Than "Surviving": An Argument for a Non-Inclusion Model for Camps." *Camping Magazine*. Vol. 84, No. 1, January/February.

10. National Camp Executives Group. 1992. *Camp Director's Primer to the Americans with Disabilities Act of 1990*. Glen Allen, VA: Markel Insurance Company. p. 17.

11. Ibid., pp. 17–20.

12. The Americans with Disabilities Act of 1990, U.S. Department of Justice, Washington, D.C. www.usdoj.gov/crt/ada; 800-514-0381.

13. Clarice M. Bowman. 1954. *Spiritual Values in Camping*. New York: Association Press (YMCA of the USA). pp. 39–40.

PERSONNEL
ORGANIZATION

Belvoir Terrace (Lenox, MA)

Chapter Six

The quality of the camp staff is of the greatest importance in the successful operation of a camp program. Comparisons of the relative success that different camps have with their programs show that the physical factors, such as size, layout, buildings, and equipment, are also important. But camps with similar or comparable facilities vary considerably in the quality of their programs. The differences are largely explainable by the variations in the ability of the personnel who make up the camp staff. [1]

—Reuel A. Benson and Jacob A. Goldberg

Over 60 years later, that statement stands. The accomplishment of a camp's mission and goals is largely dependent upon the staff who work directly with the participants in that camp. The qualifications, commitment, and effectiveness of those staff members are largely dependent upon the camp director and that individual's ability to recruit and train that staff. Each and every staff member is an important component in accomplishing those goals and outcomes. One staff member who does not understand and follow the camp's policies and procedures can not only be an impediment, but can also demonstrate negligence that can trigger an injury or lawsuit.

It is important that all prospective staff members be given a clear picture of the camp's mission and philosophy as well as the type of the staff and camper community in which they will work. Since most positions in camp have duties that are responsible to the changing and immediate needs of a situation, it can be very difficult for everyone if a staff member is rigid or inflexible. The ability or willingness of the staff person to accommodate change will be as vital to a good experience as the flexibility of the camper and staff community.

Background of a prospective staff member is another factor to consider in hiring. If a person comes from a cultural or ethnic background different from the majority of the staff, that person may add an exciting dimension to the experience of both campers and staff. These staff members, like all other staff members, should be made aware of the degree of diversity in the camper and staff population.

Elements of Organization

It is important to design a staff organizational model that parallels the camp's mission, goals, and desired outcomes and the resulting program, and which matches the camp's philosophy at each of these junctures. The camp director may then proceed to outline the following elements:
- Job responsibilities that will be required by the program design
- Determination of the number of each position required in relation to the number of campers
- Line of supervision for each position
- Job description for each position

Job Responsibilities

Starting with broad general areas of the camp operation—such as food service, health and wellness, facility maintenance, and program—the director should identify both the general responsibility and as many specific responsibilities of each staff position as possible. For example, the food service supervisor's general responsibility may be to provide healthy meals for campers and staff. The specific responsibilities would be to supervise the kitchen staff, oversee meal preparation, direct cleanup, and such. Only one person performs this job. On the other hand, some positions' responsibilities—such as those of the living group counselor—will be performed by more than one staff member.

Determination of the Number of Positions Needed

The number of individuals necessary to be employed in each position should be determined by an examination of the number of campers that position can supervise while still accomplishing the camp's desired outcomes. Staff:camper ratios are critical in terms of accomplishing goals and desired outcomes, as well as ensuring health and safety. Some industry ratios are clearer than others. For example, the American Camp Association standards identify minimum ratios of staff on duty with campers in living groups and activities (Figure 6-1). The type of program, environment, or the presence of campers with special physical, medical, or behavioral needs may require a higher ratio of staff to campers.

Camper Age	Number of Staff	Number of Residential Campers	Number of Day Campers
4–5	1	5	6
6–8	1	6	8
9–14	1	8	10
15–18	1	10	12

Figure 6-1. ACA minimum staff:camper ratios

No such standard ratios are found in other areas of camp administration based on camper population. However, some general guidelines for ratios can be projected as follows:

- *Food service*: One cook and one dish and pan washer for every 50 to 60 campers. The type of food service offered certainly affects this ratio.
- *Health service*: One nurse for the first 125 to 150 campers and one additional nurse for each 100 campers over 175. The presence of a camp physician and the nature of the camp clientele may alter these ratios.

Each program activity will require analysis of a variety of factors to determine the ratio of activity leadership to campers. For example, the ACA standards ask the camp director to determine the number of lifeguards or lookouts needed for supervision of a given number of campers in a swimming situation. Many varying factors can help the director determine that ratio: type of swimming area (pool, river, or lake), size of the swimming area, size of the group that will be swimming at one time, design of the swimming area, the type of swimming activity, characteristics and age of participants, and such. State or local statute may also dictate this ratio. Each program activity should be evaluated separately, and once ratios are determined, they should be put in writing and reviewed each year.

Maintenance ratios are almost impossible to generalize because of the variation from camp to camp in the number and complexity of facilities. Camps vary with respect to running water, electricity, buildings, lodging, dining, laundry, and plumbing. The employment of a year-round, full-time caretaker or ranger may lessen, to some degree, the number of seasonal maintenance employees needed. The establishment of year-round usage will also affect the number of employees needed in several areas.

Line of Supervision

At this point, consideration should be given to which position will supervise other positions. Except in the smallest camp, it will become apparent that the camp director cannot supervise everyone. The amount of emphasis placed on various positions will depend on the degree of centralization and structure desired, and the size of the camp will determine the number, experience, and complexity of the staff. A generally good rule for supervisory ratios is that one person cannot adequately supervise more than seven people.

The camp's program philosophy will also affect the number of supervisory personnel needed. A *centralized* program will most often require a number of program department heads, such as waterfront, crafts, sports (which can be broken down by individual sports), as well as a unit leader or head counselor who supervises a certain number of living units and their counselors. In a more structured centralized camp, program scheduling and a camper's individual schedules are determined by a director or program director in conjunction with the unit leaders or head counselors and department heads. Counselors usually have cabin responsibilities and assist in various program areas.

A *decentralized* program will usually require fewer department heads in specific program areas and more unit leaders or head counselors. Counselors will typically concentrate on the living group and either develop the program or help campers plan their program as part of the ongoing group-living process. A program director in a decentralized program serves more as a program resource, supervisor, and coordinator of unit leaders and program areas in which a certified specialist is needed as a resource or for safety. An overall or basic camp schedule may or may not be drawn, depending on whether meals or other all-camp activities are done together. Some decentralized camps require the counselor—or at least the counselors in a unit—to have appropriate certifications.

Most directors find that in determining supervision patterns, a diagram begins to take form. Endless time can be spent on the best type of diagram. Though the symbolism of any design is important, the clarity of the diagram to show the relationship of one position to another is the most important element. The diagram will be primarily used for the director and supervisory staff, but all staff should know the reporting and accountability hierarchy. A general ground rule of organization is that a person should not be supervised by more than one person. If it is essential to split supervision, careful consideration should be given as to how that supervision will be coordinated. Solid lines in an organizational chart indicate supervision, enabling a person to follow the solid line to the next box identifying the supervisor. Dotted lines indicate advisory or consultative relationships. An arrow in the direction of supervision is helpful if a nontraditional diagram is developed (Figure 6-2). Several sample organizational charts for camp staff are shown in Figure 6-3. The size of the camper population will determine, to a large degree, the size of various program and support departments.

However, it must be emphasized that it would be unwise to adopt any one of these organizational patterns until the camp has established clear program goals and desired outcomes. Staff organizational patterns grow naturally out of goals and outcomes, and the examples shown are meant to be illustrative and adapted for specific uses. The overall design, whether narrative or diagrammatic, should be outlined and analyzed carefully.

Job Descriptions

Once jobs have been identified and lines of supervision developed, it is time to begin the development of job descriptions for each position. Descriptions are essential in helping each staff member understand the specific elements of the job for which they are responsible and the abilities and skills needed in the performance of that position. A good job description shows how one particular position correlates with others in the staff organization and provides the basis for performance appraisals. A sample job description of a camp counselor is shown in Figure 6-4, as well as others in Appendix A. www.acacamps.org/sites/default/files/images/members/jobdesc/drafts/camp_director.pdf provides examples, as does www.acacamps.org/members/jobdesc/titles.

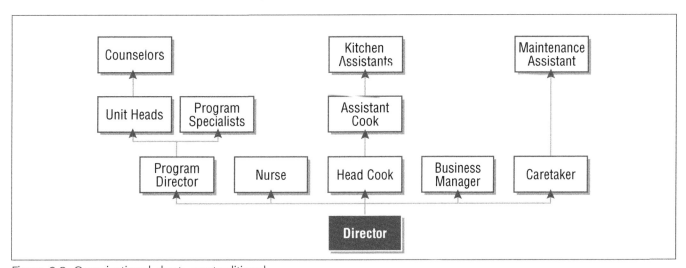

Figure 6-2. Organizational chart—nontraditional

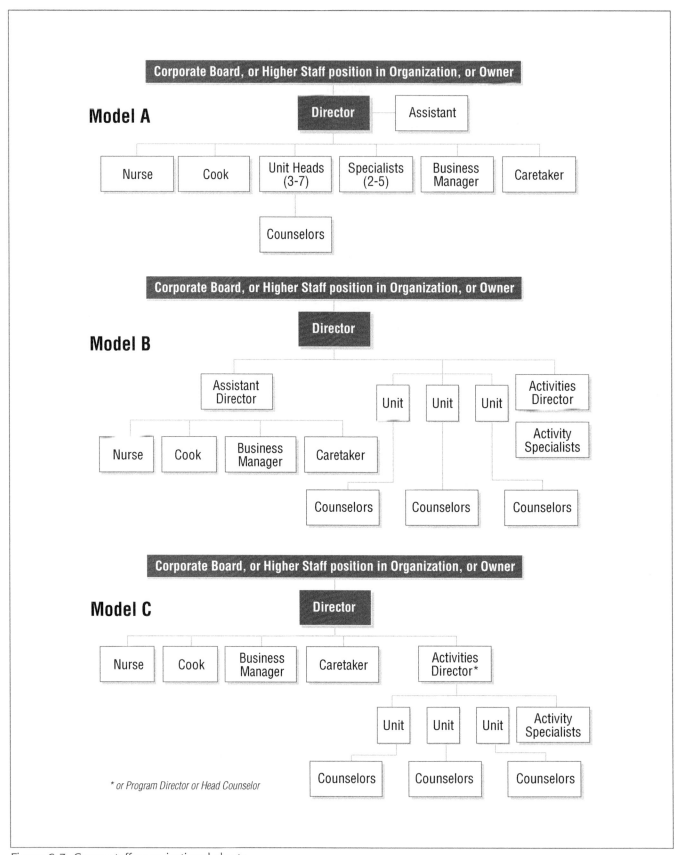

Figure 6-3. Camp staff organizational charts

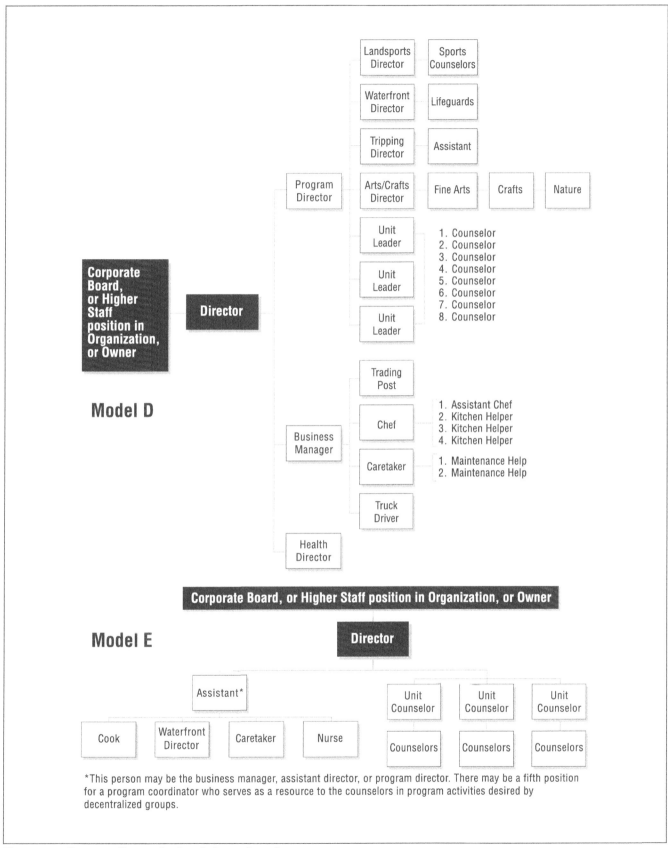

Figure 6-3. Camp staff organizational charts (cont.)

Camp Wonderful
Job Description

Job Title: Camp Counselor
Incumbent: insert name of person currently in position
Classification: Nonexempt
Reports to: This description lists the immediate supervisor for this position. It may be a unit leader or head counselor or other administrative person, including the camp director, depending on the size and structure of the camp and staff.

Position Purpose
Counselors are the primary caregivers for each camper. The counselor is responsible for planning, teaching, coordinating, and carrying out activities and guiding campers in their personal growth and daily living skills.

Essential Job Functions
- Assist in the direction, supervision, and organization of campers in their living unit, within activities and throughout the camp in order to meet the intended camper outcomes.
  - ✓ Apply basic youth-development principles in working with campers through communication, relationship development, respect for diversity, involvement, and empowerment of young people.
  - ✓ Assure campers are properly supervised at all times.
  - ✓ Be aware of and implement safety guidelines.
- Participate in the development and implementation of program activities for campers within the mission and outcomes
  - ✓ Lead and assist with the teaching of activities.
  - ✓ Actively participate in all program areas as assigned.
  - ✓ Provide for the progression of activities within the framework of individual and group interests and abilities.
  - ✓ Assist in program areas such as waterfront, nature, all-camp activities, and arts and crafts as directed.
- Maintain high standards of health and safety in all activities for campers and staff.
  - ✓ Provide the daily care of each camper within your supervision, including recognition of personal health needs.
  - ✓ Ensure that campers receive their medications as directed by healthcare manager.
  - ✓ Be alert to campers' and staff needs, assist them with personal and/or health problems, and discuss with camp health manager and/or resident camp director when appropriate.
  - ✓ Be alert to equipment and facilities to ensure utilization, proper care, and maintenance is adhered to; report repairs needed promptly to camp director.
- Be a role model to campers and staff in your attitude and behavior.
  - ✓ Follow and uphold all safety and security rules and procedures.
  - ✓ Set a good example to campers and others in regard to general camp procedures and practices, including sanitation, schedule, and sportsmanship.

Other Job Duties
- Contribute to verbal and written evaluations and communication as requested.
- Participate enthusiastically in all camp activities, planning and leading those activities as assigned.

Figure 6-4. Sample job description

- Participate as a member of the camp staff team to deliver and supervise evening programs, special events, overnights, and other all-camp activities and camp functions.
- Assist in the planning of any special events on or near the waterfront.
- Identify other tasks or duties that this position may be expected to perform but are not necessarily the primary focus of this position.

Relationships
Counselors generally have regular relationships with kitchen staff, program specialists, and business and maintenance staff. It is helpful to identify the expectations of those relationships and communication between these groups of staff members.

Equipment Used
Counselors may be asked to use fire-protection equipment, washers and dryers, dishwashers, and specialty program equipment. Some counselors may be asked to drive camp vehicles or watercraft.

Qualifications (minimum education and experience)
- Must be 18 years of age or a high school graduate.
- Must be able to obtain or become certified in first aid and CPR.
- Must submit health history record and examination form prior to first day of work.
- Must have the ability to interact with all age levels.

Knowledge, Skills, and Abilities
- Understand the development needs of young people.
- Possess the ability to relate to youth and adults in a positive manner.
- Demonstrate knowledge and skill in program areas designated camp program areas.

Physical Aspects of the Job
- Ability to communicate and work with groups participating (age and skill levels) and provide necessary instruction to campers and staff
- Ability to observe camper behavior, assess its appropriateness, enforce appropriate safety regulations and emergency procedures, and apply appropriate behavior-management techniques
- Ability to observe staff behavior, assess its appropriateness, enforce appropriate safety regulations and emergency procedures, and apply appropriate management techniques
- Visual and auditory ability to identify and respond to environmental and other hazards related to the activity
- Physical ability to respond appropriately to situations requiring first aid. Must be able to assist campers in an emergency (fire, evacuation, illness, or injury) and possess strength and endurance required to maintain constant supervision of campers.

Some physical requirements of a general counselor position could be: endurance, including prolonged standing, some bending, stooping, walking long distances, hiking, climbing, and stretching; requires eye-hand coordination and manual dexterity to manipulate outdoor equipment and camp activities; requires normal range of hearing and eyesight to record, prepare, and communicate appropriate camper activities/programs and the ability to lift up to 50 pounds; willing to live in a camp setting and work irregular hours with limited or simple equipment and facilities; and with daily exposure to the sun, heat, and animals such as bugs, snakes, bats, and such.

Figure 6-4. Sample job description (cont.)

By definition, a job description is a written statement of the minimum qualifications, general responsibilities, specific responsibilities, and essential functions pertinent to a particular position. It also identifies the supervisor by title. A general outline for a job description includes the following areas:

- Position title
- Responsible to (the name of the supervising position)
- General responsibility or purpose of position (a simple descriptive statement)
- Essential functions of position (relates to the general responsibility)
- Other job duties
- Relationships to other members of staff or outside service providers
- Equipment used in performance of duties
- Qualifications (minimum education and minimum type/length of experience)
- Knowledge, skills, and abilities needed
- Physical expectation as to aspects of the position (relates to essential functions)

The position title should be as clear as possible and relate directly to the responsibilities of that position. A position title should be assigned that clearly identifies to other staff, campers, and the public what the staff member does. Fancy titles only tend to confuse others. It also may be helpful to identify in a job description that the person in that position is the next responsible person, such as "assistant."

Clarity as to whom the person in the position is responsible is critical. To whom one reports implies authority as well as the source of counsel and performance appraisal. It also establishes the chain of command for reporting and assistance purposes.

The general responsibility of a position is identified in the early stages of outlining staff organization. Refining the language into a basic descriptive statement of the purpose of the position should be relatively simple.

To determine essential functions, go back to the general and specific responsibilities to identify the physical, cognitive, visual, auditory, and other abilities essential for an individual to fulfill these responsibilities, with or without reasonable accommodations. For instance, does the position require physical ability to lift a certain weight, walk or climb a certain distance, or swim? Reasonable accommodations include making existing facilities readily accessible to and usable by persons with disabilities, restructuring the job, or making accommodations in order for a person with a disability to perform the job (e.g., modifications of equipment, providing devices, interpreters).

Since the Americans with Disabilities Act was passed in 1990, it has given employers a renewed awareness of their responsibility to avoid unlawful discrimination against a qualified individual with a disability because of that disability. "The term 'qualified individual with a disability' refers to a person with a disability who, with or without reasonable accommodations, can perform the essential functions of the job. All employers must therefore identify the essential functions, as opposed to the marginal functions, of each job."[2]

Many camp directors also find it prudent to include in every job description any other job duties along with a statement that additional tasks may be assigned at the discretion of the director or supervisor.

Once the specific responsibilities and essential functions of a position have been identified, it is wise to identify the relationships the person in this position will have with people in other positions, including any outside providers (hospital, vendors, etc.).

A list of the equipment to be used by the person in the given position alerts applicants to certain experience or skills required and presents an area of query for the interview process.

Based upon the information developed in the previous areas of this description, the qualifications for the position require additional review. This review enables appropriate adjustments and additions to those qualifications. The qualifications for the position grow not only out of the general responsibility identified, but also describe the minimum age, education, experience, and characteristics essential to the particular position. Other descriptions may grow out of related governmental regulations, as well as accreditation and organizational standards. For instance, specific certifications or being of a certain age may be required by law. If a position demands a particular level of education, this requirement should be clearly stated, and any mandated training should be communicated.

Age is a primary employment factor that must be considered carefully. Often industry standards, certification criteria, or government regulations will specify minimum ages for certain functions, such as drivers of vehicles or waterfront personnel. For instance, requiring that a person be an adult depends upon the legal age of adulthood in the governing state. These factors must be researched carefully, even though the director may choose to require an older age or higher skill level if specific responsibilities are beyond the ordinary. For example, the group may be a considerable distance from the central camp support or public assistance, or the individuals in the group may have special characteristics. In both cases, increased skill levels and more maturity are required from the responsible staff member.

In the camp field, the accepted age for camp counselors is 18 or older. Certainly, age is no guarantee of maturity, but experience has shown that, generally, individuals over 18 tend to be more mature. Federal labor regulations affect other positions by prohibiting individuals less than 18 years of age from being employed to operate or clean slicing machines or mixers in kitchens or to operate vehicles in excess of 6,000 pounds.

It is essential to have a person of legal adult age in certain positions—such as in waterfront supervision, supervision of camper groups taken off site for extended trips or travel, and driving of passenger vehicles. Supervisors should generally be at least two or more years older than the staff they supervise.

Gender appears to be less of a factor in camp employment, except where counselors are assigned to live in the same quarters as campers of the same sex. Some camps with very young campers may not find gender to be a factor. Of course, neither sex nor age can legally be used to discriminate in employment. Where a certain age or gender is a requirement of a particular position, that factor should be carefully documented in the job description.

Experience is a plus in any position, but for certain staff positions it is essential to hire staff with previous experience. Obviously, the value of a potential staff member's experience depends upon the situation in which it was acquired. A camp director can best determine the value of such experience from references, though an interview may assist greatly in that evaluation. Both of these methods are discussed in detail in Chapter 7.

The camp director must consider skill as well as experience when hiring staff. All camps have areas that require employees to have specific outside certification, ranging from registered nurse to a commercial driver's license. For staff expected to drive vehicles carrying passengers, a current driver's license appropriate for the vehicle to be driven and from the state in which the camp is located is required. It is critical to run a check of driving history for the past four months before camp opens for seasonally hired drivers and within the past 12 months for year-round drivers.

Various skill certifications are available in such areas as aquatics, riflery, campcraft, and horsemanship. Certification is available in the skills of waterfront, archery, boating, riflery, water-skiing, and horsemanship. For example, equestrian programs offer an area of potential danger unless properly staffed and administered. Safety factors and the importance of animal care require staff members with experience and instructional skills in this area. Horsemanship training is available at various universities, riding academies, and the U.S. Army, and certification is available through some horsemanship associations (see Appendix C).

In other areas, where certification is not available, documented evidence of experience and expertise, as well as instructional skills in that specific program, needs to be provided. The director must go beyond the applicant's statement of experience and skill to talk to or correspond with people who have actually supervised the applicant in the specific area or who have observed the person in action. If the person is going to be an instructor in a skill area, then questions about teaching ability are as important as the person's technical skills.

Though adventure or challenge programs—such as ropes courses, rappelling, initiative courses, and climbing—have multiplied in recent years, no nationally recognized certification of instructors is in place at this time. Authorities in the field recommend that accreditation of a site-specific program is more appropriate than certification of individuals in these activities. However, several reputable organizations and regional resources provide training in these skills; 20 hours of such instruction and experience should be the minimum expectation of an applicant to supervise such programs (see Appendix C).

No area of camp program has consistently contributed to as many deaths in camps nationwide as water-related injuries. Therefore, extreme care needs to be taken in the selection of the person responsible for overseeing the aquatic program, staff, and facilities. That person should be at least 21 years of age with previous experience in the supervision of an aquatic area for at least one season. In addition, the person should hold current certification in lifeguard training from a nationally recognized certifying body, and if any instruction is involved in aquatic activities, certification as a swim instructor from a nationally recognized certifying body such as the American Red Cross or Boy Scouts of America. The aquatics supervisor must be a person with the maturity and judgment to train and supervise other members of the aquatic staff, as well as to recognize any potentially dangerous situations in the specific aquatic environment. Where recreational swimming is conducted, lifeguards should hold certification from a nationally recognized certifying body (such as American Red Cross, YMCA, Boy Scouts of America, Royal Lifesaving Society, etc.). Swimming instructors should hold a certification from similar bodies. See Appendix C for organizational resources providing aquatic training and/or certification.

If aquatic activities other than swimming are offered, the individual supervising each specific activity should have skills specific to that activity. The staff member should be certified through a nationally recognized certifying organization and have documented experience in the knowledge and skills required to teach and supervise the program, as well as in rescue and emergency procedures specific to the aquatic area and activities. In addition, any staff working with boats should be conversant with U.S. Coast Guard boating safety standards and the proper registration labels for recreational boats. Instructor certification programs are available through the American Canoe Association, U.S. Sailing, the American Water Ski Association, and from some chapters of the American Red Cross. Additional training in powerboat operation is available through the U.S. Coast Guard Auxiliary, the U.S. Power Squadrons, and state boating agencies. Many states have mandatory education requirements for individuals who operate any motor-powered vessel. Courses from the preceding organizations will fulfill those requirements (see Appendix C for contact information).

At each location of aquatic activity, one staff member should hold certification in first aid including in the handling of bloodborne pathogens, providing cardiopulmonary resuscitation (CPR) for the age level served, with training in AEDs that includes the use of breathing devices by a nationally recognized certifying body such as the American Red Cross. It is not possible to identify a ratio of lifeguards to swimmers that applies to every situation. Therefore, the camp director, along with the aquatic supervisor, needs to carefully study the various aquatic locations, activities, and the participant skill levels, and then establish an overall aquatic policy that includes reasonable ratios of lifeguards to swimmers. This policy will determine the number of certified persons the director needs to employ.

Note: The Occupational Safety and Health Administration (OSHA) has defined a lifeguard as someone who has a legal "duty to act" or is a professional rescuer. Where an employee by designation is required to perform a task, it is implied that the employer must provide the appropriate tools for the job. For example, rescues that include mouth-to-mouth resuscitation or treatment of wounds require equipment to protect the rescuer from communicable diseases and bloodborne pathogens. In this case, required tools include protective breathing devices and latex gloves, which should be provided by the camp.

In a job description, personal qualifications such as knowledge, skills, and abilities should be listed separately. For example, flexibility or ability to work with others may be included if they are essential. However, according to equal employment regulations, all qualifications must be directly related to the job. In every job description, it is wise to have a statement that identifies that the position has responsibility for the health and welfare of campers.

In starting the process of writing new or revising existing job descriptions, the director can gain insights by asking supervisors and staff to organize a checklist of tasks related to their individual positions. This step may also identify some misconceptions as to the actual responsibilities of the position. "Job descriptions require systematic thought and continual revision. They cannot be written in a vacuum; careful consideration of how the camp operates is an integral part of the job description."[3] Changes may have to be made in initial descriptions after individuals are employed and the summer staff is in residence, but it should be done with the full participation of the staff members concerned. The American Camp Association provides information on the hiring process, job descriptions, ADA compliance, background checks, and related matters on its website at: www.acacamps.org/knowledge/human.

Salary and Benefits

In advance of staff recruitment, careful consideration should be given to the camp policy of compensation and benefits for staff. Obviously, the philosophy of the organization will dictate the plan to some degree. For example, Girl Scout day camps or local church camps may be staffed by volunteers. However, even camps with a predominantly volunteer staff need such a compensation policy.

In addition to wages, benefits can include meals, lodging, transportation, laundry, babysitting, insurance, and/or a camp experience for children of staff members. Each benefit costs the camp money and saves money for the staff member or provides the employee with something of value; such benefits should be clearly identified in a statement of personnel policy. In addition to salary, the camp director should also consider what portion of the benefit has FICA or income tax implications associated with it. Each situation will be different, so guidelines should be developed before staff recruitment begins.

Meals: Most camps that serve meals automatically provide meals to staff members at no additional charge for the convenience of the camp. However, meals for the staff member's dependents are a negotiable matter. Some camps charge cost and deduct it from salary; some camps include meals as a benefit. Others require families to prepare their own meals in separate living quarters, while the camp takes responsibility for the staff member's meals only when they eat with the staff and campers.

Lodging: Resident camps generally provide lodging for staff members, most often in multiple-living units. Counselors are usually required to live with campers, although a privacy division or room in the same building may be provided. Lodging for dependents of staff members is sometimes charged against salary, or in other cases, given as a benefit of employment. Many camps provide housing for families in order to secure or retain older or returning staff.

Transportation: Day camps generally require some staff members to ride on camper buses and usually provide space for any staff member at no charge. Resident camps often meet staff at central locations. Some camps provide a transportation allowance, particularly for staff members who travel more than a minimum number of miles to get to camp.

Babysitting: Day camps utilizing volunteers often provide a central babysitting service for children of staff members or reimburse volunteers for the cost of home babysitting. Resident camps sometimes provide babysitters at the camp for younger children of a camp employee.

Insurance: Worker's compensation, automobile, and liability insurance are covered later in this chapter. Many camps provide a health and accident insurance policy to staff members as a benefit of employment, or offer it as an option that the staff member may purchase.

Camp experience: Where a single parent or both parents come as staff members to camp and have camper-age children, it is not unusual for those children to be enrolled as campers in their proper age group as a credit against wages. Even for volunteers, the value of this benefit may be considered income and be subject to taxes.

Salary: If any amount is agreed upon and paid to a staff member in advance (whether it is called an honorarium, a stipend, a scholarship, or a gift), that remuneration is considered salary. Initially, the director should secure information on the state's minimum-wage laws as well as the applicability of federal minimum-wage laws. It may also be helpful to visit with camp directors of comparable camps in the area to learn what salaries are being paid in similar circumstances.

If minimum wage is applicable, rooms or other facilities provided by the employer may generally be counted as a part of the minimum-wage calculation. The rule of thumb for determining the value of these services is to document the average cost of the meals including overhead, labor, and raw food. For lodging, the documentation should include the value of the lodging provided based upon the local community market, with consideration given to whether the lodging is private, semiprivate, or dormitory style. It is best to check with a human resources expert or a lawyer, since federal and state wage-hour laws change frequently.

Increments in salary levels are decided in a variety of ways:
- By number of years on the staff
- By age and experience
- By certain qualifications (cook, nurse, waterfront certification, outdoor living skills certification)
- By position in the organizational chart
- By need (i.e., the camp finds that the only way to secure staffers from the inner city is to pay considerably over the going rate because of economic circumstances)

The camp director should give careful thought to salary scales, to any increases built into those scales, and to their fairness to staff members. Though most people do not work in camps solely for the monetary benefit, sensitivity in such a close community to differences or inequities in wages can interfere with the more important parts of camp life. It is essential that it not be implied that counselors are the lowest point on the scale because there is probably no more important person in terms of health and safety or camper relationships than the living-group counselor. The program philosophy and goals will emphasize that responsibility more in some camps than in others; however, in every case, it is vital that the nature of the counselor's responsibility be fairly recognized.

In an effort to be competitive, you should compare the camp's salary scale with comparable camps. The American Camp Association conducts a salary study regularly and makes the results available online through its bookstore. This resource offers a comparison to salary scales nationally and regionally.

Personnel Policies

Although camp directors may be covered by the personnel policies of their employer, seasonal staff may not be. It is generally the camp director's responsibility to develop personnel policies that define the guidelines and expectations for seasonal staff. Each staff member should be given a copy of the personnel policies. See Figure 6-5 for a sample of some personnel policies. Ideally, these policies should be attached to an employment agreement and should be reviewed by the staff member before a contract is signed.

Personnel policies generally cover the following issues:
- Pay periods (dates, deductions, method of payment, overtime, compensation time, salary ranges)
- Overall benefits
- Workday hours
- Termination (length of notice necessary, termination pay, causes)

Sample Personnel Policies for Seasonal Staff

The camp wishes to make your employment period with us as enjoyable and beneficial as possible. Camp is a community, and the actions of each member of that community affect the other members. Certain policies help clarify the expectations of the employee and the employer, and minimize any difficulties within the community.

It should be recognized that employment at camp is "at will." Either party can terminate the relationship at any time, for any or no reason, with or without notice, under the state's at-will doctrine.

Camper Welfare

The first responsibility of each and every staff member is the health and welfare of the campers. Each staff member is expected to take every care to protect the privacy and person of each camper. Physical punishment or any sexual contact between staff and campers is inappropriate, and will be grounds for dismissal. Staff members should never touch campers in any area covered by a bathing suit or show outward signs of affection that could be misinterpreted as sexual abuse.

Insurance

Worker's compensation and health insurance is carried by the camp on each employee for work-related injuries or illnesses. This insurance does not cover non-work-related injuries or illnesses.

Liability insurance carried by the camp covers each employee when carrying out assigned camp responsibilities, as long as the employee is not negligent in carrying out those responsibilities, is following the policies and procedures of the camp, and is acting within the authority of their job.

Pay Periods

For the convenience of the camp office, the wage agreement is based on a weekly rate. It is impossible to clock the actual work hours in the camp setting for counselors, program personnel, and program supervisors. However, the kitchen and maintenance employees must furnish a daily record of the hours worked on the cards provided. The camp will issue paychecks on the first and 15th of each month during contracted time.

Time Off

Time-off periods will be scheduled as regularly as possible, but necessarily at the convenience of the camp program. Each week, staff can typically expect one 24-hour period free of duties, agreed upon with the employee's supervisor a week ahead. In some cases, days off may be accumulated for a two-week period to provide two successive days off. Days off cannot be accumulated without advance permission.

At least two hours daily will be freed up for persons related to living groups. A plan for coverage of the living group should be worked out with the staff member's supervisor.

Figure 6-5. Sample personnel policies

Sick Leave

If a staff member is sick, a camp director, supervisor, or health director may request that the staff member see a doctor or go home to recuperate from an illness or injury without pay.

Alcohol/Tobacco/Controlled Substances

Alcohol and controlled substances are not allowed on the camp property. Employees are expected to follow this policy. In addition, employees are not to return to the camp grounds under the influence of alcohol or controlled substances. Breaking this policy is grounds for immediate dismissal.

Smoking and chewing tobacco is discouraged, but is permitted in the staff lounge or the living quarters of staff not living with campers. All employees are asked to refrain from smoking in any areas of camp frequented by campers, as well as in the kitchen.

Staff are asked to be sensitive to the people in the communities near the camp. Each staff member represents the camp in dealing with members of the local communities, as well as in behavior off the camp grounds.

Tips/Gratuities

Staff members are asked not to accept any tips or gratuities from the parents or relatives of campers.

Health Services

A registered nurse is on duty at camp, and staff members have access to health services as needed. The cost of prescriptions and doctor or hospital visits must be covered under personal insurance or that purchased through the camp, unless the injury or illness is work-related (refer to section about insurance).

Grievances

Should a disagreement over the interpretation of camp policies or a grievance related to duties or relationships with fellow staff members occur, it should be reported to the supervisor promptly. Should the supervisor be the source of the grievance, the staff member may report the grievance to the supervisor of that supervisor or to the camp director.

Performance Appraisal

In an effort to help each staff member perform the requisite duties at an optimum level, each staff member is evaluated on a regular basis. The employee's supervisor will indicate the frequency of the supervisory conferences, and at the conclusion of each conference, the supervisor will share a written evaluation with the employee. The employee and supervisor will both sign the agreed-upon evaluation, and it will be filed in the staff member's personnel file.

A staff member does not have to wait for a scheduled supervisory conference to seek advice or counsel from his supervisor. The primary responsibility of a supervisor is to be available to deal with the day-to-day problems of his supervisees.

Figure 6-5. Sample personnel policies (cont.)

- Time off (amount to be expected, method of determination, scheduling, sick and personal leave days, jury duty, holidays)
- Work rules (use of tobacco, alcohol, and/or controlled substances, a specific sexual harassment policy, etc.)
- Other regulations (use of personal automobiles or equipment in conjunction with camp program, use of communications systems such as computers, e-mail, Internet, and phones, etc.)
- Workers' compensation information and procedures
- Equal employment opportunity statement
- Performance appraisal system (discipline, grievance procedures, etc.)
- A policy statement concerning the welfare of children (actions to be taken in case of child or sexual abuse by the employee, as well as other forms of harassment)
- A statement that a health examination and history is required. Because camps serve as the first line of defense for medical treatment for camp staff, such critical medical information is necessary to determine whether a doctor or additional professional medical care is required, and without the appropriate information, camp health staff cannot make an informed decision.[4]

Because of the current litigious climate, the camp director may do well to include in the personnel policies a statement indicating that the policies are designed to clarify; generally, the employer-employee relationship and should not be considered as a contract nor as a guarantee of employment. Any contract should also stipulate that the employer-employee relationship is an "at will" relationship, which may be terminated with appropriate notice by either party at any time. (Termination is discussed in more detail later in this chapter.)

The camp director should also pay careful attention to providing time off for resident camp staff. The living situation at a resident camp demands 24-hour responsibilities from most personnel; however, because of that continuing day-to-day situation, it is vital that time off be arranged for each staff member. In addition, some free time to pursue personal needs should also be available.

That time will occur naturally for many staff who work given hours, but program and counseling personnel, in particular, need a plan. For safety reasons, those plans should be coordinated carefully, and counselors should always know how their camper-group responsibilities will be supervised in their absence. A minimum of two free hours a day, apart from sleep time or eating with campers, is the accepted norm.

In addition to daily free time, every staff member needs a minimum of 12 consecutive hours free each week (or 24 hours every two weeks) so that there is time to get away from the camp community or to find uninterrupted time for personal needs in camp. Obviously, such time has to be scheduled and, in most jobs, personnel replacements arranged. Adequate flexibility in job descriptions and numbers of staff is needed so that other staff can substitute for those staff members who are off duty and still maintain an appropriate camper-staff ratio. Provision for time off is an obligation of the camp as an employer, but scheduling may be at the employer's convenience. It is important that the camp director also take a day off, for personal well-being and for the benefit of staff.

If the new director begins after staff recruitment has been completed, the director should make a careful review of the program to determine how it is affected by the individual abilities and skills of the staff. Program plans should then be adjusted accordingly. Of course, it is desirable that the new director has the opportunity to develop an ideal organizational plan for the staff before beginning recruitment.

Early Termination

Termination is a matter that a director seldom considers until faced with a staff member who is not fulfilling essential responsibilities. Discussion, prior to the season, with other camp directors concerning their termination practices can be helpful. It is important to recognize that, despite a likely concern for the employee as a person, termination of that person may be the most beneficial action for the total camp community and for that person. Because of the 24-hour living situation in a residential camp and the short season of many camps, termination becomes necessary where, in other settings, more time could be given to coaching or waiting and seeing whether the problems could be resolved. For these same reasons, it may also be better to pay the terminated employee for the notice period and have that person leave camp immediately rather than to have a disgruntled employee in the living situation for that period. Specific guidelines regarding termination are discussed in more detail in Chapter 9.

Checkpoints

- List the positions that the camp program design necessitates and to whom each reports.
- Review present job descriptions for each position. Check them, if possible, with persons who have filled the positions previously.
- Outline the general responsibilities and specific functions of each position.
- Outline the qualifications necessary to accomplish the functions as well as those imposed by position or regulations (i.e., age, certificates, degrees).
- Test the number of counselors against the number of campers at one given time to find the optimal camper-counselor ratio.
- List all of the various sorts of remuneration the camp will be giving staff, and determine the actual cost for each one. Compare this cost with line items in the budget.

Related Standards

American Camp Association's Accreditation Standards for Camp Programs and Services: HR.2, HR.6–9, HR.21

Endnotes

1. Reuel A. Benson and Jacob A. Goldberg. 1951. *The Camp Counselor*. New York: McGraw-Hill. p. 41.
2. Edie Klein. 1992. *It's My Job*. Martinsville, IN: American Camping Association. p. 3.
3. Karla A. Henderson. 1990. "Job Descriptions Help Measure Staff Performance." *Camping Magazine*. Vol. 62, No. 4, February, p. 24–25.
4. "Interviewing and the American with Disabilities Act." 2003. *The CampLine*. Vol. XI, No. 3, Winter, p. 6.

PERSONNEL RECRUITMENT

Camp Northway (Canada)

Chapter Seven

> *The director must adjust his or her own thinking about staff in the light of his or her … purposes. It now becomes obvious … that the most important single staff member is the counselor living with his or her group of campers. Even the waterfront head, the dietician, the nurse … needs to be so well-rounded and camp oriented that the special aspect he or she has to offer is thought of as a part of the natural good camp living.[1]*
>
> —Lois Goodrich

After developing a clear organizational design and job descriptions, the director can effectively begin the recruitment process. A director cannot approach this task lightly, for finding qualified staff is a challenge, takes considerable time and effort, and is an ongoing process.

The director should organize the recruitment materials and examine them for clarity, attractiveness, and appeal. Such recruitment materials may be made available on the camp website, and should include job descriptions, an application form, and a description of the job benefits and unique aspects of the camp. The materials must compete with similar materials from many other seasonal jobs and camps trying to recruit the same personnel.

Sources

Where does a director find staff? Following are a variety of different possibilities.

Former and present staff: Ask former and present staff to participate in the search. Obviously, staff members have a clear understanding of the camp's philosophy, working conditions, and the type of personality that will be most effective in this setting. Beware, however, of primarily staffing with friends; cliques may be formed, and newcomers can be excluded. Some camps provide a bonus to previous staff members who recruit someone who is hired and stays for the entire summer.

Colleges and universities: Find a contact person in the university setting. Such contacts could be former or present staff members or someone in the summer placement office, in the recreation, physical education, or education departments, or internship coordinators. Internships may be a possibility for students to gain credits. Residence-hall assistants also often have experiences that prepare them for camp supervision. Make sure the contact knows about the camp's website and has the camp's brochures, applications, and job descriptions. The director may also want to arrange for a day of interviews on campus.

Job fairs: Take advantage of college and university campus job fairs, and plan a tour of fairs in schools in the same state. Fairs often have so many participating camps and summer employers that it is difficult to attract the attention of students unless the camp's booth showcases an unusual display or graphic that includes video or pictures of the camp. Bring a laptop so potential staff can view the camp's website. Most directors soon find that some college and university profiles better match their camp program, location, and staffing "personality," and concentrate on those fairs.

Former campers: Former campers, and particularly past participants in counselor-in-training or leader-in-training programs, are already familiar with the camp. Many directors feel that this is the best resource for recruiting staff.

Faculties: Educators and administrators from elementary, middle, and high schools, colleges, universities, and private schools have valuable experience with young participants and can assist in recruiting quality staff.

Membership of the sponsoring organization: The membership is the first source of volunteer staff of a camp sponsored by an organization. The local Volunteer Bureau may also be helpful in the search for volunteers.

Placement services: Placement services offer an opportunity for the director to file a list of positions along with job requirements. These staffing agencies include departments of employment services in many states as well as some American Camp Association field offices.

Community groups: Neighborhood or community centers, block clubs, churches, and youth boards are good sources.

The Internet: A camp website with great multimedia, program descriptions, location, and a list of jobs available will attract the attention of students and others. The website can also act as a networking tool for keeping in touch with previous campers and staff. It may assist in recruiting staff through such online networks. The camp may also want to post its job listings on sites that students use to check for summer employment. The American Camp Association website (www.acacamps.org) provides resources for summer-camp positions, as well as year-round camp jobs.

Advertising: Advertising is effective, if the camp can do so in a publication specific to the skill or type of position needed.

Parents: Parents may be quite willing to take a camp position if their child can attend camp at a reduced rate.

Seniors: An alternative source of staff which many camps have found productive is to hire senior adults. Seniors have discovered the joys of being with children in a beautiful setting and of being able to continue to use skills and abilities gained from previous jobs. Camp administrators have discovered a wealth of practical work experience among seniors unmatched by younger staff. "Camps that employ seniors can enrich the camper's experience and provide a great summer for senior adults. This attractive staffing alternative is gaining momentum."[2]

Although these sources may provide most of the program and counseling staff, the camp director will probably need to turn to more specialized sources for cooks and nurses. A state employment agency, schools with cafeterias, and fraternity and sorority houses are good sources for recruiting cooks. Similarly, a state nursing association, state employment agency, nursing schools, and other medical-school systems can provide leads for camp nurse candidates.

As Christy L. Phillips writes, in the recruitment process, it is important to "remember that there are good people who are just waiting to work in your camp. Now, all you have to do is find them. Make a staff recruitment calendar and work with camp associations and other camp professionals. With some persistence, your staff recruitment efforts will be successful."[3]

International Staff

Over the past three decades, camps have come to recognize the value and richness that international staff can bring to their camp community. In addition, camps have come to rely on international staff to fill a number of positions. With increasing restrictions on visas more recently, the numbers of international staff have decreased somewhat. Having international staff members has great advantages, if those individuals are well prepared for the particular camp setting, possess the skills for the position for which they are employed, and are used to stimulate international education through the camp program.

Several excellent agencies screen potential staff applicants at different overseas locations and provide applications and interview information to the camp director. Individuals from other countries can broaden and stimulate the camp experience for campers and staff alike. Addresses of such organizations (Bunacamp, Camp America, Camp Counselors USA, International Camp Counselor Exchange Program, International Camp Counselor Program) can be found on ACA's website. In addition, the International Camping Fellowship website (www.campingfellowship.org) and its member camps often provide resources and contacts for camp staff looking for an international camp experience.

Some international exchange organizations are able to sponsor visas for year-round international interns. Environmental education programs and conference centers may find this option helpful in maintaining an international presence and program during the fall, winter, and spring seasons. Nancy Halliday of Hofstra University states:

> Campers and staff from the United States gain valuable insights into other cultures—their language, history, ways of thinking and looking at the world, customs, food, and dress. Learning from staff with whom they interact on a daily basis can be a ... powerful learning experience ... . International staff members have allowed us to view our program and staff training through fresh eyes.[4]

However, to simply employ such staff because it is the easiest way to fill difficult positions is unfair to the camp and to the international applicant. It is critical that information be shared with all applicants so that they understand not only the scope of duties, but also the type of living accommodations, working conditions, and proximity (or lack thereof) to cities. If a personal interview is not available, it is essential that the camp director take extra steps to communicate with the applicant and a former employer. Faxes, e-mail, and video-chat capabilities have sped up communication with potential international staff and made vetting them more efficient and effective. Certainly e-mail offers an inexpensive method of communication, but an interview by an international phone/video call is vital. It is particularly important for applicants who would be working directly with campers on a day-to-day basis, where ability to work with children and fluency of the language spoken in camp are both important.

The American Camp Association has developed an outline of Best Practices for International Staff that details exemplary as well as expected practices of camp directors, and is shown in Appendix D. Directors would do well to study this document before ever beginning to search out international staff. Delegating responsibility for recruitment of a staff member does not absolve the employer from careful and responsible actions in the employment process, as well as the normal humane concerns shown to the staff.

It is well to remember that international staff have the same needs and concerns that the other same age staff have (developmental need of the late adolescent and/or young adult, the transition from the classroom/dorm to the camp setting). However, they also face the adjustment to new cultures, language oddities and clarity, loneliness, and homesickness. These factors certainly have implications to the entire training plan for such personnel over and beyond the typical staff training and any training that might have been given international staff by their sponsoring organization.

Negligent Hiring

A lawsuit for negligent hiring is based on the theory that the employer is liable for the actions of an employee who was unfit or who created an unreasonable risk of harm.[5] To translate this process into camp vernacular, negligent hiring is an action wherein a parent sues a camp for injuries sustained by a camper that were caused by the careless actions of a staff member or of an unqualified staff member. Camps have also been sued for negligent hiring of staff who had previously been convicted of sexually abusing children. The expectation of the parent is that the director should discover this fact before hiring the person.

Many of the steps described in this chapter are designed to provide protection against such suits: clear job descriptions, complete application forms, references, and a thorough screening process including background checks, interviews, and documentation of each step. All of these steps are equally important for the camp that has a volunteer staff. Though some steps may be more difficult in a camp where staff changes from week to week, it is critical that a modified plan of hiring be developed which covers the same basic steps.

To further document these procedures, it is important to have a statement of the camp's overall employment policies and practices with identification of any differences in application to seasonal and year-round staff. Each of the steps identified should be stated in this portion of the camp's policy manual and reviewed at least every three years by the camp's legal counsel. To maintain consistency in hiring practices, a log of all of the steps taken for each applicant should be kept. A sample hiring log is shown in Appendix G.

Screening

Applications

Beyond the data ordinarily required for employment, a camp staff application form should emphasize the skills and experience required in the job description. It usually means a slightly different application for each category of employees (kitchen, maintenance, counseling, etc.).

A director should be aware of the importance of eliciting only that information which is legally needed for a decision about the job, and on the other hand, of requiring all information which is needed to determine if an applicant meets all personnel selection qualifications. For example, it is permissible to ask the applicant's gender or whether the person is at least a certain age only if the job requirements demand a certain gender or minimum age. Asking for that information when the job does not require it may open the camp director to charges of discrimination. Figure 7-1 shows an application developed by the American Camp Association.

It is also wise to provide enough space on the application form so that every previous job may be listed, enabling the director to check for gaps in employment. Such gaps give the interviewer an opportunity to ask questions about that period in the event that such incidents were due to convictions of a felony or crime related to abuse.

Where a license or certain level of experience is required, a copy of the license—or in the case of experience, outside documentation—should be required.

The steps taken after an application is received are critical in the selection of competent and conscientious staff. The type of references desired, the format of the interview, and the delineation of the camp's philosophy and policies should be carefully planned before implementing these steps. Training and supervision cannot mitigate the employment of an incompetent and potentially negligent person in a staff position.

Specific questions should be asked about previous convictions for child abuse; however, one should clear those questions with the camp's attorney. For instance, the application might ask: "Have you been previously convicted of a felony or misdemeanor? If the answer is yes, please indicate on a separate sheet of paper the convictions, dates, and circumstances," or "Have you been previously charged with any crime related to the abuse, mistreatment, or molestation of children?"

Camp Staff Application   Form FM 10N

Return to:

Developed by American Camp Association
Expires 10/01/08

(Please type or print.)   Date of Application_____

Name_____   Social Security Number_____

Permanent Address _____
                                    Street & Number   City   State   Zip

Phone_____   Fax_____   E-mail_____
              Area & Number   Area & Number

School or Business Address _____
                                              Street & Number   City   State   Zip

Phone_____   Fax_____   E-mail_____
              Area & Number   Area & Number

Dates available From _____To _____

What type of position do you want at camp? _____   Salary desired?_____

Do you meet or exceed any minimum age requirements for that position?   ☐ Don't know minimum age   ☐ Yes ☐ No

Can you perform the essential functions of the job for which you have applied,
with or without reasonable accommodation?   ☐ Yes ☐ No

If you are hired would you desire or need housing for any person(s) other than yourself at the camp?   ☐ Yes ☐ No

Past Work History Provide a full record of all employment — paid and volunteer — and explain any gaps in employment. Include any positions on camp staff. Use a separate sheet, if necessary.

Dates	Employer/Supervisor	Address & Phone	Nature of Work	Reason for Leaving

Indicate any employer you **do not** wish us to contact, and the reason _____

_____

_____

This form has been drafted to comply with federal employment laws; however, ACA assumes no responsibility or liability for the use of this form.

american CAMP association®   Copyright 1979 by American Camping Association, Inc. Revised 1990, 1991, 1992, 1994, 1996, 1998, 1999, 2004, 2007.

Figure 7-1. Camp Staff Application

References Give names and addresses of three persons [not relatives] having knowledge of your character, experience, work habits, and ability.

Name	Address & City	Phone

Camp Experience

Dates	Camp & Director	Location	Camper or Staff?

Education High School and Beyond

Years	School	Major Subjects	Degree Granted

Write a brief biographical sketch, including specialized training in camping, and experience or training in other fields which might have a bearing on the position(s) for which you are applying. Attach a separate sheet if necessary.

_____

_____

_____

_____

_____

_____

_____

_____

_____

_____

Figure 7-1. Camp Staff Application (cont.)

Camp Program Skills   In the following list, put a "T" *before* those activities you can organize and teach as an expert, and an "A" for those activities in which you can assist. Put a "C" *after* those in which you have *current* certification and attach a copy of your certification.

Adventure/Challenge
_____ challenge/ropes course
_____ climbing/rappelling
_____ spelunking/caving
_____ _____

Arts/Crafts
_____ ceramics/pottery
_____ drawing/painting
_____ leather craft
_____ metal work
_____ photography
_____ woodworking
_____ _____
_____ _____

Campcraft/Pioneering
_____ backpacking
_____ campcraft
_____ hiking
_____ orienteering
_____ outdoor cooking
_____ outdoor living skills
_____ overnights
_____ wilderness trips
_____ _____

Dance (list)
_____ _____
_____ _____

Drama
_____ clowning
_____ theater
_____ _____

Music
_____ singing
_____ instrument (list)
_____ _____
_____ _____
_____ _____

Nature
_____ animals/animal care
_____ astronomy
_____ birds
_____ environmental studies
_____ flowers
_____ forestry
_____ insects
_____ rocks/minerals
_____ weather

Sports/Fitness
_____ aerobics/exercise
_____ archery
_____ baseball/softball
_____ basketball
_____ bicycling/biking
_____ boxing
_____ fencing
_____ fishing
_____ football
_____ golf
_____ gymnastics
_____ hockey (ice/in-line)
_____ horseback riding (English)
_____ horseback riding (Western)
_____ informal games
_____ martial arts
_____ riflery
_____ skating (ice, roller, in-line)
_____ soccer
_____ snow sports (list)
_____ _____
_____ tennis
_____ track/field
_____ volleyball
_____ wrestling

Waterfront Activities
_____ board sailing/wind surfing
_____ canoeing
_____ diving
_____ kayaking
_____ rafting
_____ rowing
_____ sailing
_____ SCUBA
_____ swimming
_____ synchronized swimming
_____ water skiing
_____ _____

Miscellaneous
_____ academics
_____ aviation
_____ community service
_____ farming/ranching/gardening
_____ foreign language
_____ leadership development/CIT
_____ radio/TV/video
_____ storytelling
_____ team building
_____ worship services/religious studies
_____ _____
_____ _____

Certifications and Camp Support Staff Skills   In the following list, please check those items in which you have experience and skills. Mark with a "C" those for which you hold current certification and attach a copy of your certification.

Business/Administration
_____ bookkeeping/accounting
_____ computer/technical
_____ computer/software (list)
_____ _____
_____ _____

Health/Safety
_____ CPR
_____ first aid
_____ lifeguard
_____ nursing
_____ _____

Maintenance
_____ auto mechanics
_____ carpentry
_____ electrical
_____ plumbing
_____ _____

Food Service
_____ cooking/meal preparation
_____ Food Handler's Permit/Certification
_____ menu planning
_____ purchasing
_____ sanitation
_____ _____

Answer these questions *only* if applying for a position requiring driving

Do you have a valid driver's license?   ☐ Yes ☐ No   State_____

Do you have current chauffeur's-type license?   ☐ Yes ☐ No

Do you have a commercial driver's license?   ☐ Yes ☐ No

Figure 7-1. Camp Staff Application (cont.)

What contributions do you think you can make at camp?_____
_____
_____
_____
_____
_____
_____
_____

What contributions do you think a well-run camp can make to children?_____
_____
_____
_____
_____
_____
_____
_____

Harassment The camp's policy is to prohibit all forms of harassment by our employees. This includes sexual, racial, religious, and other forms of harassment. Have you ever been accused of harassment of any person including, but not limited to, workplace harassment? (Note: a prior accusation is not an automatic bar to employment. The type of accusation and when it occurred will be evaluated by the camp before any decision is made.) ☐ Yes ☐ No

Explain_____
_____
_____

Criminal Record Have you ever been convicted of a crime, other than a minor traffic offense? If yes, please describe. (Note: a prior conviction is not an automatic bar to employment. The type of conviction and when it occurred will be evaluated by the camp before any decision is made.) ☐ Yes ☐ No

Explain_____
_____
_____

I authorize investigation of all statements herein, including any checks of criminal records, and release the camp and all others from liability in connection with same. I understand that , if employed, I will be an at-will employee unless there is an agreement or law which alters that status. Furthermore, I understand that any agreement must be in writing and signed by the designated camp official. I also understand that misrepresentations or falsifications herein or in other documents completed or submitted by the applicant will result in dismissal, regardless of the date of discovery by the camp.

Signature _____ Date_____

All statements become part of any future employee personnel files.

Figure 7-1. Camp Staff Application (cont.)

References and Background Checks

In the development of the application form, a director will need to decide the number of references required and how they will be utilized. Generally, applicants request references from people they know will provide favorable recommendations, and it is unusual for persons giving written references to make negative comments. This tendency does not necessarily mean that references are useless, but rather that care should be exercised in requesting them.

If the director's concern is job performance, ask for the names of an applicant's supervisors for the last three jobs, rather than for general references. At this stage, it is important to ask the previous supervisors specific questions about performance as an employee, any dismissal, and if so, the reason for it. If the concern is the applicant's ability to relate to children, then ask for the names of persons who have had the opportunity to observe the applicant in a position where he taught or led children of specified ages. Questions about judgment and disciplinary methods should be included. If the concern is performance in a certain skill area, then ask for persons who have observed the applicant as a teacher of that skill or as a member of a team practicing that skill. If simple character references are desired, they should not be from relatives. If written references are requested, it is courteous to include a stamped return envelope. A sample reference questionnaire is shown in Figure 7-2.

While it is often difficult to get former employers to be frank about an applicant, it is unwise to employ a person without some check of references. Figure 7-3 shows an example of a document the applicant would sign releasing former employers from any liability while providing information about the skills and work habits of former employees.[6] The use of such a release may encourage the person giving references to relate negative information that a potential employer should know about an applicant.

A telephone check of references may be the most effective approach to references, since some people are more willing to make negative observations verbally than in writing. However, if telephone references are used, a system should be developed for recording notes on the conversation that can be filed with the job application. The recorded notes should be dated and signed by the person making the call. To address questions about an applicant after having received written references, make a final telephone check.

If references are received by e-mail, procedures are needed to verify the reference was sent by the person who signed the e-mail. For instance, asking for a reference written on the letterhead of the organization/business with a signature shown on the letter sent as an attachment rather than in the body of an e-mail.

References are more important than ever with the new awareness of the potential of employing child abuse offenders. Questions should be asked to determine whether the applicant may have any proclivity toward child or sexual abuse. See the last two questions in Figure 7-4.

Reference Questionnaire

Confidential

_____ has applied to work on the staff at Camp _____ for this summer. This person has given your name as a reference who could evaluate his/her past performance as well as potential for the listed position. Please give careful consideration to the ratings below.

Objective Rating

Under each general heading, check the phrase that most accurately describes the applicant's habitual behavior with regard to that specific trait. Please remember that it will be the truly exceptional person who ranks high in all categories.

How well is the applicant able to direct and influence others along definite lines of action?
❑ Poor leader; incapable of directing others
❑ Usually follows the lead of others
❑ Normally successful in directing and controlling others
❑ Very successful in leading others
❑ Exceptional leader; inspires others along desirable lines of action

How well does individual work with associates and others for the good of the group?
❑ Cooperates grudgingly; makes trouble, obstructionist
❑ Gives limited cooperation; neglects common good for own interests
❑ Cooperates with others toward accomplishment of common cause
❑ Cooperates willingly and actively regardless of self-benefit; makes things go smoothly
❑ Exceptionally successful in working with others and inspiring confidence

How does this person react to suggestions or criticisms by others?
❑ Takes criticism as a personal insult
❑ Resents suggestions
❑ Listens to suggestions but may act without considering them
❑ Follows suggestions willingly
❑ Asks for criticisms and suggestions

How responsible is applicant? Able to competently get things done on own?
❑ Irresponsible even under supervision
❑ With constant supervision, will do satisfactory work
❑ Usually needs detailed instructions with regular checks of work
❑ Carries out routine activity on own responsibility
❑ Exceptionally able to accomplish work without close supervision

How well does individual put principles and convictions into action?
❑ Fails to carry out convictions under adverse circumstances
❑ Acts according to convictions under normal circumstances
❑ Carries out principles and convictions constantly and boldly, even in face of obstacles

Figure 7-2. Reference questionnaire

How well does this person apply energy and persistence in following a job through?
❏ Needs much prodding to complete work
❏ Rather indifferent; does not finish job
❏ Completes assigned tasks of own accord
❏ Industrious, energetic; dependable at all times
❏ Unusual perseverance; does more than expected

How well does applicant control emotions?
❏ Easily depressed, irritated, or elated
❏ Tends to be overemotional
❏ Unresponsive; apathetic
❏ Tends to be unresponsive
❏ Usually well-balanced
❏ Well-balanced
❏ Unusual balance between responsiveness and control

Narrative Report

Please briefly state specific instances in which you have observed the applicant's behavior as it applies to any of these items. If you have no knowledge, please say so.
  • *Impression of suitability as a camp counselor.* Would you be willing to have your children under individual's supervision for a period of weeks in a camp situation? If not, why not?
  • *Maturity of judgment.* How does this person react in situations of stress (i.e., make decisions)?
  • *Ability to lead campers toward spiritual objectives of the camp.* Ability to lead devotionals, worship? Influence of life?
  • *Nature of associates.* Describe the types of people with whom individual habitually associates.
  • Dependability. Can be relied upon? Does person weaken in absence of authority?
  • How long have you known the applicant? _____ How have you observed applicant?
  • Have you seen the applicant in a leadership role with youngsters? _____ What role?
  • To what extent does the individual use drugs or alcohol?
  • To your knowledge, does the applicant have any proclivity toward child or sexual abuse?

Please return promptly to:

Name _____   _____

Address _____   _____

City _____State _____Zip _____

Position _____

Employed by _____

Figure 7-2. Reference questionnaire (cont.)

**Job Applicant's Release to Prospective Employer
to Request Information About the Applicant**

I_____ (applicant's name), have requested consideration for employment by _____ _____ (camp). I am aware and have been informed by _____(name) of _____ (camp) that the statements I have made on my job application (and during interviews) will be completely checked out by_____ (camp).

As consideration for the above-named employer's agreement to consider my job application, I hereby authorize him/her to engage in background checks regarding any and all statements I have made on the job application (and during job interviews) and, further, to obtain any other information regarding my previous employment, my veracity, my skills and/or abilities which the above-named employer may deem relevant.

I hereby release any individual, firm, partnership, corporation, public official or public entity from any liability on any theory whatsoever for providing such information as described in the previous sentence to _____ (name of camp).

_____   _____
Signature of Applicant   Signature of Witness

_____   _____
Social Security Number   Date

_____
Date of Birth*

_____
Current Address of Applicant

*This information should only be requested if it is necessary to obtain criminal background information. A footnote on the form should state the sole purpose of the use of this information.

Figure 7-3. Sample release form

Voluntary Disclosure Statement
All Camp Staff   FM 16

Developed and approved by the
American Camp Association
Expires 10/01/08

Mail this form to the address below by _____ (date)

Name _____ Birth date _____
            Last   First   Middle

Home address _____
                  Street Address   City   State   Zip

Social Security # _____ Other names by which known (e.g., maiden name) _____

Home phone _____ Business phone (if applicable) _____

Cell phone (optional) _____ E-mail address (optional) _____

School or College _____

Address _____
                  Street Address   City   State   Zip

Driver's License # _____ State _____ Expiration Date _____

1. Previous residence(s) for last five years (include college and home residences):

   City _____ State _____ Years _____

   City _____ State _____ Years _____

   City _____ State _____ Years _____

   City _____ State _____ Years _____

   (Continue on separate sheet, if necessary.)

2. Have you ever been arrested and/or charged with a crime? (This includes charges that have been dismissed, deemed nolle prosequi, deferred adjudication, or found not guilty.)   ☐ Yes ☐ No

3. Have you ever been convicted of any crime relating in any manner to children and/or your conduct with them?   ☐ Yes ☐ No

   If yes, please explain: (Use a separate sheet, if necessary.)

   _____

   _____

   _____

   _____

4. Have you ever been convicted of any crime including, but not limited to, those listed below and/or any crime similar in any manner to those listed below?   ☐ Yes ☐ No

   • Indecent assault and battery on a child under fourteen
   • Indecent assault and battery on a mentally retarded person
   • Indecent assault and battery on a person who has obtained the age of fourteen
   • Rape
   • Rape of a child under sixteen with force
   • Assault with intent to commit rape
   • Kidnapping of a child under sixteen with intent to commit rape
   • Distribution and trafficking of narcotics or other controlled substances
   • Intent to commit any of the above crimes

american CAMP association®   © 1997 by American Camping Association, Inc. Revised 1998, 2002, 2005, 2007.   (over)

Figure 7-4. ACA voluntary disclosure statement

If yes, please explain: (Use a separate sheet, if necessary.)

_____

_____

_____

_____

5. Have you ever been adjudged liable for civil penalties or damages involving
   sexual or physical abuse of children?   ☐ Yes ☐ No

   If yes, please explain: (Use a separate sheet, if necessary.)

_____

_____

_____

_____

_____

6. Are you now or have you ever been subject to any court order involving sexual or physical
   abuse of a minor, including, but not limited to a domestic order or protection?   ☐ Yes ☐ No

   If yes, please explain: (Use a separate sheet, if necessary.)

_____

_____

_____

_____

7. Have your parental rights ever been terminated for reasons involving
   sexual or physical abuse of children?   ☐ Yes ☐ No

   If yes, please explain:

_____

_____

_____

_____

_____

I understand that:

a. The camp may deny employment to any person who answers "yes" to any one of questions 2-6. If hired and the employer later discovers circumstances that would indicate a "yes" answer to any of the above questions, employment may be terminated immediately.

b. The information provided on this form is subject to verification, which may include a criminal history check and request from any Central Registry of child abusers.

c. The camp may terminate employment or volunteer service of any person if that person is found, regardless of when discovered, to:

   1) have a history of complaints of abuse of a minor;
   2) have resigned, been terminated or been asked to resign from a position whether paid or unpaid, due to complaint(s) of sexual abuse of a minor; and/or
   3) have falsified or omitted information in this disclosure statement.

d. This disclosure statement must be updated yearly.

Signature _____ Date_____

Signature of Minor's Parent or Guardian _____ Date_____

Figure 7-4. ACA voluntary disclosure statement (cont.)

In addition to references, the director must consider the question of background checks. The American Camp Association standards require a name-based check of the U.S. Justice Department National Sex Offender Public Registry (www.nsopw.gov) annually and a criminal background check for all new staff. Though the FBI maintains the most complete criminal database in the country, a large number of states bar access to the registry. A sexual-offender registry may exist in the state in which the applicant resided, but the standards call specifically for a check of the Department of Justice registry annually. The application form should include a statement to give permission for the camp to conduct such checks as well as a fingerprint and criminal record check and be signed by the applicant. In addition, a voluntary disclosure statement for each employee must be required annually. See Figure 7-4 for a sample voluntary disclosure statement.

Where such a background check is not required by the state, the camp can require the applicant to obtain a check as a requirement of employment. Commercial companies will perform background checks for a fee. These companies are subject to the Federal Credit Reporting Act (FCRA), which places an obligation on the camp as the employer to obtain permission from the applicant to secure the check, preferably with a copy of the applicant's rights under FCRA. Should negative information result from the check that causes the director not to employ the applicant, the applicant must be notified of the decision and given a copy of the report, the address of the agency providing the report, and another copy of the rights under FCRA.

Such checks are generally not available for minors and international counselors. Legally, the cost of such checks should be borne by the camp as a condition of employment. The usefulness of such checks in the seasonal-camp employment situation is questionable if most of the staff members are of college age, since they may be only one or two years beyond the age where such a record could be documented. In this situation, the voluntary disclosure statement is vitally important, especially with international counselors.

On the other hand, for persons over 21 or employed year-round, such a check can be a valuable precaution. It is also wise to secure an FBI fingerprint check on such employees if the state in which the camp is located has passed legislation enabling access to the Criminal History Records Repository. The most practical approach is to contact the state law-enforcement agency regarding the process and fees. Despite the lack of uniformity of reporting to the national system (and that some states do not require such checks be made of volunteers and employees), questions of liability can arise if an alleged incident occurs and a camp has not made such checks. It is, therefore, important for a camp to make a policy determination about whether such checks and/or voluntary disclosure statements will be required.

Should an applicant's name come back with a criminal or sexual offense record, it is wise to double-check it to make sure it is the same full name and same social security number. "False positives" can occur where the record actually belongs to another individual with the same or similar name.

Another means of vetting the background of potential employees is to visit various social networking websites to search for that person. Potential employees may have profiles on sites such as Facebook and MySpace. These sites provide information about applicants' interests and extracurricular activities. As an employer, look for pictures or depictions of inappropriate behavior of the potential employee. If the applicant's site is blocked, search that person's friends' profiles to see if inappropriate material regarding the applicant is a part of the friends' site. The Internet can be a useful tool for finding additional, unfiltered information about the applicant.

Child Abuse as an Issue in the Employment Process

The camp director should take steps in the employment process to minimize the risk of child abuse. The director should examine job descriptions, application forms, interview checklists, reference forms, contract forms, and staff-training outlines to make sure that all opportunities to uncover clues as to past abuse history or the proclivity toward such abuse exist. It means checking references, doing a background check, investigating for a criminal record, asking questions in the interview about the applicant's experience, and checking gaps in employment history. While many states recognize claims for negligent hiring, most courts protect employers who can document a reasonable job of checking prior to employment.

The application form offers an opportunity to document the applicant's own statement as to previous convictions, as well as to alert the applicant that abuse is a concern of the camp. Specific questions are noted later in this chapter.

Wherever statements are made about the position and the requirements (i.e., on job descriptions, in the interview, and in the staff manual), clear statements should be included that abuse will not be tolerated and that the welfare of the camper is a primary job responsibility of every staff member.

During the interview, questions should be posed that delve into areas that may give clues or danger signals. Robert Ditter, a licensed social worker specializing in adolescent treatment, suggests several such questions to be asked 20 minutes or so into the interview:

> Do you have a best friend? Tell me about them—how long have you known them? What's one thing they've taught or done for you? Would you say you are most comfortable with people your own age, older or younger? (Explore this.) How were you punished as a child? What did you think of it then? Now? What do you think works best with children?[7]

In her book, *For Their Sake*, Becca Cowan Johnson points out that, while a camp director may have no way to determine whether or not a person is a molester from traits alone, traits and characteristics can be used as guidelines for identifying potential abusers. She states that, generally, the abuser will have a negative attitude and a hot temper, and will blame others—either the child or a circumstance. Continuing further, Johnson provides listings of the traits common to potential physical, emotional, and sexual offenders.[8]

Employment Interview

The employment interview is probably the most traditional and widely used method of selecting individuals to fill job openings. It can generally be defined as a purposeful exchange of ideas through the asking and answering of questions. Studies by various management associations have shown that training in interviewing guidelines can effectively increase the ability of the interviewer to select the candidate with the best potential for the job, and that experience in conducting interviews over a period of time increases the accuracy of selection.

A 1995 study conducted by the American Bar Association revealed that personal interviews were perceived as the most effective screening practice by youth development organizations. The second most effective tool was previous-employer reference checks.

Before the Interview

A number of things should be in place prior to an interview so that the time available can be used to the best advantage. Ideally, certain information should be in the hands of the applicant prior to the face-to-face interview:

- *Job description*: A job description as outlined previously in this chapter, plus an outline of salary, benefits, starting and closing dates of the position, number of hours of work expected, and time off. If food and housing costs are to be deducted from salary, specific amounts should be noted. In addition, if food and housing are provided as part of a salary, their relative worth should also be noted. Job descriptions are helpful in the interviewing process since they will help to give the applicant a more comprehensive understanding of the position for which this person may be applying.
- *Information about the camp*: Brochures, material describing the general focus, general goals and objectives, and pertinent information about the age of campers served, fees, length of sessions, type of program, and copies of recent newsletters. The applicant should also be familiar with the camp website.
- *Organizational chart*: The interviewee should have some means of knowing where in the line-up the position in question falls, the immediate supervising position, and the relation of that position to others on the staff.

Ideally the interviewer can review all the facts available on the candidate through pertinent correspondence, the completed application form, written references received, or the notes from telephone calls or e-mail correspondence made to individuals given as references. These materials will help the interviewer plan for the areas in which more information is wanted and will serve to pinpoint trouble or blank spots that need further inquiry. In order to avoid possible charges of discrimination, the questions need to be confined to job-related material.

Under the Americans with Disabilities Act of 1990, it can be viewed as discriminatory if a potential employer asks questions about an individual and his abilities that are not directly related to abilities necessary to perform job related functions. It is inappropriate to ask whether the applicant has any disability. On the other hand, a question which takes the focus away from the disability and places it on the completion of essential job functions is appropriate. For instance, "Are there any reasons you would have difficulty performing any of the essential elements of the job?"[9] Figure 7-5 lists some of the questions that may and may not be asked in this area.

May Ask	May Not Ask
Can you perform the essential functions of this job?	Do you have a disability?
Describe or demonstrate how you would perform this job or function.	Do you need reasonable accommodations to perform functions?
Can you meet attendance requirements?	What number of days were you absent on your last job?
Are you currently using illegal drugs?	Were you ever addicted to drugs or treated for drug addiction or abuse?
Have you had prior illegal drug use?	Do you take legal drugs?
What are your drinking habits?	What is your worker's compensation history?

Figure 7-5. Questions that may and may not be asked during a job interview

After a director has offered a position to a person with a disability, it is possible to ask additional questions or pose additional requirements before the person begins work. At this point, inquire about the individual's worker's compensation history, illnesses/disease/impairments, prior sick-leave history, and require the same physical examination required of other entering employees.[10]

Interview Setting

The setting of the interview provides an important background that may help or hinder these efforts. The time set aside should be free from distractions, telephone calls, or interruptions by other people. The room where the interview takes place should have adequate lighting and ventilation and comfortable chairs. Avoid placing the desk between the interviewer and the interviewee to reduce the interviewer's dominant role and help break the ice. Sit side by side in comfortable chairs for a more relaxing and less threatening environment. Privacy is an important factor, so the interview should not be held in an area where other people can pass through or look on, or where the conversation can be overheard.

The Interview Plan

After the available information has been organized, a specific plan for the interview should be developed. It is helpful to prepare a list of questions to ask all candidates for a particular job, as well as specific questions that relate to the information provided by the particular applicant. Generally, the director needs to explore five basic factors with applicants:

- *Intellectual skills and aptitudes*: Look both to their intellectual capacity (or the ability to solve problems) and to their application or effectiveness (how well the applicant applies and uses intellectual capacity). This information can be obtained from a general survey of a scholastic record, together with pertinent questions on work experience and performance.

- *Motivational characteristics*: Primarily, these characteristics may be evaluated by discovering what a person likes to do or finds satisfaction in doing: interests, activities, best subjects in school. These aspects may well come to light in discussing long-term goals and aspirations and reasons for applying for the position in question.

- *Personality strengths and limitations*: Behavior, traits, characteristics, and temperament all reveal how a person interacts with work environments and with others. Questions regarding relationships with people with whom the applicant has worked on prior jobs may open this area for more information. Interpersonal relationships indicate what a person is like: shy, confident, aggressive, withdrawn, forceful, arrogant, open, outgoing, passive, or dependent. Occasionally, the interviewer may begin to get vague, negative feelings in this area, along with subtle and nonverbal clues. These clues should be heeded; if the interviewer reacts negatively to the person, it is possible that others will also.

- *Knowledge and experience*: From the applicant's past record, which of the job experiences will be most helpful in the job that is open? Will any of the past experiences hinder the applicant in the current job?

- *Degree of comfort with the philosophy and approach of the camp*: Rather than seeking acquiescence to the camp's philosophy, questions should be asked which reveal whether the person's individual approach is consistent with the camp's approach. Richard M. Strean suggests that the director:

> *Take advantage of the hiring process as the first, often overlooked step in counselor management, an opportunity to hire people who share the camp's philosophy and understand directors' expectations. … Such a candidate is far more likely to do what the director would want done when supervisors are not watching for the simple reason that the candidate would tend to do it anyway.*[11]

In the light of these five areas, another look at the application and reference material will aid in blocking out areas where additional conversation is needed. A list of these questions in logical order will serve as a reminder during the interview, and also provide documentation of specific questions used in interviewing candidates.

General Approach

- *Note taking*: During the interview, the taking of notes provides an organized way of recording data that may be overlooked, and of ensuring that a significant response or reaction not be forgotten. It is difficult to take notes and give attention to what is being said at the same time, and the note taking may serve to distract the person being interviewed. The pad should be placed as unobtrusively as possible, preferably in a position where the interviewee cannot read what is being written. In this way, the process becomes an integral part of the situation and can be more readily accepted by the applicant.

- *Establishing a good climate*: Applicants are often ill at ease and apprehensive as well as threatened in the face of authority. If an interviewer can show a friendly and interested acceptance at the beginning, the interviewee may be willing to respond in a frank and open manner. If the applicant seems reluctant to talk, a genuine compliment or sincere praise on some past experience or achievement noted in the application may put the person at ease. If an open, frank, and relatively non-threatening climate can be established, the desired response on the part of the interviewee will generally follow.

- *Leading questions*: Questions phrased in such a way as to indicate the response desired should be avoided. The question, "Did you take part in extracurricular activities in college?" indicates to the applicant that this factor is important, and the applicant will begin to search his experience for a suitable reply. A more general approach to the question might be, "Tell me about your college experience. What did you find particularly helpful?"

- *Open-ended questions*: It is good to open each topic area with a broad, open-ended question. For instance the interviewer might ask, "Would you tell me something about your high school days?" The interviewer will then be free to take notes and observe mannerisms and behavior patterns while the applicant has to determine how much or how little to tell. Questions can be used to guide the direction of the interview, to open areas for discussion, and to encourage participation.

- *General to specific questions*: Questions should move gradually from the general to the more specific. From "Would you tell me about your work with the YMCA?" (general question) to "What did you like least and most about that job?" (specific question).

- *Self-appraisal questions*: Questions should be directed to motivating self appraisal. "Do you feel that you effectively accomplished that particular job?" Or, "If you could repeat that experience, what would you do differently?"

- *Controlling the flow*: Although the interviewer should be in control of the interview at all times, it is to his advantage to listen and to try not to interrupt. Natural pauses can be used to check the sequence of points on the interview plan, to see that facts in each area are adequate, and to keep the communication moving along. While the applicant provides the factual answers, the interviewer can determine the answers to some other intangible questions: How does the applicant communicate ideas? Can the applicant conceptualize effectively? Is the applicant's thinking shallow or superficial? Is the applicant perceptive to the social situation?

Conducting the Interview

An interviewer should remain impartial, neither condemning nor condoning what he hears. To provide a positive setting, the person conducting the interview should not react negatively to new ideas or unfamiliar subjects. Opinions should be disassociated from facts, and time should not be wasted in disagreeing with an opinion. Time should not be taken up with facts contained on the application, but the emphasis should be on moving in the direction the interview needs to go. Although first impressions are important, it is essential that the interviewer try not to form conclusions too quickly.

If it is necessary to secure information that may not be comfortable for the applicant to reveal (e.g., why a particular job was held for a short period or details on a problem with a particular supervisor), the interviewer should indicate that such discomfort is understandable. Essential questions may be asked more than once in different ways to find out from the reaction how strongly the applicant may feel about a particular topic.

Concluding the Interview

An effective technique for ending the appointment is to summarize the interview. At this point, the applicant may be more relaxed and relay additional information. If it is determined during the interview that the person is not qualified for the position, the applicant should be told so at this time. If additional information is needed, the interviewer must be sure that the interviewee understands specifically what is required, and a time should be set for receipt of the information. The applicant should also be told the time at which he may expect to hear the decision regarding the position.

Documentation

As soon as the applicant has departed, it would be wise for the interviewer to make any additional notes. If the director is interviewing a number of applicants in close sequence, making notes immediately after each interview will help to crystallize facts and impressions and help distinguish one applicant from another. Answers to critical questions such as those about abuse and discipline are important to record. The notes from the interview should be dated and signed by the interviewer and placed in the personnel file. This provides further documentation in the endless task of showing that every precaution was taken in employing a competent individual in case there is an allegation of a child abuse incident and subsequent litigation or unfounded litigation. Some interviewers find it useful to review by making a list of positive and negative facts ascertained during the interview and to rate job qualifications against a predetermined list.

Evaluation of the Interview

One effective way of developing and refining skills essential to good interviewing is to make a personal evaluation of the performance immediately after the session. One approach is to take a look at the original interview plan and compare it to the actual interview. Was the general plan followed? Did the interviewer miss any important category? Did the interviewer succeed in putting the applicant at ease? Did the questions elicit the responses needed? Did the interview move smoothly and stay on track, or was it sporadic and difficult to control?

Another means of evaluating is to work from the personal angle. Did the interviewer talk too much? Did personal prejudices and attitudes come through to the applicant, or was objectivity maintained? Was the interview conducted from the point of view of the applicant? Did the interviewer respond negatively in any instance? If the interviewer could redo the interview, what would be added or deleted? What approach would the interviewer change? When considering impressions from the interview, it is important to remember that the overall picture is the most important. If the interviewer is undecided, he may wish to review the interview notes and information with a colleague.

These few minutes spent in considering interview performance will pay off in terms of increased perceptiveness and flexibility in handling the next interview and in operating more effectively in the selection process. In the final analysis, of course, the litmus test of the interview is whether the result is a successful selection of a staff member who performs well on the job.

As part of an interview evaluation, Robert Ditter suggests some warning signs that he terms "red flags," which possibly characterize a personality prone to abuse children:

> Who ran the interview, the director or the candidate? If the interviewer found that he/she was answering a lot of questions or being distracted by tangential conversation consistently throughout the interview, raise a red flag. Such behavior should make the interviewer wonder what a person might be avoiding. (Such behavior could indicate a "controlling" or "insecure" personality.)
>
> How much of a peer support system does this person have? Is he or she a drifter? Currently, are there significant other adults in his or her life? Are there strong connections to others, besides children, to give a sense of balance and support? If there are a lot of negative answers, raise a red flag.
>
> Does this person spend too much time with children? Does he or she seem to plan time-off activities which sound too much like work (typical of a physical abuser) or involve more time spent with children? If he or she also has weak peer relationships, this is a serious cause for a red flag alert.[12]

Becca Cowan Johnson, author of *For Their Sake*, would add:

> How does this person describe how he or she was disciplined while growing up? Was it strict, appropriate, abusive? That is, does a person report an abusive past? Was the abuse emotional, physical, and/or sexual? Studies indicate a strong tendency toward repetition of experiences.[13]

Employment Agreement

It is accepted practice to provide each staff member with an employment agreement at the time of hire. The formality of the written agreement will vary from situation to situation; but, in any event, the staff member and the director should each have a copy of the document, which they have both signed. A signed agreement between a director and a volunteer can serve to clarify obligations on both sides and demonstrate the responsibilities assumed by the volunteer.

In many states, employees are regarded to be at-will employees unless a written agreement specifies an employment period. The advantage of at-will status is that the employer can release the person earlier than had been anticipated if enrollment is slow or conditions warrant. An employment agreement may specify the dates of expected employment and indicate that the employment is at-will. Of course, an employment agreement does not force the employee to remain should the staff member decide to terminate. Using the word contract instead of employment agreement may imply an independent contract or relationship. It is wise to have the format and wording of such an agreement reviewed by the camp's legal counsel, since legal implications may be binding.

A sample employment agreement is shown in Figure 7-6. Such a letter usually contains the following items:

- Dates of employment or time commitment, with expected termination date
- Title of the position and reference to job description
- Remuneration
- A statement that employment is "at-will" and may be terminated by either party
- Policy for termination by the staff member or the camp
- A statement of agreement by the staff member that he will abide by the personnel policies which are attached, or the specific policies included in the agreement
- Dates of signing
- Signatures of staff member and director (where the staff member is under the state legal adult age, the director may wish to have the letter cosigned by one parent)

Personnel Files

Personnel files that include the application, references, contract, and eventual performance appraisal reports are typically kept for each staff member. These confidential files should be kept out of reach of all but supervisory personnel, or if managed electronically, they should be password protected. Medical records on staff members should be kept separate from personnel files, and are subject to the privacy provisions of the Health Insurance Portability and Accountability Act (HIPAA). It should be noted an employee may request to see his file. All of these files should be kept for a lengthy period of time, at least until the youngest camper at the time of that person's employment has reached 6 to 18 months beyond the age of majority in the state of operation. While state laws vary, minors usually have up to two years after they reach the age of majority to instigate litigation on their own behalf. Records of staff persons who have had exposure to bloodborne pathogens are required by OSHA to be maintained

---

Staff Employment Agreement

Dear _____:

Camp ___ _____ is happy to offer you a position as a _____ (insert position) on our staff. The position of _____ is described in detail in the attached job description, but do keep in mind that, from time to time, the administration may assign other duties deemed appropriate.

Your employment will begin on _____, 20___, and we expect that it will terminate on _____, 20___. Your salary will be based on the gross rate of $_____ per week. Deductions from your gross salary will include:
• Federal and state withholding tax
• Health insurance of $_____
• Resulting in a net weekly rate of $_____

It should be noted that all of our employees are employed on an at-will basis.

Attached is a copy of the camp's personnel policies, outlining time off, behavioral expectations, and related matters. Your signature to a copy of this letter indicates your acceptance of the terms of employment and agreement to these personnel policies. Please return no later than _____ (date).

The camp community provides a unique opportunity for teamwork, leadership, and service to our participants. We trust you will join us in our endeavor to make this a successful season for our campers, and for you.

Sincerely,

Camp Director

I accept this position as outlined.

Signature _____

Date _____

Figure 7-6. Staff employment agreement

for the period of employment plus 30 years. Other staff health records are to be maintained for 30 years, according to OSHA. Again, this matter should be reviewed with legal counsel.

Rehiring

Returning staff are important in the entire recruitment process. A director counts on retaining a significant number of staff from the previous season in order to maintain quality, continuity, and tradition. However, rehiring previous staff must not be done blindly. It must be recognized that often nine months or more has transpired since the last experience with the person. Much can happen during that period to change a person's attitude, experience level, and relationships.

Some directors go as far as to require returning staff to go through the entire employment process again: application, references, background checks, and such. Other directors use a form to ask the person to update the earlier application, perhaps by attaching a photocopy of the face sheet of the previous application and asking once again about driving record or criminal convictions. At the same time, the applicant can share additional experiences relative to the camp setting that would enable him to expand his duties. Where a staff member has responsibility for or access to children, a background check should be done annually. The director has a responsibility for developing a specific plan for assuring his confidence in the background, suitability, and fitness of every individual on the staff, including persons returning to the camp staff, however tremendous they may have been the previous year.

The ACA Standards call for new camp staff to have a criminal background check; this standard is mandatory. Staff are considered "new" upon initial hiring and/or if there is a break in employment of 12 months or more. Year-round staff, including directors, must be screened upon entry and thereafter according to the policy of the camp.

A criminal background check seeks information regarding additional criminal behavior, reported according to "levels" indicating the nature of the crime and the risk of repeat offense. The camp must have a specific plan for securing criminal background checks based on state laws, availability of data, cost, and type of staff. In many cases, a criminal record for minors may be available if a crime was committed in which the individual was charged as an adult. If a staff member is not 18 years of age at the start of employment, a criminal background check should be completed within three months of the individual turning 18 if the person is still employed by the camp at that time. Camps that hire international staff should take into account the screening practices of international placement agencies; in many cases, criminal background checks are provided through those agencies.

Appendix B provides a checklist for risk management in the recruitment and screening of employees.

Counselors in Training

Many camps have developed programs to prepare older campers to become camp staff in the future, often called counselors-in-training (CITs). Such programs can be invaluable in interesting young people in the possibility of working in camp. They also provide another method of retaining older campers and promoting their leadership skills before becoming a camp counselor.

Such programs require a carefully designed curriculum, trained, mature leadership, and careful interpretation to the camper and the camper's family. The group most often served is 16 to 17 years of age.

A curriculum may be developed from the camp's basic precamp training program, excerpting the material most appropriate to the age group and beginning staff member. Resource materials should be adapted from the camp's staff manual and from appropriate professional publications. The curriculum should be put into written form and vetted with current key camp staff.

Leadership for the program should be carefully selected, with one qualification being the ability to teach adolescents. Though many key staff may take teaching roles in their areas, one staff member should be designated as CIT trainer and act as camp counselor to the group. Since the age of participants is most often pre-adult, it is vital that the counselor role not be neglected.

Interpretation of the program is critical in the expectations of both the camper and the family. The completion of the training program does not guarantee a position on the camp staff. The role of the CIT is not equivalent to a counselor or program leader, and at no time does the CIT have complete responsibility for a group of campers. The CIT is a helper to the counselor or program specialist, and may be given an opportunity to experiment with group leadership or teaching or supervising a program skill under the supervision of an adult staff member. In most camps, the position is not a paid employee position. Some camps waive or lessen the camper fee for participants, whereas others charge the full fee.

The difference between a camp staff member and the CIT should be clearly defined to the entire camp staff. Camp staff should understand that CITs are not adults, and that it is important for the staff members to be role models not only when they are on duty, but also when they are off duty and in the presence of CITs. Similarly the camp bears an in loco parentis responsibility for these pre-adults when they are out of camp as well.

Checkpoints

- Identify the different steps taken during the staff screening and employment process to prevent employing persons with a proclivity toward child or sexual abuse. Identify the steps taken to protect the camp in case of an incident.
- Write out a series of questions to ask in a job interview. Read them aloud to see how they sound. After revision, try them in an interview. Keep adapting them as necessary.
- Outline the process the camp will use to screen returning staff members.

Related Standards

American Camp Association's Accreditation Standards for Camp Programs and Services: HR.1–7

Additional Professional Practices: Human Resources Additional Professional Practices

Endnotes

1. Lois Goodrich. l959. Decentralized Camping. Martinsville, IN: American Camping Association, pp.11, 13.

2. William A. Becker and Dawn Shelar. 1991. "Employing Seniors at Camp." Camping Magazine. Vol. 63, No. 4, February, p. 49.

3. Christy L. Phillips. 1996. "Find the Staff You Need." Camping Magazine. Vol. 69, No. 2, November/December, p. 4.

4. Nancy Halliday. 1998. "International Flavor: The Value of Including Internationals on Your Staff This Summer." Christian Camp and Conference Journal by CCI/USA. Vol. 2, No. 1, January/February, p. 12. Reprinted with permission.

5. Marge Scanlin. 1993. "Getting References: The Task of Finding Good Staff." The CampLine. Vol. 2, No. 2, October, p. 1.

6. Ibid, p. 4.

7. Robert Ditter. 1986. "Protecting Our Campers: How to Recognize Various Forms of Child Abuse." Camping Magazine. Vol. 58, No. 3, January, p. 23.

8. Becca Cowan Johnson. 1992. For Their Sake. Martinsville, IN: American Camping Association. pp. 103–113.

9. National Camp Executives Group. 1992. Camp Director's Primer to the Americans with Disabilities Act of 1990. Glen Allen, VA: Markel Insurance Company. p. 17.

10. "Interviewing and the Americans with Disabilities Act" (condensed from EEOC Preemployment Guidelines Under the ADA, October 10, 1995). 2003. The CampLine. Vol. XI, No. 3, Winter, p. 7.

11. Richard M. Strean. 1996. "Invisible Counselors: Managing What You Don't See." Camping Magazine. Vol. 69, No. 1, September/October, p. 34.

12. Robert Ditter. 1986. "Protecting Our Campers: How to Recognize Various Forms of Child Abuse." Camping Magazine. Vol. 58, No. 3, January, p. 23.

13. Becca Cowan Johnson. 1992. p. 116.

STAFF ORIENTATION AND TRAINING

Cali Camp Summer Day Camp (Topanga, CA)

Chapter Eight

To the camp director falls the task of taking a number of individuals and helping them to achieve this peak of know-how-on-the-job, at the same time welding the total staff into a smoothly functioning team. It is no simple job, but one to which the camp director must turn much of his energy and planning.[1]

—Catherine T. Hammett

Staff training is probably one of the most difficult but potentially productive functions for a camp director who seeks to create a favorable climate and to set the tone for the summer season. The training of staff falls into three general categories:

- *Orientation*: The period from the signing of the employment agreement to the staff member's arrival at camp
- *Precamp training*: The intensive period at camp set aside before the arrival of campers
- *In-service training*: During the camp season, the period of ongoing supervisory conferences, day-to-day problem solving, and staff meetings that include training components

Orientation

The preparation of the staff member for this job begins with the materials that are presented with the application for employment and the subsequent interview. It is essential that the prospective staff member understands the philosophy and goals of the camp as well as the unique makeup of a camp community, since the interplay within that community has much to do with the accomplishments of the camp's goals. The information given a staff member in the interview, in correspondence, and on the camp website must cover not only the job functions, but also the living conditions, transportation arrangements, philosophy of operation, and patterns of staff relationships.

During staff recruitment and interviews, the interviewee's concern for securing the job and the director's intent on hiring a staff member often push concerns about the details of camp living into the background. The director cannot, therefore, depend on the description given at the interview or in prospective employee materials to thoroughly familiarize the employee with the setting and responsibilities. The time between recruitment and reporting to camp is longer than it is for many other jobs, and provides candidates a long time for second thoughts and opportunities for other jobs. This timing issue, added to the potential for a last-minute vacancy, makes it even more important to use the time between a staff member's hiring and reporting to camp for additional orientation.

If staffers come from within a 100-mile radius, a number of face-to-face orientation approaches are possible, which cannot usually be used by a camp whose staff comes from across the country. In the former case, two or three meetings can be planned at a central location over the spring, giving new staff an opportunity to meet each other and former staff, to begin developing relationships, and to secure informal orientation. Local authorities or resource persons, who would ordinarily be unable to travel a longer distance or to come for a more extended period to precamp training, can often be recruited for presentations at such meetings.

A winter sport weekend, spring work weekend, or day at the camp can provide orientation to the facilities and property, as well as give further opportunity for new employees to get acquainted with returning staff and to experience the camp living situation. These events also give the director a firsthand look at the new staff members and a chance to determine what approaches or content should be included in staff training.

A spring meeting of the local area of the American Camp Association or Christian Camp and Conference Association usually provides a number of workshops and opportunities for additional certifications that are of interest to newly hired camp staff, as well as to returning staff. In addition to workshops, these local office meetings provide the opportunity of interaction with staff from other camps in the area. Such interaction provides a broader insight into the camp profession, and, often, as the staff member gets involved, can lead to a commitment beyond the current summer. Many camp directors encourage membership in one or both organizations, and may financially contribute in order for staff to attend workshops or join organizations. ACA also offers online training opportunities to help employees understand their roles as leaders of young people.

In the case of camps with geographically scattered staff, orientation will most often depend upon a visit with the director, e-mail communication, online training, or printed materials. Frequent newsletters, which can be e-mailed or mailed, help stimulate interest and familiarize staff members with other staff, place names, and other features of camp. In addition, a staff manual can be a valuable orientation and training device, as well as a helpful administrative tool for outlining policy and procedures.

It takes a great deal of time, cooperative assistance from key staff, and constant revision to prepare and maintain the most useful staff manual. "Current employment law emphasizes ... that a carefully written employee handbook is essential."[2] A staff manual should include the following:

- A brief history of the camp
  - ✓ A description of the operating body (agency, religious group, corporation, etc.) and its mission
  - ✓ A description of the population served by the camp in terms of age, gender, background, special needs, and such
  - ✓ The camp's purpose, goals, and desired outcomes, and how these needs are met in the program and structure
  - ✓ Program activities with particular reference to how the activities address the desired outcomes, developmental needs of campers, and progression from various levels of skills and needs*

* This item and other items of similar nature may be better added to the manual during precamp training, as the matters are discussed.

- A map of the property
- An organizational chart of staff, clearly delineating supervisory lines
- A job description for each position
- The personnel policies, including a statement concerning compliance with local, state, and federal nondiscrimination laws and child-abuse reporting
- Other policies and operational procedures
  - ✓ Rules with specific philosophy of behavior management and disciplinary actions*
  - ✓ A description of compensation policies including a statement that all raises—other than uniform or automatic wage increases—are at the discretion of the employer
  - ✓ Any laws affecting the duty of the employee
- A description of the operating body (agency, church, corporation)
- A list of items staff members will need to bring to camp
- A bibliography of helpful materials
- General counseling tips*
- Emergency procedures (e.g., for lost campers and natural disasters)*
- A statement that the staff manual/employee handbook does not constitute a contract of employment, and that the camp reserves the right to terminate employment at any time

Online training can also provide a fun and interactive way for future employees to internalize some of the preceding information. An online training program can take employees on a virtual tour of the camp, provide information about the camp and its background and philosophy, cover important policies and procedures, discuss the employee's role in relation to the camper, and assess the employee's learning. Online training can be done anytime and anywhere, so it can be used to free up time for more effective face-to-face training on site before the campers arrive.

Some directors use a rotating library of three or four books or articles that best describe the camp's program and counseling philosophy for staff orientation. Some materials can be posted on the camp's website, giving staff the ability to more readily access information. The assignment of certain articles or portions of the books for discussion by individual staff during staff training may motivate further reading and focus interest.

Whatever information is sent to new staff before camp, it is vital that it be condensed as much as possible and its importance or value highlighted. If the staff member is a teacher or student, classes will occupy much of their attention and only a limited amount of preparation or reading can logically be expected. Therefore, the director should choose material carefully and plan to get it to staff well in advance.

Orientation is equally as important in day camp as in resident camp. Since day camp staff members tend to be from the same community and many

---

* This item and other items of similar nature may be better added to the manual during precamp training, as the matters are discussed

times hold full-time jobs, staff sessions on Saturdays or Sundays may provide the orientation and training time needed prior to staff training immediately preceding camp.

It is important that the camp director plan ahead to ensure that staff members receive needed camp information as early as possible. Students can often use school health service personnel for their physicals if they receive the form early enough. Providing a list of clothing and equipment needed at camp soon after employment will enable the staff member to shop carefully. Other information sent to staff should include: the date and time they are expected at camp, the transportation available, the phone number and address of camp, and directions to camp.

However experienced in camp life a new staff member may be, that person will always feel a degree of concern about a new site, a new camp community, and a new employer. Every step the director takes to relieve this concern and to help the new employee adjust and feel more confident will better the chances of success upon arrival at camp.

Precamp Training

A precamp staff-training program is one of the most effective forms of staff development and of assuring that the camp will fulfill its mission. The purpose is to bring staff together to develop personal skills and competencies for the job, and to mold individuals into a functional team for accomplishing the camp's goals and desired outcomes. Precamp sessions also seek to provide opportunities for personal evaluation and growth.

In order to plan the most productive type of staff training, the camp director should begin early in the year to pull together possible topics and activities, and to see what suggestions can be found in evaluations of the preceding year's training. If at all possible, the planning should include members of the program and administrative staff for the coming season; it is often good to add one or two experienced counselors to the group. As the planning begins, a number of factors need to be considered:

- *Staff come from varied backgrounds*: Many staff members will have experience in other types of camps and will be prone to making comparisons, while others may not have been exposed to the demands of camp living. Some may come from sections of the country remote to the camp location and will have no knowledge of or familiarity with the natural environment or other resources of the new area.

- *New staff and inexperienced staff will be trained together*: Some difficulties are usually involved in planning the training with returning staff and new or inexperienced staff in the same group. Variation in the format and schedule of the training from year to year and the use of experienced staff to share their abilities with the new group can help to alleviate some of the problems. Working in small groups, when possible, gives new staff a chance to integrate more easily into the larger staff.

- *All staff need to participate in the training process*: Every staff member does not need to participate in every session of training, but certain sessions apply to all staff—administrative, support, counseling, returning, and new staff. For example, it is very important that kitchen staff or maintenance staff understand the philosophy of the camp and the importance and goals of the program operation, but they may not need the additional sessions related to camper behavior or conflict resolution. All staff members need to have a review of personnel policies and practices as well as camp rules so that the chances of misunderstanding are lessened.
- *Training usually centers on counselors and staff who work directly with campers*: Because they make up the largest portion of the staff and are primarily responsible for carrying out the camp's goals and outcomes, the training usually centers around counseling staff. The difficulty is that this group is probably composed primarily of individuals whose age and lack of experience may mean that they are at a loss about how to translate such goals or outcomes into everyday activities. The director's task is complicated by the necessity of clarifying for them the connection between the camp's *mission* and its procedures and policies of operation. Such understanding will, it is hoped, be gained in precamp training.

Experiential Training

Some directors find it helpful to organize the training period, to some degree, after the pattern in which counselors will work with campers. The counselors, in this plan, are divided into small living groups under the supervision of an administrative staff member or experienced counselor acting as counselor, mentor and facilitator. Within these groups, they can function the same way their camper groups later in the season will. They move through the usual opening schedule: check in at the office, report to the health center with their health-examination forms, tour the campsite, eat a meal in the dining hall, practice dining procedures, clean their cabin, and so forth. This plan has the potential of orienting the counselor more swiftly and provides a small living group to whom new counselors can more easily relate. This pattern can be continued daily throughout the training time and can be related to the camper experience in as detailed a manner as is desirable.

Trainers often refer to the acronym MUD to recap the essential ingredients of training: Memory, Understanding, and Doing.[3] Training needs to be experientially based. Bob Ditter suggests that activities used in staff training "either provide a shared experience for counselors or tap into the counselors' own experience to make them more sensitive to children." He further quotes Ray Diamond of Camp Kokanda as suggesting, "If my Group Heads and Head Counselors have seen it first and have had a chance to practice it, they are less worried that some activity they might do with staff will be a flop."[4]

During the initial training period, habits will be formed, patterns established, attitudes developed, and relationships with peers and supervisors begun. Regardless of the necessarily high concentration of time spent on the factors which create a good experience for the campers, the staff members' greatest gains should be in their own growth, maturity, and development of potential.

The advantage, of course, is that such personal development among staff members results in increased benefit to the campers with whom staffers will live and work.

On the practical side, some basic goals and outcomes need to be reached during staff training:

- Infusing staff with the basic philosophy, mission, and desired outcomes of the camp, and defining their implications for program procedures and operations
- Fostering a sense of pride in the camp job, and developing a harmonious working relationship among staff
- Developing an understanding of the developmental needs of various age groups being served, providing an insight into working with them, and providing them with an atmosphere of emotional safety
- Teaching and providing practice of necessary program skills, with emphasis on how the campers' developmental needs influences the use of those program skills
- Providing the opportunity for staff to understand working policies and procedures as they relate to individual staff responsibilities and the camp as a whole, with particular emphasis on sexual harassment policies and child abuse policies, recognition, and prevention
- Age-appropriate behavior management and the degrees of supervision needed for various age groups for an emotionally and physically safe environment
- Sharing individual and group skills in working with people, with emphasis on respect for the individual camper, and for his background, beliefs, and abilities, as well as placing camper needs ahead of an individual staff member's needs
- Emergency procedures and specific roles of various staff members

On a more individual and personal level, there are other desired outcomes. Opportunities should be provided during the training for personal interaction so individuals find it easy to establish personal relationships with peers, immediate supervisors, and administrative staff. The use of experiential training activities can help guide a staff member to an increased self-knowledge and understanding of himself.

Scheduling

To deal successfully with all these factors and to accomplish the desired results in the time allotted demands careful planning. The time set aside for training never seems to be sufficient to cover all the priorities; even an experienced director who has worked at staff training over a period of years may not be pleased with the results.

The time allotted to precamp training varies. Day camps often plan training sessions on certain weekend days during school months and then plan for at least one day before starting camp. Resident camps' precamp training ranges from one week to three weeks, depending upon the program and size of staff.

A period of 6 to 10 days will usually suffice. Shorter time periods seldom allow sufficient time for building the spirit of camaraderie so important in a camp community. Generally, staff are contracted to arrive for and are paid for this training period.

Before beginning to fill in a time schedule or consider topics, a director may find it helpful to review training schedules and postcamp evaluations from previous years. Discussions with staff who were present for some of those periods may provide insights into the character and effectiveness of the methods used. The evaluations at the end of the previous training sessions and the summer season can add additional data.

Once a block of time is set aside, a director is ready to decide what he expects to accomplish during the training period. Setting these intentions and desired outcomes will do much to help choose and prioritize subjects and activities.

As the schedule is developed, the progression of the activities and sessions during the week should be considered. Early get-acquainted activities in the larger group will help put new and old staff at ease and provide an opportunity for new relationships. From this point, it is easier to move toward team-building activities in smaller groups. As staff members experience various program elements, the flow of camp will become more real. At this point, the group will be more open to child-centered training, and various techniques and approaches can be tied into the camp's program design and goals. The smaller the living or working group (up to five or six persons), the greater the personal involvement and commitment will be.

Child Abuse

One of the topics that should be dealt with during training is child abuse. The topic should be presented in such a way as to reinforce the alliance between the director, staff members, and parents, rather than to create an atmosphere of mistrust or fear. Placing comments about child abuse in the context of the stress or wear and tear that camp life can have on everyone provides an opportunity to talk about the possibility of impatience or unintentional meanness of counselors toward campers, which is one of the chief symptoms of burnout. Including this topic in staff training will send a clear, specific message that the director is concerned about this issue and is working to ensure the quality of care for all campers.

The discussion should include a clear and frank detailing of the basic definitions, tips for helping staff monitor their own level of fatigue, and guidelines for handling a situation that may have the potential for child abuse or child abuse accusations. Legal ramifications should be clearly pointed out. The camp administration has a responsibility to report such alleged abuse if observed at camp. Legal responsibility for reporting suspected child abuse differs from state to state, but every state has a reporting requirement today. Make certain that all staff members are aware of state mandated reporter laws and reporting methods. Some states, such as California, require every staff member in contact with children to sign a form acknowledging their awareness of state laws that mandate them to report any suspected or known incidents of child abuse. In addition, ground rules concerning the continued employment of a staff member alleged to have abused a child should be concisely stated.

In addition, staff should be alerted to watch for signs of physical or sexual abuse that may have occurred to the child prior to the arrival at camp. Symptoms outlined in Chapter 4 should be discussed with counselors, and policy concerning notification of the appropriate camp administrators should be outlined.

In her book *For Their Sake*, Becca Cowan Johnson suggests two different formats that can be used to cover this topic for staff training. The book also provides a wealth of reference material and current information, which can form an excellent basis for staff discussion.[5]

Varying Training Sessions

Actual training sessions should be planned for variety and balance. For instance, sessions requiring physical activity should be alternated with sessions requiring sitting and listening. A variety of teaching techniques should be employed to assure maximum attention and comprehension: guest speakers, demonstrations, films, charts, discussions, panels, and human relations games and activities. Variation in numbers can stimulate participation; group sessions where everyone participates may be alternated with small-group gatherings. Many programs now employ the use of online training prior to staff arriving at camp. The American Camp Association e-Institute includes a number of courses that support precamp training. Additionally ACA offers Certificates of Added Qualification that address foundational requirements for staff who work with youth.

In any case, the training needs to provide participation, demonstration, and interaction around the learning. Since many staff members are college students, they have been exposed to all types of academic techniques and may have some resistance to being bombarded with facts and theories beyond the end of the school year. They may well expect to be far removed from the formal presentation of knowledge and anxious to have physical exercise.

Practical examples of behavior management should be discussed. Roleplaying can be helpful device to illustrate reaction to different behavior problems and methods of management discussed afterward. Some material may be reviewed individually online in order to provide more time for face-to-face sessions.

Work sessions, with specific tasks assigned to small groups, can get necessary work done before camp opening and provide an opportunity for small groups of staff to work together. However, the director should avoid the temptation to spend 50 percent or more of the staff training time on the physical tasks required to open camp. The painting, cleanup, and repairs should be completed by a work crew well in advance of staff arrival so that the time set aside for training can be devoted primarily to camp goals.

In searching for ways to accomplish the desired outcomes from training, it is important for the director to assess the needs and feelings of individual staff members. An open-ended discussion early in the period can reveal needs identified by a number of staff. Some directors also use a written needs assessment to identify needs that a staff member may be hesitant to mention early in the camp relationship. The size and experience of the staff will, in part, determine the method the director uses to gain an understanding of staff members' individual needs and objectives. Staff participation can be increased by assigning sessions or topics to individual staff members with expertise in a specific area.

Outside resource individuals from universities, county health departments, the U.S. Forest Service, or state natural resources departments, as well as consultants in the camp field, can often provide additional expertise for specific presentations. The involvement of such people may also build relationships in the local area. However, the selection and spacing of such presenters should be carefully scheduled so that they do not interfere with the development of group spirit and the overall thrust of the training.

Several other processes should be included in the training period. Specialty program directors or department heads should have an opportunity to confer with staff, who will work under their immediate supervision. Procedures and responsibilities of each staff member can then be defined before actual operations begin. A tour of the campsite should also be included, along with an orientation about the region in which the camp is located. Having the staff run and participate in each activity area is also useful in allowing staff to practice what they will actually be doing in a non-threatening environment. Health and safety procedures, as well as emergency management plans, need to be covered in detail, as do rules and procedures regarding the dining room, waterfront, and camp store. Some opportunities should also be set aside for relaxation and fun—and simply for talking together. Appendix F offers a list of training topics suggested to meet ACA standards.

Training can also provide an overwhelming amount of information for staff. Varying training in this manner can alleviate some of the intensity and retention issues inherent in traditional training. For example, an overnight camping trip (or one slightly longer) can be a productive part of staff training. Such a trip would allow time for practice of camping or outdoor living skills and latitude for working and relaxing together in a more informal setting. This type of overnight trip is even more important in a day camp where training may be day-only sessions that do not allow the time needed for socialization.

When setting the time schedule for training week, the director should plan a day off for staff between the close of training and the arrival of campers. The intensity of the training period can often be exhausting, and staff need the relaxation and some free time to gain perspective.

Training for Supervisory Staff

Supervisory staff need training in specific areas that will not be of general interest or profit to other staff. However, since these supervisors are responsible for the staff, whose responsibility is to seek to achieve the camp's desired outcomes directly with the campers, it is important that supervision skills be addressed. A good supervisor with the framework of a well-executed supervisory program can effect changes in staff performance and skills resulting in better experiences for campers, and more personal development and a higher return rate among staff.

As a result of a study of 100 camps and how they train supervisors, Becker and Shepherd state: "In many cases, however, new supervisors are often thrown to the wolves with little or no supervisory training. Camp administrators almost never start a summer without extensive, comprehensive precamp training. So, then, why do many camps skimp on training and orientation for head counselors?"[6]

The New Director Orientation course, an eight-hour training resource, available through the American Camp Association, outlines the roles supervisors play, a process for analyzing skills and handling appropriate and inappropriate behaviors, as well as individual supervision plans for each staff member. The curriculum also covers many of the following responsibilities that should be addressed in supervisory training:

- *How to oversee staff*: What are the specific functions and roles the director expects supervisors to carry out? How does the director observe and monitor performance of staff members?

- *How to treat staff members as individuals*: It is important that a supervisor learn early in his experience the importance of treating staff as individuals and respecting that individuality. In the beginning, the supervisor ought to learn all the details about the staff: likes and dislikes, talents, skills, motivations, and how they react to different situations and to their supervisor.

- *How to praise staff*: Recognition of work well done has long been known as an important factor in motivating staff. This recognition can be given on a personal basis, at staff meetings, or as part of a supervisory conference. Public recognition or recognition before the staff member's peers is even more effective as a motivator.

- *How to challenge staff*: A supervisor who believes in the potential of individuals can inspire them to accomplish a task simply because he believes that an individual has the ability to do the job. It is essential that a supervisor always remember to look beyond current job performance to the capacity a person has for achieving.

- *How to deal with inappropriate behavior*: Dealing with inappropriate behavior is an important function of a supervisor, especially in a camp setting, since staff problems may quickly exert a negative impact on other staff and campers. The biggest hurdle is to get the staff member to recognize the problem; if this is accomplished, methods of solving the problem can follow. An important part of the supervisor's effectiveness with problems is to address the behavior and to be supportive without condemning the individual.

- *How to conduct supervisory conferences*: Supervisory conferences may be difficult for new supervisors, particularly if negative points are to be discussed. It is essential that the new supervisor learn how to conduct such conferences with the proper balance of support, praise, and constructive criticism. A supervisor needs to comprehend how to make negative feedback a more positive experience by suggesting ways in which the staff member can improve his performance. And, most importantly, the supervisor needs to convey that his regard for the staff member has not changed because of problems.

- *How to provide on-the-spot supervision*: Not all supervisory comments can wait until a supervisory conference. On the other hand, pointing out an improper method or a violation of a procedure in front of other staff or campers at the time of occurrence will likely be embarrassing and difficult, and it is not appropriate unless the issue is one of immediate health and safety. Supervisors need help in learning the best way to share tips and observations with staff soon after such behavior is observed.

- *How to work with the camp director*: Supervisors should be able to solve routine camper and staff problems in a consistent manner without having to consult with the director. However, some problems should be discussed in full; the dilemma is to identify which is which. The director needs to be kept in the picture since he is usually one step removed from the day-to-day operation, but the director does not need to be consulted about every detail.

- *How to handle framework*: A clear understanding of the underlying philosophy and desired outcomes should be discussed so that supervisors know how their responsibilities and the responsibilities of their subordinates fit into the total framework; doing so allows them to work from a secure base of full understanding of the whys and wherefores.

- *How to handle the supervisor's role*: It is often difficult for a new supervisor to understand how much his role has changed as he moves into supervising other staff. To be adequately prepared for this role, the new supervisor must recognize that, with such leadership, comes a difference in the way that person is viewed by subordinate staff. As the person ultimately responsible for performance of staff, the new supervisor may become the motivating force behind goals and outcomes that staff may not share.

- *How to deal with an alleged abuser*: The general rules for reporting an alleged abuse situation and the protection of the abused child are covered earlier in this chapter. In most camps, a policy is in place for the process of handling an accusation. The staff member is usually suspended, with or without pay. The director should give advance thought to any role the supervisor might play with the alleged abuser (e.g., reporting to director, being with the accused until he leaves camp).

The supervisory and appraisal process is discussed in detail in Chapter 9. As John Durall suggests:

> *The abusing staff person may feel anxious or depressed. He may be preoccupied with immediate issues, such as being arrested and going to jail. He may be embarrassed to face coworkers and the director. He also may be worried about going to court, being sentenced to jail, handling the effects*

the incident may have on his future, and facing family and friends. On a deeper level, he may feel shame, guilt, and self devaluation, as well as hopeless and desperate.[7]

Documentation

A schedule of the entire precamp training period with annotations about content and presenters should be kept in the permanent written or electronic file. In fact, Gregg and Stamp suggest that "the curriculum for counselor training should be written, followed consistently, and updated frequently. If there is a question about what a counselor was told on a particular matter during training, management should be able to point to the relevant item in a training manual or agenda."[8] Having a written curriculum for training may also be helpful in legal actions relating to staff responsibilities.

It is also wise to have an attendance sheet for each session for staff to sign as they enter the training area. If precamp online training is required, documentation regarding the completion of the online material should also be collected. Staff should understand that this process is a protection for them, in the sense that it documents that they have had training in the identified areas, in case their qualifications are challenged after an alleged incident at camp. The director should also document how staff who are new or miss precamp training eventually received instruction. Again, all of these steps are part of the risk-management plan and a protection package that the camp director develops and preserves in case of a change in directorship, lawsuit, or alleged abuse incident.

In-Service Training

When precamp training concludes and campers arrive, the training of staff does not end. With seasonal staff, training must be continued throughout the season: first, in effort to continually assure a quality experience for the participant, and second, to address issues that arise during camp. Also, many of the staff will return for another season, and the training will bear further dividends. After precamp training and during supervision, supervisors often have the best sense of what topics need to be covered in such training and can help develop the format. Common problems or voids in performance will appear in a number of staff members as the season goes along. These situations can necessitate a meeting or staff-training module designed to fill that void or deal with a specific problem. Since time is precious and staff is under pressure, such training periods should be planned carefully and developed for a succinct and practical presentation.

A meeting devoted solely to a training problem or concept focuses staff attention on the training without the time competition and attention pressures of a regular staff meeting. However, it is often from the regular staff meeting, supervisory observation, or conference that topics for the special training sessions are derived.

In-service training sessions may also be an extension of topics begun during precamp training, where time, readiness, or lack of experience of staff members did not allow more substantive discussion. In fact, many training topics become more meaningful after the staff members have had experience in their program areas or with participants. Because of the experience gained at this point, it is vital that some time in the training module be allowed for discussion and sharing among group members.

The use of outside resource individuals is most effective in these in-service training sessions when the topic requires a certain expertise or authority. For example, if abuse is the topic, a psychologist or social worker with experience in the field can add a certain level of authority to the issue, answering questions from experience. Similarly, a naturalist with knowledge of local flora and fauna can bring expertise to a nature walk or presentation that may not have been possible during precamp training.

It is critical that the topics chosen for in-service training events be timely and of practical use by the staff at that point of the season. Staff will be under considerable pressure from ongoing program and relationships and will exhibit impatience and inattention if they do not find the session pertinent to their current day-to-day experiences.

Also, one of the realities of a camp staff group is that some individuals arrive in the middle of or after staff training. For example, the termination of an employee necessitates a replacement early or midseason. A returning staff member cannot leave university classes until midway through staff training. A weak link is created each time a director assumes that a returning staff member understands all of the assigned responsibilities or that a new employee can "pick up" the needed information along the way. Therefore, it is important to have a plan to make sure that the training topics such a staff member missed are covered and documentation collected before the person assumes assigned duties.

Staff Meetings

In-service training modules are different from administrative staff meetings or all-staff meetings held on a regular basis throughout the season. The purpose of regular administrative staff meetings is the coordination of program events, operational details, personnel, and personal concerns. An opportunity should be given for all staff members to share concerns, to clear up details, or to explain decisions. It is important that matters announced or discussed at all staff meetings be distributed in some fashion to those not present, who may be on duty with campers or in other operations. Some immediate behavioral problems may be resolved at such meetings or identified for future in-service training. Staff may learn by leadership behavior modeled by the director or other administrators. These staff meetings can be considered training only in a limited sense.

Checkpoints

- Have the dates for precamp training been clearly identified to staff at the time of the contract?
- What are the specific outcomes desired to be accomplished during the precamp training period?
- Have staff applications and interview records been reviewed to determine areas in which particular help or instruction will be needed by individuals?
- Which staff members with particular expertise can be used during staff training as group leaders, presenters, or instructors?
- Are any outside resource persons within 50 miles of camp who can be helpful?
- Which training topics could be offered online, and what format would effectively cover those topics?
- Will the director assume the leadership role in staff training, or collaborate with other key staff or delegate the training to others entirely? How are those roles to differ?
- Has the director involved staff in designing a needs assessment to try to uncover the training needs identified by individual staff?
- How will the director evaluate the effectiveness of the camp's training programs?

Related Standards

American Camp Association's Accreditation Standards for Camp Programs and Services: HR.1–20

Additional Professional Practices: Human Resources

Endnotes

1. Catherine T. Hammett. n.d. *A Camp Director Trains His Own Staff*. Martinsville, IN: American Camping Association. p. 7.

2. "Written Employment Policies." 1996. *Trendlines* Vol. VIII, No. 3, January/February, p. 1.

3. Beryl Hesketh and Stephen Bochner. 1994. "Technological Change in a Multicultural Context: Implications for Training and Career Planning" in *Handbook of Industrial and Organizational Psychology* by H.S. Triandis, M.D. Dunette, and L.M. Hough [eds.], Palo Alto, CA: Consulting Psychologists Press.

4. Bob Ditter. 1995. "New Direction in Staff Training and Development." *Camping Magazine*. Vol. 67, No. 3, January/February, p. 38.

5. Becca Cowan Johnson. 1992. *For Their Sake*. Martinsville, IN: American Camping Association. pp. 121–128.

6. William. A. Becker and Tony Shepard. 1989. "Study Suggestions to Improve Camp Supervisory Training." *Camping Magazine*. Vol. 61, No. 1, January, pp. 32–35.

7. John J. Durall. 1997. "Encountering Child Abuse at Camp." *Camping Magazine*. Vol. 70, No. 6, November/December, p. 33.

8. Charles R. Gregg and Catherine Hansen-Stamp. 2009. "Staff Training and Risk Management: Key Risk Information for Front Line Staff." *The CampLine*. Spring, p. 7.

STAFF SUPERVISION AND PERFORMANCE APPRAISAL

Chapter Nine

Coleman Country Day (Merrick, NY)

Supervision is seen to be—first, last, and all the time—a relationship of persons; as such, it calls for deep qualities of heart and mind and spirit, and for acceptance of whatever disciplines and plain hard work are necessary to develop the needed abilities and skills.[1]

—Margaret Williamson

Possibly one of the most overlooked and underestimated procedures in general camp administration is a regular system of supervision and performance appraisal for staff. Under the pressures of the summer season, it is difficult to allot sufficient time for supervisory functions unless a plan is developed prior to camp. A regular program of supervisory conferences provides countless opportunities for stimulation of individual growth, for a deepening of supervisor and staff relationships, and, ultimately, for upgraded job performance.

This supervisory process, if carried out in a relationship of mutual trust and respect, can be a major factor in the retention and effectiveness of staff. As staff become conscious of their own personal growth through the supervisory procedure, the usual result is on-the-job satisfaction and a desire to repeat the experience. Few jobs are available to young people today that provide such a climate of interested and productive supervision.

The director has no more valuable asset for ensuring good job performance than his personal knowledge and relationship with supervisory staff who assess individuals' job performances. This interplay of relationships provides an opportunity for the director to share in the lives of individuals with a people oriented commitment to the camp and its programs.

Functions of a Supervisor

A supervisor has been defined as a person who holds the following responsibilities:
- Overseeing the conduct of others in the achievement of a particular task
- Maintaining quality standards
- Protecting and caring for materials and/or people under his control
- Rendering services to those under his control

The functions of supervisors can be categorized in numerous ways. Writers and trainers generally identify the following functions of supervision:
- Teaching staff their job
  - ✓ Understanding all the tasks required in the job being supervised
  - ✓ Teaching skills in a progressive manner (i.e., what has to be learned first, second)
  - ✓ Assessing whether and how well the skill has been learned

- Delegating responsibility
  - ✓ Assigning staff to program areas, activities, and functions
  - ✓ Delegating tasks (e.g., ordering supplies, planning an event, supervising the wash house)
  - ✓ Determining time off and related coverage for staff responsibilities (e.g., days off, rovers)
- Evaluating performance and accountability within the camp's performance review system
  - ✓ Observing performance
  - ✓ Providing verbal feedback on a regular basis, both praise and constructive criticism
  - ✓ Writing reviews of staff performance
  - ✓ Holding supervisory conferences
- Improving performance
  - ✓ Observing behavior
  - ✓ Analyzing skill performance
  - ✓ Determining what has to be improved and how to improve it
  - ✓ Establishing and maintaining a positive relationship with staff so that they accept instruction and commit to change
  - ✓ Communicating what is being done well or what needs to be changed
- Dealing with problems
  - ✓ Listening and observing
  - ✓ Mediating conflict
  - ✓ Confronting problems rather than letting them fester
  - ✓ Recognizing the difference between a complaint and a real problem

Guidelines in Supervision

Further guidelines concerning relationships may be helpful to a supervisor who has little experience directing others.

- *Trust*: This factor is basic to establishing a meaningful relationship, both for job performance and for personal interaction. Each staff member needs to know that the supervisor can be trusted to deal objectively and unemotionally with problems and discussions that arise. He must also know that the supervisor can deal with matters involving other individuals, seeing several sides of personal problems and concerns. The staff member also must know that job performance and discussions with the supervisor will remain confidential (unless the disclosure must be shared with the camp director, in which case the staff member should be informed of the intent to do so). To maintain this relationship of trust with staff, the supervisor must show staffers that he values and respects them, regardless of job performance. It may be difficult, at times, for the supervisor to maintain this attitude, but it should grow out of an inherent respect for the worth of every individual—a respect which can transcend differences or personality conflicts.

- *Rapport*: The ability of a supervisor to quickly establish communication and a relaxed interaction with staff members who may be unaccustomed to and wary of the supervisory framework is paramount. Along with the belief in individual worth, a genuine liking for all kinds of people and skills in human relations will help create the desired climate.
- *Sharing*: The supervisor should cultivate the habit of sharing with employees, individually and collectively, appreciation of the job being done. Regular commendation of a job well done will also help to prepare the staff member to accept criticism when it is necessary. It is also helpful if the supervisor has a plan to regularly observe the people he supervises "on the job" (while with campers, while teaching, while interacting at meals, etc.). If staff find that this supervision is done in a benevolent spirit, they will gradually become less self-conscious about observation. A supervisor's support and appreciation may not be perceived by others unless it is expressed verbally and reinforced by benevolent treatment.

The details of the staff-supervision process should be shared with the group during staff training. Further, it is helpful to give an idea of general expectations and the criteria to be used in performance appraisals. If written notes from supervisory conferences and observations are to be added to personnel folders, the staff should be told about this procedure.

How to Begin?

As preparation for beginning a staff-supervision program, time can well be spent in reviewing personnel information folders of returning staff and the application and interview documents of new staff. Acquaintance with staff backgrounds is an asset when meeting the individuals, since it helps establish them in memory. Before the opening of the camp season, the supervisor might well seek opportunities to become personally acquainted with local staff who are new and with returning staff whom the supervisor may not know well. With out-of-town staff, beginning a relationship is more difficult and perhaps limited to letters and e-mail, but is still important.

With the opening of camp and the beginning of staff training, personal contact can be broadened through discussion sessions, small group activities, human-relations training, unstructured social occasions, group work projects, and staff overnights or trips. Any personal interplay that strengthens a relationship between supervisor and staff is a major plus in beginning a supervisory relationship.

Legal Negligence and the Supervisory Process

In court cases where a camp is being sued for negligence in failing to protect a camper against accident or abuse, one of the lines of defense is to show that a plan or process for supervision is in practice consistently for all staff. To be adequate, this plan or process for supervision should include the following points:

- Each employee must be given information as to who will be his immediate supervisor, as well as the employee's specific job responsibilities.

- A definitive, written plan for supervision should be in place, which should include observations, formal conferences, informal conferences, written reprimands signed by supervisor, and a performance appraisal system.
- Supervisors should have a clear understanding of their authority and the options available to them when staff behavior does not match expectations.
- A specific plan should be in place for dealing with an alleged abuser.
- A system should be in place for dealing with alleged harassment—camper to camper, staff to camper, or staff to staff.
- Special training must be provided for supervisors and should deal with a uniform performance-appraisal system of monitoring, observing, and recording methods, appropriate and inappropriate staff behavior, and conference formats, recording, and techniques. This training should include written guidelines for supervisors in monitoring performance of staff they supervise, identifying and reinforcing or correcting behavior as appropriate.
- A formal plan should be in place that includes authority for terminating an employee, documented evidence of events leading to firing, and a plan for the final interview.

Techniques for Supervising Others

The following is a range of possible supervisory techniques that help define the supervisory relationship and the behaviors, attitudes, knowledge, or situations supervisors may encounter. Supervisors need to be able to quickly access factors that are motivating behavior and select a course of action.

- *Teaching*: Teaching assumes the person being supervised lacks knowledge or has incomplete knowledge. This lack may be because information has yet to be presented on the topic or because the staff member has forgotten the presentation or is unable to apply the knowledge to a different set of facts. The role of the teacher includes:
  - ✓ Directing
  - ✓ Providing instruction
- *Coaching*: Coaching assumes the person being supervised lacks experience or confidence in performing appropriately or with great skill. The individual may not have connected the intellectual knowledge he has with its application in a given situation. The role of the coach includes:
  - ✓ Reminding about key principles
  - ✓ Encouraging where necessary
  - ✓ Instructing in the fundamentals of the skill where necessary
  - ✓ Indicating confidence that staff will get it right
  - ✓ Helping staff "walk through" the potential experience and rehearsing the skills
- *Modeling*: Modeling assumes the supervisor is being observed and should be constantly demonstrating the skills and attitudes expected of staff members. Staff members will notice if the supervisor expects others to be consistent in enforcing policies with campers, but is not consistent with

himself in enforcing policies with staff. Staff will perceive if the supervisor is not responsive to their problems, but expects them to be responsive to camper problems. Modeling roles include:

✓ Always demonstrating positive attitudes

✓ Always demonstrating compliance with camp rules and philosophy

✓ Always taking problems to the source or to the immediate supervisor, and never gossiping or revealing information on the problem to other staff

✓ Working hard and showing initiative

✓ Acting in the best interests of the camp and the campers, not in the supervisor's own best interest

- *Reinforcing*: Reinforcing assumes a supervisor observes staff frequently enough to find them doing things right. It further assumes that positive feedback is provided when a supervisor observes appropriate behavior, recognizing positive changes the staff member has made, or noting a positive attitude in difficult circumstances. Reinforcing good behavior prepares the staff member to hear constructive criticism. They then know the supervisor is not just looking for fault, but also praises the good. This approach creates an organizational culture where positive behavior thrives.

- The role of the reinforcer includes:

✓ Being a frequent observer of each staff member

✓ Complimenting and praising each staff member frequently

✓ Searching for things staff members are doing well

- *Correcting*: Correcting occurs when a supervisor observes behaviors that have not changed in spite of teaching, coaching, modeling, and reinforcing. Except in cases where safety requires immediate intervention to correct a behavior, supervisors should generally use one of the first four techniques in dealing with staff behavior prior to correcting or disciplining. Correcting should be done in private, and in a manner that focuses on the behavior rather than the person. The one exception to this rule is a situation where a serious health or safety issue is involved and immediate intervention is required. The role of the corrector includes:

✓ Maintaining the self-esteem of the person being corrected

✓ Focusing on the behavior, not the person

✓ Teaching, coaching, reinforcing, and modeling prior to correcting, except when safety demands immediate correction

Christopher Thurber points out that "the biggest obstacle to providing effective feedback is that relationships are at stake. Supervisors naturally worry: 'Will this person react badly? Will he or she get angry or defensive?' Ironically, without feedback, those who need it may not even be aware of a need for improvement. It takes time and effort to create a culture at your camp where clear, bidirectional feedback is frequent and welcome, but the alternative is stagnation and weakness."[2]

Appendix B provides a checklist for risk management in the recruitment, screening, training, and supervision of employees to help administrators in the area of negligence. The American Camp Association maintains a Knowledge Center on its website that provides training resources that may be helpful to the camp director.[3]

The Supervisory Process: Counselors

Since counselors are the majority of staff members, a supervisory plan for counselors and the persons supervising them (whether a unit director, head counselor, or the camp director) will be outlined in this section. However, this program can easily be broadened and adapted to other staff and departments.

In the case of each of the supervisory conferences, written records—either paper copies or electronic documents—need to be kept by the supervisor, along with pertinent reports and appraisals, and filed in the individual's personnel folder. It provides a permanent, on-going performance record while the person is employed by the camp. It also becomes a valuable resource during rehiring decisions and when references are requested by future employers. The overall goal is to help all staff members perform their jobs as expected, feel successful in their job, and receive appreciation for their success. Waiting until midseason or the end of camp to let people know how they are doing will not help job performance improve quickly and may be interpreted implicitly by staff as satisfaction with their job performance on the part of the supervisor. During precamp training, supervisors will want to assess their staff's attitudes and participation to determine if some staff will need additional training in certain areas and to see if they understood the training content.

Post-Staff-Training Interview

It is often effective for the supervisor to schedule 20- or 30-minute conferences with each counselor at the end of staff training and before the arrival of campers. Some specific questions can help the supervisor increase his knowledge of the staff member. Other questions can help get feedback on the training period, and at the same time, assist the staff member in solidifying and expressing his own personal reactions. Questions to be included in the appraisal may be:

- What areas of the job, as you see it now, do you feel confident in handling?
- Are there any areas about which you feel apprehensive?
- Are there still areas where you feel less than competent? (If teaching skills, is there an area where you have difficulty with organizing and teaching material?)
- If age groups have not been assigned, is there a particular age group of campers you would prefer and why?
- How do you feel about your relationship with other staff? (Although the counselor's answer to this question is important, the supervisor's observations may be necessary to complete the picture.)
- With which areas of staff training did you feel most comfortable?
- Were there sessions of training that were of little or no interest to you?

• What are your goals for the summer? (These outcomes should be measurable and attainable, which can be evaluated in an objective manner later through agreed-upon indicators. These goals should include job-related goals as well as personal-growth goals. It might be beneficial to write them down.)

One very positive factor in avoiding a climate which may be favorable to child abuse is to encourage staff to set personal goals. Another is to persuade staff, at this point, to plan ahead to spend some time each day refreshing and recharging themselves, without neglecting responsibilities. This revitalizing time will help them deal with stress and will prevent them from being overly drained.

Observation

A planned program of informal observation provides a supervisor with occasions to observe the counselor in various activities that are a part of his performance—in the living situation, in skills teaching, and while participating in program activities with campers and other staff. These observations, which should be carried out informally and on a regular basis, will provide information about the counselor's ability and potential. A concerted effort should also be made to talk with campers in informal situations, since these contacts may give further indication as to the job the counselor is doing. The frequent presence of the supervisor in daily activities will also provide the means for interchanges that may not otherwise happen. Although these drop-in practices may cause some anxiety in the beginning, staff and campers will usually come to accept them as part of the routine.

Gwynn M. Powell, a University of Georgia associate professor, suggests:

> *The periodic occurrence of brief conversations and observations, as opposed to setting up blocks of time, were viewed as both more helpful and easier to accomplish during busy days. Setting a goal of a certain number of contacts per week allows for mentoring to become an integral part of patterns within camp routines instead of viewing the mentoring time as an interruption.*[4]

The best performance feedback to the counselor is that given immediately after the observation. However, since the feedback should not be given when others are present, the opportunity may not present itself in a timely manner. In any case, notes of each observation should be written as quickly as possible after leaving the observation area. Such notes can be tucked into the counselor's personnel folder or recorded electronically and used at the time of the next supervisory meeting. It is important that these notes include positive feedback as well as criticism, and they should show the date, place, and conditions of the observation (e.g., counselor teaching group canoeing). These notes also provide another link in the protective chain for the counselor and the camp if child abuse or negligence should be alleged. It may be possible to develop a checklist that can be used in observation of all personnel in similar positions.

Bob Ditter notes that being a good observer includes: watching carefully, waiting to draw conclusions, checking assumptions and appearances, and observing personal biases. He also suggests that using an observation guide will help keep the observer on track. The guide could include such things as: eye contact, appropriate touch, one-on-one communications, pitching in, and working well with co-counselors.[5]

Periodic Conferences

Depending upon the length of the camp's sessions, another supervisory conference should be scheduled with each counselor after a primary period of working with campers. The conference should come at a logical program point within the first two weeks. This timeframe gives an opportunity for acknowledging strengths, as well as mistakes to be corrected or habits changed before the lapse of too much time. This conference should deal with a number of topics such as:

- The counselor's comments on each camper in his group, and the relation of each to the group as a whole. The discussion on this topic has a dual purpose. First, the supervisor receives information helpful in dealing with the individual campers. Second, the supervisor has a chance to check on the counselor's ability to relate to and observe campers in order to articulate understanding both of individuals and of the group-living process.

- Any problems or conflicts that arose or currently exist, and whether they have been worked out. This subject probably will arise naturally out of the first topic; if not, it is good to include it as an indicator of how the counselor interacts and makes decisions concerning campers.

- The counselor's conclusions about what things he might handle differently if the time could be redone

- The counselor's evaluation of personal job performance, including frustrations and high points

- The counselor's assessment of the accomplishment of any goals, and establishment of new or modified goals for the next period

- A brief review of the supervisor's observations of the counselor in action. Good points should be given first, followed by any problems or suggestions for a more effective performance. It may be a good idea to introduce this area by asking the counselor to evaluate the weaker and stronger points of his own performance during the period. This approach often opens the topic on a more positive note, and sometimes brings up the very areas the supervisor wishes to discuss.

Drawing a sociogram (Figure 9-1) is sometimes used as a part of this type of conference, particularly if the camp's program is focused on small group living and camper relationships. Such a diagram serves as a visual reminder of questions that should be covered during this and subsequent discussions, as well as compares observations of members of the living group. This type of conference can be repeated at the end of each camp session where a change in camper assignments occurs, or on a regular basis if the camper group remains longer. The topics can be adjusted to deal more specifically with problem areas and with progress since the previous conference.

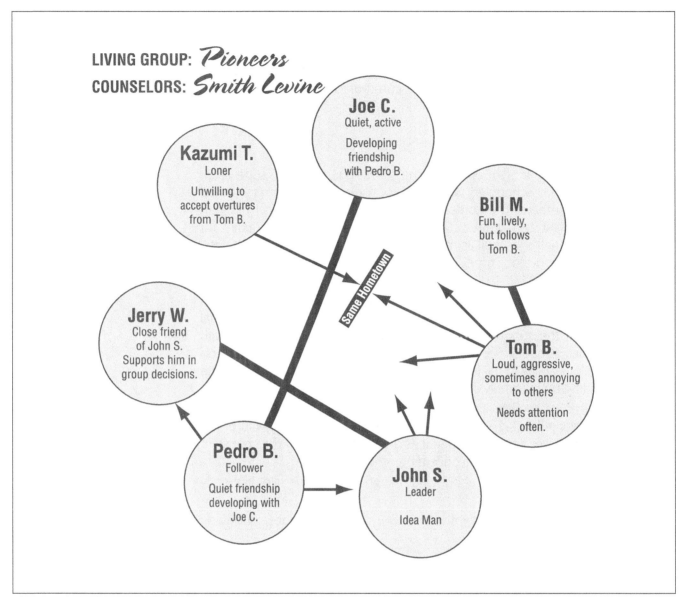

Figure 9-1. Sociogram

End-of-Season Performance Appraisal

The goal of any good supervisor is to enable the staff member to come to the point of effective self-appraisal followed by appropriate responsive behavior. However, certainly near the end of a summer season or a three- to four-month period with a year-round employee, the performance appraisal emerges as a responsibility of the supervisor. Any performance appraisal should relate to the employee's job description and especially the essential functions the employee is expected to perform. Other areas of evaluation may also be tied to performance, which are related to stated job functions.

So far, only the evaluation from the viewpoint of the counselor and the immediate supervisor has been pinpointed. However, this perspective only provides a partial view of the counselor's job performance. In addition, some system should be devised for evaluation of the counselor by supervisory personnel in other departments or areas of camp with whom the counselor has had some contact during the summer. Some other performance appraisers, depending upon the basic staff organization, may be the nurse, the program or unit directors, the assistant director, the business manager, specialty staff, the food-service director, and the waterfront director. It is helpful if these evaluations can be devised in such a manner that they can be added together to get a numerical average in various areas of concern that can be readily communicated to the counselor. See Figure 9-2 for a sample staff performance-appraisal form. Note that the evaluation form is for a camp counselor position, such as the one outlined in the sample job description shown in Figure 6-4.

The counselor should have few surprises in the end-of-season performance appraisal. Any major performance concern or problems will have been dealt with as the occasion arose during the summer. The final conference of the season should begin with an end-of-period appraisal for the last camper session of the summer. This conference also offers other opportunities to the supervisor:

- To share the evaluation of the counselor's performance over the summer along with any comments and evaluations from other staff gained through the evaluations mentioned previously
- To hear the counselor's feelings about camp, the experience, and his own performance
- To hear the counselor's assessment of his accomplishment of job related and personal goals for the summer, related to the outcomes developed in the first conference of the season

---

Performance Appraisal Form

Directions:
- Person doing the rating studies each square in the horizontal row and then circles one number (1 to 10), indicating appropriate level of skill. High numbers indicate a high rating; low numbers indicate less satisfactory performance or areas that need work. Particularly appropriate phrases can be circled, and inappropriate phrases can be crossed through.
- The averages of various persons' ratings are recorded on a central form, and a line is drawn through the form connecting the average rating for each row (see bold vertical line).
- Employee being evaluated is invited to mark a form on himself at the beginning of the conference, with the supervisor pointing out the importance of self-evaluation as a growth tool.
- The employee's evaluation line is marked in a different color on the central form (see dashed vertical line), and the comparison of the two lines is used as a basis of the supervisory conference. Again, emphasis is placed on self-perception in the evaluation process.

Figure 9-2. Sample staff performance-appraisal form

PERFORMANCE APPRAISAL FORM

Confidential Appraisal of _____ by _____

Please circle a number in each row which best approximates your position of staff member or skill area noted in the first column. Mark through words or phrases that do not apply.

Understanding of and Relationship with Campers	• limited understanding of groups/individuals • communication on basic level only • no close relationships with campers **1** **2**	• beginning comprehension of groups/individuals • begins to communicate • occasionally develops close relationships with campers **3** **4**
Manner/Responsiveness	• timid • overbearing • withdrawn • cocky • dominates conversations • curses, vulgarity **1** **2**	• quick tempered • irritating • indifferent • does not volunteer information • evasive • inappropriate language **3** **4**
Motivation	• just wanted a job • not interested **1** **2**	• primarily interested in camp life, not campers • self-centered **3** **4**
Appearance	• untidy • sloppy • often dirty • disheveled **1** **2**	• careless in dress/cleanliness **3** **4**
Attitudes Toward Camp Operation	• avoids participating in certain camp activities • complains about assignments • sees only small part of total operation of camp as important **1** **2**	• participates but avoids active leader-ship in activities • attitude discourages participation of campers • ill at ease before a group – timid, hesitant • lacks confidence to secure group's attention **3** **4**
Teaching of Specific Skill	• disorganized • wordy • unsure of self • limited ability in skill area **1** **2**	• ill at ease • knows basic skills • lacks organization/confidence in teaching **3** **4**

Notable strengths

Notable weaknesses

If you were director, would you employ this person another year? ❏ *Yes*   ❏ *No*

Figure 9-2. Sample staff performance-appraisal form (cont.)

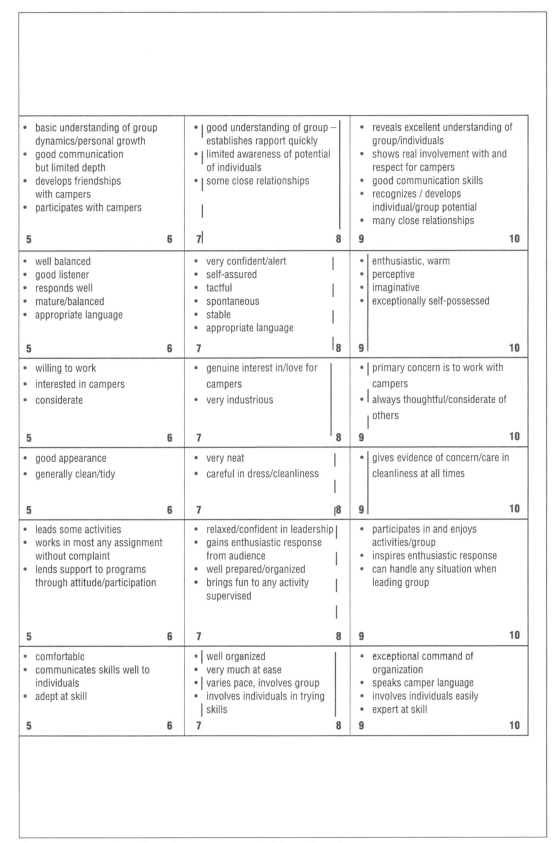

Figure 9-2. Sample staff performance-appraisal form (cont.)

- Through this closing conference, the supervisor should seek to guide the counselor in understanding the importance of self-evaluation as a necessary part of growth and development. It is also an occasion for the supervisor to share his support of the counselor along with an expression of appreciation for a job well done.

The Supervisory Process: Noncounseling Staff

A supervisory process similar to that designed for counselors is applicable to noncounseling positions and administrative staff. The supervisor can follow similar principles and steps:

- Establish initial ground rules, understandings of responsibilities and performance outcomes with the staff member in a conference at the close of the training period.
- Observe the staff member at work, and make notes of these observations.
- Establish a scheduled time for periodic conferences to discuss the staff member's concerns, job performance, personal goals, and accuracy of the job description.
- Hold an end-of-season performance appraisal in which some feedback is given, pointing out improvements over the season and evaluating together the staff member's accomplishment of agreed-upon outcomes. Again, this appraisal of performance should be related to the specific responsibilities and essential functions from the job description and should not be a surprise to the subordinate. This discussion should open the way for any feedback from the staff member and for his self-evaluation of job performance, as well as suggestions about improving the area of his responsibility.

For administrative staff, a plan should also be in place for securing evaluations from counselors and other staff who work with and for them. A summary of these evaluations should be shared at the final performance appraisal at the end of the summer. The form shown in Figure 9-3 gives one example of a form for administrative staff evaluation.

If the camp director does not supervise certain staff directly, he can benefit from the supervisor's notes on each appraisal conference that have been filed in the employee's personnel record. The director can also learn from administrative staff meetings and written records of the overall individual needs and performance of staff members whom he may not be able to observe directly.

The supervisory program for full-time, year-round staff can operate under the same framework as that for summer administrative staff. The timing of supervisory appraisals could parallel that of summer administrative staff and then be adjusted to long appraisal periods for the remainder of the year. A yearly performance appraisal should be scheduled according to the organization's personnel policies (e.g., end of year, end of fiscal year, or anniversary date). On the other hand, if the job description of the full-time staff member does not essentially change during the summer season, evaluation might be more effective on a periodic basis apart from other members of the summer administrative staff.

Evaluation of Administrative Staff by Counselors

❑ Program director
❑ Naturalist
❑ Tripping counselor
❑ Nurse
❑ Waterfront director
❑ Office secretary
❑ Hostess
❑ Arts/crafts counselor
❑ Aquatic director
❑ Camp director
❑ Head cook
❑ Unit director (seniors)
❑ Truck driver
❑ Second cook
❑ Unit director (juniors)

It is helpful to have feedback from counseling staff on the listed personnel. Please check the appropriate square as you complete the form. Positive and negative comments can be helpful.

Comment on:

- Ability in assigned job (listed previously)
- Helpfulness to you in doing a better job as a counselor
- Congeniality
- Efficiency
- Attitude toward individuals (campers/counselors)
- Interest in total camp program
- Any other comments or observations

Figure 9-3. Evaluation of administrative staff by counselors

Stress and Camp Staff

In any program of supervision at camp, the camp director and department supervisors need to be aware of the potential problems of stress. The intensity of living in the camp community provides its own proclivity to stressful situations. It is essential that the director and all supervisors have a technical understanding of stress, its symptoms and effects, and how to help alleviate those effects in themselves and the staff they supervise. Stress management in staff has been previously named as one factor in risk management as well as in staff retention. Attention to the symptoms of stress has been shown to significantly decrease the number of accidents/incidents.

Definition of Stress

Stress is a physical, chemical, or emotional reaction that causes bodily or mental tension. Stress results from factors that tend to alter an existing equilibrium. These stressors are external demands or internal attitudes and thoughts that require us to adapt. Stress triggers a response from a complex part of our brains and bodies called the autonomic nervous system. This system creates the fight-or-flight response, which provides for bodily changes that enable humans to fight or flee from physical dangers to ensure their survival.

Stress may cause people to experience some of the following symptoms:

- Digestion slows so that blood may be directed to the muscles and brain—commonly experienced as "butterflies in the stomach"
- Breathing gets faster to supply more oxygen for the needed muscles—often experienced as a shortness of breath
- The heart speeds up, and blood pressure soars, forcing blood to parts of the body that need it—commonly experienced as a pounding heart
- Perspiration increases to cool the body, allowing it to burn more energy—usually experienced as increased sweating
- Muscles tense in preparation for important action—generally experienced as a stiff back or neck after a stressful day
- Chemicals are released to make the blood clot more rapidly
- Sugars and fats pour into the blood to provide fuel for quick energy—often experienced as a surprising increase in strength and endurance during an emergency

Response to Stress

Camp often triggers stress and its symptoms, but it provides few outlets for relief. Unlike other jobs where an individual can go home and find outlets for relieving stress, the seasonal staff work long hours with little contact from their home or from others who might help them relax. Further, camp staff are often accountable for campers 24 hours a day and do not receive many breaks from this responsibility. When human beings cannot run from anxieties or physically fight their fears, the result is emotional stress. Even if the chemicals produced by emotional stress could be safely burned off, the resulting psychological distress can interfere with productivity, learning, and interpersonal relationships. When stress reactions continue without relief, people become less and less able to handle even minor stress.

Short-Term Stress

In the short term (a period of hours), stress responses often manifest themselves through the following symptoms: a jittery stomach, a lump in the throat, a tight feeling in the chest, a racing pulse and pounding heart, a pain in the neck and shoulders from tension, or a tendency to lose control of emotions.

Long-Term Stress

In the long term (a period of weeks), stress responses become chronic and incessant, and they have much wider implications for the staff member. It is at this point that the supervisor may first become aware of the presence of stress, because the staff member exhibits some of these symptoms:

- Becomes less productive
- Never has enough time
- Becomes withdrawn and depressed
- Has increased smoking or drinking problems
- Experiences an increase in pain associated with chronic diseases (arthritis, headaches)
- May eat more and gain weight, or eat less and lose weight
- Is subject to daydreaming and has difficulty concentrating
- Experiences sleeplessness or sleepiness
- Has feelings of worthlessness, inadequacy, and rejection
- Has difficulty dealing with campers and other staff

Stress Management

To help the stressed staff member cope with the situation, the supervisor needs a basic understanding of the biological systems related to stress factors. The major system, the autonomic nervous system, has two divisions. The first, called the sympathetic nervous system, is the one that triggers the fight-or-flight response to danger and is responsible for the changes in the physical body. It is the second system—the parasympathetic—that influences the body in ways that are almost the exact opposite of those of the sympathetic. This second division is responsible for conservation and replenishment of energy and modification of the sympathetic nervous system response. Some evidence suggests that the parasympathetic nervous system can be activated through relaxation procedures, thus minimizing and negating the physical responses of the sympathetic nervous system.

A supervisor who observes the symptoms of stress can counsel the affected staff member to take practical steps toward managing the stress. Most stress can be divided into three main categories: stress from the situation, stress from the mind, and stress from the body. Within these categories, staff can be educated to use certain immediate solutions or ways of handling stress.

Situational Stress

- Assert yourself; say no, or ask for exactly what you need.
- Remove yourself or escape from the problem.
- Plan specific steps to avoid, reduce, or correct the problem in the future.
- Pace yourself and schedule time to relax.

Mental Stress

- Avoid jumping to conclusions, taking things personally, or attaching much importance to a minor event.
- Mentally yell, "Stop!"
- Replace negative or anxious thoughts with positive thinking or a happy memory.
- Imagine taking charge in a relaxed and confident way.

Physical Stress

- Breathe in deeply, counting slowly to five; exhale completely, count slowly back to one, and relax all muscles.
- Imagine the body is loose and relaxed from head to toe.
- Avoid caffeine, nicotine, or any stress-causing chemicals; substitute a quick stretch or a brief walk.
- Find ways to exercise regularly and blow off steam.

It should be noted that these solutions are of a temporary, stop-gap, or preventative nature. They may be effective in some cases of short-term stress and may help to alleviate some problems. However, in some individual cases, medical or psychiatric assistance may be necessary if symptoms seem severe and if the person is unable to function normally under daily demands.

Burnout

Some degree of stress is healthy and helps the individual be productive and competitive in day-to-day situations. However, if stress is unrelieved or moves to long-term stress, burnout can result. Burnout is a condition of emotional and physical collapse brought on by the unchecked escalation of pressure or stress. Signals can alert the supervisor to the potential burnout of a staff member. Particularly in the resident camp situation, where staff members are often with campers 24 hours a day, day after day, even with time off, a counselor can find himself burnt out by the end of the fifth or sixth week of camp. Time off may actually cause additional stress when it is accompanied by pressure to be with friends, do laundry, drive distances, and the like.

People who are overly enthusiastic are prone to burnout. They become so involved in the job and situation that they feel everything is wonderful and do not hesitate to share that with one and all. Antagonism toward others sometimes arises at this point, and the individual often moves away from peers who are less enthusiastic or tire of the individual's enthusiasm. People who frequent the health center with colds, neck pain, back pain, rashes, and other similar conditions are often actually exhibiting the early signs of burnout.

With burnout, the individual begins to sense that his commitment level is lessening or something is wrong with the assignment. The person may feel that he needs something more challenging, indicating that this person is not enjoying the present assignment as much as in the past. Similarly, a request may be made for more time off to provide a new viewpoint. Days off may be spent in frenzied activity to relieve this feeling or tension. However, the relief of time off does not seem to last; within a day or two, the old symptoms often return.

At this point, the individual begins to find it difficult to function as efficiently as in the past, and often tries to cover up inefficiencies or mistakes by making excuses or lying. Relationships seem to deteriorate, and it is difficult to find peers who are willing to help or support the individual. The person may appear nervous, forgetful, or distracted. From this point, burnout can progress to desperate efforts to combat the feeling of defeat, and it can resemble depression. Day-to-day tasks become more difficult, and the person uses lies or deception to cover up the problem.

A well-developed supervisory process lends itself to helping the potential burnout candidate recognize the problem and the symptoms and develop a program to utilize his free time and days off for relaxation rather than for frenzied activities. The supervisor and other staff may try to provide support and nurturing concern for the individual, but at the same time, the supervisor should help the individual recognize the importance of opening himself to those people who are supportive.

Careful attention to providing the adequate and appropriate time off and days off for all staff is important to prevent burnout and relieve stress in all staff. Though some types of personalities are more prone to burnout than others, the pressure of the camp living situation can bring on burnout in people who otherwise would not be as susceptible. Therefore, as the season progresses and staff tend to get more tired, providing relaxing events for groups of staff and careful coaching for individuals can help prevent burnout.

The Supervisor and Termination

If a supervisor utilizes all the techniques of supervision and does everything possible to encourage a staff member to function as expected, but the employee still does not have the skill, does not cooperate, or for some other reason cannot fulfill the position's responsibilities, it may be time to dismiss the employee. Today's increased awareness of many employment issues such as sexual harassment means that employers must terminate employees as a result of such unacceptable behavior. Failure to do so puts the supervisor, as well as the camp, at risk. Training and supervision, however, are designed to minimize the possibility of having to dismiss staff because of inappropriate behavior or inadequate job performance. A copy of the staff manual (containing termination policies) in the hand of each staff member assures that the "no one told me" excuse cannot be used. Most supervisors do not have the authority to fire a staff member without discussing it with the director.

If a supervisor is having difficulty with an employee, the first action is to confront the employee regarding the problem and take steps to correct the behavior. Rob Crawford recommends a three-step process:

1. Sit down with the employee and talk it over—and, what is more important, listen to the employee. Most employees want to do the right thing; it may be that they need more direction or training, which the supervisor needs to provide. Following the conversation should be a follow-up memo to the individual, stating the problem and the appropriate action decided upon. If step 1 has not resolved the problem, proceed to step 2.

2. The supervisor and the staff member, together, agree upon a more formal process, which is agreeable to both. The agreement must stipulate the objective, measurable behavior that is required. A timeline is set, and the consequences clearly set out. The consequence might not be termination; other disciplinary measures might be chosen. Everything should be clearly defined, with a reasonable penalty for failure to comply.

3. Follow through with what was agreed upon in step 2.

If all else fails and termination is the only answer, do it quickly. Once the supervisor realizes that it is beyond the point of no return, give the employee a final check with a fair severance pay and request that he leave the property as soon as possible. To protect against the potential charge of discrimination, the supervisor needs to see to it that all employment policies treat everyone equally. It is also essential that the supervisor refuse to discuss the circumstances of firing with other staff.[6]

On the other hand, it is wise for the director to communicate the departure of a staff member from camp, while, of course, keeping the reasons confidential. Further, information as to how the person's responsibilities will be reassigned should be communicated. For example: "We wanted to let you know that [staff member's name] has been asked to leave camp. All camper activities and staff responsibilities will be reassigned .... We believe that these actions were necessary and in the best interest of the camp's mission and all concerned."

Oddly enough firing a staff member can have a positive side. It will confirm to other staff members, who may have witnessed the continuing problem, that the ongoing, disruptive behavior brought its own result. In addition, upon reflection, the termination may actually prove to be a new beginning and a more positive move for the employee.

Checkpoints

- Outline who supervises whom.
- What is the supervisory plan (including conferences, observation, and group meetings) for staff the director directly supervises?
- How does that plan relate to the overall plan of supervision?
- Outline performance appraisal tools to be used.

Related Standards

American Camp Association's Accreditation Standards for Programs and Services: HR.7, HR.8, HR.19, HR.20; PD.12, PD.16, PD.21

Endnotes

1. Margaret Williamson. 1950. *Supervision: Principles and Methods*. New York: Women's ress. p. 4.
2. Christopher Thurber. 2010. "They've Done Their Jobs…Now What Will You Tell Them?" *Camping Magazine*. Vol. 83. No. 5, p. 47.
3. www.acacamps.org/knowledge.
4. Gwynn M. Powell. 2002. "Leadership Directions: Where Are We Going This Summer?" *Camping Magazine*. Vol. 75, No. 3, pp. 58–59.
5. Bob Ditter. 1996. "Skills for Staff Supervisors." *Camping Magazine*. Vol. 68, No. 5, May/June, pp. 15–16.
6. Rob Crawford. 1995. "The Firing Line." *Journal of Christian Camping*. Vol. 27, No. 3, May/June, pp. 16–19. Reprinted by permission from CCI/USA.

SELECTION, DEVELOPMENT, AND MAINTENANCE OF THE SITE

Chapter Ten

Camp Pemigewassett (Wentworth, NH)

To guide the orderly development of any camp site, a plan is needed. This will govern the total development that may take place over a period of years. ... While it may seem a lot easier and much more fun to skip planning more or less completely, such a course ... can only lead to headaches, trouble, and possibly disaster. Impatience to get the job done and over with and unwillingness to spend money for professional planning services are poor excuses for not using hard won ... funds to produce the best possible result.[1]

—Julian Harris Salomon

Physical Facility as an Asset

The physical setting of the camp is an important element in the planning of program, and therefore, in meeting the camp's goals and desired outcomes. If used to its greatest potential, the setting can make the best experience even better. On the other hand, the neglect of the physical property of a camp can make even the best program a disappointing one for participants and staff.

Whether a camper, a parent, or new staff member, the first impression a person has of a camp is its appearance. A camp director should go to camp one day and try to see it as a first-time visitor would. What strikes the director: cleanliness and loving care, or neglect and disarray? Clear signage or confusion?

The most valuable physical asset a camp owns is its camp site and the buildings on it. With less and less suitable land available for camping, and with land values continuing to escalate, the camp director has a tremendous responsibility to protect that asset. Part of the camp director's responsibility is to help safeguard and preserve a physical site and property for future generations of campers, as a camp, conference center, and/or outdoor education facility. Today, camps face many pressures—from outside developers and urban sprawl, and from within financially struggling parent organizations—to use camp properties for other purposes or to gain capital from their sale. The camp director becomes the guardian of this asset, not only from the viewpoint of discouraging the sale of the property, but also for making sure the property is accomplishing its purpose so well that discussion of its sale can be effectively fended off.

Selection of a Site

Though most camp directors inherit a physical site, other camp directors rent facilities and therefore have the opportunity from time to time to select a site. The most fortunate of all camp directors are those who get to select a site and build a facility from the ground up. However, this book is not designed to provide all the steps necessary in that process.

As a camp director reviews a variety of camp facilities in the process of selecting a site, especially in regard to rental, the following guidelines may be helpful:

- Check to see if the appropriate local and state permits and licenses are available for review. Have there been appropriate water tests? When were they taken? Is the sanitation system approved and in working order? Has an inspection been made by the fire authorities? States and localities vary in their permitting systems and regulations, and the absence of certain permitting processes or regulations means that the director must be more knowledgeable and more careful regarding inspections and questions during the selection process.

- Review the camp site for health and safety factors. Are apparent natural hazards present? Are buildings well maintained, or does their condition signal hazards? Are those hazards easily corrected, or does the condition of a given building require major repair or replacement? What is the condition of the swimming facility in terms of water quality, location, ease of control, and safety? Is the kitchen clean and rodent-free? What is the condition of major equipment such as walk-ins, refrigerators, ranges, and dishwashers?

- Has the camp met the Site and Food Service standards of the American Camp Association?

- Look at the layout of the property, location of buildings, the natural environment of the camp, and program facilities. Do they complement the camp program's philosophy and goals? How would the camp's program have to be adapted in this setting?

- Check the location. Is it convenient enough for transportation to and from the areas from which the camp draws campers or from major transportation terminals?

- Check for utility availability. Are sewer and electrical lines connected to the site? Will phone, Internet, and television services be available at the site? Would an assistance program enable access to such services through grants or other offers?

- Determine the distance to the closest medical, fire, and other emergency services.

- Survey the camp's closest neighbors. Do the homes or activities surrounding the camp create potential problems currently? What is the zoning of surrounding properties? What potential development could occur that might affect the camp in the future? Is a major highway or thoroughfare planned?

- Look for security problems. Are any obvious problems present that might endanger campers or staff? How many access points into camp are available? How easy is it to control those access points?

When a site is rented for seasonal use, it should not be assumed that the owner is routinely taking care of maintenance upkeep and problems. At the time the lease agreement is signed, a careful inspection of facilities and a list of expected repairs and maintenance should be made and incorporated into the lease agreement. An advance understanding between the director and renter about meeting state and local regulations, as well as any standards set by the director's organization, is vital. A clear understanding about cleaning and other advance preparations should save some frustration later. Be prepared upon leaving to fulfill the camp's obligations to the owner as stated in the agreement.

Before signing a lease agreement, the director should study it carefully to understand the responsibilities of both parties. It is advisable to have it checked by an attorney. Similarly, closer to the time of use of the property, an informal inspection should be made and reminders given to the owner about items not yet completed.

Development of an Owned Site

Most camp properties are in perpetual change, and every camp director is faced with decisions about these changes at some time: building new structures, remodeling and repairing older structures, or constructing roads or sewer lines, and the like. Such concerns may not be the primary interest or strength of the camp director, and it may seem to be an interruption of the more important aspects of programming and service to others. However, the camp director must develop a plan to effectively deal with those changes, both in the acquisition of funding as well as designating staff to supervise and/or accomplish the changes.

Long-Term Planning

The wise camp director understands that form follows function and will work to help develop a facility that serves and enhances the program functions of the camp. If the camp does not have a master site plan, resulting from a long-term look at the camp's philosophy, market, program, finances, and facilities, then this should become the first priority of the director, owner, or volunteer board or committee. To make extensive changes in the property without an overall plan could be both costly and frustrating.

A master site plan requires a commitment to study the overall camp situation and its potential. A site plan should focus anywhere from 5 to 20 years in the future and could include five-year installments for incremental change. In most cases, an outside consultant will be most valuable from the beginning of the process. Whether that person is paid or a volunteer, it is critical that the consultant should be objective, have an understanding of organized camping with some depth of knowledge of camps beyond this particular camp, and have basic planning skills. Eventually, the need for the expertise of an engineer, architect, and perhaps a landscape architect will likely arise. Professional camp-site planning firms, as well as individual consultants, offer services in this field.

A comprehensive site plan will encompass a number of procedures:
- A review and evaluation of the camp's purpose and philosophy
- An analysis of the clientele now served and a review of what potential markets the camp may desire to serve in the future (i.e., projected demographic changes in the surrounding areas)
- Statements by the director, owner, and, in nonprofit camps, the committee or board about the purpose, new or existing target markets, overall program of the camp, and desired uses year-round
- A careful cost analysis of existing services and programs, as well as a look at potential funding sources

- An inventory of present facilities and property
- A preventative maintenance plan
- An inventory of present uses of each facility and each portion of the property year-round
- Evaluation of the accessibility of the buildings and program facilities for staff or campers with disabilities, and the difficulty with which modifications/adaptations can be made
- Development of a schematic site plan that would best use the existing buildings and the natural resources of the property, showing where new buildings or program areas might be constructed
- Development of a timeline and plan to accomplish whatever site plan is agreed upon after input and discussion among the planner, the director, the owner, and any volunteer structure

Often the first thought after securing proposals for a master site plan is that the cost of such a plan could easily offset some of the direct expenses of the actual development. Many camp directors or boards may be tempted to shortcut the process and simply do it in-house. Though this approach may save money initially, most often it will cost a great deal more in the long term due to the lack of objectivity or expertise. Dan Smith points out:

> *While there are basic principles of design, arriving at a well designed solution is not a simple cookbook process. Even though computers have placed the means to draw floor plans within the reach of almost everyone with a keyboard, there is more to good design than a wide selection of fonts and a big assortment of furniture symbols. Good design includes both a knowledge of design principles and an understanding of the concepts behind these principles. Also needed is an 'eye for design.' It is this knowledge, understanding, and 'eye' that consultants in the field bring to the camp.*[2]

Short-Term Planning

Though development of a master site plan is ideal, not every director will be able to wait on such a plan before instituting development. However, some steps will assist in making immediate decisions about such development. They will also be invaluable when retaining a planner and starting a master site plan.

First, make sure that accurate maps of the property, topographical as well as schematic, are available. If no topographical map is on file and the camp budget precludes having one made, purchase the U.S. Geological Survey map for the area. An aerial map will also prove valuable. A survey map of the property, which was secured at the time of purchase of the property, should be available; however, that is not always the case. A survey map should indicate property lines, highways and/or roads, and rights-of-way or easements. Major buildings and utility lines should have been added to this map as they were built. If any questionable property lines have not been surveyed, addressing this situation should be the first order of business.

Second, make sure all utility and sanitation lines are correctly drawn on a property map so that water lines, phone lines, cable lines, electrical lines, and gas lines (with cutoff points and valves) are clearly identified. Blueprints of buildings should also be gathered in one location.

Third, secure as much information about the land, soil, vegetation, wildlife, and water resources as possible. State or county foresters, fish and wildlife personnel, university professors, and conservationists will often be willing to walk the property with the director and provide suggestions on reforestation, improving wildlife habitat, protecting and improving the lakes and streams, and other conservation measures that can be undertaken. All of this information will provide clues to areas that should not be developed with buildings or program activity areas, and to other areas where development will have less of an impact.

Fourth, if the camp does not have copies of the state, county, and local regulations and building codes that specifically apply to camps, they should be secured at this time. Obviously, these issues become the first priority in the development of the site, should the camp not already comply. New development may be required to meet higher standards to come into compliance. Also, state, county, and local health and sanitation officials often can provide guidance to developmental concerns in their areas as well as to the adequacy of the camp's waste disposal system, water system, and related sanitation concerns.

The director should give careful attention to the implications the Americans with Disabilities Act of 1990 (ADA) has for providing accessible facilities:

> Camps must consider needs of persons with physical disabilities in relation to the site, facilities, and program. A camp is not relieved of its legal responsibility to make "reasonable accommodations" simply because it is not currently serving any persons with disabilities. As public accommodations, all camps must adhere to applicable laws. For the purpose of the ADA, camps must also consider hearing and visual impairments, emotional disturbance, developmental delays, and so forth.
>
> For specific guidance, refer to the "Americans with Disabilities Act Accessibility Guidelines for Buildings and Facilities" (ADAAG), which is available through the U.S. Access Board. ADAAG standards refer mainly to buildings, toilets, bathing facilities, and parking .... .
>
> Full compliance with ADAAG is required only for new construction and alterations. Existing facilities can be made more accessible through some "readily achievable" changes in which barriers are removed.
>
> States will vary on accessibility regulations. Camps must comply with the most stringent requirements (that which provides the greatest access for individuals with disabilities) of the local, state, and federal codes that apply.[3]

Fifth, uncover the inventories of the physical facilities and major equipment. If an updated inventory is not available, then one should be made, noting the years of construction of buildings and acquisition dates and identification numbers for all equipment. When a new facility is constructed, it is important to retain as-built drawings and catalogue cuts from the contractor. These documents will help current maintenance staff to know what materials and equipment were used in construction and where things are located. Maintenance personnel can then know how to access important areas in buildings where problems may occur and where to locate replacement parts. Further, the contractor who built the facility needs to include an operations manual, which will assist maintenance staff in operating and maintaining facilities and equipment.

Once this information is gathered, more intelligent planning may begin. Take a walk through the camp's property and examine each building and program area. Note where improvements are needed, such as areas with erosion problems or natural hazards, areas where energy efficiency can be improved, buildings needing modifications to comply with the ADA, as well as where additional development may complement program and appearance or provide new opportunities to serve new groups. Divide this list into repairs or corrections that can be done quickly and easily or need to be made immediately to alleviate risks, and those which may require more funding or assistance than is immediately available.

It is the list of repairs that can be made immediately that will start a development plan. These items should be prioritized, with those that affect health or safety receiving earlier priority than those that are cosmetic or programmatic in nature. Each development project should be evaluated against the information secured in earlier surveys to determine its effect on the natural environment, its fit in the overall aesthetics of the camp, its seasonal use, and as far as possible, carefree maintenance. With this background, detailed plans should be developed, involving a structural architect, landscape architect, or engineer where necessary. Only then can budget development and a timeline for completion begin. This process becomes the camp's short-range plan until such time as an overall master site plan can be developed.

Maintenance

A Maintenance Plan

The first list of immediate repairs and corrections will fall under maintenance as opposed to development, and should be resolved as part of an ongoing maintenance plan. This overall plan is one that should be developed in collaboration with the year-round caretaker or ranger who normally supervises camp maintenance. It should include:

- A routine inspection of all facilities after their use by a group, to assess any damages and identify cleaning needs, as well as areas where energy use can be reduced or less environmental impact made
- A regular schedule of painting or application of protective finishes to exteriors and interiors of buildings

- A schedule of draining, unhooking, and connecting water lines if the camp is located in the freeze zone and lines are not winterized
- A plan for checking and correcting erosion throughout the camp grounds that includes a plan for alternating activity areas or traffic patterns to restore a setting to a healthy state
- A routine inspection schedule of all water and sewage systems, including the swimming pool and its maintenance, and a regular testing schedule of drinking water, the swimming pool, and any natural bodies of water used for swimming
- A routine schedule for cleaning, lubricating, and checking each piece of machinery and equipment with moving parts, including tests of smoke detection equipment, sprinkler systems, carbon monoxide detectors, and replacement of filters, where appropriate
- A schedule for routine inspection, replacement, and repair of screens, windows, railings, steps, docks, and roofs
- Inspection of storage areas, especially those where flammable materials, fuel, gas and liquid flammables, explosives, livestock medications, and other hazardous materials are to be stored
- An annual inspection of all electrical service, heating systems, fireplaces, chimneys, and cooking areas
- When these various routines have been established for cleaning, repairs, and testing, a written record giving scheduled and completion dates, person responsible, and specifics of what is done, is wise. The keeping of a maintenance logbook will greatly assist other staff and preserve a record of all work done and help to ensure accountability. Preventative maintenance will lengthen the life of buildings and equipment and make the facilities more attractive to guests. Samples of two forms that may be adapted for use in routine inspections are shown in Figures 10-1 and 10-2.

A daily schedule can then be prepared of the prioritized tasks with specific assignments made to staff who may be assisting. Emergency repairs will come up on a day-to-day basis, sometimes pushing scheduled projects to the next day.

As part of the maintenance plan, a strategy should be developed for the cleaning and upkeep of high-traffic areas in camp: bathrooms, the dining hall, meeting areas, pathways, and such. In most camps, the day-to-day cleaning of living areas—such as cabins or dorm rooms—is left to the camper groups that occupy the areas through camper assignments or group projects. However, in rental situations with certain types of adult groups, cleaning of rooms may also need to be assigned to staff. Many camps depend on campers to clean the bathrooms, but supplemental cleaning and checks by staff will help. Campers and staff should use rubber gloves and follow procedures for handling bloodborne pathogens when cleaning the bathrooms.

Most camps have a large number of older buildings that require constant maintenance and upgrading to extend their lifespan. Not enough can be said about the importance of regular annual maintenance of each and every building in camp. Camps in a budget squeeze often look first to see which repairs or

General Maintenance Inspection Checklist

Camp Name: _____ Date: _____

Check as okay, or indicate assigned job card number.

Utilities	Food Handling	Swimming Pool	Communication equipment
Water System	Arrangement	Fence	Office furniture
Well casing	Stoves	Walks	
Well cover	Refrigeration	Pool walls	Inspected by:
Spring protection	Freezer	Pool floor	Date:
Intake screen	Mixer	Gutters	
Pump(s)	Ovens	Drainage	**Program Areas**
Pump motor(s)	Dishwasher	Dressing rooms	*Waterfront*
Chlorinator	Sterilization	Showers	Piers
Filter	Sinks	Toilets	Floats
Control system	Tables/counters	Filters	Boat dock
Pipe lines	Dishes	Chlorine equipment	Guard tower
Storage tank	Dish storage	Cleaning equipment	Beach
Valves	Utensils		Control fence
Winter drains	Storage space	Inspected by:	Check board
	Ventilation	Date:	Boats
	Lighting		Oars
Sanitation	Garbage	**Land Management**	Canoes
Sewer lines		*Lakes/Ponds*	Paddles
Septic tanks		Silt control	Sailboats
Seepage pits	Inspected by:	Aquatic weeds	Lifesaving equipment
Disposal field	Date:	Dam	PFDs
Garbage disposal		Spillway	
Grease trap	**Maintenance**	Control gate	*Tripping/OLS Equipment*
	Trucks		Rope
Electrical	Tractor	*Conservation*	Axes
Power lines	Tractor equipment	Erosion control	Saws
Line clearance	Trailers	Wildlife management	Compasses
Telephone	Power tools	Stream management	Cooking equipment
Telephone lines	Hand tools	Forest management	Shovels
Line supports	Spare parts	Landscaping	Tents
	Standby equipment	Foot trails	Packs
Gas/Oil	Fire equipment	Soil conservation	
Gas lines	Fire extinguishers	Obnoxious plants	*Other Program Areas*
Storage tanks	Camp signs	Conservation equipment	Archery range
Regulating equipment	Flammable/hazardous		Archery equipment
	material	*Public Areas*	Rifle range
Inspected by:	MSD sheets	Picnic area	Rifles/guns
Date:	Basic records	Boundary fence	Fishing gear
	Utility maps	Lawns	Ropes course
Roads/Parking	Mechanical equipment		Ropes course
Surface	records		equipment
Ditches	Vehicle records	Inspected by:	
Drainage	Smoke detectors	Date:	
Bridges	CO2 detectors		Inspected by:
Culverts	Sprinkler system	**Office**	Date:
Service roads		Computers	
Gates	Inspected by:	Printer	
Barriers	Date:	Copy machines	
		Phone system	
Inspected by:		Answering machine	
Date:		Fax machine	

Figure 10-1. General maintenance inspection checklist

Building Maintenance Inspection Checklist
Camp name _____ Date _____
Person making inspections_____
Check as okay, or indicate assigned job card number.

NAME OF BUILDING OR STRUCTURE ⇨																				
Foundation																				
Sills																				
Floors																				
Outside walls																				
Inside walls																				
Doors																				
Windows																				
Screens																				
Roof																				
Steps/rails																				
Chimney																				
Fireplace																				
Wiring																				
Plumbing																				
Fire protection																				
Building																				
Gutters																				
Drainage around bldg.																				
Housekeeping																				

Figure 10-2. Building maintenance inspection checklist

improvements can be postponed. However, to postpone maintenance—whether it is painting, replacing screens or water pipes, or roof repair—is "penny-wise and pound-foolish." Delay only increases the wear and tear and the eventual cost, as well as often leaving the camp open for potential accidents or injuries.

In the day-to-day maintenance of a facility with a large number of staff and campers, it is important to have a system for reporting needed repairs. Oral transmission of such requests through the camp director or directly to the maintenance supervisor is unfair since it relies on the memory of a busy person. A form should be available so any staff member can report an item needing repair or attention by placing the form in a given location. See Figure 10-3 for an example of such a form. Providing a tear-off or duplicate copy enables the director or supervisor to keep a copy while forwarding a copy to the person charged with the repair. That person returns the duplicate copy indicating the date of completion and circumstances of the repair. It is wise to maintain a file

---

Request for Maintenance

Director (copy)

Date _____

Check one: ❑ Building repair ❑ Equipment repair ❑ Grounds repair
What building or piece of equipment?
Nature of problem _____

_____
_____

Signed _____

— — — — — — — — — — — — — — — — — —

For Maintenance Department Use Only
Action taken _____
Date completed_____ By whom _____

Figure 10-3. Request for maintenance

of such forms for risk-management purposes. This system may be simplified by an e-mail and/or maintenance software program, which handles the reporting and progress of maintenance tasks. Using this type of program can help the director track and report on what maintenance projects are getting done, where they are located, and how long tasks are taking. All of this information could then be used in the planning process.

Essential to any extensive maintenance program is a building that houses tools, equipment, and vehicles, and provides dry, heated or cooled workshop space with sufficient electric power to conduct repairs and build replacement items as needed. Adequate storage space is needed for supplies and extra beds, mattresses, and other equipment. Scott King points out:

> At many facilities, one of the first things a guest sees is the maintenance building and the assorted objects and vehicles around it. Screen this area and other undesirable elements from the guest's view. A pleasing entry to your facility sets the tone for what guests expect when they arrive.[4]

Care should be taken to make the screen blend into the natural environment without detracting from the natural aesthetics of the camp.

Where the camp director has a supervisor or a volunteer committee off site, it is vital to share information concerning facility needs and problems with the proper party on a regular basis. The maintenance software program could enable the director to send monthly maintenance reports to the appropriate party. In this situation, it becomes a shared responsibility because the camp director may not be in a position to free the funds needed to undertake certain projects or to make a final decision about location and construction. When supervisors and committees are kept well-informed and involved, they will be more likely to help in finding unbudgeted funds to solve problems or expand facilities.

Personnel

Careful selection of property management personnel is as important to a camp as the selection of camp counselors. To provide year-round maintenance and control, it is essential that responsibility be assigned to one individual. That person is most likely the ranger or caretaker who lives on the property and becomes the property or site manager by default. It is important that such a designation carry with it the appropriate job description, level of responsibility, and compensation plan. However, not just any person will possess the skills to do the job. On the other hand, some onsite managers get so accustomed to being in control for nine months that they take on a feeling of ownership, and seasonal directors and guests feel as though they are intruding on private land.

As a maintenance plan is developed and scheduled, it should help identify the pressure points where additional part-time or full-time maintenance assistance is needed or where certain contract services will alleviate that necessity. It will also show downtime when maintenance personnel can take time off. Much will depend upon the skills the caretaker or ranger brings to the job, and some skills may need to be supplemented by additional help, training, or contractors.

The director should give some thought to the potential involvement of volunteers in repairs. A work weekend at a resident camp site or a work day on a day camp site can accomplish quite a bit at very little cost if adequate energy and time has gone into the planning. One of the most important elements is recruitment of skilled parents, organizations, members, staffers, and volunteers, as well as campers and less skilled volunteers for general labor.

Thought should be given to who supervises the volunteers. Some property managers may have the skills to work with and supervise volunteers, where others may feel inadequate or uncomfortable in such a role. If the latter is the case, the camp director or another staff or committee member may need to team with the property manager to ease relationships, while the property manager supervises the projects and ensures that projects are completed properly.

Careful organization of the projects—including assignments of teams, proper tools and materials, and clear, written instructions—are essential to the success of such volunteer experiences. Some projects are too lengthy or involved to be accomplished in a weekend, and others require licensed personnel or have potential risk attached and should not be attempted during a volunteer weekend. The food service at such an event may be a volunteer effort where everyone brings a food item and the camp furnishes basic food and supplies, or the camp might provide total food service.

It is always a temptation to leave much of the cleaning and minor repairs for the week when staff arrive for precamp training. Except where certain work projects are used for a one- to three-hour period to build staff teamwork and ownership of the site, it is unwise to use this valuable training period for such routine cleaning and maintenance.

Written Records

Reference has been made to the importance of written plans, records, and reports. The importance of written records will be further commented on in Chapter 11. However, aside from alleviating liability concerns, if the property is truly the camp's most valuable asset, then written records to ensure its health and longevity are not too burdensome. These records should include:

- A surveyor's map of the property
- A topographical map of the property
- An aerial map of the property
- A schematic map of the property, showing facilities and program areas
- A map of the property, showing all utility lines, cutoffs, disconnects, and valves
- The property deed and any related easements or rights-of-way
- The blueprints or construction drawings of buildings
    - ✓ As-built drawings, catalogue cuts, and an operations manual from the contractor who built the facility
- A record of each structure, its construction date, and subsequent repairs
- A master site plan
- Any written reports of land or resource conservation management
- Inventory of all mechanical equipment, including dates acquired, serial numbers, and repairs made
- All warranty information on equipment, along with instructional manuals and manufacturers' catalogs
- The ongoing maintenance schedule, with written checklist showing dates and work completed
- Inventories of supplies and minor equipment

A clear designation of which staff member is responsible for securing, storing, and maintaining these records should be made in job descriptions. A specific location should be identified where these records are maintained if the process is not computerized.

Winterization

Many camps have traditionally been summer-only operations, and their buildings have often been built without protection of water lines from freezing temperatures and without insulation and heat. Camps have steadily moved to operating longer than the summer months. New camp buildings are almost universally being winterized for use in non-summer months.

The modification of summer-only buildings into winterized facilities is often an expensive and unsatisfactory proposition. An analysis of the types of use that are desired and the nature of possible user groups should be made before any steps are taken toward winterization. A careful assessment should be made to see if the need for such facilities is being met in the area by other camps or conference/retreat centers, or if a real interest is documented for a new program. A market analysis, as described in Chapter 15, is a logical exercise at this point. After this analysis, a camp is better able to judge the type of facilities that will attract these groups as customers, and to determine whether it is feasible to modify existing buildings or whether the volume of business or service will justify the construction of new winterized facilities.

A camp should carefully consider the distance from the nearest metropolitan area, which is most often the source of extensive nonsummer use, as well as existing competition from other camps or conference/retreat centers in the area. Does a demand exist for weekday as well as weekend use? It is without question that year-round operations can spread the cost of maintenance and staff over a larger number of users, allowing better cash flow, broader accomplishment of purpose and goals, and certain savings. However, without the appropriate market or facilities, the opposite may occur. Certain costs will increase with winter use. For example, buildings will need to be kept at a minimum temperature even when not in use, and additional cleaning and maintenance will be necessary, so energy and personnel costs will rise. The facilities will have increased wear and tear as well. Careful study should precede a move toward a four-season facility to make sure that increased usage will more than cover the increased expenses.

Another critical factor in the decision to winterize or expand a summer program to other seasons of the year relates to the camp's overall purpose and philosophy. What is the overall mission, and how will moving to year-round operation affect that mission? Will changes in the character or design of buildings have any effect on the summer program? Will expansion of the program beyond the summer create different demands for the time and skills of staff? Will continuous use of existing buildings or grounds over a year have any detrimental effects for their use during the summer?

Checkpoints

- Does the camp have the appropriate maps of the property: topographical, survey, schematic?
- Does the camp have a map showing all current buildings with utility lines, cutoffs, disconnects, and valves?
- Does the camp have an inventory of all equipment?
- Does the camp have a maintenance schedule for all mechanical equipment on the grounds? For all buildings (painting, caulking, repairs)?
- Does the camp have a master site plan? If not, are individuals working toward securing such?
- Has an inspection occurred of all buildings and program areas, listing needed repairs and corrections? Have repairs and corrections been prioritized, and has a plan been outlined for their correction?
- Have present buildings and program areas been evaluated to determine what modifications are needed to bring them into compliance with the Americans with Disabilities Act of 1990?

Related Standards

American Camp Association's Accreditation Standards for Camp Programs and Services: SF.1 through SF.13
Additional Professional Practices: Site and Food Service

Endnotes

1. Julian Harris Salomon. 1959. *Camp Site Development*. New York: Girl Scouts of the United States of America. p. 29. Reprinted by permission.

2. Dan Smith. 1995. "Design—Good or Bad—Influences Your Ministry." *Journal of Christian Camping*. Vol. 27, No. 5, September/October, p. 19. Reprinted with permission from CCI/USA.

3. American Camp Association. 1998. *Standards for Camp Programs and Services*. Martinsville, IN: American Camping Association. p. 197.

4. Scott King. 1988. "The ABC's of Facilities and Maintenance." *Journal of Christian Camping*. Vol. 20, No. 5, September/October, p. 9. Reprinted by permission from CCI/USA.

RISK
MANAGEMENT

Camp Echo (Burlingham, NY)

Chapter Eleven

Risk management is one of the most important tasks of camp administration. ... The board must establish risk management policies in conjunction with the director, and the director must work with the staff and campers in implementing the policies. ... The quality of the camp experience deteriorates in direct proportion to the extent of unreasonable risks to which the camper is subjected. A camper must be able to participate with confidence that the experience will be a safe one in regard to instruction given, the nature of supervision, and in environmental conditions. A safe experience is a primary responsibility in the conduct of a camp. However, fear of legal liability ... should never be the reason for not having adventurous, challenging activities. Such activities are needed in today's society.[1]

—Betty van der Smissen

Definitions

Risk is an uncertainty or probability concerning the loss of resources. The loss of resources, depending on their importance and value, can endanger the very life of an organization. Through a poorly managed risk, camps can potentially suffer losses with regard to the reputation of the camp, the health and safety of staff, the loss of camp property or financial resources, and ultimately, the loss of the camp as a resource for future generations. Some of those aspects are very tangible (money and property), while others are intangible, such as the camp's reputation and public attitudes toward the camp.

Although camps have always been concerned about the health and safety of the campers, it is the litigious climate of the past four decades that has caused camps to broaden their understanding of the risks involved in camp and conference center operations. In this process, a term developed that has become a critical facet of camp administration: *risk management.* This term implies an overall integrated plan that seeks to manage the risks that might occur in any and every aspect of camp life.

A risk-management plan is a system to identify a camp's physical, human, operational, and financial resources and to develop a plan to evaluate, reduce, or control the losses that might result from the operation. It is first an attitude— the attitude that risks can be managed and minimized even if they cannot be eliminated. It is impossible to remove all risk from camp life. Therefore, developing a system to identify and handle those risks in a variety of ways in advance of such losses is wise and necessary.

The areas in which camps are exposed to risk are generally categorized as physical assets, human resources (e.g., personnel or participants), operational financial resources, and standard of care or third-party liabilities. Physical or property assets can be lost through fire, floods, theft, vandalism, poor maintenance, and negligence. Risks affecting people—whether campers, staff, or the public—include death, injury, abuse (physical, mental, sexual, emotional, or verbal), and loss of their service or property. Operational financial risks involve fidelity and income risk. Fidelity risks involve the loss of financial resources through theft, nonperformance of duties, or mismanagement.

Similarly, risks to income include events that close the camp or prevent continuance of a camper session, thus requiring refunds or the nonpayment of fees. Third-party liabilities are those imposed by law or assumed under contract (contractual or tort liability).

Incidents and accidents are often used interchangeably, but a differentiation in meaning is helpful. Ed Schirick, of Schirick and Associates Insurance Brokers, suggests, "An *incident* is generally considered to be an event specific as to date and time that could have resulted in injury to people, damage to property, or financial loss to the business. ... An *accident* is an incident that results in unintended injury to people or damage to property that will cause a loss to the enterprise."[2]

Legal Aspects

With both incidents and accidents, the camp may suffer direct loss and may become entangled in litigation. Of course, the goal of good risk management planning is to avoid loss *and* litigation. When a suit is brought against a camp, both the corporate entity and an individual can be involved in the legal action.

Litigation has become a byword in today's society, and no camp is exempt from lawsuits. To avoid them, camp officials need good legal advice as well as advice concerning camp management and public relations. The camp needs regular access to an attorney who has a sound understanding of the camp program and operation. This goal will require a period of orientation and education of the attorney by the camp director. A good risk-management plan requires obtaining advice from that attorney, among others, about avoiding legal entanglements without hampering the camp program. Regardless of how capable an attorney the camp retains, the director should possess some basic understanding of both civil and criminal law. Some legal terms and principles of law need review by the administrator.

The *duty of care* is a foundational principle in risk management. The camp and its staff owe a duty of care to the campers and their families to protect those participants from any *unreasonable* risks. That is often tested on the basis that the individual (or individuals) has performed in a manner any reasonable staff member or perhaps a parent would act in a similar situation. Obviously, the reasonable factor is not easily measured and places a significant responsibility on the camp for the highest duty of care and documentation.

The term *in loco parentis* ("in place of the parent") applies to camps/conference centers at any time the entity assumes the responsibility for a minor "in place of the parent." The entity, whether the corporation or a cabin counselor, has the responsibility of maintaining the same or better level of care of that minor than would be expected from the minor's parents.

The director should understand the *doctrine of respondeat superior* (the master must answer for the acts of his servants), implying that a corporate entity is accountable for the actions of employees (including volunteers) *if* acting within the scope of their responsibility or authority. Understanding this concept gives the corporate chief employed officer and board reason to make sure that the responsibility and authority given employees is clearly identified in job descriptions and training. Similarly, helping an employee understand this concept encourages that employee to carefully carry out the responsibilities outlined in the job description, follow camp policies and procedures, and use only the amount of authority so delegated.

Individuals in camps can be guilty of *criminal acts*, where the offender is punished for actions that might include child abuse, drug usage, harassment, theft, and such. However, it is far more likely that camps will get entangled in *civil law*, where an injured party seeks financial compensation for negligent actions of the camp or an individual at the camp. Such litigation is likely to be very costly, even if the camp has not been negligent.

Much of the litigation in camps involves either *contractual* or *tort liability*. The camp enters into written and verbal contracts with various businesses, individuals, campers, parents, groups, and employees. Where a disagreement concerning the terms of that contract develops, whether it relates to the refund of a camper fee or the purchase of equipment or service, litigation can occur. The development of language in implied contracts such as camper registrations, staff agreements, and rental agreements needs careful thought by the author and review by legal counsel. Verbal contracts are even more difficult, and clear policy statements should be developed about who can make alterations in written policy or commit the camp to financial or other obligations.

Tort liability involves wrongful acts against a person other than through contracts. Torts may be *intentional* or *unintentional*. Camps can avoid the intentional torts relatively easily since they include such actions as slander, physical attack, or invasion of privacy. However, camps are exposed to unintentional torts wherever an allegation of *negligence* arises. Some evidence of negligence is needed, which involves proof that all four of the following occurred:

- The person in charge had a legal duty to the individual injured.
- The person in charge violated that duty to prevent an accident or incident that was foreseeable.
- Breach of that duty was directly related to the incident.
- Actual loss or damage resulting from the incident was caused by the breach (e.g., emotional, physical, mental).

All of the aforementioned acts most often involve a member of the camp staff underlining the importance of selection, training and supervision of the staff members. As mentioned in Chapters 8 and 9, the training and supervision of the staff are key elements of prevention in this area. An outline of areas of concern is shown in Appendix B.

Identification of Risk Exposures

The camp director should list all the assets he can identify that might be exposed to risk before methods of managing those risks can be chosen. Organizing those risks first by category (who or what is exposed) and then within those categories by types of exposure should help in this process. For example, risks can involve:

- Physical property or equipment (fire, theft, vandalism, lightning, power surges)
- Personnel and participant (injury, death, loss of personal property)
- Operational financial (cancellation or interruption of a camp session, embezzlement)
- Standard of care or third-party liabilities (contractual, tort action)

  Types of exposures within these four areas could include:
- Program activities (swimming, tripping, rappelling)
- Business operations (contracts, tax status and documentation, trademark, camp website)
- Natural hazards (poisonous animals or insects, insects that transmit diseases, lightning, cliffs near trail, rushing rivers)
- Natural disaster (floods, hurricanes, tornadoes, earthquakes, forest fires, etc.)
- Operation, maintenance, and supervision of facilities and equipment (loose steps, faulty personal flotation devices, weapons on the property)
- Behavior of people including campers, staff, visitors, or others, such as trespassers (abduction; inappropriate use of the Internet, chat rooms, blogs, or e-mails; illegal downloading of copyrighted material)
- Preexisting medical conditions (asthma, epilepsy, allergy to bee stings)
- National emergencies (terrorism)
- Environmental impairment risks (pollution, dangers from discarded substances, power outages shutting down business operations)
- Privacy issues (copyright laws, health records, unauthorized access to electronic records and e-mail history, compliance with the Children's Online Privacy Protection Act of 1998 (COPPA), posting a privacy notice on the website home page and where data is collected, etc.)[3]

A review of accident and insurance reports, health service records, and any history of lawsuits will reveal the frequency with which previous losses from these risks occur. Those that show up most frequently should be noted and analyzed. The analysis should include review of types of injury, locations of accident, times of day, days of week, ages of injured, types of activity, and amounts of supervision in place.

With the integration of cyberspace in all elements of business and personal life, it is important to give thought to management of related risks. Ed Schirick suggests that "if you haven't taken time to consider the threats/risks to your computer network resources, take time to do so in the very near future. Impacts may involve first-party (your camp) or third-party (others) interests."[4]

Consideration should be given also to how severe various losses might be. For instance, though the camp has had no record of a drowning or head injury from rappelling, either loss could be quite severe, involving long-term effects upon the participant, lawsuits, and negative public relations. Those losses with greatest severity should also be noted and analyzed. Obviously, risks that appear in both lists (frequency and severity) provide the areas of first concern.

Regulations

No risk-management planning is complete without careful consideration of the laws and regulations governing the camp operation. These laws and regulations arise at the federal, state, county, and local level; and, except for the federal regulations, they vary considerably from state to state.

The first step is to secure a copy of those regulations. If no one in a camp is knowledgeable about them, the director should make an effort to talk with other camp directors or the offices and staff of the local area American Camp Association or Christian Camp and Conference Association. The department of health or social services and the Occupational Safety and Health Administration (OSHA) will often have regulations affecting camps, including specifics on how health records are maintained and what training is mandated for staff. Some states will require a permit or license to operate; some licenses will require an inspection by state or county personnel, and some will not. Regulations also may be applicable to camps in other jurisdictions: fire, water, pollution, natural resources, building codes, sanitation, and such. Some states have integrated most regulations affecting camp into a single Camp Safety Act. Most states, however, have regulations affecting camps in areas such as health, labor, childcare, human services, agriculture, or even education.

If, after study of the regulations, the director finds some that are unclear or very difficult for the camp to comply with, the director should call for an appointment with a person in the appropriate office. The role of the state or local official is to help the director know how to comply with regulations and to give some assistance in problem situations. It is wise to check on the pattern of inspections. Some departments require a pre-opening inspection as well as during-operation inspections; others inspect annually or biannually.

Where a camp has its home office or its incorporated parent organization in one state and the camp's physical location in another, the regulations of both states need to be examined. Although the governmental unit and state in which the camp is physically located may have jurisdiction over health, sanitation, vehicles, fire protection, and pollution control, the state of incorporation may have primary jurisdiction over payroll, employment practices, and tax laws.

Management of Risks

Four methods of managing risks have been identified. In general, risks can be avoided, transferred, retained, or reduced. Choices will have to be made as to which method or methods best fit the risk exposure.

Avoidance of Risks

First, the director should review risks to see if the camp can simply avoid any unnecessary risks. The director may eliminate an activity that is not essential to the accomplishment of camp goals. A practice such as allowing anyone to ride in the back of an open-bed truck can (and should) be eliminated. An old, dilapidated wooden shed that could easily catch fire may be a risk that can be avoided by simply tearing down the shed.

Transfer of Risks

Many of the risks in a camp are transferred to another party through insurance or specific agreements or contracts.

Releases

The camp attorney may develop "hold harmless" statements, which can transfer responsibility for certain actions to the participant or sponsoring group. Leases are one method of transferring certain risks to the lessor. Some debate exists in the legal community about "waivers," "hold harmless" statements, or "releases."

A minor or even a minor's parents cannot waive the minor's rights. It is one reason a minor may file suit against a camp for a supposedly negligent act some months or years (depending on the state) after the minor reaches the age of majority. Of course, such releases can never release the camp from gross negligence or wanton, willful, reckless misconduct by the administration or staff.

However, properly worded permissions and releases can have the parent give informed consent rather than a general overall consent to participate. These releases have been accepted in the courts of all 50 states as showing that the parent was knowledgeable that the minor was participating in a given activity, was told that risks were inherent in the activities and environment of the camp, and risks specific to a special activity are described. Releases can be effective tools in helping bar recovery by the parents or guardians when their child is injured. However, "releases are not a sure bet," state Charles R. Gregg and Catherine Hansen-Stamp. They "will generally be enforced only on a case-by- case basis in the jurisdictions where they are allowed. Although the laws of most states allow the use of releases, the enforceability issues emphasize the need for careful draftsmanship and wise use of legal counsel."[5]

On the other hand, a waiver by adult participants may be more binding or carry more weight in court. Janna S. Rankin states that "with regard to adult activities in a recreational setting, a release may be upheld if it is carefully worded, concerned with a risk normally associated with that activity, and the recreation service provider has not been clearly negligent."[6]

A general permission to participate and a release or a waiver should both be considered. A signed *permission* form is the consent by the parent or guardian for a minor to participate in a specific activity or activities of the camp generally, depending on the wording. The camp enrollment process should provide a full description of the activities, including the nature of risks and potential dangers of any activities that are not commonly known to the average person. The camp should then seek a signed *specific* parental permission for that type activity. In this way, the parent is giving informed consent, which is an essential ingredient of permission forms and waivers. In many cases, this requires two or more forms to be completed by the parents or guardian.

Many camps are now requiring releases in addition to permission forms. A signed *release* is an act whereby the participant, parent, or guardian gives up some claim, right, or interest to the persons against whom the claim could be made. A parent may release rights to sue the camp, but the parent may not waive or release the rights of the child. Beyond the permission form and release, some camps are now also using an *indemnity agreement*, which requests the parent or guardian to reimburse the camp for any expenses (e.g., legal, medical) incurred by the camp as a result of providing services to the camper.[7] Such permissions and releases need to be developed in consultation with the camp's attorney. An example of a permission form can be found in Figure 11-1.

Certainly, an organization can assume responsibility for its own members or participants when renting a facility, if the contractual responsibilities of both parties are clearly drawn. However, requiring a certificate of insurance from the organization is often a safeguard to the written agreement.

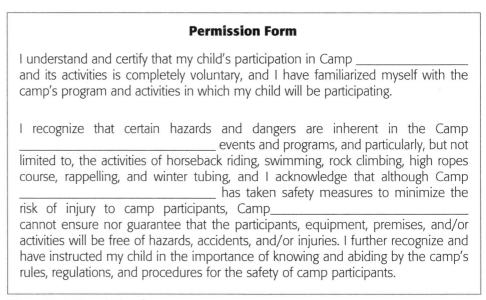

Permission Form

I understand and certify that my child's participation in Camp _____ and its activities is completely voluntary, and I have familiarized myself with the camp's program and activities in which my child will be participating.

I recognize that certain hazards and dangers are inherent in the Camp _____ events and programs, and particularly, but not limited to, the activities of horseback riding, swimming, rock climbing, high ropes course, rappelling, and winter tubing, and I acknowledge that although Camp _____ has taken safety measures to minimize the risk of injury to camp participants, Camp_____ cannot ensure nor guarantee that the participants, equipment, premises, and/or activities will be free of hazards, accidents, and/or injuries. I further recognize and have instructed my child in the importance of knowing and abiding by the camp's rules, regulations, and procedures for the safety of camp participants.

Figure 11-1. Permission form

Insurance

A critical ingredient of any risk-management planning is risk transfer. One risk transfer technique is buying insurance. Though some camps may be in a position to self-insure, buying insurance is the most common method camp directors use to transfer risk. The careful selection of an insurance agent or broker is the first step in securing insurance. If possible, an agent should be found who has some understanding of camps and does not cringe at each program activity that, on the surface, seems to pose a risk. If the agent has the designation CPCU (Chartered Property Casualty Underwriter) or CIC (Certified Insurance Counselor), ARM (Associate Risk Manager), CRM (Certified Risk Manager) or similar designations it indicates the person has taken the time to seek the certification and has acquired a broad background in insurance. However, many qualified agents can be found without either of these designations.

It is important also that the director be familiar with the various types of insurance that need to be considered. Following are seven general categories or types:

• Property Insurance

Property insurance may be purchased for camp buildings and personal property. Coverage options are available for basic causes of loss, broad causes of loss, or special causes of loss. Basic causes of loss coverage, previously known as named perils insurance, covers damage from events such as fire, lightning, windstorm, and vandalism. Broad causes of loss adds a few additional events to these causes of loss, such as collapse due to weight of ice and snow. The most comprehensive coverage for camp property is offered by the special causes of loss form. The difference between the forms is that the basic and broad causes of loss forms cover only those events named in the form, where the special causes of loss covers all events, except those excluded.

Some directors choose to insure the buildings and business personal property at their camp using replacement costs. Buying an appropriate amount of insurance is an important matter because of possible penalties for buying too little insurance compared to values at the time of the loss. Directors should obtain appraisals from real estate professionals, or replacement-cost estimates on buildings from local contractors as a basis for selecting the proper amount of insurance. Inventories of personal property and equipment should also be maintained and evaluated periodically to ensure that the amount of insurance purchased is not too little, or too much. All property values should be adjusted annually to keep pace with inflation in subsequent years, even in years when inflation is relatively low.

If insuring all camp buildings at replacement value does not fit into your budget, an option to consider is insuring only the most valuable or essential buildings in this fashion. It is well to consider which buildings are the most valuable and without which it would be difficult to operate. In recent years, laws/ordinances regarding construction have been passed at the local, state, and federal levels that may increase the cost of reconstructing a building after a loss. The additional cost of reconstruction is not automatically included under replacement cost insurance. Optional coverage for application of these building laws—including demolition and increased cost of construction—is available. Insurance against catastrophic loss, such as a flood or earthquake, which might destroy the entire camp, should also be considered. Protection may be available depending upon where your camp is located.

If insuring all camp buildings at replacement value does not fit into your budget, an option is to insure buildings and business personal property for their actual cash value (ACV), or depreciated value. Under these circumstances, if a building were damaged or destroyed, the camp would receive only the value at the time of the loss, and the difference between the depreciated value and replacement cost would have to be funded by the camp. This option brings a reduction in rates in proportion to the reduction in value. Depreciation is a subject of negotiation. How much the camp property is depreciated depends on a variety of factors. Ed Schirick notes "factors that reduce depreciation (and increase value) include proper maintenance, renovation and repair practices. While there is some subjectivity in determining depreciation and actual cash value, detailed records of repair, maintenance and improvements help you negotiate successfully on this issue."[8]

Another option is to insure buildings and camp personal property on a functional replacement cost basis. This differs from the replacement cost valuation method. Instead of providing for replacement "with material of like kind and quality" in the event of total loss, functional replacement cost provides for the replacement of the building's useable square footage with less costly material than was in the original building. Partial losses requiring repairs would be paid for in the same architectural style, but with less costly materials.

Directors should realize that some camp property is so unique that the materials to replace the building may no longer be available, or may be so costly that the replacement cost is increased well beyond usual construction parameters. Unique camp personal property and memorabilia also present valuation challenges. If directors have particularly valuable or unique items in buildings, they may wish to consider having them insured for their fine art, or antique value. While functional replacement cost represents another option, directors should exercise caution and get proper advice about the use of "less costly materials." Appropriate planning is required in advance if this approach is to have any chance of working properly.

In any case, it is good risk-management and business-management practice to have a schedule of all buildings—insured or uninsured—and an inventory of their contents with their estimated replacement cost, actual cash value, functional replacement, fine art, or antique value noted. In this fashion, the difference between an item's value and amount of insurance is known. Accurate, up-to-date inventories, pictures or video of buildings and especially their valuable contents should be kept to document the loss should a fire or some other loss occur. Certain financial-management software packages enable camp directors to photograph and inventory buildings and assets. These records should be stored at an off-site office or in a fireproof safe, or if the records are digital, backed up in several locations both on site and off. Best practices require reevaluation and appraisal to ensure proper insurance to value given inflation or diminished value.

The amount of the deductible the camp assumes will also affect the premium. As premiums for insurance coverage have increased, camps have tended to partially retain the loss (self-insure) through higher deductibles (for example, $1,000, $2,500, $5,000 or more).

• Commercial General Liability

A liability policy is designed to provide protection for the camp if lawsuits are brought as a result of alleged negligence. Such allegations may be brought as the result of property damage, bodily injury, personal and advertising injury liability (e.g., libel, slander, false arrest, infringement of another's copyright, trade dress, or slogan in the camp's advertising).

It is important that the camp director help the insurance agent understand the camp and its different risk exposures provided in the individual program and setting. It is at this point that risk-management planning will help the agent understand the precautions and steps needed to minimize risks. The insurance company generally evaluates all conditions that increase or decrease risk. For example, the number, experience, and training of horses for horseback riding, the number of motorboats for waterskiing, and the number of staff all affect the risk factors as viewed by the insurance company. The insurance agent should also have exposure and understanding of the camp's American Camp Association camp accreditation. Many insurance companies offer reduced rates to camps that hold ACA accreditation.

The liability insurance policy should be checked in detail to see if it provides professional liability insurance for camp directors, medical personnel, and other professional employees of the camp. Protection should also include product liability coverage for food service, and any type of coverage for independent contractors who may work at camp in construction or program. It is wise coverage to have. It is prudent to check the policy carefully for any exclusions.

Many new exclusions and restrictions of general liability coverage have occurred in recent years, including terrorism, mold, bacteria, fungus, employment practices and communicable disease. Limitations may be placed in certain activities, such as amusement devices and the height of water slides in pools. Similarly, many risks are related to the use of the Internet and bulletin boards/chat rooms that are excluded from automatic coverage, as well as breach of privacy and other issues related to doing business online. These cyber risks are accelerating and changing rapidly.

Given the increased awareness of inappropriate sexual behavior in recent years, camps should be sure that their policies provide coverage for the risks of sexual misconduct and physical abuse. The director must not assume that coverage is provided when contracts are silent on this subject. It is advisable to have an affirmative statement that the policy provides this coverage through an endorsement to the general liability policy. Most insurance underwriters require a criminal background-check program for all staff, including volunteers, as one of the methods for managing this risk.

Further, the director should question whether protection is extended to allegations of sexual harassment of employees. An additional coverage, employment practice liability, may be necessary to cover sexual harassment, along with allegations such as discrimination and wrongful termination. In addition, for camps with several year-round, full-time staff who receive employee benefits, consideration should be given to the purchase of employee benefits liability coverage. This covers the camp against mistakes in the administration of their employee benefits plan.

Where the camp has a governing board, consideration should be given to coverage for directors and officers (D-and-O insurance). Directors and officers insurance provides management liability and insurance against wrongful acts such as misleading statements, misfeasance, and malfeasance. The insurance provides protection to those volunteer board members for their actions on behalf of the camp. In addition, if volunteers are used in any fashion in the camp operation, coverage should be checked to make sure volunteer workers are insured.

Economics and outside forces often alter the insurance marketplace. When a hard market for insurance develops, camps may have to look into secondary markets. Non-standard insurance sometimes becomes an option in such a market. Examples include surplus lines placements, claims made insurance policies, captive insurance companies, and risk-purchasing group programs which may not provide the scope of coverage camp directors have been accustomed to finding from camp-insurance specialists. The director should be very careful in exploring these sorts of nonstandard insurance solutions because such approaches are often confusing and may result in an incomplete risk transfer. The camp director should be realistic in setting the limits of coverage to be purchased. In an increasingly litigious environment, camps have to be careful to have enough insurance to cover a major incident.

• Umbrella or Excess Liability Insurance

Umbrella insurance is aptly named because it is designed to sit over the top of primary liability insurance policies such as general liability, auto liability, and the employers' liability coverage in workers' compensation insurance. This type of policy is also known as a catastrophe liability policy.

Over the years, coverage under most umbrella policies offered to camps has been scaled back to the point where the umbrella has become an excess policy. Excess policies usually provide higher limits than primary policies, but provide no broader coverage than that provided by the primary policy itself. True umbrella policies provide broader coverage than the primary policies underneath and are subject to a self-insured retention (SIR), thus filling in the gaps in some primary policies. Such policies have become very rare.

Buying umbrella or excess insurance is another area where the camp needs to be particularly careful in scrutinizing the detail, because they have no standardization. Specific attention should be given to sexual misconduct liability coverage, as this coverage can vary greatly.

• Workers' Compensation

Required by law, this policy covers medical and hospitalization costs and loss-of-time (wages) compensation incurred for employees injured at work or suffering a work-related illness. The requirements for workers' compensation limits vary from state to state. The experience rating of a camp can affect the premium in certain situations, so the control of staff accidents is an important part of risk-management planning. In most states, international staff are considered employees and as such are covered under workers' compensation insurance laws. Directors should be certain to show income paid to international staff as part of their payroll records in this case.

• Motor Vehicle Insurance

Vehicles, particularly where they carry passengers, are a major risk. It is vital that the vehicles owned or used by the camp be covered by insurance. Coverage should include liability, property damage, medical payments, and uninsured motorist coverage. Collision and comprehensive coverage is available but must be examined in light of the value of the vehicles and the additional premium. If the camp uses staff-owned vehicles for any purpose whatsoever, non-owner coverage should be secured. If the camp hires or leases vehicles to be driven by camp staff, the camp is typically expected to carry the insurance. This includes liability and physical damage. Consult with your insurance agent or broker before signing any agreement for leased vehicles to ensure proper insurance protection is arranged.

Concerns about the use of 15-passenger vans have grown in recent years, and some insurance companies will no longer insure 15-passenger vans. Some manufacturers have stopped making 15-passenger vans, and others are attempting to provide additional stabilizing mechanisms to reduce risk of rollover accidents. Directors considering the use of such vehicles should carefully check safety records, insurance implications, prohibit roof racks, and overloading, as well as limit the use of trailers. Consideration should also be given to how the decision to use such vehicles can be defended in court.

• Health and Accident Insurance

Health and accident insurance is designed to help pay the costs of medical services and hospitalization for camper and staff accidents or illnesses occurring or contracted during the camp stay. Various kinds of coverage are available under such policies. The increasing costs of health care and the increasing number of families without health insurance give a camp director cause for careful consideration about the need of health and accident insurance for campers and staff.

For those camps that continue to offer primary camper accident and sickness insurance, some automatically cover campers and offer coverage to staff as a benefit. Other camps offer campers and staff the option of taking the insurance or relying on their own family policy. Many camps in an attempt to reduce costs have stopped buying camper accident and sickness insurance and chosen to rely entirely on the camper family's health insurance. As more families are uninsured, or are being forced by employers to retain more of their family health insurance costs uninsured gaps are developing. The gaps represent large deductibles, out-of-network penalties, coinsurance, and copayments families are being forced to absorb.

If the policy covers staff, work-related injuries are still covered first under workers' compensation insurance. Health and accident insurance that covers the cost of treatment may show the camp's concern for the well-being of all persons, reduce costs to parents, and, thus, help minimize the likelihood of a lawsuit.

It is possible to secure a policy that covers the camper in coordination with the family's insurance. These policies are secondary or excess policies. They are designed to pay after the family's primary health insurance is exhausted. Where no family insurance exists, then the policy becomes the primary insurance. This type of policy generally costs less than covering all campers directly.

Day camps typically buy accident only insurance. Resident camps can also buy sickness medical expense insurance. Limits in these policies tend to be low. However, higher limits are desirable today. There is usually an accidental death and dismemberment benefit. Some insurers provide a catastrophe medical benefit in the event a claimant is totally or partially paralyzed. Coverage can be primary or excess. Rates vary and are experience rated. Coverage can be purchased with or without a deductible. Preexisting conditions are usually excluded. Since policies vary greatly, the director should examine a prospective policy carefully before purchase.

• Business Interruption/Loss of Income Insurance

Business interruption or loss of income and extra expense insurance is designed to insure a camp for loss of business net income and added expenses when the camp's standard operation is interrupted or suspended. It is not intended to cover the loss of the property that may have caused the cancellation of a session, as that usually would be covered under property and casualty. Business income and extra expense insurance typically requires a direct physical loss or damage to property that results in a loss of business income. Directors should consult with their insurance agents and complete a business income worksheet to ensure selection of an appropriate limit of insurance.

Standard business income insurance usually includes a clause that provides coverage for a limited time period when access to camp is prevented by order of a civil authority, as has occurred during various forest fires and floods. Under these circumstances, loss of income insurance may respond even if your camp did not suffer direct damage. The requirement is that the damage to adjacent premises which triggered the order of the civil authority is a covered cause of loss under your camp property policy.

Standard business income insurance policies do not extend to interruption or suspension of your camp program as the result of food contamination or communicable disease (e.g., H1N1 or food poisoning). Some insurance companies will offer an extension of loss of income insurance for these events. Coverage is also triggered by order of civil authority. Voluntary closings in these situations do not trigger the policy coverage.

With the increased reliance camp administration has on electronic records and communication and cyber risks evolve, it is wise to examine how any potential interruption of business or loss of income could occur from a breakdown or infringement in this area as well.

• Insurance Binders

The director should request and receive binders on each insurance policy on or before the date the policy takes effect, if the policy is not available on that date. A binder assures the director that the policy is in effect for a given time. It is wise to inquire of the agent as to the A M Best rating of the insurance companies issuing policies; the rating should be a B++ (very good) or higher, if at all possible.

Retention of Risk

Certain risks may be retained in instances where it is not possible to avoid or transfer the total risk. Insurance to completely cover all physical losses is too expensive for most camps, so some risk must be retained by the camp. Certain activities are so important to the mission and goals of the camp that the director would not consider eliminating them. For example, though drowning may be a severe risk, a camp likely would not eliminate all aquatic activities.

The retention of a risk should be a deliberate decision of the administration and the sponsoring organization (if there is one). Each risk should be identified and outlined with the potential consequences and measures developed to minimize such consequences. The potential financial consequences of such risks should be estimated.

Where insurance is used to transfer part of the risk, the camp must usually retain a financial deductible or threshold. The insurance company must pay the costs beyond the amount of the deductible. A reserve or contingency fund should be set aside that can be tapped if such risks materialize.

Reduction of Risks

When a camp retains a risk, then the management of that risk is examined to see how much of the risk can be reduced. Once the camp has identified which risks are to be eliminated or avoided, the balance of risk-management planning is developing the policies and practices that will reduce the remaining risks to an acceptable level. The plan for reducing risks examines what can be done before and during the operation of the risk. Much of the reduction of risks is akin to practices that also reduce incidents that may increase insurance premiums or prove to be issues in public relations.

Staff other than the director should be involved in identifying risks, for other staff members are much closer to many risks. "All managers should be given the opportunity to brainstorm ways to reduce risk. They should constantly monitor their staff for behaviors that reduce … the opportunity for incidents to occur," states Chris Rollins.[9]

For example, the camp's administration feels that providing a certain activity to every participant in a certain unit is important in attaining certain goals or outcomes in the camp experience. In advance of the activity, several steps are taken to reduce the risk:

- Leadership is selected on the basis of documented experience and maturity, and on demonstrated ability to work with types of campers being served.
- Leaders' skills are tested and verified during precamp training.
- Written operating procedures that include safety regulations and prerequisites for participation or eligibility are followed and used as the basis for all staff training.
- Participants are given adequate training and tested on the skills essential to their participation in the activity. Leaders are trained to watch for fatigue, overcompetitiveness, stress, and other signs that may bring a greater human risk factor to an otherwise safe situation.
- Equipment that is appropriate and safe is provided for use in the activity.
- The location where the activity is to take place is examined for potential hazards, such as natural hazards or outside interference from other activities and events.
- A proper ratio of leaders to participants ensures adequate supervision is established and carried out.
- Leaders are trained to implement a clear action plan for emergencies that might arise in participation in the activity.

It is equally important that during the operation of the activity, the following steps be taken to reduce risk:

- Supervision of the activity by one or more of the leaders is carried out at all times. Most activities should require a minimum of two leaders at all times.
- Appropriate clothing and equipment are required of the participant during the activity.
- An unsafe practice or violation of operational procedures is stopped immediately upon observation.

The foci of lawsuits in camps over the years have centered on supervision of the activity, the manner in which the activity is conducted, and the availability and condition of facilities or equipment related to the activity. With this knowledge, it is possible to carefully examine program activities, establishing clear policies by the camp administration and regular supervision to see that policies are continually implemented. Since the courts hold camp staff to the standard of care of a "reasonably prudent professional," the recruitment, training, and supervision of staff are critical to help prevent allegations of negligence. Not only is it important that such steps be taken, but the camp needs documentation that appropriate recruitment, training, and supervision of staff occurred.

In addition, clear policies need to be put in writing and in the hands of all staff. A notebook or staff manual that organizes all such policies and procedures in an orderly fashion is perhaps the best method for preservation and annual review. Nothing is as helpful in litigation as producing written documentation that can be attested to as being available and used in an orientation or training process.

However, everything cannot be written. For instance, though the camp may have a written policy for the supervision of an activity, that policy does not ensure that the supervision did occur at a particular time and place. Where the risk in question is severe, it is wise to have at least two leaders present so that a second person can attest to the supervision given.

Handling Incidents

However well a plan is put into practice to reduce risks, incidents will occur. Action taken at the time of the incident is as important as the preventive steps taken before the incident. As much as possible, the steps to be taken at the time of an incident should be identified in advance.

The first step is to develop a crisis communication plan with a designated crisis-response team while there is no crisis and there is time to carefully outline the critical steps and responsibilities. *The CampLine* suggests that the team be "interdisciplinary and include people from the camp administration, maintenance, health care, your owners/sponsors (of the camp), a mental health resource (counselor, social worker, community health services) and perhaps a clergy member."[10]

Key staff representing various areas of camp operation should do an analysis of possible crises and their implications for camp operation. Linda Ebner Erceg suggests that completing a chart such as shown in Figure 11-2 be a starting point in risk analysis.[11]

Staff members in leadership positions should be given training and directions in writing to cover such points as:
- Providing immediate care of the individuals involved in the incident, both injured and uninjured
- Notifying staff's supervisor or designated person as soon as possible
- Securing outside assistance, if necessary
- Writing a report of the incident, documenting as many facts as possible (see OSHA requirements later in this chapter)
- If serious, reporting to appropriate persons outside of the camp (e.g., government agencies, parents of the participant, camp's home office)
- Diverting or organizing the persons not involved in the incident into other activities or other areas of the camp

Functional Role	Core Person	Understudy
Emergency Operations Center Location where crisis response team functions		
Director of Crisis Management Coordinates the response plan from the Operations Center.		
Transportation Coordinator Secures transport as needed to move people and/or supplies.		
Communication Coordinator Provides and coordinates communications system, including web support, prepares key messages for media, provides and coordinates phone team, documents incident.		
Mass Care/Operations Manages and coordinates shelter and food service for displaced population, provides for bulk distribution of relief supplies.		
Health and Medical Services Coordinates care for injured/ill people, makes decisions related to health of population, coordinates search and rescue until external provider takes over.		
Physical Plant Needs Restores power or secures alternate to run emergency services, restores essential services (e.g. toilets, running water, heat) and facilities (including site for Operations Center).		
Financial Support Tracks costs of incident, has access to funds to support plan.		
Personnel Management Assigns other employees to specific tasks, sets up training and materials to support these tasks, attends to camper needs and those of their families.		

Figure 11-2. Risk analysis chart

- Referring media and determining who speaks for the camp/organization. On this point, it should be recognized that media relations can be as critical of an element in risk management as notifying parents. Adverse and incorrect publicity can account for long-term damages to the camp. As Bari S. Dworken points out, "In many cases, reporters and photographers often arrive at camp even before the emergency crew. This can create more than just the initial emergency to deal with."[12]
- Identifying the types of incidents that require special attention to the feelings of staff members and campers, and the person/s responsible for securing expertise to help those persons

In the same outline, it should be clearly stated as to which staff member is accountable for certain responsibilities or actions at the time of the crisis.

Some of the incidents will be emergencies, and others will not be. It is equally important in non-emergencies to take the aforementioned steps where applicable. However, certain types of emergencies can be explored in advance and procedures developed to cover them (e.g., drowning, fire, tornado, evacuation of camp, injury requiring medical assistance). For each different type of emergency:

- Procedures should be put in writing, reviewed by various experts, and given to staff.
- Procedures should be rehearsed during staff training, where practical.
- Emergency phone numbers and contact information should be posted in critical places, such as the swimming area, maintenance building, kitchen, and office (communication is very important).
- Staff trained in basic first aid/CPR should be assigned to pertinent areas where emergencies might occur.

Thought should be given not only to the first aid for physical injuries, but also to how to deal with the stress brought on by the emergency. Stress in general should be discussed during staff training. Particularly where the participants are children, staff should be helped to understand the signs of mental and emotional stress, the areas where stress can increase the possibility of an accident, the behaviors in which stress can manifest itself once an incident is underway, and the appropriate responses.

For instance, where an alleged incident of abuse occurs, the first concern should be for the welfare of the camper(s). Therefore, the accused staff member should be relieved of responsibilities, and a staff member with expertise and experience in dealing with children should be assigned to the camper group. Camp staff must not assume that the staff member is guilty just because an accusation has been made. That guideline should be made clear at the outset to the accused staff member and any other staff involved. However, to protect the campers, the staff member, and the camp, the staff member in question should be separated from any camper group.

A clear understanding of the accusation and situation must be secured before making a report. It is important to get the facts but not interrogate the child involved and any other children who are witnesses. Any questions to the child must be kept very low key and witnessed by another staff member. Every effort to ease the child's emotional stress should be taken. Remember, it is not the director's responsibility to determine whether the abuse occurred; that is the responsibility of trained professionals. If an accusation or indicator of some type of physical, emotional, or sexual abuse occurs, the proper authorities should be notified. Reporting allegations of abuse is mandated in all 50 states, though the procedures vary from state to state. Specifics on reporting should be determined before camp and be readily accessible during camp.[13]

From this point on, the role of the director is related to controlling the impact of the incident by communicating with the parents of the child, the balance of the staff and campers, the owner of the camp or board of directors, the media, and perhaps the parents of other campers in the camp session at the time. Legal advice, as well as advice from a communications or public relations specialist, may be warranted in addressing concerns with parents of other campers in the living group or total camp, as well as with the media. At this point, a written plan for such incidents made prior to camp is extremely valuable in helping the director act and react carefully and logically.

Recent events have made camp directors more sensitive to the ways in which incidents outside of the camp itself can affect the feelings, attitudes, and behaviors of staff and campers. However isolated the camp may be, today's communication systems make it impossible for camps to be isolated from knowledge of such incidents. The camp's crisis communication plan should recognize external forces and the type of measures the camp can use to assist campers and staff at such a time.

Maintaining Records

One of the functions for which the camp director must take responsibility is seeing that accurate records are kept of the entire camp operation. As Ed Schirick states, "Defining relationships and responsibilities, as well as terms of agreements with other parties, are examples of responsible risk management and represent good business practice."[14] Though the director will not be able to do this alone, it is important that he identify the types of records to be kept, who is to keep them, where they are to be stored, and for how long. Records serve a number of purposes:

- To provide documentation that shows what, when, and why things were done
- To provide information about the current financial state of the organization
- To provide information to analyze operations and costs for efficiency, health, safety, and effectiveness
- To demonstrate the operation is in compliance with local, state, and federal regulations and American Camp Association standards
- To protect against and be available as evidence in case of litigation
- To maintain a history of the camp

Certain records and information are needed so that those who follow the present personnel know what significant events and actions occurred over a period of years.

Health Records

The isolated setting of many camps means that the camp is the primary healthcare provider for campers and staff. To provide the best healthcare possible, a camp must collect information about each camper's and staff member's health (e.g., health history, medications, allergies) and inform the appropriate staff of any health considerations of persons in their areas. For example, unit counselors and kitchen staff should be aware of food allergies, unit counselors should be aware of campers who need to receive medications at the health center, and program staff should be aware of campers with illnesses or other medical conditions.

The collection of this information can be difficult because parents and staff do not always understand the significance of providing this information. For instance, the fact that a camper has recently traveled overseas may not seem significant to the parent, but may be important to know should certain symptoms appear while at camp. Parents may not recognize mental or emotional problems as part of the camper's health history that would give camp health staff clues to behavior.

While the forms may be separate from camper registration forms, the process for collecting this information should be part of registration and follow-up. Forms on which to collect this information should be mailed to parents and staff in advance, accompanied by an explanation of the importance of providing this information. See Chapter 12 for an example of the health history and examination form developed by the American Camp Association, as well as more specific information on the type of information that should be collected and retained.

It is important to recognize that information collected about a camper's or staff member's health history is to be used solely to provide accurate and helpful information to those providing health care to the individual and must not be used to refuse the individual a position as a camper or a staff member. In fact, regulations in the Americans with Disabilities Act require that the health information on staff members be collected *after* a position has been offered and before camp begins.

It is also true that most of an individual's health history needs to be maintained confidentially, and some of that history need not be shared with the camp. For example, knowing an individual's HIV status should not change the health care given at camp because all staff with healthcare functions should be trained in the use of universal precautions that would protect the staff member from transmission of such a bloodborne disease. Additionally, under the Americans with Disabilities Act, persons who have tested positive for HIV may not be denied enrollment due to their HIV status.

Any health care provided to campers or staff members while they are in the camp's charge should be recorded. Various regulations affect health records, and a variety of methods are used for maintaining the health care given at camp. OSHA requires that camper healthcare records and medical logs be kept separate from staff healthcare records. Other federal regulations require that healthcare information on staff be maintained apart from their personnel files.

The Health Insurance Portability and Accountability Act of 1996 (HIPPA) places responsibilities on businesses and organizations alike in terms of health records that need careful study. The rules require a provider of health care who has a direct treatment relationship with an individual to obtain consent regarding the use and disposition of the individual's health information. A camp needs to make sure that its release/waiver statement on the camp registration form and/or health history/exam includes permission to disclose health information to appropriate parties such as the insurance carrier, related external healthcare providers, appropriate staff, and the like. Legal counsel should review that release/waiver statement for red flags in light of the Act's provisions that required compliance by April 2003. In addition, a camp needs to examine its electronic communication in terms of health care, and double-check the applicability of the law. In any case, the camp should have a clear policy on how healthcare information is handled in terms of access and transmission to others.

Incident Reports

It is particularly vital that reports be made of all accidents or incidents and that uniform information be recorded each time an accident or incident occurs. The term incident is used deliberately, for certain occurrences in camp are not accidents, but are of such a significant nature that a record should be kept in case questions arise at a later date. These questions tend to relate to emotional stress, alleged abuse, outside intruders breaching security, and the like. No form will cover all potential types of incidents, so a narrative identifying the witnesses and dates, precautions taken, actions taken, and any specific results will usually suffice.

The American Camp Association has designed an accident/incident report form, which serves as a good model (Figure 11-3). Such reports should be attached to insurance claims where applicable and filed along with all records of treatment of injuries and illnesses until the injured is at least one to four years beyond the age of majority or for the period of statutory limits in the state where the camp is located, whichever is greater. It is also important to complete appropriate workers' compensation and OSHA forms recording incidents involving employees. Any reports of possible child abuse should be carefully documented as this can be the basis of a criminal action. ACA has a form available that provides a checklist record of possible indications of abuse that are reported by individuals at camp (Figure 11-4). The appropriate recordkeeping of injuries and illnesses is also discussed in Chapter 12.

Keeping the records of injuries, accidents and incidents is only the first step. One important use of these records is to assist the camp director and health manager in analyzing the frequency and severity of certain types of injuries and incidents in light of the location where those injuries occurred. Between the camper health record (see Chapter 12), the accident or incident reports, and insurance claims, the director has a clear source of data that requires tallying and analysis at the end of each season. A comparison of such data after several seasons will be most meaningful in risk-management planning. This is best done with an outside advisor from the health, insurance, or consultancy fields that brings an objective viewpoint and is aware of current practices. With that person, a review and revision of procedures can be identified as a measure of prevention for the coming season.

Record Retention

It should be noted that a minor may sue up to one to four years beyond the age of majority, for the period of statutory limits in the state where the camp is located, whichever is greater. Therefore a child of the minimum age at the camp (for example, seven years old) would have 13 years to bring suit, making it wise to maintain all records concerning campers involved in accidents or incidents for 13 years (e.g., health records, accident reports, registration forms, and permissions signed by the parent, insurance coverage records, witness statements). Consideration of maintaining a file of verifiable parental consent for data and pictures collected for children under 13, in compliance with COPPA (Children's Online Privacy Act of 1998), needs consideration. Further information on record retention is found in Chapter 16. Storing these files in a digital format, where appropriate, can greatly increase the effectiveness of retaining records for such a long period of time. Such a format requires that protections be in place to prevent changing any of the information originally recorded.

Many different statutes of limitations exist, with time periods that vary from law to law and state to state, especially in regard to tax, unemployment, and workers' compensation records. Therefore, the director should give careful thought to record retention and should obtain legal advice. The policy of the organization or camp on recordkeeping and record retention should be developed on the basis of law, the rule of reason, and the risk involved. Such a policy should be in writing. In many cases, some records may be digitized and serve as a legal record, but this approach needs to be verified with an attorney for the specific state ruling.

OSHA regulations require employers with 11 or more employees to maintain OSHA 200 forms, record all employee injuries, and post the summary of the form from February 1 to March 1 each year at a location where employees can read it. In addition, a supplementary record of each individual injury and illness must be kept on the OSHA 101 form and retained for five years. In some cases, a workers' compensation First Report of Injury form may serve both purposes if it covers all information required. An OSHA poster must also be posted in a location where it can be seen by all employees. Copies of the forms are available directly from the state OSHA office and, in some cases, the state labor department. See Chapter 12 for other OSHA requirements.

Accreditation

Accreditation by an outside body has proven to be an invaluable step in all types of institutions across the country, from schools to hospitals. It gives validity to the concern of the camp, in this case, to meet professional standards and to stay abreast of the latest information concerning health and safety in the field. The fact that an outside body comes in to examine all aspects of the operation provides not only a checkpoint for the administrator, but also a backup if litigation ever occurs.

Accident/Incident Report Form   FM 01
Developed by the *American Camping Association*®
(Fill out 1 on each incident or person)

Camp Name_____Date_____

Address _____
          Street & Number   *City*   *State*   *Zip*

Name of person involved _____ Age_____ Sex_____ ☐ Camper ☐ Staff ☐ Visitor
                          Last   *First*   *Middle*

Address _____Phone_____
          Street & Number   *City*   *State*   *Zip*   *Area/Number*

Name of Parent/Guardian *(if minor)* _____

Address _____Phone_____
          Street & Number   *City*   *State*   *Zip*   *Area/Number*

Name/Addresses of Witnesses *(You may wish to attach signed statements.)*

1. _____

2. _____

3. _____

Type of incident   ☐ Behavioral   ☐ Accident   ☐ Epidemic illness   ☐ Other (describe)

Date of Incident/Accident _____ Hour_____ ☐ a.m. ☐ p.m.
                            Day of Week   *Month*   *Day*   *Year*

Describe the sequence of activity in detail including what the (injured) person was doing at the time _____

_____

_____

_____

_____

_____

_____

Where occurred? *(Specify location, including location of injured and witnesses. Use diagram to locate persons/objects.)*

Was injured participating in an activity at time of injury?   ☐ Yes ☐ No If so, what activity? _____

Any equipment involved in accident?   ☐ Yes ☐ No If so, what kind? _____

What could the injured have done to prevent injury?_____

_____

Emergency procedures followed at time of incident/accident _____

_____

_____

By whom?_____

Submitted by_____Position_____Date_____

Phone number _____

Figure 11-3. Accident/Incident Report Form

Medical Report of Accident

Were parents notified? _____ ☐ Yes ☐ No   By ☐ Writing ☐ Phone ☐ Other

By whom? _____ Title _____ When _____
                                                                                                                    Time   Date

Parent's Response _____

_____

Where was treatment given (check and complete all that apply)?

☐ At Accident Site: Where? _____ By whom? _____

      Treatment given _____ Date _____

☐ Camp Health Service: By whom? _____ Title _____

      Treatment given _____ Date _____

      Released to   ☐ Camp Activities ☐ Home ☐ Other _____ Date _____

☐ Doctor's Office: By whom? _____ Title _____

      Treatment given _____ Date _____

      Released to   ☐ Camp Activities ☐ Camp Health Service ☐ Home ☐ Other _____

☐ Hospital: By whom? _____ Title _____

      Was injured retained overnight in hospital?   ☐ Yes   ☐ No   If so, which? _____

      Where? _____ Date _____   ☐ Out-patient   ☐ In-patient

      Name of physician in attendance _____

      Date released from hospital _____

      Released to   ☐ Camp   ☐ Home   ☐ Other _____

Comments _____

_____

_____

Persons notified such as camp owner/sponsor, board of directors, etc.

Name	Position	Date
_____	_____	_____
_____	_____	_____
_____	_____	_____

Describe any contact made with/by the media regarding this situation _____

_____

Signed _____ Position _____ Date _____

Insurance Notification

                                                                                                          Date

1. ☐ Parent's Insurance   By ☐ Parent   ☐ Camp   _____

2. ☐ Camp Health Insurance   _____

3. ☐ Worker's Compensation   _____

4. ☐ Camp Liability Insurance   _____

Figure 11-3. Accident/Incident Report Form (cont.)

Checklist of Possible Indicators of Abuse   FM 15A

american CAMP association®

Name _____ Nickname _____

Address_____

City _____ State _____ Zip_____ Phone Number _____
                                                                    Area/Number

Parent/Guardian_____ Relationship_____

Parent/Guardian_____ Relationship_____

Observations

If more than one person utilizes this form, it is beneficial to use different marks.
The first person could use check marks (✓), the second pluses (+), etc.

Observer #1 _____ Date ____ / ____ / _____

Observer #2 _____ Date ____ / ____ / _____

Observer #3 _____ Date ____ / ____ / _____

NEGLECT

Indicate on the following diagram the areas in which physical injury is evident, using "X" to indicate the location of superficial injuries, "O" to indicate the location of deep injuries and "shaded areas" to indicate areas of apparent burn. Beside each injury or apparent burn, please note the color, size, pattern, texture, and degree of pain.

Behavioral Indicators

1. Is truant or tardy often or arrives early and stays late.
2. Begs or steals food.
3. Attempts suicide.
4. Uses or abuses alcohol and/or other drugs.
5. Is extremely dependent or detached.
6. Engages in delinquent behavior, such as prostitution or stealing.
7. Appears to be exhausted.
8. States frequent or continual absence of parent or guardian.

Physical Indicators

1. Frequently is dirty, unwashed, hungry, or inappropriately dressed.
2. Engages in dangerous activities (possibly because he/she generally is unsupervised).
3. Is tired and listless.
4. Has unattended physical problems.
5. May appear to be overworked and/or exploited.

Right   Left

Front   Back

Name

Date Observed

Cabin or Group

Year

Figure 11-4. Checklist of Possible Indicators of Abuse

SEXUAL ABUSE

Behavioral Indicators

☐ 1. Is reluctant to change clothes in front of others.
☐ 2. Is withdrawn.
☐ 3. Exhibits unusual sexual behavior and/or knowledge beyond that which is common for his/her developmental stage.
☐ 4. Has poor peer relationships.
☐ 5. Either avoids or seeks out adults.
☐ 6. Is pseudo-mature.
☐ 7. Is manipulative.
☐ 8. Is self-conscious.
☐ 9. Has problems with authority and rules.
☐ 10. Exhibits eating disorders.
☐ 11. Is self-mutilating.
☐ 12. Is obsessively clean.
☐ 13. Uses or abuses alcohol and/or other drugs.
☐ 14. Exhibits delinquent behavior, such as running away from home.
☐ 15. Exhibits extreme compliance or defiance.
☐ 16. Is fearful or anxious.
☐ 17. Exhibits suicidal gestures and/or attempts suicide.
☐ 18. Is promiscuous.
☐ 19. Engages in fantasy or infantile behavior.
☐ 20. Is unwilling to participate in sports activities.
☐ 21. Has school difficulties.

Physical Indicators

☐ 1. Has pain and/or itching in the genital area.
☐ 2. Has bruises or bleeding in the genital area.
☐ 3. Has venereal disease.
☐ 4. Has swollen private parts.
☐ 5. Has difficulty walking or sitting.
☐ 6. Has torn, bloody, and/or stained underclothing.
☐ 7. Experiences pain when urinating.
☐ 8. Is pregnant.
☐ 9. Has vaginal or penile discharge.
☐ 10. Wets the bed.

EMOTIONAL ABUSE

Behavioral Indicators

☐ 1. Is overly eager to please.
☐ 2. Seeks out adult contact.
☐ 3. Views abuse as being warranted.
☐ 4. Exhibits changes in behavior.
☐ 5. Is excessively anxious.
☐ 6. Is depressed.
☐ 7. Is unwilling to discuss problems.
☐ 8. Exhibits aggressive or bizarre behavior.
☐ 9. Is withdrawn.
☐ 10. Is apathetic.
☐ 11. Is passive.
☐ 12. Has unprovoked fits of yelling or screaming.
☐ 13. Exhibits inconsistent behaviors.
☐ 14. Feels responsible for the abuser.
☐ 15. Runs away from home.
☐ 16. Attempts suicide.
☐ 17. Has low self-esteem.
☐ 18. Exhibits a gradual impairment of health and/or personality.
☐ 19. Has difficulty sustaining relationships.
☐ 20. Has unrealistic goal setting.
☐ 21. Is impatient.
☐ 22. Is unable to communicate or express his/her feelings, needs, or desires.
☐ 23. Sabotages his/her chances of success.
☐ 24. Lacks self-confidence.
☐ 25. Is self-deprecating and has a negative self-image.

Physical Indicators

☐ 1. Has a sleep disorder (nightmares or restlessness).
☐ 2. Wets the bed.
☐ 3. Exhibits developmental lags (stunting of his/her physical, emotional, and/or mental growth).
☐ 4. Is hyperactive.
☐ 5. Exhibits eating disorders.

PHYSICAL ABUSE

Behavioral Indicators

☐ 1. Is wary of adults.
☐ 2. Is either extremely aggressive or withdrawn.
☐ 3. Is dependent and indiscriminate in his/her attachments.
☐ 4. Is uncomfortable when other children cry.
☐ 5. Generally controls his/her own crying.
☐ 6. Exhibits a drastic behavior change when not with parents or caregiver.
☐ 7. Is manipulative.
☐ 8. Has poor self-concept.
☐ 9. Exhibits delinquent behavior, such as running away from home.
☐ 10. Uses or abuses alcohol and/or other drugs.
☐ 11. Is self-mutilating.
☐ 12. Is frightened of parents or going home.
☐ 13. Is overprotective of or responsible for parents.
☐ 14. Exhibits suicidal gestures and/or attempts suicide.
☐ 15. Has behavior problems at school.

Physical Indicators

☐ 1. Has unexplained* bruises or welts, often clustered or in a pattern.
☐ 2. Has unexplained* and/or unusual burns (cigarettes, doughnut-shaped, immersion-lines, object-patterned).
☐ 3. Has unexplained* bite marks.
☐ 4. Has unexplained* fractures or dislocations.
☐ 5. Has unexplained* abrasions and lacerations.
☐ 6. Wets the bed.

(*Or explanation is inconsistent or improbable.)

This form may be used by camp staff to record observations of possible indicators of abuse. Staff should be trained to recognize indicators of abuse, to understand their reporting responsibilities, and to know when to get professionals involved. Find additional resources about child abuse awareness and staff training from the ACA Bookstore at www.ACABookstore.org or from the ACA Knowledge Center at www.ACAcamps.org/child-health-safety/child-abuse.

Figure 11-4. Checklist of Possible Indicators of Abuse (cont.)

The American Camp Association is currently the only national organization with an independent accreditation program for all types of camps. Its long history of developing standards in the field as well as its research and constant updating of those standards has led courts and government bodies to hold these standards as industry standards. In other words, actions of a camp involved in a lawsuit will be measured against American Camp Association standards, whether or not the camp is affiliated with or accredited by the association. Since ACA accreditation does not require a camp to meet every standard for accreditation, an ACA-accredited camp may find that in court, questions are asked about standards the camp chose not to meet. Therefore, a camp needs to be prepared to provide rationale and documentation for standards not met, as well as carefully considering where the camp needs to exceed ACA standards. The ACA is careful to point out that the standards are minimum standards. Some activities and situations require having more stringent standards and practices in place.

Over 90 percent of the ACA standards relate to risk management, and the paperwork related to those standards would meet many of the suggestions provided in this chapter. Local offices of the American Camp Association offer annual courses that explain the standards and the type of preparation that is needed for an accreditation visit. These courses are invaluable for directors, even if accreditation is not sought.

The single-most effective step a camp can take in risk-management planning is to become accredited by the American Camp Association, and to annually update all of the written procedures and policies. Of course, that step is effective only if the camp continues to comply with the standards after the accreditation visit.

Verification

This book relies upon various sources to provide the best information in regard to the legal, insurance, financial and other risk issues. However, in all legal, financial and insurance matters, the director should consult with professionals familiar with the location of their camp operation. In some cases, locations in multiple states will complicate the legal and insurance aspects of risk management.

┌───┐

Checkpoints

- Which state and local regulations apply to the camp?
- Prepare a list of the risks that exist in the camp, starring those that appear to happen most frequently and those that carry the highest potential risk.
- Identify on that list which risks can be avoided or transferred to others.
- Develop risk-reduction steps for all risks to be kept or transferred.
- Review which insurance of the camp and identify areas that need updating.
- Is the camp covered with fire and casualty, liability, workers' compensation, vehicle insurance?
- Has the camp been accredited, or have camp officials investigated what is involved in accreditation?
- What is the camp's information-collection and record-retention plan?
- Is there an annual review of accidents, incidents and injuries completed with a revision of related procedures?

└───┘

Related Standards

American Camp Association's Accreditation Standards for Camp Programs and Services: Nearly all of the standards apply to risk management. However, standards OM.1 through OM.15 are not referenced in other chapters and should be considered with the other standards. In fact, the preparation of *American Camp Association's Accreditation Process Guide* is probably the easiest way to develop risk-management planning materials and to keep in one place most of the records necessary for such documentation.

Additional Professional Practices: Items in each of these sections should be considered in the broader risk-management picture.

Endnotes

1. Betty van der Smissen. 1993. Foreword. *Management of Risks and Emergencies: A Workbook for Program Administrators*. Kansas City, MO: Camp Fire Boys and Girls, Inc. p. v.

2. Ed Schirick. 2000. "Risk Analysis and Evaluations." *Camping Magazine*. Vol. 73, No. 4, July/August, pp.12–13.

3. Andrew Ackerman. 2004. "Three Years of Coping with COPPA." *The CampLine*. Vol. XII, No. 3, Winter. p. 7ff.

4. Edward A. Schirick. 2006. "Cyberspace: Risks in a Networked World." *Camping Magazine*. Vol. 79, No. 4, July/August, p. 13.

5. Charles R. Gregg and Catherine Hansen-Stamp. 2007. "Releases Revisited." *The CampLine*. Vol. XVI, No. 1, Spring, p. 6ff.

6. Janna S. Rankin. 1986. "Waivers." *Camping Magazine*. Vol. 58, No. 3, January, p. 24.

7. Marge Scanlin and Richard Smikle. 1994. "Reviewed Your Permission Form Lately?" *The CampLine*. Vol. 5, No. 2, October, pp. 3–4.

8. Ed Schirick. 1997. "Risk Management: Insuring Your Camp's Buildings and Contents." *Camping Magazine*. Vol. 70, No. 3, May/June, p. 9. and e-mail of October 2011.

9. Chris Rollins. 1998. "Train Away Risk." *Camping Magazine*. Vol. 71, No. 5, September/October, p. 39.

10. "Crisis Response in a Troubled World." 2003. *The CampLine*. Vol. XII, No. 1, Spring 2003. Martinsville, IN: American Camp Association. p. 15.

11. Linda Ebner Erceg. 2003. "Emergency and Disaster Planning: Responding to Camp Needs Using Updated Disaster Planning Paradigms." *ACN Compass Point*, Vol. 13, No.1, March, p. 15.

12. Bari S. Dworken. 1998. "10 Commandments of Risk Management." *Camping Magazine*. Vol. 71, No. 5, September/October, p. 20.

13. Becca Cowan Johnson. 1992. *For Their Sake*. Martinsville, IN: American Camping Association. p. 68.

14. Ed Schirick. 1997. "Get It in Writing." *Camping Magazine*. Vol. 70, No. 4, July/August, p. 12.

HEALTH AND WELLNESS SERVICES

Concordia Language Villages (Bemidji, MN)

Chapter Twelve

An effective administration relieves program of all nonessential detail … . The tracks must be kept clear if program is to operate at its maximum degree of economy and effectiveness. Such matters as health, safety, and sanitation, although vitally important in program considerations are as much the concern of administration as feeding, housing, and transportation. In fact, it is hard to draw the line, when discussing responsibility, as to just what parts of the total camp life are administrative in contrast to those of program.[1]

—Gerald P. Burns

Though every operation in camp is part of the overall program, certain services tend to be seen in a more supportive role to the direct program operation. The importance of these services in complementing direct program activities, as well as their role in the risk-management plan, cannot be overemphasized.

Health Service

Following are three broad functions of a camp health service:

- *To manage resources for health care*: The purpose of this function is to maintain an effort to promote a healthier, safer camp community and to make policy decisions in the area of camp health. Tasks include defining the scope of health care which the camp will provide, writing job descriptions for health service staff and supervising that group, determining budget, deciding what parents are told about camp health services and how that is communicated, arranging out-of-camp health service, signing medical protocols, and defining the chain-of-command of health-service personnel. These elements comprise the function of camp health care administration, and it is most often fulfilled by the camp director in collaboration with the camp's supervising physician; however, in a very large camp or a camp serving a population with special medical needs, duties may be assigned to the physician-in-residence at the camp.

- *To provide care*: The purpose of this function is to meet the individual health care needs of staff and campers and to manage the health of the total camp community. Tasks include medication management; screening practices, assessment, care, and evaluation of illness or injury situations; surveillance of the camp community health concerns; collaboration with out-of-camp providers to support recovery of ill or injured individuals; collaboration with other camp staff to provide a safe and well camp experience; collaboration with camp administration in an effort to improve camp health practices; and communication with external medical and health resources. This function is often performed by the camp nurse or camp physician, as the camp health care provider.

- *To respond to emergencies*: The purpose of this function is to develop, implement, and evaluate the camp emergency-response system. Tasks include plans to be followed by camp staff for site emergencies and coordinating with external providers. These tasks are usually identified by the camp director and completed by a group of camp staff, including the health care personnel. Persons with training in CPR/AED (cardiopulmonary resuscitation and the use of an automated external defibrillator) and certifications in aquatics and wilderness medicine often are involved in this process.[2]

Personnel

All camps need to clearly identify two positions:

- *Health services administrator*: The person who develops the health care plan and coordinates all health services functions. This position is responsible for the first functional area of health services. The position might include overseeing health care but more often coordinates various health care providers.
- *Health care provider*: The person or persons with day-to-day responsibility to implement the health care plan.

In some camps, both positions may be assumed by one individual who reports to the camp director. Within these positions, various other health care personnel may be involved. Figure 12-1 provides a clearer picture of the variety of health care certifications that may come into play within the camp's health service.[3]

The term *supervising physician* is used to describe a physician who provides the medical oversight for the camp, both in terms of helping develop the health care plan and in terms of establishing the medical protocols to be followed. Such a person may or may not reside at or near the camp. If the supervising physician is not in residence at camp or in the nearby community, a camp physician who resides in the nearby community should be secured. The title *camp physician* is used to designate the physician who is in residence at the camp or is available by telephone in the nearby locale to treat an injury and/or illness, delegate some medical authority to a nurse via standing orders for an individual, and provide liaison with the external medical and health resources in the local community. It is critical that this person be comfortable with the camp's health care plan and protocols and has had communication with the camp's supervising physician. Of course, one person may serve in both of these capacities.

Careful attention to the early selection of a supervising physician and the camp health care administrator, along with the development of comprehensive health care policies and procedures, will save the camp director considerable time and worry later in the season. The director should be comfortable with the physician and/or registered nurse. This person's knowledge of camp and the age groups served goes a long way in making sure the camp's health services support the health needs of campers and/or staff. Although the camp director can seldom be an expert in today's health care world, this person should be very familiar with this particular part of camp life.

Camp Health Care Providers: A Comparison of Selected Characteristics

Note: Chart information is meant only as a guide; state regulations supersede chart information.

Title of Provider	Conditions That Impact Ability to Practice at Camp	Primary Skill Based on Educational Preparation	Ability to Diagnose and Prescribe Medication	Ability to Handle Emergencies	Skill With Individual and Community Health Needs	Equipment Needed to Function in Role
Physician (MD)	Must be licensed to practice in the state. Works autonomously in medical role.	Diagnosis and treatment of injury and illness.	Priority skill; ability to diagnosis and treat at camp may be limited by lack of access to lab and other supporting services.	Varies; depends on person's experience in camp's pre-hospital setting and camp's limited equipment.	Well-skilled in individual needs related to injury or illness. Ability in psychosocial and community health domains vary.	Varies. Access to lab, x-ray, and other routine items; strong physical assessment skill.
Physician's Assistant (PA)	Must be credentialed by state in which camp is located; check State regs for limits of practice.	Assists MD with diagnosis and treatment of selected injuries and illness.	Skill generally limited to common injuries and illness per directives of supervising MD.	Generally limited since training focuses on clinic setting, not EMS.	Works best with individual needs related to injury or illness. Varied ability in community health.	Varies: some access to lab and x-ray. Physical assessment skill varies with experience.
Registered Nurse (RN)	Must be licensed by the state in which the camp is located. Works autonomously in nursing role.	Diagnosis and treatment of people's responses to health issues, actual or potential.	Provides nursing diagnosis. Does not prescribe meds; gives meds per MD direction. May direct treatments.	Generally limited unless RN has pre-hospital, field experience.	Skilled in meeting individual needs including psycho-social. Community skills if educated at BSN level.	Equipment need is usually minimal and of a general nature. Physical assessment skill varies with experience and education.
Nurse Practitioner (NP) *Note: NPs Are Also RNs.*	Varies. Some states limit the scope of practice (e.g., no prescriptive ability). Check state regs. Also licensed as RN.	Diagnosis and treatment of both injuries and illnesses as well as people's responses to health issues; combines RN and PA abilities.	Varies based on experience, credential and State regulations (may have some prescriptive authority).	Generally limited unless NP has pre-hospital, field experience.	Skill in individual needs including psycho-social. Community skills vary based on practitioner's education.	Varies: some access to lab and x-ray. Physical assessment skill varies with experience.
Licensed Practical Nurse (LPN or LVN)	Must be licensed by state in which camp is located. Supervision required; state regs define by whom.	Assists with care of ill or injured under supervision of RN and/or MD (state defined).	Limited; gives medication under orders of MD or as delegated by supervising RN.	Very limited; works under direction of RN or MD.	Skill in individual needs but limited psycho-social skills. Not skilled in community health.	Equipment need is usually minimal and of a general nature. Minimal assessment skill.
Emergency Medical Technician (EMT) Also W-EMT	Varies by state.	Responds to emergency situations; this is their domain!	Recognizes emergency situations; does not prescribe or diagnose.	Emergency response is a primary skill. More training needed for wilderness setting.	Focused on individual needs related to crisis. Limited community health skill.	Uses equipment common to emergency work (e.g. ambulance supplies).
First Aider Also WFA	"Duty to act" by virtue of being camp employee.	Responds to life-threatening situations.	Recognizes life-threatening crises; does not prescribe.	Limited to scope of training and experience.	Individual needs related to life-support; no community skills.	"Makes do" with items in the area.

Figure 12-1. Health care providers comparison

Camps with boards or committees may have a health committee that includes a physician and/or nurse to help recommend such policies to the operating board or committee. It would be ideal if a camp could have a physician and a nurse to provide most of the care of the camp population, since both professions fulfill unique roles in the health care field. However, having both a physician and a nurse on staff is often impractical for the majority of camps, except where the camp has a population with special medical needs or is a larger, long-term camp. Subsequently, a registered nurse is typically placed in the role of camp health provider.

A registered nurse treats people's reactions to injury, illness, and life events, and provides medical care as directed by a physician's signed protocol. In many camps, the nurse is the principal camp health provider. A separate scope of practice has been developed for the camp nursing practice, and the camp director should become familiar with that scope.

In selecting a nurse, a careful examination of the nurse's experience and approach is critical if it is to be a good experience for both the camp and the nurse. A nurse who has spent an entire nursing career in a hospital or doctor's office may be reluctant to take any step in a camp health center without direct, immediate orders from a doctor. Experience in an emergency room, as a school nurse, or in pediatrics is more likely to provide the experience comparable to the camp health situation. The nurse also needs direct experience in first aid, because many of the minor ailments of camp life require that sort of attention rather than diagnosis or long-term treatment.

The role of the nurse in health education with both the camp staff and campers is not to be overlooked. Kris Miller Lishner points out:

> *The camp nurse is a health education resource person, collaborator, and consultant for the staff … Everyone in camp is a health educator and has some responsibility for health teaching. Activity directors, kitchen managers, and administrative staff engage in health education when they point out safe ways to do activities, perform jobs and maintain environmental health and safety. In their daily routines with campers, counselors are their primary health teachers.*[4]

Some camps use several physicians and nurses who are camper parents or former campers or staff to rotate in for a couple of weeks each over the summer. Where such a turnover of personnel occurs, the health care administrator needs to establish a system to ensure consistency in day-to-day operation and practices.

American Camp Association standards recommend that, in a day camp, if a physician or registered nurse is not available, the camp should have a previous written arrangement with a physician or registered nurse to provide consultation and daily health care support. In resident camps where such personnel are not available, it is acceptable to make similar arrangements with a nurse or physician who comes to the camp site daily to consult. Of course, in camps that primarily serve persons with special medical needs, it is crucial to have a resident physician or registered nurse on site. As noted previously, the Health and Wellness (HW) standards of the American Camp Association are minimum standards and each camp needs to assess its own needs based upon program, location, and persons served. Those needs may be different from the camp down the road.

In addition to these requirements, it is essential to have individuals in camp at all times who have training in first aid and CPR/AED. ACA acknowledges variations in the degree of training needed by the health care provider, depending on the proximity of the camp to an emergency medical system. If professional medical help is 30 minutes or less away, certifications in first aid and CPR/AED are minimum qualifications. Where the time for access is more than 30 minutes, at minimum, certification from a nationally recognized provider of training in wilderness first aid plus CPR/AED is required. In all cases, previous arrangements with health care personnel and facilities away from the camp site should be made in writing.

Health Care Planning

The camp administrator holds primary responsibility for health care planning; however, planning should be done with input from key people such as the camp's supervising physician, the camp's lead health care professional, and the camp's insurance (liability) carrier. With the input from these persons, the camp administrator should develop a comprehensive camp health plan, which defines the scope of health care the camp will provide, the various positions required, written job descriptions for health-service positions, a supervision plan for staff and campers, what parents are told about camp health services and how that is communicated, the external camp health services required, and signed medical protocols.

In developing a camp health plan, a director should not only consult with the camp's physician and principal health care provider, but also examine related literature. A review of the standards of the American Camp Association related to health care is critical. As well, a review the Standards of Camp Nursing Practice provides more detailed information, especially from the suggested practices relative to the principal health care provider.[5]

Policies

A set of written policies should address the following points:
- What is the scope and limits of health care, including emergency care, to be provided at the camp site as opposed to at external health facilities?
- What are the qualifications, authority, and responsibilities of the health care administrator, providers, assistants, and other camp staff to provide health and emergency care?
- With what external health-support resources does the camp need relationships (e.g., emergency room, hospital, dentist, mental health, pharmacy, crisis team, clinic/lab)?

- What are the health care policies and procedures to be followed during the camp's operation?
- What determines the use of external health care resources, including a clear understanding about hospitalization and emergency provisions?
- What treatment procedures are allowed under the scope of practice of the designated health care provider(s) for dealing with reasonably anticipated illnesses and injuries?
- Is a physical examination to be a requirement of the camp, and if so, what is the maximum time acceptable between physical examinations by licensed medical personnel and arrival at camp for staff and campers?
- What is the maximum time between submission of a health history and arrival of the person at camp?
- Is a system in place for evaluating the camp's ability to meet a participant's special medical needs prior to enrollment?
- What is the communication plan for parents about the camp's health service and treatments, and the line of responsibility and timing for that communication?
- What is the status of the privacy of health information and records as discussed in Chapter 11?
- What health and lifesaving equipment will be required and where will these be located?

Determining the need for a physical exam or recommendation for participation in a camp's program by a licensed physician should be based upon the camp's program, length of sessions, and any state regulations germane to this topic. The camp's program may have activities that require significant physical exertion or extended trips out of camp in areas at a distance from emergency services. Camp sessions may extend to three weeks or longer. The final determination should be made by the director or by the director and board after consultation with medical and legal personnel.

If it is determined a recommendation or examination form be required, it should indicate an examination to have been performed no more than six months (ACA standards) prior to their arrival at camp, signed by a licensed medical provider, specifying date of exam, any current medications, and treatments or medical conditions requiring restrictions on participation. A sample health care recommendations form is shown in Figure 12-2, and a sample health examination form is shown in Figure 12-3.

A health history form with names, e-mail addresses, phone numbers, and addresses of persons to be contacted in case of a medical emergency plus a detailed health history of the individual is an essential for any camp. A sample health history form is shown in Figure 12-4. Less ordinary questions may be helpful, depending on the camp's clientele, such as whether the participant has traveled outside the country recently, and if so, where or if the participant has piercings or tattoos. In other words, the camp director should review the standard health history form to see if additional information may be helpful in light of the camp's clientele, program, or location.

CAMPER HEALTH-CARE RECOMMENDATIONS by LICENSED MEDICAL PERSONNEL FORM 2

Developed and reviewed by: *American Camp Association, American Academy of Pediatrics Council on School Health, & Association of Camp Nurses*

Mail this form to the address below by _____ (date)

To Parent(s)/Guardian(s): **Complete this section** and give **this form (FORM 2)** and **a copy of your** completed CAMPER HEALTH HISTORY FORM (FORM 1) to your child's health-care provider for review.

Dates will attend camp: from _____ to _____
Month/Day/Year   Month/Day/Year

Camper Name: _____
First   Middle   Last

☐ Male   ☐ Female   Birth Date _____   Age on arrival at camp _____
Month/Day/Year

Camper home address: _____

_____
City   State   Zip Code

Custodial parent(s)/guardian(s) phone: (_____)_____ (_____)_____

Parent(s)/guardian(s) stop here. Rest of form to be completed by medical personnel.

The following non-prescription medications are commonly stocked in camp Health Centers and are used on an <u>as needed basis</u> to manage illness and injury. ***Medical personnel: Cross out those items the camper should <u>not</u> be given.***

Acetaminophen (Tylenol)
Ibuprofen (Advil, Motrin)
Phenylephrine (Sudafed PE)
Pseudoephedrine (Sudafed)
Chlorpheneramine maleate
Guaifenesin
Dextromethorphan
Diphenhydramine (Benadryl)
Generic cough drops
Chloraseptic (Sore throat spray)
Lice shampoo or scabies cream (Nix or Elimite)
Calamine lotion
Bismuth subsalicylate (Pepto-Bismol)
Laxatives for constipation (Ex-Lax)
Hydrocortisone 1% cream
Topical antibiotic cream
Calamine lotion
Aloe

Medical Personnel: Please review the CAMPER HEALTH HISTORY FORM (FORM 1) and complete all remaining sections of this form (FORM 2). Attach additional information if needed.

<u>Physical exam done today:</u> ☐ Yes ☐ No **(If "No," date of last physical:_____)**
Month/Day/Year
ACA accreditation standards specify physical exam within last 24 months.

Weight: _____ lbs Height: _____ft_____in Blood Pressure_____/_____

<u>Allergies:</u> ☐ No Known Allergies

☐ To foods *(list):*

☐ To medications: *(list):*

☐ To the environment **(insect stings, hay f... etc.– l...**

☐ Other allergies: *(list):*

Describe previous reactions:

<u>Diet, Nutrition:</u> ☐ Eats a regular diet. ☐ Has a medical... scribe... ... or ...tary restrictions: *(describe below)*

<u>The camper is undergoing treatment at thi...</u> ...for the ...owing conditions: *(describe below)* ☐ None.

<u>Medication:</u> ☐ No daily medications. ☐ Will take the following prescribed medication(s) while at camp: *(name, dose, frequency—describe below)*

<u>Other treatments/therapies to be continued at camp:</u> *(describe below)* ☐ None needed.

Do you feel that the camper will require limitations or restrictions to activity while at camp? ☐ No ☐ Yes

*If you answered "Yes" to the question above, what do you recommend? **(describe below—attach additional information if needed)***

"I have reviewed the CAMPER HEALTH HISTORY FORM (FORM 1), and have discussed the camp program with the camper's parent(s)/guardian(s). It is my opinion that the camper is physically and emotionally fit to participate in an active camp program (except as noted above.)

Name of licensed provider (please print): _____ Signature: _____ Title: _____

Office Address _____
Street   City   State   Zip Code

Telephone: (_____)_____ Date:_____

Copyright 2008 by American Camping Association, Inc.   Rev. 2/07 LEE/EAW

(right margin, vertical text) Camper Name: First ____ Middle ____ Last ____ (For Camp Use) Cabin or Group ____ (For Camp Use) Session Code(s): ____

Figure 12-2. ACA Camper Health Care Recommendations by Licensed Medical Personnel Form 2

For Office Use

Year — *Cabin or Group* — *Name*

Health History and Examination Form for Children, Youth and Adults Attending Camps   FM 08N

Suggested for resident camp use.

Developed and approved by American Camp Association with the American Academy of Pediatrics

Dates of Camp Attendance_____

Mail this form to the address below by _____ (date)

The information on this form is not part of the camper or staff acceptance process, but is gathered to assist us in identifying appropriate care. Health history (first three pages) must be filled out by parents/guardians of minors or by adults themselves. Update required annually. Health exam (back page) must be completed by approved licensed medical personnel at least every two years.

Name _____ Birth date_____ Age at camp_____
       Last   First   Middle

Home address _____
                Street Address   City   State   Zip

Social security number of participant_____ Gender: ☐ Male ☐ Female

Custodial parent/guardian _____ Phone_____

Home address _____
(if different from above)   Street Address   City   State   Zip

Business address_____ Phone_____
                   Street Address   City   State   Zip

Second parent or guardian or emergency contact_____

Address _____ Phone_____
          Street Address   City   State   Zip

Business address_____ Phone_____
                  Street Address   City   State   Zip

If not available in an emergency, notify _____

Relationship _____ Phone_____

Address _____
          Street Address   City   State   Zip

Insurance Information

Is the participant covered by family medical/hospital insurance? ☐ Yes ☐ No

If so, indicate carrier or plan name_____ Group #_____

▶ Photocopy of front and back of health insurance card must be attached to this form.

Important — These boxes must be complete for attendance*

This health history is correct and complete as far as I know. The person herein named has permission to engage in all camp activities except as noted.

I hereby give permission to the camp to provide, seek, and consent to routine health care, administration of prescribed medications, and emergency treatment for me/my child, as may be necessary, including, but not limited to x-rays, routine tests and treatment, and/or hospitalization. I also give permission for the camp to arrange related transportation. I agree to the release of any records necessary for treatment, referral, billing, or insurance purposes.

It is my intention that the camp be treated as acting *in loco parentis* if the person herein named is a minor. Further, it is my intention that the appropriate representatives of the camp be treated as "personal

representatives" for the purposes of disclosing protected health information pursuant to the privacy regulations promulgated pursuant to the Health Insurance Portability and Accountability Act of 1996. I hereby agree (pursuant to 45 CFR § 164.510(b)) to the disclosure to camp representatives of the protected health information of the person herein described, as necessary: (i) to provide relevant information to the camp representatives related to the person's ability to participate in camp activities; and (ii) in the case of minors, to provide relevant information to the camp representatives to keep me informed of my child's health status.

In the event I cannot be reached in an emergency, I hereby give permission to the physician selected by the camp to secure and administer treatment, including hospitalization, for the person named above. This completed form may be photocopied for trips out of camp.

Signature of parent or guardian or adult camper/staffer _____

Printed Name _____ Date_____

I also understand and agree to abide by any restrictions placed on my participation in camp activities.

Signature of minor or adult camper/staffer_____ Date_____

*If for religious reasons you cannot sign this, contact the camp for a legal waiver which must be signed for attendance.

american CAMP association™   © 1983 by American Camping Association, Inc. Revised 1990, 1992, 1994, 1995, 1996, 1998, 1999, 2000, 2001, 2004.

Figure 12-3. ACA Health Examination Form for Children, Youth, and Adults Attending Camps

Health History

The following information must be filled in by the parent/ guardian, or adult camper or staff member. The intent of this information is to provide camp health care personnel the background to provide appropriate care. Keep a copy of the completed form for your records.

Any changes to this form should be provided to camp health personnel upon participant's arrival in camp. Provide complete information so that the camp can be aware of your needs.

ALLERGIES List all known.   Describe reaction and management of the reaction.

Medication allergies (list)

_____   _____
_____   _____
_____   _____
_____   _____

Food allergies (list)

_____   _____
_____   _____
_____   _____

Other allergies (list) — include insect stings, hay fever, asthma, animal dander, etc.

_____   _____
_____   _____
_____   _____

MEDICATIONS BEING TAKEN

Please list ALL medications (including over-the-counter or nonprescription drugs) taken routinely. Bring enough medication to last the entire time at camp. Keep it in the original packaging/bottle that identifies the prescribing physician (if a prescription drug), the name of the medication, the dosage, and the frequency of administration.

☐ This person takes NO medications on a routine basis.

☐ This person takes medications as follows:

Med #1_____ Dosage_____ Specific times taken each day_____

Reason for taking_____

Med #2_____ Dosage_____ Specific times taken each day_____

Reason for taking_____

Med #3_____ Dosage_____ Specific times taken each day_____

Reason for taking_____

Attach additional pages for more medications.
Identify any medications taken during the school year that participant does/may not take during the summer:_____
_____

RESTRICTIONS

The following restrictions apply to this individual.

Dietary

☐ Does not eat red meat   ☐ Does not eat pork   ☐ Does not eat eggs
☐ Does not eat poultry   ☐ Does not eat seafood   ☐ Does not eat dairy products
☐ Other (describe) _____

Explain any restrictions to activity (e.g., what cannot be done, what adaptations or limitations are necessary)

_____
_____
_____

Figure 12-3. ACA Health Examination Form for Children, Youth, and Adults Attending Camps (cont.)

General Questions (Explain "yes" answers below.)

Has/does the participant: Yes No   Yes No

1. Had any recent injury, illness or infectious
   disease? .... ☐   ☐   17. Ever had problems with joints
2. Have a chronic or recurring illness/condition? .... ☐   ☐   (e.g., knees, ankles)? .... ☐   ☐
3. Ever been hospitalized? .... ☐   ☐   18. Have an orthodontic appliance being
4. Ever had surgery? .... ☐   ☐   brought to camp? .... ☐   ☐
5. Have frequent headaches? .... ☐   ☐   19. Have any skin problems (e.g., itching,
6. Ever had a head injury? .... ☐   ☐   rash, acne)? .... ☐   ☐
7. Ever been knocked unconscious? .... ☐   ☐   20. Have diabetes? .... ☐   ☐
8. Wear glasses, contacts or protective   21. Have asthma? .... ☐   ☐
   eye wear? .... ☐   ☐   22. Had mononucleosis in the past 12 months? ..... ☐   ☐
9. Ever had frequent ear infections? .... ☐   ☐   23. Had problems with diarrhea/constipation? .... ☐   ☐
10. Ever passed out during or after exercise? .... ☐   ☐   24. Have problems with sleepwalking? .... ☐   ☐
11. Ever been dizzy during or after exercise? .... ☐   ☐   25. If female, have an abnormal menstrual
12. Ever had seizures? .... ☐   ☐   history? .... ☐   ☐
13. Ever had chest pain during or after exercise? .... ☐   ☐   26. Have a history of bed-wetting? .... ☐   ☐
14. Ever had high blood pressure? .... ☐   ☐   27. Ever had an eating disorder? .... ☐   ☐
15. Ever been diagnosed with a heart murmur? .... ☐   ☐   28. Ever had emotional difficulties for which professional
16. Ever had back problems? .... ☐   ☐   help was sought? .... ☐   ☐

Please explain any "yes" answers, noting the number of the questions.

_____

_____

_____

_____

_____

Which of the following   Please give all dates of immunization for:
has the participant had?   Vaccine: Dates: Mo/Yr   Mo/Yr   Mo/Yr   Mo/Yr   Mo/Yr   Mo/Yr

☐ Measles   DTP   _____   _____   _____   _____   _____   _____
☐ Chicken pox   TD (tetanus/diphtheria) _____   _____   _____   _____   _____
☐ German measles   Tetanus   _____   _____   _____   _____   _____
☐ Mumps   Polio   _____   _____   _____   _____   _____
☐ Hepatitis A   MMR   _____   _____
☐ Hepatitis B   or Measles   _____   _____
☐ Hepatitis C   or Mumps   _____   _____
                                      or Rubella   _____   _____
TB Mantoux Test   Haemophilus influenza B _____   _____   _____   _____
Date of last test _____   Hepatitis B   _____   _____   _____
Result: ☐ Positive ☐ Negative   Varicella (chicken pox) _____   _____

**Use this space to provide any additional information about the participant's behavior
and physical, emotional, or mental health about which the camp should be aware.**

_____

_____

_____

_____

_____

_____

Name of family physician_____ Phone_____

Address _____

Name of family dentist/orthodontist_____ Phone_____

Address _____

Figure 12-3. ACA Health Examination Form for Children, Youth, and Adults Attending Camps (cont.)

Health Care Recommendations by Licensed Medical Personnel

I examined this individual on _____. (ACA-accreditation requirements specify exams within 24 months of camp attendance. Individual camps may require annual exams. A new exam is not necessarily required for camp attendance.)

BP _____ Weight _____ Height _____

In my opinion, the above applicant ☐ is ☐ is not able to participate in an active camp program.

The applicant is under the care of a physician for the following conditions

_____

_____

_____

_____

Recommendations and Restrictions at Camp

Treatment to be continued at camp _____

_____

Medications to be administered at camp (name, dosage, frequency)_____

_____

Any medically-prescribed meal plan or dietary restrictions _____

_____

Known allergies_____

_____

Description of any limitation or restriction on camp activities _____

_____

Additional information for health care staff at the camp_____

_____

| Signature of Licensed Medical Personnel_____ |
| Printed_____ Title_____ |
| Address _____ |
| Phone _____ Date_____ |

For camp use only

| Screening Record |
| Date screened_____ Time_____ am / pm |
| Meds received_____ |
| _____ |
| Updates/additions to health history noted ☐ Yes ☐ No ☐ None required |
| Current health needs identified _____ |
| _____ |
| Observational notes_____ |
| _____ |
| Screened by _____ |

Figure 12-3. ACA Health Examination Form for Children, Youth, and Adults Attending Camps (cont.)

CAMPER HEALTH HISTORY FORM 1

Developed and reviewed by: *American Camp Association, American Academy of Pediatrics Council on School Health, & Association of Camp Nurses*

Mail this form to the address below by _____ (date)

Dates will attend camp: from _____ to _____
Month/Day/Year   Month/Day/Year

Camper Name: _____
First   Middle   Last

☐ Male   ☐ Female   Birth Date _____   Age on arrival at camp: _____
Month/Day/Year

To Parent(s)/Guardian(s): Please follow the instructions below. Attach additional information if needed.

1) Complete *pages 1, 2 and 3* of this form (*FORM 1*) and *make a copy.*
2) Send the *original, signed FORM 1* to camp by the requested date.
3) Complete the top of FORM 2 (CAMPER HEALTH-CARE RECOMMENDATIONS) and provide the *copy of FORM 1* with *FORM 2* to your *child's health-care provider* for review and completion.
4) After it has been *completed and signed* by your child's health-care provider, return *FORM 2* to camp by the requested date.

Camper Home Address: _____
Street Address   City   State   Zip Code

Parent/guardian with legal custody to be contacted in case of illness or injury:

Name: _____ Relationship to Camper: _____ Preferred Phones: (____) _____ (____) _____

Email: _____

Home Address: _____
(If different from above)   Street Address   City   State   Zip Code

Second parent/guardian or other emergency contact:

Name: _____ Relationship to Camper: _____ Preferred Phones: (____) ____ _____ (____) _____

Email: _____

Additional contact in event parent(s)/guardian(s) can not be reached:

Name(s): _____ Relationship to Camper: _____ Preferred Ph___ ___ ___ (____) _____

Allergies: ☐ No known allergies.   ☐ This camper is allergic to: ☐ Food ☐ Medicine ☐ environment (insect stings, hay fever, etc.) ☐ Other
(Please describe below what the camper is allergic to and the reaction seen.)

Diet, Nutrition: ☐ This camper eats a regular diet. ☐ This camper eats a regular vegetarian diet.
☐ This camper has special *(Please describe below.)*

Restrictions: ☐ I have reviewed the program and activities of the camp and feel the camper can participate without restrictions.
☐ I have reviewed the program and activities of the camp and feel the camper can participate with the following restrictions or adaptations. *(Please describe below.)*

Medical Insurance Information:

This camper is covered by family medical/hospital insurance ☐ Yes ☐ No

Include a copy of your insurance card if appropriate; copy both sides of the card so information is readable.

Insurance Company_____   Policy Number_____

Subscriber_____   Insurance Company Phone Number (____) _____

Parent/Guardian Authorization for Health Care:

This health history is correct and accurately reflects the health status of the camper to whom it pertains. The person described has permission to participate in all camp activities except as noted by me and/or an examining physician. I give permission to the physician selected by the camp to order x-rays, routine tests, and treatment related to the health of my child for both routine health care and in emergency situations. If I cannot be reached in an emergency, I give my permission to the physician to hospitalize, secure proper treatment for, and order injection, anesthesia, or surgery for this child. I understand the information on this form will be shared on a "need to know" basis with camp staff. I give permission to photocopy this form. In addition, the camp has permission to obtain a copy of my child's health record from providers who treat my child and these providers may talk with the program's staff about my child's health status.

Signature of Custodial
Parent/Guardian _____ Date: _____ Relationship to Camper: _____

If for religious or other reasons you cannot sign this, contact the camp for a legal waiver which must be signed for attendance.   Page 1/4

Camper Name / First / Middle / Last / (For Camp Use) Cabin or Group / (For Camp Use) Session Code(s)

Figure 12-4. ACA Camper Health History Form 1

CAMPER HEALTH HISTORY FORM 1

Developed and reviewed by: *American Camp Association, American Academy of Pediatrics Council on School Health, & Association of Camp Nurses*

Camper Name: _____
First   Middle   Last

Birth Date: _____
Month/Day/Year

Immunization History: Provide the month and year for each immunization. Starred (★) immunizations must be current. Copies of immunization forms from health-care providers or state or local government are acceptable; please attach to this form.

Immunization	Dose 1 Month/Year	Dose 2 Month/Year	Dose 3 Month/Year	Dose 4 Month/Year	Dose 5 Month/Year	Most Recent Dose Month/Year
Diptheria, tetanus, pertussis ★ (DTaP) or (TdaP)						
Tetanus booster ★ (dT) or (TdaP)						
Mumps, measles, rubella ★ (MMR)						
Polio ★ (IPV)						
Haemophilus influenzae type B (HIB)						
Pneumococcal (PCV)						
Hepatitis B						
Hepatitis A						
Varicella (chicken pox) ☐ Had chicken pox Date:						
Meningococcal meningitis (MCV4)						

Tuberculosis (TB) test	Date:	☐ Negative	Positive

If your camper has not been fully immunized, please sign the following statement. I understand and accept the risks to my child from not being fully immunized.

Signature of Custodial Parent/Guardian: _____ Date: _____ Relationship to Camper: _____

Medication: ☐ This camper will not take any daily medication while attending camp.

☐ This camper will take the following daily medication(s) while at camp:

"Medication" is any substance a person takes to maintain and/or improve their health. This includes vitamins & natural remedies. *Please review camp instructions about required packaging/containers. Many states require original pharmacy containers with labels which show the camper's name and how the medication should be given. Provide enough of each medication to last the entire time the camper will be at camp.*

Name of medication	Date started	Reason for taking it	When it is given	Amount or dose given	How it is given
			☐Breakfast ☐Lunch ☐Dinner ☐Bedtime ☐Other time:_____		
			☐Breakfast ☐Lunch ☐Dinner ☐Bedtime ☐Other time:_____		
			☐Breakfast ☐Lunch ☐Dinner ☐Bedtime ☐Other time:_____		

The following non-prescription medications may be stocked in the camp Health Center and are used on an <u>as needed basis</u> to manage illness and injury. *Cross out those the camper should <u>not</u> be given.*

Acetaminophen (Tylenol)
Phenylephrine decongestant (Sudafed PE)
Antihistamine/allergy medicine
Diphenhydramine antihistamine/allergy medicine (Benadryl)
Sore throat spray
Lice shampoo or cream (Nix or Elimite)
Calamine lotion
Laxatives for constipation (Ex-Lax)

Ibuprofen (Advil, Motrin)
Pseudoephedrine decongestant (Sudafed)
Guaifenesin cough syrup (Robitussin)
Dextromethorphan cough syrup (Robitussin DM)
Generic cough drops
Antibiotic cream
Aloe
Bismuth subsalicylate for diarrhea (Kaopectate, Pepto-Bismol)

Copyright 2008 by American Camping Association, Inc.   Page 2/4   Rev. 1/2007 LEE/EAW

Figure 12-4. ACA Camper Health History Form 1 (cont.)

CAMPER HEALTH HISTORY FORM 1
Developed and reviewed by: *American Camp Association, American Academy of Pediatrics Council on School Health, & Association of Camp Nurses*

Camper Name: _____
First   Middle   Last
Birth Date: _____
Month/Day/Year

General Health History: *Check "Yes" or "No" for each statement. Explain "Yes" answers below.*

Has/does the camper:

1. Ever been hospitalized? ☐ Yes ☐ No	11. Had fainting or dizziness? ☐ Yes ☐ No
2. Ever had surgery? ☐ Yes ☐ No	12. Passed out/had chest pain during exercise? ☐ Yes ☐ No
3. Have recurrent/chronic illnesses? ☐ Yes ☐ No	13. Had mononucleosis ("mono") during the past 12 months? ☐ Yes ☐ No
4. Had a recent infectious disease? ☐ Yes ☐ No	14. If female, have problems with periods/menstruation? ☐ Yes ☐ No
5. Had a recent injury? ☐ Yes ☐ No	15. Have problems with falling asleep/sleepwalking? ☐ Yes ☐ No
6. Had asthma/wheezing/shortness of breath? ☐ Yes ☐ No	16. Ever had back/joint problems? ☐ Yes ☐ No
7. Have diabetes? ☐ Yes ☐ No	17. Have a history of bedwetting? ☐ Yes ☐ No
8. Had seizures? ☐ Yes ☐ No	18. Have problems with diarrhea/constipation? ☐ Yes ☐ No
9. Had headaches? ☐ Yes ☐ No	19. Have any skin problems? ☐ Yes ☐ No
10. Wear glasses, contacts, or protective eyewear? ☐ Yes ☐ No	20. Traveled outside the country in the past 9 months? ☐ Yes ☐ No

Please explain "Yes" answers in the space below, noting the number of the questions. For travel outside the country, please name countries visited and dates of travel.

Mental, Emotional, and Social Health: *Check "Yes" or "No" for each statement.*

Has the camper:

1. Ever been treated for attention deficit disorder (ADD) or attention deficit hyperactivity disorder (AD/HD)? ☐ Yes ☐ No
2. Ever been treated for emotional or behavioral difficulties or an eating disorder? ☐ Yes ☐ No
3. During the past 12 months, seen a professional to address mental/emotional health concerns? ☐ Yes ☐ No
4. Had a significant life event that continues to affect the camper's life? ☐ Yes ☐ No
   (History of abuse, death of a loved one, family change, adoption, foster care, new sibling, survived a disaster, others)

Please explain "Yes" answers in the space below, noting the number of the questions. The camp may contact you for additional information.

Health-Care Providers:

Name of camper's primary doctor(s): _____ Phone: (_____) _____
Name of dentist(s): _____ Phone: (_____) _____
Name of orthodontist(s): _____ Phone: (_____) _____

What Have We Forgotten to Ask? *Please provide in the space below* any additional information about the camper's health that you think important or that may affect the camper's ability to fully participate in the camp program. *Attach additional information if needed.*

Parents/Guardians: STOP here. The rest of this is form is completed when the camper arrives at camp. Keep a copy for your records.

Figure 12-4. ACA Camper Health History Form 1 (cont.)

CAMPER HEALTH HISTORY FORM 1

Developed and reviewed by: *American Camp Association, American Academy of Pediatrics Council on School Health, & Association of Camp Nurses*

Camper Name: _____
             First   Middle   Last

Birth Date: _____
            Month/Day/Year

Individual Health Record (For Camp Use Only)

Initial Screening   Date/Time: _____   Initials: _____

☐ **Screening** has been conducted according to camp protocol and significant findings noted as follows:

A. Any signs/symptoms of illness or injury upon arrival?......................☐ No   ☐ Yes as noted below

B. History of exposure to communicable disease?................................☐ No   ☐ Yes as noted below

C. Additions or corrections to information on this health history?...........☐ No   ☐ Yes as noted below

D. Medication given to health-care staff?..   ☐ No   ☐ Yes as noted below

E. Any signs/symptoms of head lice?..☐ No   ☐ Yes as noted below

Provider notes: (date/time/initial all entries) _____

_____

_____

_____

_____

_____

_____

_____

_____

_____

_____

_____

_____

_____

_____

_____

_____

_____

_____

_____

_____

_____

_____

_____

_____

_____

_____

_____

Exit Note: Check one of the following:

☐ Left camp this day with no reported illness or injury symptoms.

☐ Left camp this day with the following problem/concern:

_____

_____

This person was told about the problem and instructed about follow-up as noted above: _____

Date/Time: _____ Initials: _____

Page 4/4   Rev. 1/2007 LEE/EAW

Figure 12-4. ACA Camper Health History Form 1 (cont.)

A health history is a current record of a person's past and present health status that is completed and signed by an adult camper or the custodial adult of a minor. "Current" means prepared specifically for the camp season. The required signature serves as evidence that the adult camper or the custodial adult has supplied complete and accurate health information related to the camper participation in specific activities. The ACA Standards (2012) has a separate health history standard for staff, where the required signature serves as evidence that the staff member has supplied complete and accurate health information related to the job description.

Similarly, a record of health screening done at camp within 24 hours of the arrival of campers is an essential part of health care. It should include:

- A check for observable evidence of illness, injury, or communicable disease or condition
- Verification and updating of health history information to identify any medication, changes in health status since the health exam, or special needs that may require further follow-up
- A review and collection of any medications to be dispensed during the camper's stay at camp

The person and method of this health check should be determined in the development of the health care policies. A sample health-screening record is shown in Figure 12-5.

Procedures

A set of written procedures should address the following matters and may comprise a health care manual to serve as a practice guide for the health care provider:

- Name, qualifications, and location on site of all camp health providers, including where first aid and CPR certified personnel are required to be present, and location of all AEDs and other lifesaving equipment
- Supplies and equipment, including a plan for maintaining an inventory of stock medications, supplies, and medical equipment; ordering additional supplies; and storing existing supplies (for example, in a locked cabinet or refrigerator for narcotics and prescription drugs)
- Identification of information to be collected in health histories of campers and staff, and timeline for reviewing the histories and method for sharing pertinent information affecting health or participation of individual campers with appropriate staff
- Method of health screening, in resident camps, of campers and staff upon arrival and return (if leaving on extended trips), including what records are kept. In day camps, what routine visual health check for observable evidence of illness, injury, or communicable disease is accomplished for all campers on the first day, and what the plan is for daily follow-up.
- Treatment procedures for routine health care emergencies in situations where health care personnel are not readily available (e.g., out-of-camp excursions, camping and canoe trips)

Language Villages Nursing

_____
date/time

SCREENING has been conducted according to Concordia Language Villages protocol and significant findings noted.

A. Any signs/symptoms of illness or injury upon arrival? .... ☐ No ☐ Yes as noted below

B. History of exposure to communicable disease? .... ☐ No ☐ Yes as noted below

C. Additions or corrections to information on this health history? .... ☐ No ☐ Yes as noted below

D. Medication given to healthcare staff? .... ☐ No ☐ Yes as noted below

E. Any signs/symptoms of head lice? .... ☐ No ☐ Yes as noted below

Screening done by_____

Name of Villager

EXIT NOTE – Check one of the following:

☐ Left Village this day with no reported illness or injury symptoms

☐ Left Village this day with the following problem/concern: _____

_____

Date: _____

Initial: _____

This person was told about the problem and instructed about follow-up as noted above: _____

1536_1/700/0110

Page 4 of 4

Figure 12-5. Sample health-screening record

- What information is to be sent with staff on out-of-camp excursions, and how it is protected from being seen by non-authorized personnel? (A list of campers with names, home addresses and phone numbers, birth dates, and emergency contact numbers for people responsible for minors, along with all medical treatment permission forms)
- How campers and staff who have special medical needs are to be assessed for service and the conditions under which any portion of that information may be shared with the appropriate staff members
- Management of stock medications kept by the camp, and how medications brought to camp by campers are collected, stored, and dispensed
- Emergency medical assistance may take the form of a written and practiced emergency action plan.
- How life-threatening medical emergencies are to be handled in situations where health care personnel are not readily available (e.g., out-of-camp excursions, camping and canoe trips) as well as when they are available.
- Methods of prevention of an emergence of communicable illness and how any outbreak of communicable illness would be handled
- Emergency transportation, permission for use of private cars for such purposes
- Procedures for monitoring health and sanitation—identification of general routines to be followed for monitoring health and sanitation throughout camp, specifying the roles of counselors, kitchen staff, and maintenance staff, and including:
  - ✓ Sanitary procedures to be followed in dealing with medical wastes and bodily fluids
  - ✓ A plan for storage, pick-up, and disposal of trash and garbage throughout the camp
  - ✓ Identification of person(s) to whom the health care provider expresses concerns about observations in area(s) outside his supervision
  - ✓ A plan for monitoring the health of staff who handle food and areas used for food preparation
- Recordkeeping. Type of records to be kept by the camp health care administrator and/or providers including:
  - ✓ Health examination forms or health care recommendation forms
  - ✓ Health historics
  - ✓ Health screening records
  - ✓ A day-to-day bound health log with numbered pages for recording in ink (which cannot be altered or removed) all treatments of campers and staff
  - ✓ Injury/incident reports
  - ✓ OSHA forms
  - ✓ Any health care documentation required by a state licensing agency, and/or the license held by the camp's health care provider, as well as any other supplementary records

✓ Review of previous years' injury/illness data for risk-reduction purposes (Linda Ebner Erceg suggests that the health care center in the average camp sees 10 to 15 percent of its population on any given day.[6] This figure may provide a measuring stick as the director reviews the previous year's record.)

- Who has access to health records, and what privacy protection is provided under the standards resulting from the Health Insurance Portability and Accountability Act of 1996?

- How will these records be secured and backed-up?

These health care policies and procedures and the health care provider's manual are a vital part of the camp's risk-management plan and should be maintained within it as well as being located at the health center. The supervision of these health care policies and procedures is the responsibility of the health care administrator, even though specific portions of it may be assigned by the camp director to non–health-care personnel (e.g., maintenance or kitchen staff).

In advance of staff training, those providing leadership to the camp's health services should have an in-depth discussion that reviews the camp's written health care plan that should include a review of the written camp health care plan that includes policies and procedures describing the scope of health services provided by the camp, and an update of such items as:

- Arrangements in writing with the hospital chosen by the physician, and with providers of other emergency services, such as dental and mental-health services

- Mealtime procedures for people admitted to the health center, including how to obtain meals from the kitchen, as well as arrangements for special menu requirements

- Laundering of health-center linens and removal of trash and medical waste

- Disposal of biohazardous materials, including sharps (These materials require a dedicated type of waste collection and labeling.)

- Emergency transportation with names of drivers, location of vehicle keys, and gas

- Regular hours for the health center, and how the health care provider(s) can be reached at night or when not in the health center

- Daily procedures for living-group counselors to follow in the supervision of camper health, including procedures for regular check-ins at the health center or area

- A plan for regular inspection of the entire camp (for example, who accompanies the health care provider on inspection of living quarters)

- A clear statement of insurance and billing procedures

This conference of the health administrator, the director, the health care provider, and the camp physician should also include a discussion of the medical protocols or treatment procedures under which the camp health provider will operate. *Medical protocols* are given by the physician so that an RN may carry out certain procedures for the camp population without further consultation, whereas *standing orders* are often provided in the treatment of an individual. Even if a camp does not employ an RN but uses an EMT or other certified personnel, the camp's medical protocols should include procedures and responsibilities in first aid, emergency medical care, routine health care by staff other than the health care provider, initial health screening, and professional therapy (if any).

These procedures should be discussed carefully, modified as needed, signed by the doctor at least every three years, and a copy kept by the camp health care administrator, camp health care providers, camp director, and the doctor. Using the camp's previous year's protocols as a sample may make it easier for the physician to review and suggest adjustments according to his viewpoint. In the current litigation climate, some physicians may be reluctant to sign protocols, especially if they are part of a larger practice. Where such resistance is encountered, it is wise for the camp director and camp health manager to develop written health care procedures based upon conversations with the physician, and then ask the physician to review and suggest corrections or additions.

Before staff training begins, it is wise for the camp director to have a conference with major supervisors on the camp staff to review the health care procedures and identify their role in the training and supervision process.

The camp director has an important role in orienting health care providers and providing the support that will make their time and work effective. Since a health care provider is often the only person in camp in that profession, opportunities should be sought to put the provider in touch with other camp health care providers by encouraging visits to other camps or workshops during the year. The Association of Camp Nurses has proven to be a rich resource for sharing experiences and knowledge among camp nurses across the country.

Louise Czupryna, a camp nurse, points out:

> *Camp directors can play a vital role in welcoming a nurse to camp, especially newcomers to the field, and giving them the support they need to become a part of the "camp team." They often need to be "helped along a bit." One of camp nurses' biggest complaints, especially new ones, is the lack of deliberate effort to help them feel a part of the camp operation. Without the interaction and assistance of fellow health professionals that they receive in a hospital or clinic, new camp nurses are apt to feel lonely and disconnected in the rustic camp environment.[7]*

A camp director, being in a people-oriented business, should understand the need for this personal attention to someone arriving into a setting to which they are unaccustomed. The director can develop a plan for orientation during the early weeks, using key staff, and helping integrate the nurse into the team.

Training Staff for Individual Health Care Roles

During the precamp training for all staff, the camp health administrator and/ or the camp health care provider should be given time to work with staff concerning their individual roles in the health care procedures. Everyone should be given a copy of emergency procedures and required to rehearse any drills. All staff should be given some training in basic first-aid techniques. Training should include identification of the dangers of bloodborne pathogens and hepatitis B, precautions that should be taken to avoid exposure, and steps to be taken should exposure occur. A clear delineation should be made between the types of medical situations general staff can care for and what should be referred to the health center.

Staff should be given the impression that the health center is not simply a place for the treatment of serious illness and injury, but a friendly, integrated part of camp life that ministers to many diverse needs in the camp community. Often, the health care provider will deal with homesickness and ailments growing out of stress or other emotional and psychological issues. The involvement of the health care personnel in the fun activities of camp, whether as an occasional helper at the waterfront, in the craft shop, or as a participant in skits or stunts at a campfire, can endear the person to the camp. With the proper attitude, health care personnel can become a listening ear for many of the problems of campers and staff that have little to do with medical treatment.

Living-group counselors need additional time with the health care provider to better understand their day-to-day role in the health care of the campers entrusted to their care. They should understand how they are to be informed of special health problems of individual campers in their group, when they are to bring campers to the health center, and what symptoms or problems to watch for in their daily living routines (e.g., during dressing, personal hygiene routines, eating, and sleeping). The importance of cabin cleanup, daily inspections, and their relationship to the health of campers and staff should be stressed.

Those daily inspections, the "walk around," along with regular visits to other parts of camp (e.g., the kitchen, maintenance shop, program activity areas, and staff living quarters), are a key part of health supervision. It is important that the health care provider not be considered a spy by other departments or counselors. However, the health care administrator should be alert to possible health hazards, and when a hazard is spotted should report it immediately to the department supervisor or to the director. Naturally, it is not wise for the health care provider or administrator to approach the counselor, kitchen helper, or individual staffer on the spot unless it is an emergency. Rather, the problem should be called to the attention of the person's immediate supervisor.

Staff should also be trained in prevention as well as symptom recognition and first aid or treatment for any health problems specific to the geographic location. This training is especially important when staff come from other areas of the country or the world. Topics to cover here might include local poisonous plants or other similar health hazards, such as Lyme disease. International staff should be given some orientation to the health standards of the USA, personal and group, since the standards and practice in their home country may differ.

If the camp health care provider is to perform the role of overall health, sanitation, and wellness supervision of the camp, careful interpretation of that role must be given to the staff during training. In addition, a clarification of the manner in which the health care provider deals with problems observed in areas outside of his direct supervision needs to be determined early on.

Staff training should also include information about disease transmittal and precautions to prevent transmission, including hand washing. As employers, camps are now mandated to provide training on disease transmission, including bloodborne pathogens, and on universal precautions to prevent their transmission. Specific mention should also be made of HIV/AIDS and hepatitis as bloodborne pathogens. In light of having a staff that is old enough to be sexually active, it would be a serious omission not to also discuss sexually transmitted diseases.

OSHA has a number of regulations regarding employee health and safety that should be a part of staff training. As Ed Schirick reports, certain OSHA regulations require:

> *… providing personal protective equipment [for employees]. In the pool area, for example, OSHA requires a respirator, rubber gloves, and eye protection in the filter room. An eye wash station is also needed when chlorine is handled by employees … In addition … employers are expected to examine workplace conditions to ensure they conform to applicable health and safety requirements.*[8]

Hazards are a key factor in OSHA regulations, which typically require that they be removed or guarded against. A written Hazard Communication Plan is required and includes:

- A list of the hazardous chemicals on the site
- Details on how the staff is trained in the use of such substances
- The requirements for labeling and storing containers of such substances
- Posting material-safety data sheets in appropriate locations

Employers are required to distribute to employees information on any hazardous substances in work areas. Robert Bush states, "The OSHA definition of a 'hazardous chemical' is *very* broad" and identifies examples such as: chemicals used in photography, pool cleaning, arts and crafts, industrial-strength cleaning materials, and the like. These substances come with material-safety data sheets (MSDS), which must be kept in a place accessible to employees.

In addition, a safety program should be developed with specific procedures to disable or to prevent inadvertent activation of machines or equipment. These lockout/tagout requirements are designed to prevent the removal of guards or safety devices. The director must be able to show that the plan has been reviewed annually and employees have been trained in the plan.[9]

Records

Documentation is a vital ingredient of good health care as well as for risk management. The following types of documentation are important:

- Signed permissions for routine health care, for administering prescribed medications, and for seeking or providing emergency medical treatment for all campers and staff who are minors
- Health examination and/or health care recommendation forms
- Health histories
- Records of health screening
- A health center log chronologically lists people who sought care at the health center by date and time and briefly describes why that care was sought. Used to capture the health status of the camp community (epidemiology), logs are typically completed in ink and include the date, time, legal name of the ill or injured person, general description of why the person sought care, and the name of the individual evaluating and treating the client. From a risk-management perspective, a log should be "unalterable." For paper-based logs, this typically means the log should be bound, completed in ink, and have consecutively numbered pages; some state regulations require this. Computer-based log systems should have an administrative function that allows the ability to determine who made a change, what change was made, and the date/time of that change since a legal defense depends on having records that can be demonstrated as having not been altered. In moving to computer records, the director should consult not only with the health care administrator, but also with a computer programmer in conjunction with the camp's legal counsel. The log is the minimum reassuring record in case of legal defense in a lawsuit. A sample health log sheet is shown in Figure 12-6.
- A health record captures documentation about the health care given to a specific individual while that person was at camp. The health record will, at minimum, include: why the person sought care, date and time, presenting signs/symptoms, a description of what the health care provider did, and the provider's signature. It should be noted that these minimums may be augmented based on a state licensing agency and/or by the license held by the camp's caregiver, as well as by OSHA for staff members. For example, nurses must chart in a way that reflects the nursing process; consequently, a nurse's documentation will also include in-depth assessment notes and an evaluative statement (how the client responded to the provided care). On the other hand the record from a staff member holding first aid/CPR certification would likely include less in-depth assessment notes. A sample health record form is shown in Figure 12-7.

Some state regulations may specify how a camp must keep its health records. When setting up a health record system and in addition to legal review, it is good practice to initiate the record with a statement that captures the individual's arrival status (e.g., Opening Day health screening) and close the record with a statement that captures the date/time the person left camp and their health status at the time of leaving.

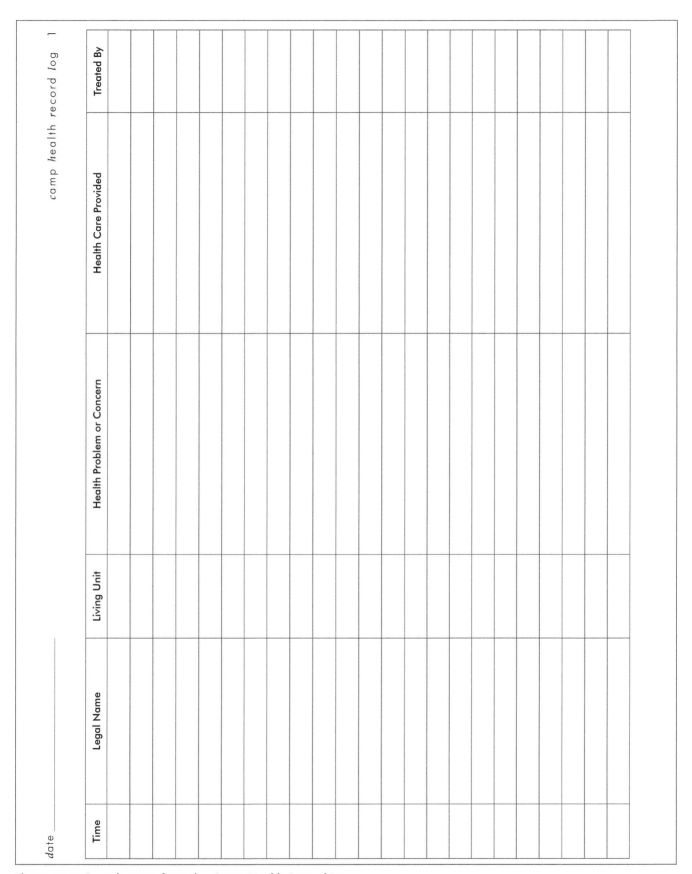

Figure 12-6. Sample page from the Camp Health Record Log

Camp Health Record
Individual at Camp Form   FM 03

Developed and approved by the
American Camp Association
with the American Academy of Pediatrics

Camp Name

Name _____ Age_____ Sex_____

Entrance Date _____ Departure Date_____

Examination Entrance by _____	Departure by _____	Important Observations to Follow While at Camp
Height		
Weight		
Temperature		
Eyes		
Nose		
Ears		
Throat		
Teeth		
Posture		
Skin		
Feet		

Meds Received _____

Dosage/Interval _____

Health Record While at Camp (include date, time, illness, treatment, initials of person treating)

_____

_____

_____

_____

_____

_____

_____

_____

american CAMP association™   © 1983 by American Camping Association, Inc.   Revised 1990, 1992, 1996, 2005.   (over)

Name

Last

First

Initial

Cabin or Group

Year

Figure 12-7. Sample health record form

Health Record While at Camp (include date, time, illness, treatment, initials of person treating)

_____
_____
_____
_____
_____
_____
_____
_____
_____
_____
_____
_____
_____
_____
_____
_____
_____
_____
_____
_____
_____
_____
_____
_____
_____
_____
_____
_____
_____
_____

Figure 12-7. Sample health record form (cont.)

Note: Some state regulations mix the concept of a health log and a health record. Reference to a "Health Record Log" may be seen If so, clarification should be sought from the appropriate state interpretive authority since a log and an individual health record are two different things.

The camp director has the ultimate responsibility for being familiar with how records are generated and stored, and making sure the following records are kept for legal defense on behalf of the camp:

- Injury/incident reports completed on all injuries. A sample accident/incident report form is shown in Figure 11-2. A different form may be required by workers' compensation or OSHA and may substitute for the form used for campers.
- Inventories of medications and supplies at the beginning and end of the season
- Records, required by OSHA, of all health information and training provided staff in the area of bloodborne pathogens, all treatments rendered to staff concerning bloodborne pathogens, and any incidents in which staff have had exposure to bloodborne pathogens. OSHA requires a written exposure control plan that includes:
  - ✓ Identification of job classes or job tasks with occupational exposure to blood and other potentially infectious materials
  - ✓ Procedures for evaluating the circumstances surrounding an exposure incident
  - ✓ A schedule and method for implementing the various parts of the plan, including training of employees[10]

All of these records should be placed together and, with the exception of the inventories, kept until one to four years after the youngest participant has reached the age of majority of the state of the camp's location and office (be sure to check the statutory limit in the state in which the camp is located). They probably need to be immediately accessible during the 12 months following the close of the camp session and could be stored in a fireproof area thereafter.

Checkpoints

- Are protocols in place from the supervising physician for the healthcare provider?
- Outline the healthcare plan for the camp.
- Identify the types of healthcare certification or training that the staff will need.
- What written records are maintained in the healthcare service?

Related Standards

Health Service *American Camp Association's Accreditation Standards for Camp Programs and Services*: HW.1–28

Endnotes

1. Gerald P. Burns. 1954. *Program of the Modern Camp*. New York: Prentice-Hall. p. 59.
2. Linda Ebner Erceg. Letter. January 1999, e-mails, August 2003 and September 2011. Bemidji, MN: Association of Camp Nurses.
3. Linda Ebner Erceg. 1994. "Who is Your Camp Healthcare Provider?" *The CampLine* Vol. 3, No. 1, May. p. 2.
4. Kris Miller Lishner and Margaret Auld Bruya. 1994. *Creating a Healthy Camp Community: a Nurse's Role*. p. 122.
5. Association of Camp Nurses. 2005. *The Scope and Standards of Camp Nursing Practice*. Bemidji, MN: Association of Camp Nurses.
6. Linda Ebner Erceg. 2005. "Your Health-Care Plan: Does It Need An Update?" *Camping Magazine*. Vol. 78, No. 5, September/October, p. 69.
7. Louise Czupryna. 1989. "Partners on the Health and Safety Team." *Camping Magazine*. Vol. 61, No. 5, April, p. 30.
8. Ed Schirick. 1998. "What is Your OSHA IQ?" *Camping Magazine*. Vol. 71, No. 2, March/April, p. 18.
9. Robert B. Bush. 1994. "A Director's Primer on Selected OSHA Requirements." *The CampLine*. Vol. III, No. 2, October, p. 2.
10. "Camp Health, Bloodborne Pathogens, and OSHA." 1992. *CampLine*. Vol. 1, No. 1, May, p. 4.

FOOD
SERVICE

Cheley Colorado Camps (Estes Park, CO)

Chapter Thirteen

> *Cooking at camp, then, was never a simple, transparent process of supplying ample quantities of wholesome food. Rather, the food axis was a locus of struggle in which camp organizers tried to reconcile their own conflicting notions about class, gender, and, eventually, the very nature of childhood. At early boys' camps, for instance, camp organizers valued the change to involve boys in food preparation and embraced military arrangements as appropriately manly settings in which to teach boys to do for themselves. Yet, they were unwilling to abandon the mealtime gentility that was a defining characteristic of middle-class respectability.[1]*
>
> —Abigail A. Van Slyck

As Abigail A. Van Slyck states here, food has always been an important part of the camp experience. Early on, it required some hands-on experience on part of the camper in food preparation. In today's camp food service, not only must the balance of keeping the camp and staff happy, balancing the budget, involving campers in helping, and maintaining a balance between camp spirit and some "gentility" be considered, but concerns are present about good nutrition, combating obesity, and a variety of individual requirements on the part of campers.

Each camp and each camp population present a challenge to the camp director in planning the best food service possible for the camp. Safety and health protocols in the food preparation and service become a key factor in the camp's risk-management program. On the other hand, food plays an important element in implementing the spirit of the camp community and mission of the camp in terms of camper development.

Day Camps

Many day camps do not have the matter of institutional food service as a day-to-day concern. Most often, campers bring their own sack lunch, except on cookout days. This approach makes appropriate planning in the following areas important:

- Care and refrigeration of lunches from campers' arrival at the site until lunch
- Refrigeration and serving of the drink for the lunch meal (e.g., milk, juice, punch)
- Provision for drinking water throughout the camp day
- Disposal of paper and scraps from the lunch period
- Supplemental snacks for campers who bring inadequate lunches
- Provision of a relaxed community atmosphere during the lunch period to aid good digestion
- Sanitation procedures for food storage and handling for cookout meals, often done with the aid of campers Some day camps do provide hot-meal service for their campers, and much of the information that follows is as applicable to them as it is to resident camps.

Food Service Supervisor

A resident camp travels on its stomach as much as an army does. Therefore, the director should turn attention to the food service early in planning for the camp season. The early recruitment of a capable food-service supervisor is one key to dealing with this important area of camp life.

The qualifications set down for that food-service supervisor will depend on the size of the camp and the type of food service desired. A small camp of 25 to 150 campers can seldom afford to employ a trained dietitian or nutritionist as food-service supervisor. A cook with experience in a school lunchroom or fraternity or sorority house can easily fill the bill if the menus are carefully planned with a dietitian or nutritionist prior to camp. A camp of 150 or more will require a food-service supervisor with more skills in meal planning and staff supervision than will a smaller camp. In fact, the larger camps need food-service supervisors whose skills are best in the areas of purchasing, planning, and staff supervision rather than cooking. An experienced first or second cook can provide the cooking ability needed to provide tasty, nutritious food. Surveys show that 15 to 25 percent of a resident camp's budget is spent on food service, and 25 to 31 percent of that cost is labor.[2] Cutting corners on the salary or living conditions of the food-service supervisor can lead to far greater costs than an increased salary would. Violation of state regulations and standard foodservice practices can lead to serious health and legal problems.

The development of menus is the first step in purchasing and summer planning. In order to give the food-service supervisor (particularly if he is new) the best information for developing the summer's menus, the camp director should include the following items in the primary discussion:
- The previous year's food budget in detail
- The previous year's menus and any camper or staff feedback
- A profile of the camp community, including any likely "special diet" requirements
- The style used for serving meals in previous years
- Whether most preparation is from scratch or from packaged foods
- The menu cycle, based on camp periods
- The average daily meal count
- The number of projected campers for the coming season

The food service supervisor should then revise the proposed menus in light of any suggestions, the current prices of foods, the amount allocated in the camp budget for raw food, personal menu favorites, and the cycle of camp periods. If the camp qualifies for provision of food or financial subsidies from state or federal programs, the food service supervisor should be given appropriate information about these items and any menu requirements prior to preparation of menus and food orders.

Upon completion of the menus, the director should review them and raise questions or concerns about them. Unless the food-service supervisor is a qualified dietitian or nutritionist, menus should be reviewed by such a person to ensure a balanced diet. Often, a specialist can be found in a district or city school office, or in the family and consumer sciences department of a nearby college or university, who will be willing to look over the menus for sound nutritional balance. When the menus have been reviewed, the dietitian should be asked to sign the menus and explain any suggestions to the director or to the food-service supervisor. Ideally, this step can be done early in the year so that adequate time is allowed for the purchasing of food. A returning foodservice supervisor or someone who lives in the area of the camp may know the best local sources for purchasing various foods. Otherwise, the director should research the best sources.

Food Purchasing

Usually, better prices can be secured on a large initial food order than on a week-by-week delivery. Therefore, it is advantageous to develop a list of the basic canned and dry foods needed for the summer and place the bulk of that order for delivery at the beginning of the season. If food orders are placed early, companies will often guarantee quoted prices at the time of the order. Mark J. Brostoff suggests seven factors to be taken into account in the selection of vendors:

- Price
- Quality
- Delivery of product
- Personal relations (with salesperson)
- Service
- Technical assistance
- Competitive position (discounts or rebates)[3]

Before placing an early order, the director should have a relatively stable count of the number of meals to be served during the period for which food is being ordered. To determine the maximum number of meals to be served on a seasonal basis: multiply the maximum number of persons (campers and staff) that can be accommodated by three meals a day, then multiply that result by the number of days feeding each period, including staff training and days between periods, and add the totals. Dividing the total by the number of days in the particular season provides the *average daily meal count*.

If enrollment is slow or the camp has a variable record of enrollment, the director should be cautious about the quantities ordered so that a large inventory does not need to carry over beyond the season. If the camp has enrolled only 75 percent of its capacity, it is foolish to order for a full camp until the camp has evidence that enrollment is climbing to that degree. The same principle follows with nonsummer groups. Where principal nonsummer usage is on the weekend, food purchases of perishables must be carefully managed to avoid waste, which is not cost effective.

With appropriate food-storage areas such as protected dry storage and freezer and refrigeration space, good prices on certain items can often be secured in advance of sudden price increases due to weather or shortage problems. For example, if the summer has been particularly dry and the fruit crop was short, it is wise to check on the availability of the previous summer's canned fruits early in the fall since a price increase by the next year's season is sure to follow. Securing bids on food orders can be helpful as a cost-saving device, but for the director, this process may be an unnecessary burden unless a system of bidding has been established in prior years. On all bids, the grade and type of produce as well as the size of container required must be specified, or the prices received may not be comparable. In a bid process, the director should secure prices from several firms (if multiple delivery sources are an option) on major food items such as milk, bread, meat, and certain canned fruits and vegetables that will be used in larger quantities. One factor in food purchasing for not-for-profit camps in the United States is government aid that is available in the form of food items or financial reimbursement for part of the cost of meals served to low-income campers. Availability and regulations continue to change in this area at the federal and state levels. Appendix E gives the information available at the time of publication.

Food Service Staff

When considering the size of food service staff, the following guidelines should be used:

Persons per Meal	Staff Required*
Up to 70	1 cook, 1 dishwasher
70 to 120	2 cooks, 1 dishwasher
140 +	3 cooks, 2 dishwashers

*The type of food service utensils and plates may affect these ratios.

The employment of staff to assist the food-service supervisor is a matter that should be clearly agreed upon between that supervisor and the director. The director and the food-service supervisor should discuss expectations about housing arrangements, salaries, the type of skills needed for each position, and expectations for behavior or clothing. Any staff to be hired who will handle food will need to secure a food handler's permit before arrival at camp as required by the state or county. It is always an advantage to everyone involved if the supervisor can meet or interview applicants before they are hired.

Though the degree to which food-service staff is involved in camp life outside the kitchen varies from camp to camp, it is always an advantage if the food-service staff feels they are a part of the total camp and participates in some of the all-camp programs. Food-service staff should be made aware that they are part of a much larger team, and that their cooperation and teamwork are essential for a successful camp.

Housing away from the busy and noisy activities of the camp is important for kitchen staff since the schedule in most camps makes it necessary for foodservice employees to rise early and consequently, retire early in the evening. If camper facilities are rustic in nature, the director should give careful thought to the quarters for kitchen staff since they may expect and need some conveniences not provided for campers.

Meal Organization

The type of food service affects the number and type of staff required as well as the quantities to be cooked. Basically, the two types of service are cafeteria and family style, though camps will often use a buffet for a special occasion or a salad bar in conjunction with one of the types of service. Both of these types of service have advantages and disadvantages, as shown in Figure 13-1.

Cafeteria Style	
Advantages	*Disadvantages*
• Portions are more easily controlled. • Quantities served are more easily controlled, as are costs. • Table setting is not required prior to the meal. • If dining area is too small for the entire community, this style enables persons at the last of the line to fill tables vacated by persons in the first of the line.	• Some people will be completing the meal while others are being served (unless the camp is very small). • It is difficult to have any all-camp activity (announcements, singing) at this type meal setting.
Family Style	
Advantages	*Disadvantages*
• The counselor can better observe how much and what each camper eats. • Family atmosphere and group spirit are better. • Everyone starts and finishes at the same time. This factor is helpful if singing and/or any announcements follow the meal, and dishes can be cleared before campers leave the table. • It provides opportunities for camper groups to share in tasks around the meal service.	• More food is wasted unless service is controlled by the kitchen and counselors. • Tables must be set in advance. • More time is generally required for the meal.

Figure 13-1. Food service comparison

If the relationship between the counselor and campers is the most important concern and a more intimate, home-like atmosphere is desired, the family type will probably serve the camp better (see Chapter 5). Other factors to be considered are:

- Who will wait tables, clear tables, clean tables, and sweep the floor following the meal? Often, campers are used for any or all of these tasks, and their duties are rotated. Other camps employ waiters who set the tables and bring food and refills.
- Who will serve the plates? Food may be passed around the table, each taking the desired amount, or the counselor may serve the plates and pass them down the table. The latter method provides for a more careful check on what the camper does or does not eat; this aspect is particularly important with younger campers. Serving the plates for younger campers also can prevent spills of foods and liquids.
- What foods must be apportioned, if any, and what foods may be refilled? This factor is dependent partially on budget, but also on nutritional desires. It is particularly important for milk, meats, and desserts, which are higher cost items.

- What is the plan for returning dishes and utensils to the kitchen for washing, or if disposable ware is used, how should it be disposed? Some camps have each table group wash its own dishes at the table. In this case, careful sterilization in compliance with state laws is essential. Dishes may be resterilized in the kitchen after table washing to ensure a 180-degree rinse. If dishes are to be scraped, stacked, and returned to the kitchen, this procedure should be established and the logistics worked out during staff training.
- How much choice should campers have? The camper may come from a school or family situation in which choices of foods are always available. To what degree does the camp feel it necessary to respond to this concern?

Cookout Meals

If a camp program calls for cookouts, overnights, or any sort of tripping program that removes campers from the dining room, the director should draw up a plan for notifying the kitchen of changes in meal counts early enough so that the proper amount of food is prepared for those meals. A plan must also be in place for those groups cooking out to secure their cooked or raw food. Groups may be required to submit a food-service requisition directly to the food-service supervisor, or some other staff members working with the food service may be in charge of filling orders. If out-of-camp meals are few in number over the course of the summer, a system can be devised in which menus, established either by the group or the kitchen, can be picked up at the close of the last in-camp meal served to the group. However, as the number of out-of-camp meals increases, the importance of a carefully planned system will become more apparent. Following are some factors to consider.

First, the type of experience that the camp wishes to give its campers will dictate the approach to planning menus for such meals. If the goal is to have a camper group plan and understand the nutritional elements of menu planning or to have free choice, then it is more important that a food list be developed to assist campers and counselors in planning the menu and determining the quantities needed. Amounts available per person or per group should be standardized and made known. If the experience of cooking is a more important part of a trip experience, it may be simpler to have them choose between menus or accept predetermined menus.

A stock of food in sizes or types not typically used in institutional cooking should be gathered in one storage and checkout facility and a staff member given responsibility for that area. A wide variety of dehydrated and freeze-dried food is available, which will make supply packs much lighter.

Foods to be secured from the kitchen (because of limited quantity or refrigeration needed) should be identified along with a method of securing them.

A checkout plan and amount of advance notice need to be clarified. The group may come with its food list at a specified time and check out the food across a counter so that they may pack and check it for themselves, or staff may accumulate the food from a list and pack it for a group in advance of departure. Careful attention should be given to procedures for keeping refrigerated foods cool and what foods (if any) can be returned to the kitchen.

Some camps operate the out-of-camp meals through a store, providing campers the opportunity not only of planning their menus, but also of learning budgeting by purchasing the food items from that store with camp money. This type of learning experience takes preparation—pricing, order sheets, and orientation of staff. The director should also consider the impact of any such program on the food-service supervisor, food purchasing, food costs, and nutritional standards before establishing the system.

Sanitation and Health

Camp kitchens range from rather rustic centers where campers take food to their units to cook over wood, charcoal, or gas fires, to fully equipped commercial kitchens with all of the appliances typically found in the finest restaurants. However simple or elaborate, some basic health and sanitation standards need to be followed in food storage, preparation, and serving. The dangers of foodborne illness in a camp setting cannot be underestimated.

Source	Percentage
Inadequate refrigeration/cooling	63
Preparing food far in advance of service	29
Hot holding at bacterial incubating temperature	27
Infected persons handling food	26
Inadequate reheating	25
Inadequate cleaning of equipment	9
Use of leftovers	7
Cross-contamination	6
Inadequate cooking	5
Storing acid food in toxic metal containers	4
Contaminated raw ingredients in uncooked foods	2
Intentional additives	2
Obtaining food from unsafe sources	1

Figure 13-2. Sources of foodborne illness

To prevent foodborne illness, a food-service supervisor should give careful attention to Hazard Analysis Critical Control Points (HACCP), which is a food safety and self-inspection system that looks at the flow of potential hazardous foods through the camp's operation—from receiving of food to serving of the food. Hazard analysis encourages food-service staff to ask where the food safety problems are most likely to occur. Critical control points suggests what steps are needed to take control of food-safety problems and where or when to take them.

A good starting point is to find the sources of dangers of foodborne illness most frequently reported. The North Dakota Department of Public Health identified the following primary sources.[4]

Storage of all food should be in areas protected from rodents and vermin. Perishable foods should be stored in *refrigerated areas* at 40 degrees Fahrenheit or below. As a safety measure, a clipboard should be mounted beside each walk-in, freezer, or cooler, providing a form with a line for each day for the assigned individual to initial and indicate the temperature at the time of the check. This step will ensure that, if the temperature begins to rise in a 24-hour period, corrective actions can be taken promptly. The walk-in will fluctuate some during mealtime when it is often opened, but it should quickly return to a safe temperature.

One of the greatest points of danger in food contamination falls in the period of thawing, or cooling after cooking, when pathogenic organisms can multiply more easily. It is best to thaw frozen items in refrigerated areas so the items will not sit after thawing in temperatures higher than 40 degrees Fahrenheit.

A minimum temperature of 140 degrees Fahrenheit should be maintained in *keeping food warm* before a meal or for serving in a cafeteria operation, and it is wise to heat the food to 170 degrees Fahrenheit before placing it in a serving container. The maximum periods in which perishable foods (e.g., meat, fish, eggs, milk, poultry, salads with dressings) should be allowed to sit in 46 to 139 degree range is two hours. Care should be taken that perishable foods be cooked in deep trays or large cooking pots that would take more than two hours to cool the center.

The food-service supervisor and healthcare provider should sit down with all food-service staff and discuss the *personal sanitary and hygiene practices* that should be followed, as well as the principles of careful food preparation and serving. Employees should be made aware that should they have a contagious condition, they should immediately notify both the food-service supervisor and the healthcare provider, so they can be relieved of food-service duties. A toilet for use by kitchen employees should be convenient to the kitchen area and display signs reminding employees about washing hands with soap after use of the toilet facilities. Other staff that may be handling foods on a cookout should be trained in food handling and sanitizing dishes, pots, and pans.

A definite system following state regulations for *washing and sanitizing* dishes, pots and pans, and utensils must be established. If the camp has a mechanical dishwasher, such regulations will require having wash water at least 100 degrees Fahrenheit, and rinse water at least 180 degrees Fahrenheit, or using an approved chemical sanitizing solution. Some camps wash dishes and utensils by hand. However, the temperatures for washing and rinsing should be maintained at 100 degrees Fahrenheit or above, and a second rinse should use an approved chemical sanitizer when washing by hand. In both cases, dishes, utensils, and pots and pans should be air-dried. As in refrigeration, it is wise to have a clipboard mounted near the dishwashing area where the temperatures are checked, recorded, and initialed at least once during each meal's dishwashing process.

The cleanliness and sanitation of the kitchen work areas is very important. All work surfaces should be cleaned after use. Special attention should be paid to slicers and can openers, which are often overlooked in the daily cleaning. Surfaces in which food comes into contact should be identified to kitchen personnel, and the procedures for cleaning those surfaces before and after every food contact established.

Garbage and rubbish should be promptly removed from the kitchen into leak-proof containers with tight-fitting lids. Daily removal and emptying of those containers should be part of the maintenance schedule. Those containers should also be cleaned regularly, even when plastic bags are used inside the containers.

Contracted Services

Many camps have chosen to contract with food-service companies to provide the entire food-service operation, eliminating the employment and supervision of staff, the purchase of food, and the related bookkeeping chores. Though some control of menus related to what is served or what the camp can afford remains, most of the control and resulting problems become those of the contracted service. Many times, the services that contract with colleges and universities find that camps are a natural customer and enable them to retain their staff between school seasons.

The applicability and affordability of such services vary from camp to camp. A careful analysis of the related costs for both types of service should be made. Current customers of the service should be interviewed and if at all possible, the food-service provider observed before making a commitment.

Checkpoints

- Does the camp have on hand menus and inventories of food, supplies, and equipment?
- Does the type of meal service used currently lend itself to the camp's program philosophy?
- To what degree will campers assume responsibility in the dining room for preparation or cleanup?
- To what degree will campers assume responsibility for their own meal planning and preparation during their camp experience?
- Check the food-service area sanitation practices against government regulations and American Camp Association standards.

Related Standards

Site and Food Service Standards *American Camp Association's Accreditation Standards for Camp Programs and Services*: SF.14–23
Additional Professional Practices: Site and Food Service

Endnotes

1. Abigail A. Van Slyck. 2006. A Manufactured Wilderness. Minneapolis & London: University of Minnesota Press. p. 148.
2. Armand Ball. 1990. "Food Service Cost Survey." *Trendlines*. May/June, p. 1.
3. Mark J. Brostoff. 1989. "The Dynamics of Camp Food Purchasing." *Camping Magazine*. Vol. 61, No. 4, February, p. 28.
4. *ACN Compass Point*. Bemidji, MN: Association of Camp Nurses.

TRANSPORTATION

Cali Camp (Topanga, CA)

Chapter Fourteen

Of the many responsibilities that rest on the shoulders of the day camp director or sponsor, probably the heaviest is transportation. Between the safety of the home and the safety of the campsite lies the danger of the public way, over which the camper must be carried twice daily. Although the director can exert reasonable control over the activities and premises of his camp, he has very little control over the external hazards of the road. He can, however, control the operation of his own vehicles.[1]

—Grace Mitchell

Though Mitchell is directing her remarks to the day camp director, the essence of this quotation applies equally to the resident or trip camp. The transportation of campers and staff provides one of the key areas of potential liability to camps. Careful planning along with careful risk management, including a thorough review of insurance coverage and safety education practices, is essential. In camps, vehicles may vary from cars, vans, and buses to boats and planes. Transportation issues in a day camp are usually major factors in the program cost and schedule, and most likely involve city driving.

The first step is to analyze what transportation is required:
- Do campers have to be transported to and from camp, or will parents or the sponsoring group arrange that?
- Do campers have to be transported in groups out of camp for program activities or events?
- Is a camp vehicle needed to haul supplies and equipment into camp?
- What vehicle will be needed for maintenance personnel?
- What vehicle will be needed in an emergency to transport injured individuals to the doctor or hospital?
- Do campers or staff members have to be transported to and from transportation terminals?
- Will staff-owned vehicles be used for certain purposes?

The use of staff-owned vehicles should be considered carefully with a review of the camp's insurance coverage for non-owned vehicles and its implications for rates. If a situation warrants the use of a staff-owned vehicle, then a clear agreement should be developed between the director and the staff member concerning insurance, reimbursement for mileage, and periods of use.

Recent lawsuits have brought into question the safety and reliability of certain types of vehicles. The safety of a vehicle for transporting groups of campers or staff is the first consideration to be made, and information on reliability of available vehicles should be checked carefully.

Owning, Leasing, or Chartering

Initially, the question of whether the camp purchases and maintains its own vehicles must be answered. Since camp situations vary greatly, no single method will be best for every camp. Figure 14-1 details the advantages and disadvantages that accompany the three usual methods of securing camp ehicles.

	Factors	Owning	Leasing/Renting	Chartering
Advantages	**Drivers**	Camp selects drivers.	Camp selects drivers.	Company provides drivers.
	Cost	Cost may be less.	Some maintenance and repair costs may be covered. No capital investment.	Maintenance covered by company. No capital investment.
	Schedule	Camp controls schedule, employee, and vehicle.	Camp controls schedule, employee, and vehicle.	Contract specifies pickup and/or arrival time and transfers much of risk to company.
	Insurance			Company provides insurance and can add the camp to their policy as "additional insured."
	Other	Can advertise on side of vehicle.	Camp may have newer vehicles earlier than if owned.	
Disadvantages	**Drivers**	Finding qualified drivers may be a problem.	Finding qualified drivers may be a problem.	No control over selection of drivers.
	Cost	Camp absorbs maintenance and repair costs. Purchase requires a large sum of cash.	Lease contracts vary and can contain much "fine print."	Cost is usually more. Multiple use increases cost.
	Schedule	Camp controls schedule. A careful maintenance schedule is required.	Camp controls schedule. A careful maintenance schedule is required.	No direct control of vehicle.
	Insurance	Insurance may be a problem.	Insurance may be a problem, requiring substantial deductible and offering only state-required minimum limits.	
	Other			

Figure 14-1. Vehicle chart

Some advantages can become disadvantages in certain circumstances, so carefully consider the cost, availability of qualified personnel, and the amount of use necessary. The number and type of vehicles required by the camp program will certainly affect the decision, since the capital investment at one time for purchase may be more difficult than renting, leasing, or chartering annually.

Although some problems are removed by chartering or leasing vehicles, it does not relieve the camp of the responsibility of double-checking that the company carries the appropriate insurance, maintains a written record of regular maintenance and vehicle upkeep, and provides a written verification of the safety record and experience of its drivers. These factors should be part of the selection and contract process, and any signs of variance from stated practice should be immediately reported to the charter or leasing company.

Drivers

The selection of the drivers for such vehicles is the key to safety and public relations. It is the driver who must regularly check that the maintenance of the vehicle is maintained, be friendly to campers, parents, or vendors, and yet maintain constant surveillance of safety factors. In a day camp, the daily nature of picking up, transporting, and dropping off campers adds an even greater element of responsibility with regards to safety and public relations.

A careful check of each driver's driving record should be made each year (within four months prior to the camp season or annually for year-round drivers), either by the camp or by the camp's insurance company. The director should also analyze the type of driving experience and how it relates to the particular vehicles to be driven. Experience with the type of vehicle is very important. Training should be provided if the person does not have previous experience with that particular type of vehicle.

State licensing laws vary. Some states require a different type of license for drivers of vehicles that carry a certain number of passengers, or where children are transported by a hired firm. State laws should be checked early so that the appropriate license for the vehicle to be driven can be included in the job requirements. Where a vehicle is designed to carry 16 or more persons or is in excess of 26,000 pounds, federal law requires a special Commercial Driver License issued at the state level. (Note: It is the design and not the number of actual passengers that determines the license requirement.) A Commercial Driver License requires drug/alcohol testing.

Every vehicle carrying campers should have a staff member, which may be the driver, trained to carry out written accident procedures for providing or securing care for any injured, supervising the uninjured, specifying whom to notify in an emergency, and obtaining appropriate accident information at the scene. When a vehicle carries 15 or more persons, an additional staff member should be assigned to give attention to the campers to manage safety and ensure appropriate group behavior. The number of staff members may need to be increased if any campers are younger than nine, or if campers have mental, emotional, or physical disabilities.

Written procedures and policies should be provided to drivers and specific training given during the pre-camp period. All drivers, even those who do not transport campers or staff, should have training in the following areas:

- Use of fire extinguishers and emergency reflectors stored in vehicle
- Safety inspection of all vehicles the person is expected to drive
- Inspection of the vehicle before use, and procedures for reporting any needed repairs
- Importance of not transporting campers in vehicles not designed for passengers (e.g., open-bed trucks or trailers)
- Procedures to follow in case of an accident, including information cards for witnesses to complete and a camera for accident pictures. A disposable camera in each vehicle is a good way to handle this aspect.

All drivers who transport campers or staff should have additional training in the following areas:

- Use of the first-aid kit kept in vehicles
- Identification of appropriate behavior for passengers in loading, unloading, and traveling in vehicles
- Use of seatbelts or, in the case of smaller children (and some persons with disabilities), restraints
- Maximum seating capacities of various vehicles
- Availability and location of medical-information forms and permission-to-treat forms
- Procedures for backing up, loading and unloading passengers, dealing with vehicular breakdowns, refueling, and dealing with illnesses of passengers (cleaning up bodily fluids)
- Procedures for rest stops and telephone use during long excursions (i.e., determining when they are needed, choosing locations, and checking to assure everyone is present at the conclusion of the stop)
- Procedures for determining when to unload campers or leave them in the vehicle
- Procedures for determining where campers are to be located during refueling of vehicle
- Procedures for evacuation in an emergency
- Division of responsibility of staff other than that of the driver
- Maintenance of an appropriate log of trips, including refueling and oil records (Figure 14-2)

One person on the staff should be responsible for checking out any staff before they are given permission to drive a camp vehicle. This step is ordinarily done during the staff-training period. In the frenzied pace of camp life, it is too easy to designate any staff member to take a vehicle and run an errand or transport campers. Drivers should be designated, in addition to the regularly assigned drivers, in order to deal with unscheduled trips as well as to allow for time off.

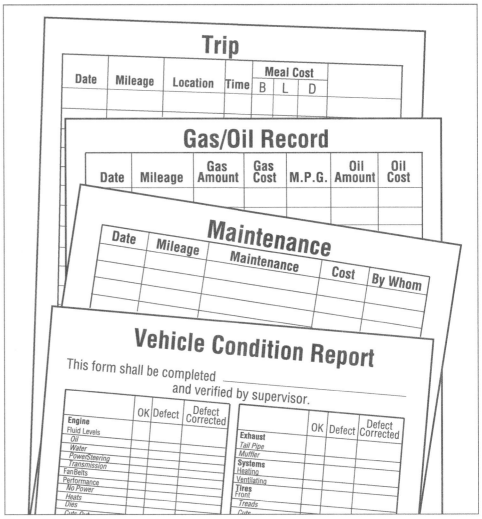

Figure 14-2. Vehicle record log

Maintenance of Vehicles

A regular plan of maintenance of vehicles is the second key to good risk management in transportation. Even the best driver is dangerous in a poorly maintained vehicle. A specific staff member should be given the responsibility of maintaining all vehicles, and a system of regular checks should be established. The written maintenance plan should include:

- Written records of all oil changes and repairs, with the mileage and date
- Regular checks to make sure that a fully stocked first-aid kit, flares, fire extinguisher, disposable camera, and appropriate tools are kept in each vehicle at all times
- A regular schedule of safety checks of lights, tires, wipers, windshield, emergency warning systems, horn, brakes, and oil and coolant levels (as shown in Figure 14-2)
- A quarterly mechanical evaluation of vehicles that carry passengers (or, in the case of a seasonal operation, within three months prior to use)

Camper Education

In addition to all of the preceding precautions, if campers are to be transported, they should be given instructions on appropriate behavior, safety regulations, use of cell phones, evacuation procedures, and use of seat belts.

Day Camps

Day camps that transport campers deal with these sorts of concerns on a daily basis and are generally very sensitive to the issues of safety and transport. Often, multiple vehicles are involved in the transport of campers, and it is vital that a plan for the orderly arrival and departure of vehicles be developed. Areas for loading and unloading, parking, waiting, and moving traffic should be clearly delineated in writing, and staff should be made available to supervise arrival and departure periods.

A written schedule of camper pickup and drop-off times and locations, as well as safety rules and precautions, should be presented to parents, along with a telephone number for contacting the central office handling transportation. Even in the well-organized transportation system, all sorts of things will occur which can delay the arrival or departure of campers. A notification system for parental cell phones and e-mail addresses that deals with delays could be developed. Any system to notify parents of unusual delays in pickups or dropoffs will go a long way toward good public relations.

Checkpoints

- For what purposes are vehicles used in/outside camp? How many and what type?
- Has the director examined the options of renting, leasing, chartering, or owning vehicles?
- In which vehicles are campers currently allowed to ride?
- Is one person responsible for upkeep of vehicles?
- Is one person responsible for selecting and checking drivers?
- If a day camp, is a plan in place for the pickup and drop-off of campers, and the notification of parents if plans change?
- What is the provision for emergency vehicles?

Related Standards

American Camp Association's Accreditation Standards for Camp Programs and Services: TR.1–15

End Notes

1. Grace Mitchell with Irwin Rhodes and Robert Rhodes. 1982. *Fundamentals of Day Camping*. Martinsville, IN: American Camping Association.

MARKETING

Chapter Fifteen

Ours is a field where the value is not experienced unless the participant is there. It becomes imperative that we become more aggressive in our advocacy of the camp experience. We cannot wait for the campers to come to us. For all directors this means earlier and more vigorous recruitment of campers. It means more talk about values, outcomes, and specifics in language that can be understood by parents, business people and organization boards.[1]

—Armand Ball

Camp Identity as the Key

The simple fact that campers are essential to the operation of a camp is often not considered early enough in camp planning. Nor do camp administrators translate the word *camper* into *customer* often enough; camps have much to learn from the business world in terms of marketing and customer relations.

Marketing is an ongoing, year-round process that involves the direct recruitment of campers and groups. It also involves the constant interpretation of the generic values of the camp experience, as well providing a clear sense of what the camp is about. It is the foundation of all good financial development, public relations, and community relations. It is an attitude that should embodied by each and every staff member, be heard in the voices that answer the telephone, reflected on the faces of those who greet campers and parents, and sensed in the response to complaints.

Dr. Dwight Jewson, a marketing guru, underlines this sentiment in the following statement:

> *Development of state-of-the-art marketing begins with defining "who we are"—the very identity of the camp, then:*
> - *Ensuring that camp identity is relevant to ("speaks to") its target audience.*
> - *Aligning everything the camp does with and around that identity.*
>   *Marketing is the external voice of a carefully considered, clearly articulated sense of what camp is all about. It is the voice through which its target audience learns of the vision, purpose, and mission—the very essence of the camp.*
>   *Ensuring the camp communicates its identity clearly and that everything the camp does is aligned around that identity is vital for service organizations where the experience people have is the product we provide. If the camp is not "walking its talk," literally "practicing what it preaches" in everything no matter how "nice sounding" its external message is, the marketing message will ring hollow to the marketplace it serves. In camps, the proof is crystal clear:*
> - *Returning campers are the primary source of enrollments.*

- *Word of mouth is the key and dominant "media channel" for camps. Camp experience, not brochures or advertising, drives word of mouth.*[2]

Therefore, marketing involves everything a camp does, both to attract and to keep customers and consumers of its services. Marketing is not just a single promotional mailing, but the total package: staff, program, communication materials, food service, grounds and buildings, and the like. Communicating the essence or identity of the camp in each and every contact with the customer/consumer requires the careful analysis of philosophy and mission discussed previously, as well as ensuring that the total package speaks the same language throughout.

That language has to "speak to" the targeted audience at their level of understanding and expectations. In camps for youth, it is usually the family who must be convinced to pay the fee for the child to attend camp, with the caveat that children's opinions have a great deal to do with a family's decision. The parent then becomes the primary customer. Early on, the director needs to recognize that the key responsibility of the camp's marketing must be information that will help the family make an informed decision in assessing whether the camp is the best fit or appropriate for their children. Such an approach protects all parties, and can often alleviate problems that could arise during or after the camp experience. Similarly, in camps that rent facilities, the organization that rents is the primary customer, needing to find the best fit in a facility and services.

Currently, surveys show that children ages 7 to 17 influence their parents' decisions concerning leisure activities in 74 percent of families.[3] Therefore, the camper is not only the consumer of the service in youth camps, but also the secondary customer and must be considered with regard to customer concerns and marketing. The individual participant in the rental situation becomes the secondary customer and consumer.

When camps are no longer solely summer camps or children's camps, the marketing approach becomes more complex, requiring more market research and strategy if the camp is to attract a variety of potential clientele to operate at full capacity in all seasons. The customer in a camp may be an adult, a child, a family, an organization, a school, a church or synagogue, or a business, so different methods to communicate the identify of the camp to that customer need to be instituted. Ultimately, the consumer is an individual, and it is that individual who must also sense the identity of the camp in his experience. Different segments of the camp operation may have different primary customers and consumers, so the marketing tools should be crafted differently for each segment.

As Edward L. Hayes states, "People form impressions about you and your camp the instant they see you advertised or mentioned in print. Even the way you handle correspondence conveys how you feel about your public. Unanswered inquiries and tardy, poorly typed letters speak worlds to your public."[4]

Early in marketing, the boundaries for marketing must be analyzed: What is the present market, target population, or customer base for the camp, and what potential markets exist? Many camps are designed for a particular type of camper based on a specific geographical area, income level, or physical challenge and those factors are usually reflected in the mission or purpose. This focus establishes the parameters of marketing efforts from the outset. In camps that serve broader geographical areas and appeal to campers with no particular physical challenge or medical condition, the potential market is much larger. The fee charged for the camp experience may limit the market to a more specific income level. A camp that operates a conference and retreat program during part of the year may be limited by mission to the members of an organization or to churches of the same persuasion. Each of these requirements shapes the tools of marketing to be used. In other words, understanding the boundaries of the camp market enables a camp to better design how the experience is packaged, how much money is spent on marketing, which markets are explored, and how the experience is promoted. Christian Camp and Conference Association reports that mean amounts camps and conference centers spent on marketing and promotion more than doubled between 1996 and 2000.[5] Such a budgetary impact requires careful consideration of the way in which that money is spent.

Market Analysis

A market analysis will be easier if the camp has previously kept good records and if a computer is available on which data can be recorded. The following eight steps need to be taken.

Step #1: Secure enrollment figures by sessions or type of program and use for the past five years. Compare shifts in total enrollment, types of program and use, and sessions.

Step #2: Break down those enrollment figures for the same period of time, using various factors. The factors will vary, based on the type of programs and length of season. Where individual enrollment is based on particular programs or different lengths of sessions, break down the enrollment for each session or program by age, sex, ZIP code, religious affiliation, school affiliation, ethnic and racial groups, general family income, or any other relevant specification.

Where the enrollment is by groups—such as schools, churches, social clubs, and businesses—break down the enrollment by type of user groups, size groups, age groups, geographical origin, type of camp services used, and seasons attended.

Next, search for patterns or segments of the market where the heaviest and lightest enrollments occur to study further what creates the difference. For example, why do enrollments reflect large numbers from certain neighborhoods and fewer from others? Which types of groups seldom rent the camp facilities? Which are the primary segments being currently served? Look back at the stated purpose and target market and compare that to the camp's existing demographics. Is the targeted audience being served?

Step #3: Examine the return rate. What percentage of campers or user groups returns from the previous year(s)? Study evaluations from customers and consumers. Are campers not returning for any specific reason?

Step #4: Look at enrollment dates. When is the earliest registration, and what are the dates when the largest number register? What prompted people to enroll more during a particular three-week period? Who enrolled earliest?

Step #5: Compare enrollment with enrollment in other camps. The American Camp Association and Christian Camp and Conference Association both conduct surveys from time to time to see what trends are occurring in camp enrollment. Talk with camps in the general area; if the camp is affiliated with an organization that has other camps in the region, seek comparative information. Any significant deviation from the pattern other camps are experiencing may give clues to problems or unique features in the camp's situation that need analysis before recruitment plans are developed or revised.

Step #6: Gather some demographic information about the area served. What is the current population by age groups, socioeconomic groups, ethnic or racial groups? What has been the trend over the past five years? Is a projection made for the next five years? Where is the largest concentration of prospective campers or groups? Has the camp's enrollment followed the trends in the general population?

Step #7: Identify the competition. Competition comes in the form of other types of programs, other camps, schools, sports, and other types of activity that involve the entire family. Competition is not bad; in fact, it is a part of our way of life. It is always wise to learn as much as possible about the competition, considering what they are offering, what fees they charge, and whom they are serving. Dr. Dwight Jewson states:

> *The camp competes with other products being marketed to youth … . The message or advertisement for the camp thus must be addressed to a specific market or markets … . That message exists in the context of many other messages or advertisements for alternatives for the summer, and thus must communicate directly with the needs and concerns of the market segment towards whom it is directed.*[6]

Step #8: Once a camp director collects the preceding data and has studied it thoroughly, it should be shared with others. Key staff, who have experience with the camp, may have insights that prove valuable. If the camp operates with a board or committee, that group should be presented with the information and given an opportunity to react to and discuss it. Another camp director or mentor may be able to offer some observations. Often, outside consultants from the camping field can provide a clearer analysis of this data and help give guidance to the director and board in developing an appropriate marketing plan.

Analysis of Current Market Strategies

Marketing efforts should be motivated by the desire to accomplish the purpose of the camp, meet customer and consumer needs, and provide a quality service that is superior to the competition or unique in some way. Having already determined the purpose of the camp, time may need to be devoted to analyzing customer needs and the quality of services provided.

Doug Herron reminds camp directors that "headache sufferers don't need aspirin—they need relief from the headache." The benefit is the relief, not the aspirin. He goes on to state:

> Benefits are the result customers and consumers derive from satisfactory use of the service. Features (the characteristics we most often talk about) are the distinguishing facts about the service that are true whether the service is ever used or not. Features are easily provable characteristics that are not debatable. They are the elements you can see, taste, touch, smell, and measure.
>
> Staff who base their selling strategy solely on a description of the program's features are hoping the prospective customer will bridge a conceptual gap and convert all the features into personal benefits. Professional salespeople and marketers know, however, that the typical prospect, no matter how well educated, does not have the time nor inclination to convert all the features into benefits. At the same time they realize that no sale starts without the prospect anticipating some benefits. You must persuade potential customers that use of your service will satisfy their needs and interests.[7]

Peg. L Smith echoes this approach in slightly different words:

> We suffer brand recognition. … in truth, we may be branding ourselves with the noun "camp" that we no longer own … We need to brand the value of the [camp] experience in the lives of children, youth, and adults.[8]

Figure 15-1 illustrates how the terms features, benefits, and derived benefits apply to the camp setting. The camp's outcome/objectives and the derived benefits should be consistent.

An analysis of the benefits offered by the camp to the potential customer and consumer needs to be made. Chapter 3 outlined some of the generic values of camp. Those values or benefits need to be outlined for the specific camp or programs within the camp. Remember that the benefits outlined in materials describing a camp will be compared by the potential customer/consumer with those outlined by other camps. Benefits need to be clear and at the same time should generate excitement.

In a 1990 study by the Maguire Associates, the top-five camp characteristics rated by parents were: caring counselors, enjoyment/fun camper has there, overall quality, safety, and personal attention given to each camper.[9] These

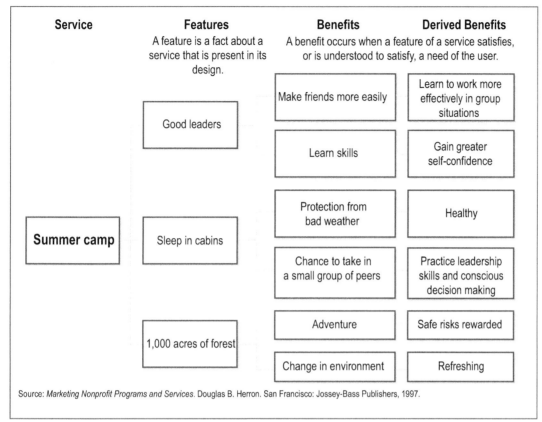

Service	Features	Benefits	Derived Benefits
	A feature is a fact about a service that is present in its design.	A benefit occurs when a feature of a service satisfies, or is understood to satisfy, a need of the user.	

Service: **Summer camp**

Features: Good leaders / Sleep in cabins / 1,000 acres of forest

Benefits and Derived Benefits:
- Make friends more easily → Learn to work more effectively in group situations
- Learn skills → Gain greater self-confidence
- Protection from bad weather → Healthy
- Chance to take in a small group of peers → Practice leadership skills and conscious decision making
- Adventure → Safe risks rewarded
- Change in environment → Refreshing

Source: *Marketing Nonprofit Programs and Services*. Douglas B. Herron. San Francisco: Jossey-Bass Publishers, 1997.

Figure 15-1. Features and benefits of the camp setting

characteristics were evidently the benefits perceived by the customers at that time, and it is likely that these characteristics rank high in the mind of camper parents. In fact, parents seem to be more concerned and more specific about what a camp contributes to their child than ever. Compare these with the benefits the camp purports as well as with the benefits campers perceive.

In analyzing customer perceived benefits, an evaluation form that is used with present campers and parents or camper groups can provide some insights into which needs are being met (i.e., what makes them happy) and which are not being met (i.e., what both current and non-returning campers disliked). The design of the evaluation form is critical, and some outside expertise or review will help hone the form to accomplish what the camp needs. Remember the questions asked of the primary customer (e.g., parent, organization that rents) may be different from the secondary customer or consumer (e.g., camper, participant). This process may necessitate more than one questionnaire.

The time when the person is given the form also can affect the outcome. For example, giving it to the leader of a rental group upon their arrival at camp or mailing an evaluation form to summer campers during the Christmas/Hanukkah season may not provide the return rate or information desired. Evaluation needs to take place soon enough after the conclusion of the experience to be fresh in the respondent's mind, but not in the moment of unpacking the suitcase. The matter of evaluation is covered more fully in Chapter 18.

At this point, a camp director needs to examine current marketing materials and practices. Everything should be examined with care—from website content, brochures, and videos to the schedule of mailings and promotional meetings— with an eye for its target populations, its accuracy, its attractiveness, and its effectiveness in identifying benefits. Make a list of all current marketing strategies and tools used by the camp.

To deal with a competitive marketplace, a camp must emphasize overall value and differentiate its identity and services from that of other camps. Simply offering more activities than the competition will not necessarily bring campers. Without a clear analysis of the identity the camp wishes to communicate, adding new program activities may actually negate or weaken that identity. Value does not necessarily imply having the nicest buildings or equipment, but rather relates more directly to having safe, clean, and comfortable facilities with capable, mature, and caring staff members.

The issue of quality cannot be treated lightly. So much of a camp's reputation depends on word-of-mouth comments that a camp must ensure it provides consistent and continuing service. News of a good camp travels fast, but today's parents are not overly loyal. When a camp does not produce what it promises, parents are quick to look for another camp.

A specific focus will often stimulate interest on the part of campers and parents. In marketing, this matching of a special focus with a particular group of customers is called "developing a niche." To emphasize a niche, a camp needs to understand the following:
- Establish a camp identity that applies to the target audience.
- Concentrate on what the camp does best. Emphasize quality and do not compromise in the area chosen.
- Make sure that the niche chosen is not too narrow, thereby limiting the audience too much.
- Prepare to give up something else (e.g., a less appealing program, staff or equipment in another program area, etc.). It is difficult to finance, staff, and ensure quality in a large number of programs.
- Choose a name for the program or experience that communicates well. It must mean something to the camper. It may involve using contemporary or classic vernacular.
- Be patient. Success does not come in one summer.
- Provide what is promised. Deliver services in accordance with marketing claims.

Site User Groups

If the site is marketed to user groups, determine the competitive niche. Unless the camp provides a program that is subsidized from some aspect of the organization, one of the goals is for revenue to exceed cost of service delivery. The camp's competitive niche includes the qualities of its site and the quality and extent of services provided for the fee the camp charges. If the camp is serving adults, the physical space may be more indoors than outdoors. That space should be physically and emotionally conducive to the program or to meeting goals of the user group. As with any good marketing strategy, match the needs of the user group with the opportunities provided by the camp. An outdoor education class or a troop camping experience will have different needs than a college class or an adult training group. The features of the site that are desirable for most adult groups include:

- Quality meeting space
- Indoor bathrooms with privacy
- Comfortable beds and mattresses
- Comfortable chairs and tables with good writing surfaces
- Accurate directions to the site and signs or maps of the site
- Hard-surfaced walkways
- Lounge furniture

In addition, the following amenities add to the desirability, comfort, and convenience for adult groups:

- Training aids (such as easels, markers, tape, digital projectors, laptops, audiovisual equipment, etc.)
- Telephones and Internet access for individual use
- Copy machine
- Fax machine
- Privacy for meetings
- Flexible mealtimes
- Lounge and deck areas
- Recreational opportunities, including walking paths, game areas, television, and the like

The hosting function is critical in working with user groups. Interest in meeting their needs from the first phone call to the checkout procedures should be carefully planned and be a part of the marketing strategy.

Developing a Marketing Plan

Having analyzed the present population served by the camp, examined the demographics of the service area, taken a look at competing services, and evaluated current marketing and services, the director should have the necessary information to develop a marketing plan for the coming year. This should be developed in conjunction with the staff and committee members who will carry out the plan. It might also be wise to include customers and consumers in an advisory role.

First, reexamine what the message is and to whom it is to be communicated. Review the mission or statement of purpose and what has been established as the camp's identity. Is it clear to others? Does it communicate the desired message? Is it concise? Also, consider the ways in which potential customers seek to learn or learned about the camp.

Determining the camp's identity is the critical step in marketing. Though this certainly relates to the purpose of the camp, it also relates to the setting, staff, and strengths of the camp operation. Some camps have found their identity as a camp centers on providing a program that is general in nature with many different activities and programs. Another camp's identity may lead to finding a specialized niche in the marketplace.

This identity may need to be communicated in a variety of ways if the camp serves multiple audiences. It is likely that a camp will identify different tools for different audiences. In today's market, most camps have determined they need more than the traditional camp brochure and will develop tools such as websites and promotional videos as primary mechanisms to reach their target audiences. Whatever tools are selected, it is critical that they are consistent in communicating the mission, desired outcomes, and identity of the camp, and that they are targeted to the desired audience.

Often camps are tempted to combine everything into one compartmentalized brochure in order to save dollars, but it is questionable whether such an approach can be effective in speaking to multiple audiences (i.e., summer campers, parents, renters, weekend programs, and day and/or resident camps) on the same property. Trying to market messages to a variety of audiences can be confusing. So this step entails actually laying out on paper the audiences to be attracted and the message to be communicated to each of those audiences. Camp websites should be created with specific areas for specific audiences. The site's home page should include prominent and clear links to each audience's specific area (e.g., links for current and campers, for current and potential campers' parents, for current and prospective staff, etc.).

Second, determine the promotional tools needed to communicate the camp's message by reviewing those currently being used, comparing them with tools used by other camps or similar types of operations (e.g., parks, recreation opportunities, conference centers, etc.). Most tools for communicating the camp's message will fall in four areas: personal interaction, promotional materials, advertising, and public relations. A mix of these tools will provide a balance of appeal.

Tools for Marketing

Personal Interaction

This tool deserves first consideration because camp is a very personal experience both for the camper and for the family. In any discussion with camp directors around the country on the topic of marketing, all agree the best way of securing campers is by word of mouth. As in the business world, referrals by satisfied customers are the best advertisement.

However effective promotional or advertising materials may be, the potential customer will be looking for identification with a person related to the camp. Confidence is instilled by some contact with a caring and informed individual. The following tools involve some person-to-person contact.

Returning Campers

Except in very unusual camp situations, the primary source of enrollment at camp is returning campers. A national survey of all types of camps shows that the average percentage of campers returning to camps is 50 to 60 percent. These percentages suggest that many camps depend upon a much higher return rate. Obviously, the lower the return, the more difficult is the task confronting the director; recruitment of new campers requires considerably more time, effort, and money.

Therefore, the director's first concentration should be on approaching previous campers. An early mailing or e-mailing about the upcoming summer's sessions, dates, and special programs for returning campers is an important step. Follow-up website postings or newsletters (digital or hard copy) can list the returning campers as they enroll. Many camps find that a regular bulletin or e-mail to campers and staff is a good means of maintaining contact, building spirit, and encouraging a return to camp. It need not be expensive, but it should be attractive and newsy with numerous names mentioned and pictures and memories from the previous summer included. Producing such communication digitally can substantially reduce costs associated with printing and mailing. Further, some camps have set up chat rooms, bulletin boards, and blogs for campers to stay in contact with each other between seasons. Building an online community is an efficient and cost-effective way of keeping, creating, and maintaining communication between anyone interested in the camp.

Camper Reunions

A camper reunion often engenders enthusiasm among the previous year's campers and staff. A reunion each year provides an opportunity to share stories, pictures, videos, and fun. The involvement of staff members coupled with a visual presentation from the previous summer are natural elements of a reunion program. Camper reunions can stir memories of the previous summer's experiences and reunite campers who have not been in touch with one another. It is important to have next summer's registration material available at a reunion.

If the majority of campers come from a number of cities or states, then a decentralized plan of reunions or parties may be required. A larger, central reunion provides more excitement and greater contact among campers and staff, but a decentralized plan provides more personal contact between the director and campers as well as a better opportunity to invite prospective campers and parents. Opportunities to share the names of prospective campers (or staffers) can be given for future follow-up. Some camps encourage attendees to bring a friend.

The camp website can also serve as a form of "virtual reunion" with slideshows, pictures, videos, and camper comments about a particular season. In this way, those who may be geographically dispersed can still be reminded of their experience at camp. Previous campers might share these pictures and experiences with their friends without friends having to schedule a trip to camp.

Fun Weekends at Camp

Where the camp property is close enough to a population center, the director can make the property available to groups for their use during the fall, winter, and spring. Day trips or overnight and weekend camping trips on the camp property offer an excellent opportunity for the group leader to describe summer-camp experiences. If camp is rented by user groups, explaining other programs open to individuals is an excellent way to promote the summer experience. The director should see that displays, slideshows, pictures, and videos are available which showcase summer activities.

An "off-season" campsite with all the "in-season" amenities stored or off premises, such as canoes, horses, waterfront and archery equipment, does not promote summer sales to visitors. Special care should be taken to have helpful staff, attractive audiovisuals, and a sampling of camp songs, games, and activities to give visitors a taste of the magic of the regular season.

Home Parties

A preplanned visit and presentation in a previous camper's home or neighborhood, where invitations have been issued to friends, is a tool that has often been used when potential campers are youngsters from upper middle income families and above. They are most effective when a parent or several parents invite prospective campers and their parents to a home for a private presentation by the camp director or staff member. An invitation from a neighbor or friend stimulates more interest than a cold invitation received by mail or from someone the person does not know. It has become harder and harder to persuade families to host such parties in a time-pressured climate where both parents often work. Where it is difficult to utilize a home, the same method may be used in a school, hotel, or church, with several parents of former campers issuing invitations.

Personal Calls

Once a prospect's name and information has been secured and appropriate information about the camp shared by mail, e-mail, or in person, a follow-up call should be made to answer questions and "close the sale." The personal interest shown, as well as the opportunity to answer even minor questions, can be a determining factor in enrollment. This factor is no less true of follow-up calls to previous campers who have not enrolled after the initial enrollment periods.

Individualized Responses to E-mail Requests

Though not as personal as the telephone or in-person visits, responses via e-mail to inquiries from the camp's website or e-mail address should be individualized. A personal interest and concern can be expressed. With the permission of parents of a returning camper, it can be suggested the person contact a given parent to secure their experience or endorsement.

Camp Representatives

Some camps recruit camper representatives—often camper family members—in certain cities or neighborhoods to seek referrals and recruitment. These persons are given training and recruitment tools. In a number of cases, these individuals receive a commission from each new camper enrolled who actually attends camp.

Visits to the Camp

It is not unusual for a family to visit a camp the season before a child is anticipating attendance, or for prospective renters to visit the conference/retreat center in advance. In both cases, this aspect of marketing should not be overlooked.

A plan should be in place for welcoming visitors who wish to see the camp facility or program in operation. A positive approach is to invite such visits on the camp website, in brochures, and in newsletters. Signs at the entrance to the property should clearly indicate where visitors are to report upon arrival.

Similarly, in recruiting rental or user groups, it is good to invite leaders of prospective groups to visit camp while other groups are in operation. Having them see firsthand the type of facilities in use and services offered can be an effective marketing tool.

It is important that the person assigned the responsibility of showing the visitors around the site be fully familiar with the operation, program, and registration questions. It is not a chore to be done quickly so that the camp employee can get on with the business of the facility, but an opportunity to interpret and sell. Similarly, when parents arrive with campers for a session or at the end of a session, it is important to provide the opportunity to meet the camper's counselor and to have any remaining questions answered.

If actual visits to the camp are not feasible, consider providing virtual visits on the camp website. This might involve providing a virtual tour of the camp and its facilities, an opportunity to view profiles of the type of staff employed at the camp, and video presentations of the programs offered at camp. Include video or textual testimonials from campers, staff, and parents. Through such a virtual visit, parents and other potential customers should feel the quality of the camp, its commitment to safety, and the opportunities it provides for fun and growth.

Promotional Materials

All materials produced by the camp should be considered promotional materials, and their quality and content should be addressed with this in mind. Where possible, materials should be developed with the help of a professional and previewed by a small number of potential customers to gauge their reaction prior to dissemination on a larger scale.

Prospective Campers and Groups

A brochure, video, or DVD presentation, however well done, is of little value without a good, qualified prospect to whom it can be presented. Developing lists of qualified prospects requires a system, consistent follow-up, and good planning. With the help of the demographics of previous marketing analyses, an interested group can then brainstorm for sources of prospects. As indicated previously, the best source is previous campers, groups, and staff. Personal referrals from previous campers and interested individuals are also beneficial. These prime prospects should be cultivated with care. Therefore, a system of asking for names of friends or children of friends must be devised. A personal contact is most effective. Providing incentives for interested individuals to provide names and addresses of potential customers is another approach. The development of a referral slip in each newsletter or mailing may be the first step.

Camps that operate under the sponsorship of organizations or churches and synagogues have a natural opportunity for obtaining referrals from other members. They may also be able to provide membership lists in specific age categories. Careful study needs to be given to how members of the organization can be reached for recruitment purposes in the most personal manner. Where members are recruited through troops, clubs, or other neighborhood groups, a natural opportunity arises for letting potential customers know about the camp through the troop, club, and group programs and activities. Many organizations try to get members of a troop, club, or group to come to camp together during the same session. Parents' meetings during the year also offer opportunities to communicate the value of camp for children. Few organizations today can rely solely on their membership for campers or groups, but certainly interpretation and promotion of camp to these organizations is much easier and more effective than to the public at large.

Many camps can cultivate schools or churches and synagogues for the opportunity of presenting a program to an assembly or a class group, or to distribute descriptive material. Though the willingness of a particular public or private body to permit this approach varies, it is worth exploration.

When following up on names received from other individuals, sending materials with a personalized note, indicating: "You were recommended by _____," helps make the materials more meaningful and increases receptivity. Of course, individualized follow-ups by telephone or in person will strengthen the chance for enrollment.

A file should be maintained on each prospective camper or group, including as much personal data as can be secured: name, address, phone number, e-mail address, name of person referring the prospect, age (if an individual), type (if a group). A file of index cards may suffice, though the more sophisticated operation computerizes the list and develops a system to transfer persons to the enrollment file as individuals or groups are signed up. All inquiries received by telephone or mail, or at events such as camper fairs or presentations, should be entered into this file.

Brochures or Flyers

The most traditional method of telling people about the camp experience is the printed word. The size and quality of printed materials marketing the camp experience varies greatly. Many camps print a high-quality, undated, four-color brochure, which is used for several years in conjunction with a rate and date sheet insert that is updated annually. Other camps print a new brochure annually. Some camps simply have to send out an announcement with an application form, but that happens less and less frequently in an increasingly competitive climate.

To be effective, a brochure must be targeted to a specific audience and seldom can speak to multiple audiences effectively. If a variety of audiences are to be reached or significantly different programs to be marketed, several smaller brochures, rather than one extensive one, may be more effective. Each brochure requires careful consideration. For example, type size may not be important in the development of a brochure aimed at youth, but adults prefer larger type for ease of reading.

A brochure need not be expensive to be attractive and effective, but it does need to look professional. A camp director may not have experience in this area and should seek the help of a design or printing professional. In the camper recruitment material for parent consumption, there must be clear definition of age and maturity of staff, type of program and instruction, refund policy, health and age requirements, and values; materials directed to the camper will concentrate on fun, adventure, specific program activities, and peer relationships. On the other hand, a brochure promoting group rental of facilities will emphasize comfort, types of facilities available, beauty of the setting, appropriate seasonal pictures, good food, and value.

Words should be used sparingly; pictures and open space should make up a large part of content. It is better to use good artwork than poor photographs, though a good photograph always speaks best. Although four-color materials are very attractive, a color stock paper with one color ink and the use of screening or reverse tools can also produce an attractive brochure at a lower cost. In a limited-budget situation, consider an enrollment card on a page of the brochure and another page as the back cover with space for an address label and postage imprint for a self-mailer.

Incentives

Incentives to returning campers who sign up by a given date and to staff or campers who sign up or recommend new campers can stimulate interest. These incentives range from pennants or t-shirts to cash discounts on camper fees or bonuses on staff salaries. Obviously volunteer referral and genuine enthusiasm are preferable.

Visual Presentations

However good a brochure may be, it is impossible to capture the full visual and emotional impact of the camp experience on paper. That aspect is more effectively captured in the voice of a person who has been there, along with pictures illustrating the camp experience. Presentations are tools that can combine both of those elements.

Again, the principle of quality prevails, for it is better to do something simply and do it well than to produce a highly technical presentation that is poorly done. Therefore, a camp director will do well to start with a simple presentation with good visuals until the time, budget, and expert assistance to move to the next level are available.

With the availability of volunteers with photographic equipment and/or experience in developing websites, it is difficult not to immediately take advantage of an offer to help develop this tool. To be effective, such efforts need to be carefully planned, scripted, photographed, and tightly edited. It is better to take the extra time and money and do it right when so much hinges upon telling the story effectively.

Try to limit audiovisual presentations for public use to eight minutes. It is a short time, but viewers' minds wander when presentations last much longer.

Supplement the show with 10 to 15 minutes of personal presentation, which may include a camper or staff-member presentation. The prospective audience must be determined first, and the presentation designed to address, captivate, and sell that audience.

Developing a website requires a different approach and also requires particular skills that make it professional and engaging. As more and more camps develop websites, it becomes critical to distinguish the camp from the many others found on the Internet.

Though many camps are utilizing videos or DVDs in place of brochures, a live person offering a visual presentation is certainly preferable to achieve a face-to-face sale. The video or DVD "brochure" has the advantage of multiple showings and the potential involvement of many friends and neighbors. On the other hand, however well made such a presentation is, the sales world knows it is best when someone is present to make the sale—to ask the prospect to enroll and sign on the dotted line. Where it is not possible (such as mailing a video/DVD or visiting a camp's website), the material must provide a clear way in which the viewer can get more information, plus receive follow-up by a staff member as soon as possible.

Outside Referrals

A plan to secure referrals from social agencies, judiciaries, churches, and synagogues can be valuable. Many camps rely on referrals from social workers, agencies, the court system, or their own membership. In these cases, early contacts with the persons responsible for such referrals are important so that the director can establish a good relationship with changing personnel at the agency and develop a plan for working together. A clear understanding of the ability of the camp to serve persons with certain needs or problems and the plan for payment is essential in this arrangement.

Camper Referral Services

These agencies will list a number of camps and refer prospective campers who inquire about a camp or camps that meet the requirements the parents and children have set forth. Some agencies charge the camp a percentage (10 to 15 percent) of the camp fee of children who actually enroll. Other agencies—particularly not-for-profit agencies that are there to serve a specific population—will refer campers as a service to the parent, with no charge to the camp.

Public Displays

Displays with quantities of brochures in public locations can stimulate interest in camp. Carefully choose the locations where the demographic profile of the camp's potential customer would shop, stop, or browse. Generally, this approach cannot be afforded except with a relatively inexpensive brochure. However, an attractive display with pictures or a self-contained audiovisual presentation and return postcards to request a brochure can lower the cost and narrow the prospects.

Advertising

Camper Fairs

Camper fairs are events where a large number of camps are invited to set up individual booths to interpret their camp for one day. A fee is normally charged the camp. The event is publicized and advertised broadly and large numbers of people flow through a fair for its duration. A booth must have a lively visual presentation and aggressive, but personable, staff to distinguish the camp from the many others in the lineup.

Magazines, Newspapers, and Other Media Advertising

This type of advertising requires an attractive, professionally designed ad, and to be effective, it must be run on a regular basis during the peak period for enrollments. Advertising on the radio or television certainly requires professional advice and development to be effective. Though many radio stations offer free time for spot announcements to non-profit organizations, the spots are often run at odd hours. In each medium, regular repetition of the ad is vital.

To advertise in any and every publication is not a wise use of funds. Diane Meckler, *The New York Times* group advertising manager, states:

> An advertising campaign is not an end unto itself in securing enrollments, but a means for securing prospects who can then be turned into enrollments. [When] you have defined

the target audience geographically, by your cost and by your specialty, you are ready to choose the right [medium] for your advertising campaign.[10]

Internet Ads

An Internet ad or banner on a compatible website—such as a youth development site or news organization—can direct the viewer to the camp website where the reader has the option to e-mail or call for further information. Collaborations can be sought with businesses that may be willing to give credence to the camp on their websites.

Since websites exist for a variety of camps, it is important to identify the unique characteristics and mission of the camp. Pictures, illustrations, and testimonials will liven up the copy and will appeal to the reader.

Billboards

Attractive, professionally designed billboards can attract attention to the camp. However, location, timing, and duration of exposure are critical ingredients. The cost factor is another consideration. Even if space is donated, the cost of design and printing is significant.

Posters

Posters must be eye-catching and should include tear-off pieces to request more information or the placement of brochures nearby.

Direct Mail and E-mail

Specialized businesses sell lists of names, addresses, and e-mail addresses based upon the specifications given by the customer. For example, a camp may wish to purchase labels or e-mail addresses for families of a certain income, in certain ZIP codes, and with children of a certain age range. The camp presents the company with three specifications that they are to meet, and the company provides a set of labels or e-mail addresses accordingly.

At this point, reference to the earlier market analysis will indicate the neighborhoods, schools, ZIP codes, or organizations from which more campers and groups have previously enrolled. It will usually prove much more effective to market in areas where sales have been made previously than to pioneer totally new territory. It takes less time and budget because of built-in recommendations and contacts, where people have already shown receptivity to the camp's message.

With the volume of bulk and junk mail received by the public at large, such a mailing must be eye-catching and have a response gimmick to make it pay for itself. One rule of thumb is that a camp may expect an inquiry rate of about four percent of the number mailed with a one percent sign-up.

Publicity and Public Relations

Public Presentations

Presenting the camp's video or slideshow along with a verbal interpretation at various service clubs and community organizations can be a different way of spreading the word about the value of the camp experience. Parents of campers, staff members, and volunteers often have relationships with churches, synagogues, or schools (both public and private) that can make it possible to make presentations to interested persons. Though the presentations may not be designed for camper recruitment, the programs can help others know about the camp.

Websites

A website can give basic information about the camp in a fashion to entice the reader (parent or prospective camper) to examine page after page, stimulating excitement about the camp program in a way that printed materials may not. The page can provide contact information so if the site visitor is interested or has questions, the visitor can follow up via e-mail, phone call, or visit. A registration form should be included with the capacity to accept a credit card deposit.

It is important to identify the unique characteristics and mission of the camp. Virtual tours, photos, videos, and testimonials will engage and excite the site visitor if done properly. As parents scan many camp websites looking for a camp, the home page is critical in enticing the reader to explore the site further. Information should be included about the staff, camp facilities, and camp activities. Dynamic content in these areas can distinguish a camp from others that merely provide static web presentations.

Social Media

Social media has opened new ways of connecting with a camp's market directly. Certainly, the camper-age prospect is already on Facebook, Twitter, YouTube, or such, conversing with friends. Why should camp not be part of that conversation?

Eric Nututlin suggests that:

> *Today, your marketing needs to speak with people, not at them with the goal of making new friends, building trust, and enhancing existing relationships. Conversations about your camp are taking place online with or without you on Facebook, Twitter, LinkedIn, YouTube, MySpace, Flickr, and Yelp, so why not join the fun?*
>
> *If your camp does not have a YouTube account, sign up today. Then start posting videos, invite viewer ratings and comments, and respond to any comments you get … . Other than Facebook, there's no place online you find more camper prospects gathered in one place than YouTube.*[11]

One of the values of the development of the Internet is the ability of individuals to share their experiences and opinions. Stephen Bransletter suggest that:

> Blogs and online news postings are excellent ways to keep your camp families informed. Typically written in an informal and personal style, blogs are like online journals and serve as an excellent way to display a camp's true personality. Make sure the author includes his or her name (or camp nickname) to personalize the message.[12]

The other side of the coin is that a camp director can often gain information about the experiences of campers that can give clues for better promotion or provide implications for the camp program. Not all of the information gained may be positive, for in the process online respondents feel very comfortable sharing negative comments as well. Such feedback should be considered with an eye toward how the consumer views the camp experience, and making appropriate amends.

E-Mail

E-mail provides not only an opportunity to confirm registrations, request information, or remind persons that payments or forms have not been received, but it provides a method of continuous communication with the camper after camp is over. For instance, many camps have sent birthday cards to their campers during the year. E-mail provides a more economical method in tune with the camper's mindset. Of course, texting would be even more in tune, but a bit more difficult.

News Stories

Camp is rich with human-interest stories. A staff member should be given the responsibility of notifying local newspapers, magazines, and radio/TV stations of potential stories. Make sure enough details are provided to interest a reporter. Though camp season may offer the most obvious opportunities, special events during the rest of the year may also stimulate stories.

Bringing Groups to the Camp

Arranging a time during the camp season for people in the local community nearest camp to visit the camp can be invaluable in developing strong community understanding and ties. Though many camps offer facilities for rental in periods other than the summer, rental groups are often looked upon as a separate program or entity. Actually, if time and energy are spent, these groups can be ideal conduits for camp promotion. These organizations offer a natural marketing target. The nature of a rental group may enable the marketing approach to be tailored in a fashion that may generate interest in specific programs or facilities. Perhaps benefits of individual participation in camp can also benefit the group, thus stimulating the support and interest of the leader of the group.

When rental groups arrive at the camp, a clear plan of check-in and orientation should be in place. The orientation should include a tour to familiarize them with facility locations and informational sessions about mealtimes, safety regulations, and how to obtain help in case of an emergency. Though much of this information will have been presented to the group in writing, it should still be presented in person, if at all possible. Helping people feel at home and comfortable is the beginning of a good experience, and the continuation of marketing. When the website effectively communicates about the camp's facilities and procedures, individuals are likely to have clearer expectations when they arrive at camp.

An initial on-site orientation provides the opportunity to explain about other camp programs and to indicate that materials are available at a given location. Attractive displays—including brochures—will stimulate interest on the part of some participants. A self-contained audiovisual could be set up in one corner of the dining hall or a lounge area.

Again, it is important that a plan for marketing be developed that selects which of these marketing devices will be used and in what fashion. The selection of the tools to be used will depend upon many factors: amount of funds available, the number of new campers desired, the camp's philosophy and message, and the audience to be addressed. It is always better to do a few things well than to use many tools and use them poorly.

Registration Forms

Regardless of whether the camp is enrolling individuals or groups, a registration form will be needed. It should be carefully designed in light of its intended use before, during, and after the campers or groups are at camp. Whether it is a card, a sheet, a half sheet, or available online should be determined by how it is to be filed and how often it will be handled. When choosing a format, also consider if the information will need to be transferred to a computer file. It should be remembered that the information gathered on the registration form will provide the beginning of the camp's database of campers and groups, so careful thought should be given to what data will be helpful for comparative purposes in the future.

Actual information on the application blank for individual campers may include:
- Address of camper (zip code sorts may reveal some of the best markets)
- Home phone number and any related cell-phone numbers
- E-mail addresses
- Birth date
- School and grade (specify the grade at the time of enrollment or the following fall)
- Parents' and guardians' names and emergency contacts
- Work address, e-mail address, and phone numbers of each parent and guardian
- Height and weight

- Religious affiliation (particularly if special arrangements are made for attending religious services out of camp)
- Name of a friend the camper wishes to have in the same living group
- Where the camper learned about camp
- Other organizational programs or activities in which the camper participates
- Any physical, psychological, or mental disabilities which may require special attention
- Gender
- Any previous outdoor camping or camp experience
- Cancellation and refund policy

In addition, a paragraph is usually included, after which the parent or guardian signs, giving permission for the child to be enrolled in camp for the given session and stating that he will pay the camper fee. In the case of adult campers, it should be a paragraph that the person signs, indicating the session for enrollment and that he will pay the given fee. A paragraph may include:

- A release for the camp to use any photos or video taken of the camper at camp
- A statement concerning family income, if the child qualifies for financial assistance through any local, county, state, or federal program
- Information about the family's or individual's health-insurance carrier (if the camp is not providing health and accident insurance on the camper, or if the family's insurance is used as the primary or secondary insurance)
- A medical and surgical release statement (in some communities, this statement must be notarized as a requirement of the local hospital)
- Information about to whom, if anyone other than the admitting parent, a minor camper is to be released
- Any special dietary requirements

Actual information on the registration form for groups may include:
- The name of the organization or group, and its office address and phone number
- The name of the responsible adult who will be in charge of the group at the time of their arrival
- The name, address, e-mail address, and phone number of the person making the reservation
- The number of persons who will be present, including some breakdown by sex and general age grouping
- How the group learned about the camp
- The planned arrival and departure times
- What services will be covered in the contract (e.g., meals, staff for program, equipment, linens, room setup, special menus)
- The conditions for the use of any equipment and facilities, such as swimming area, as well as who is responsible for such items as first aid, supervision, behavior, or program

- The rate that the group will be charged
- The amount of deposit required, the minimum fee, and cancellation policies relating to refunds and deadlines
- Any rules to which the group leadership must agree in advance on behalf of the group, such as those concerning alcoholic beverages, controlled substances, or firearms

Some camps, by their special nature, have rather specific entrance requirements or limitations necessitated by the owner's purpose and program. Those entrance requirements should be clearly spelled out in the promotional materials and on the registration form. The registration form should elicit all the information necessary to determine if an applicant meets those requirements. All camps have some requirements even though they may be only a given sex or minimum age.

In some cases, it may be essential to collect specific information to determine the suitability of the activities at camp for the camper or to ensure the placement of the camper in activities appropriate for his age and skill level.

The Americans with Disabilities Act of 1990 (ADA) requires that all camps— except those operated by religious groups and private clubs—make their programs and facilities accessible to individuals with disabilities. Religious groups and private clubs are exempted only when serving their own members and only if they are not receiving any federal funding or food or milk commodities from the U.S. Department of Agriculture.

To determine appropriate accommodations, it is permissible to ask that disabilities be identified on registration forms. It is important, however, that the information requested about a camper's health and disabilities only be used to identify appropriate health care, activities, and precautions, and to better serve the camper, not to screen out campers. It will be helpful to indicate to parents that the goal of the camp is to provide the best camp experience possible. Add wording to this effect to letters that accompany health forms where parents are asked to identify any disabilities or health problems the prospective camper has.

Some camps may find that they are unable to serve campers with certain disabilities. The Americans with Disabilities Act obligates camps to make reasonable accommodations to include individuals with disabilities in their programs, so long as the accommodations are readily achievable and do not create an undue burden on the organization or fundamentally alter the basic experience the camp is designed to provide. As Marge Scanlin notes, "For example, it would appear to fundamentally alter a wilderness backpacking experience conducted in mountainous rocky terrain where there are no paths, if persons in wheelchairs were included on the trip."[13]

Camps must also be concerned with the level of safety provided to the individual and every other camper in the program. Scanlin continues:

> *The ADA expressly states that a public accommodation may exclude an individual, if that individual poses a direct threat to the health or safety of others that cannot be mitigated by*

appropriate modifications in the camp's policies or procedures, or by the provision of auxiliary aids. [Camp directors] will be permitted to establish objective safety criteria for the operation of their camps. However, any safety standard must be based on objective requirements rather than stereotypes or generalizations about the ability of people with disabilities to participate in an activity.[14]

Therefore, decisions about participation should be on an individual basis.

Registration forms may also include an agreement to participate. Ed Schirick, vice president and division manager of Frontier Insurance Group, suggests:

There is a growing trend toward acceptance [of agreements to participate or waivers]. This is especially true when the individuals have been "properly" informed of the risks and understand what might happen to them if they participate in the activity. The basis of this is a reaffirmation by the courts, in some states, of the common law doctrine of assumption of risk.[15]

Obviously, such statements should be developed in consultation with the camp's attorney, but they can never remove the responsibility of the host to the guest. See Chapter 11 for more information about waivers and liability releases.

The third step, after identifying the message and selecting the tools to be used in marketing, is to develop a plan of implementation. A plan should outline each of the steps to accomplish the goals, and should place those steps in calendar form for a 12-month period with a deadline for each. Joanna Warren Smith recommends:

The best way to convey consistent attention to detail and excellence at every level of your program is to put your ideas on paper and publish a year-round marketing strategy … . Plan mailings, phone calls, and newsletters. Be realistic about necessary preparation time. Be clear about the personalized follow-up that every inquiry demands. Through this tracking you can see what is working, what is not, and where you have too much and not enough.[16]

The emphasis is on approaching marketing on a 12-month basis, calendaring each segment of the plan, and reviewing regularly the progress of each aspect of the plan.

It is to the director's advantage in planning, buying supplies, and employing staff, to start camper enrollment as early as possible. It takes time to develop a pattern of early enrollment, but it can be gradually encouraged. On the other hand, certain weather changes or seasons do encourage customers to begin thinking about camp (e.g., the arrival of warm days in the spring, or a vacation period when the youngsters are around the house a great deal).

It is not possible for the camp director to accomplish each of these steps alone. It is wise to enlist the assistance of staff, former staff, former campers, parents of campers, and committee members in the marketing process. This enlistment will provide a variety of energetic and enthusiastic people who, given the proper information and training, can spread the camp's story much more effectively than one person can. Most of this process can be accomplished through volunteers, though it may be necessary to employ one or two people to carry out more time-consuming or specialized portions of the plan. The next step is to implement the plan and to constantly check whether the plan is proceeding on schedule. Even the best volunteers need follow-up calls and pep talks from time to time.

Planning for the coming year will require evaluation of how well the previous year's plan worked and how it should be changed. Evaluation is discussed in greater detail in Chapter 18.

Checkpoints

- Clarify the camp's identity.
- Do a market analysis of the camp.
- Locate all materials previously used for camp promotion. Examine them in light of the clarity of the camp's identity, goals, desired outcomes, and the market analysis. Ask an outside expert to critique them, or check out the competition's marketing materials.
- Determine the ways in which potential customers seek to learn or learned about the camp.
- List the steps that can be taken in light of the market analysis; arrange them in order of importance.
- Develop a marketing plan for the camp, calendared for one year.
- Implement, and follow through.

Related Standards

American Camp Association's Accreditation Standards for Camp Programs and Services: OM.4, OM.13–15; HW.1, HW.9, HW.17, HW.20, HW.28; PD.1, PD.3; HR.1, HR.4, HR.5, HR.8, HR.12

ACA e-Institute Online Course

Marketing Essentials for the New Economy (Three Part Series) with Jodi Rudick

Endnotes

1   Armand Ball. 1982. "On the Ball." *Camping Magazine*. Vol. 54, No. 3, February. p. 2.
2. Dwight Jewson, Strategic Frameworking, Inc., Personal correspondence. Vashon, Washington, May 31, 2003.

3. "Parents Are Listening More to Kids." 1990. *USA Today*. January 24, 1990.

4. Edward L. Hayes. 1989. "Positioning Your Ministry in the Market Place." *Journal of Christian Camping*. Vol. 22, No. 3, May/June. p. 10. Reprinted with permission from CCI/USA.

5. "Survey Says…" 2001. *Christian Camps and Conference Journal*. Vol. 5, No. 5, September/October. pp. 30–33.

6. Dwight Jewson. 1978. "The Promotional Aspect of Camp Marketing." *Camping Magazine*. Vol. 50, No. 6, May. p. 17.

7. Douglas B. Herron. 1997. *Marketing Not-for-Profit Programs and Services*. San Francisco, CA: Jossey-Bass. p. 34.

8. Peg L. Smith. 2008. "The Strength of Many Voices." *Camping Magazine*. Vol. 81, No. 1, January/February. pp. 27-28.

9. Report of Maguire Associates, Inc., Concord, MA, for the American Camping Association Private Independent Camps, 1990.

10. Diane Meckler. 1988. "Marketing." *Camping Magazine*. Vol. 61, No. 1, September/October. p. 24.

11. Eric Naftulin. 2011. "Top Eight Summer Camp Marketing Strategies for 2011." *Camping Magazine*. Vol. 84, No. 2, March/April. p. 42.

12. Stephen Bransletter. 2008. "New Technologies to Improve Camp Marketing." *Camping Magazine*. Vol. 81, No. 2, March/April. p. 10.

13. Marge Scanlin. 1992. "Better Camping for All: A Beginning Look at the Americans With Disabilities Act." *Camping Magazine*. Vol. 64, No. 3, February. p. 31.

14. Ibid.

15. Ed Schirick. 1990. "Risk Management." *Camping Magazine*. Vol. 62, No. 5, March. p. 9.

16. Joanna Warren Smith. 1997. "Out-of-the-Box Marketing Strategies." *Camping Magazine*. Vol. 70, No. 5, September/October. p. 25.

BUSINESS AND FINANCE

Chapter Sixteen

Continuing success in camping is obviously dependent upon sound business procedures ... the camp business administration is just as surely a long-term means of accomplishing our camp objectives as are other phases of camp operation, such as program, staff recruiting, and property upkeep.[1]

—John A. Ledlie

The fiscal management of the camp is too often the last consideration of many camp directors, whose primary concerns lie with campers and program. To others, the bottom line is the starting point and program considerations depend upon the financing. Actually, the philosophy, program, marketing, and finances are so interdependent that each one is ineffectual without the other.

When the camp director chooses to give significant personal attention to the program of the camp when groups are on site, a support system may need to be in place to oversee the camp's operations and fiscal affairs. Often, camp directors retain the direct supervision of the program because of their interest and find an assistant who serves as business manager. A business manager typically supervises all or some of the operational systems of the camp, such as office, business, food service, transportation, property and site management, and health service. Other staffing arrangements may divide functions differently, depending on the interest and skills of the camp director and other personnel, and on camp organizational structure.

The director should assign day-to-day financial responsibilities to one staff person at camp and should provide that person with a precise job description. Lines of responsibility and accountability should be clear to all staff. The maintenance of up-to-date, accurate records is essential, so some training and experience is necessary for this job. A business manager with some accounting experience is ideal; in addition, some camps will have a bookkeeper in the office.

Accounting Practices

The specific accounting and budgetary practices of camps will vary greatly according to the volume of financial transactions and the sophistication of the operator's organization. Camps that are part of a larger organization will find that systems which the camp is expected to follow are already in place. Other camps will have the opportunity of setting up their own systems; in most cases, those systems will be tied to a computer program. Today, even the smallest camps have access to a computer and a simple bookkeeping system. However, with or without a computer, the basic principles are the same and need to be understood from the outset:

- A budget of projected income and expenses should be established.
- All income must be documented and verified.
- All monies (cash receipts and checks) should be deposited promptly.
- Internal controls should be established.
- Expenditures should be made against approved invoices.

- Regular summaries of financial activity, preferably monthly, should be planned. During more active times, weekly summaries should be scheduled.

- A system should be developed which identifies high and low points of cash flow, so that low points may be anticipated and adequate planning can occur.

- The books should be audited annually, by some person not on the staff.

Advice from a certified public accountant (CPA) or other knowledgeable source should be secured on the following matters (in some cases, a bookkeeping service will be able to answer these questions):

- Choice of a cash or accrual system of bookkeeping.

- Tax reports required by local, state, and federal governments.

- Generally Accepted Accounting Principles (GAAP) as defined by the Financial Accounting Standards Board (FASB).[2]

- Financial records to be kept—including journals and receivables, payables, and payroll—and the length of time different records should be kept.

- How and where to store and back up paper and digital records.

Annual Audit

If the camp is setting up a new financial system or reevaluating a system already in place, an operational financial risks worksheet (Figure 16-1) will be helpful in identifying office procedures to manage and safeguard financial resources.

Where camps are part of larger organizations, the organization will have already chosen a cash or accrual system of bookkeeping. In an independent camp, that choice is one the director should make in consultation with the accountant. A cash system recognizes cash when received and disbursed and treats all monies received and expended in a given period of 12 months as the operating funds. An accrual system recognizes income when earned and expenses when incurred, regardless of when cash is actually received or paid and seeks to attribute the income and expenses to the actual 12 months of operation they affect; thereby, accruing or accumulating and applying income and expense for the next year's operation to the next year's budget.

An annual audit of the financial records of a camp is an important step in identifying to the camp's public that it is being operated in a sound fashion. That audit should be done by an external person or group rather than by the person keeping the books or preparing the camp's financial statements. One of the functions of an external audit is to define any "significant deficiencies" or "material weaknesses" within the financial operation. Such points provide guidance in strengthening systems, establishing appropriate policies in the operation of the camp that give evidence of strong financial oversight.

More complex rules apply to the type of audit for nonprofit organizations with a total income of more than two million dollars, and this would affect camps that are part of a nonprofit organization with that income. Certain types of grants that entail government funds may also result in the more detailed audit.

Operational Financial Risks Worksheet

Operational financial risks are those where property, equipment, and/or money might be damaged or lost. Considerations to effectively manage and safeguard the financial resources include identifying the financial controls needed and determining procedures to control or reduce the risks. Oversight of the financial operations includes audits, preparation of financial statements, preparation of and monitoring of the annual budget and cash flow projections, and monitoring of actual cash flow.

Person responsible: _____

Petty Cash
Amount of cash available: _____ Maximum an individual may request: _____
Person responsible for maintaining: _____ Reconciling: _____
Person with access to petty cash: _____ How is cash secured? _____
Explain reimbursement requirements from petty cash: _____
Person authorizing payments: _____ How is petty cash replenished? _____

Cash Receipts
Person handling checks received by mail: _____
How and when are checks endorsed and recorded (numbered receipts reconciled with cash received)? _____
_____
How often are deposits made? _____ By: _____
Procedure for giving checks/cash to staff or volunteers: _____
Person with access to checks/cash: _____
How are checks/cash secured on-site? _____ Off-site? _____
Policy on third-party checks: _____

Cash Disbursements
Does the procedure include use of pre-numbered checks? _____
And a system to secure and account for unused checks? _____
Person authorized to sign checks: _____
Is a limit established, over which a second signature is required? _____
Are purchase orders and receiving documents required for payment? _____
Person authorizing payment: _____ Are invoices canceled after payment? _____
Explain the refund policy: _____
Person with authority to purchase or commit camp funds: _____ Are limits to this authority established? _____
Person responsible for entering into a contract on the camp's behalf: _____
When is bidding required? _____
What is considered for comparison, (e.g., quantity, quality, delivery availability and time, cost, size or minimum-order requirements, etc.)? _____
What expenses are reimbursable, and at what rate? _____
Documentation requirements: _____

Reconciliation and Analysis
Are bank statements reconciled monthly? _____ By: _____
Explain the policy on payroll and benefits accrual: _____ Person responsible for analyzing: _____
Person responsible for reviewing receivables: _____
Is a policy in place on write-offs of accounts receivables? _____
Person responsible for generating a monthly list of outstanding unpaid invoices: _____

Inventory of Equipment and Supplies
Person responsible for program supplies: _____ Person with access: _____
How are program supplies secured? _____
Person responsible for office supplies: _____ Person with access: _____
How are office supplies secured? _____
Person responsible for food supplies: _____ Person with access: _____
How are food supplies secured? _____
Person responsible for sale merchandise: _____ Person with access: _____
How is sale merchandise secured? _____

Tax Liability
Is sales tax being collected and remitted on selling of supplies? _____ By: _____
Person responsible for remitting payroll tax forms, filling 990s, paying into unemployment funds, and making provisions for any contingencies that might encumber the future operation: _____

Figure 16-1. Operational financial risks worksheet

Financial Statements

Three financial statements are important for camps. The first important statement to be considered is a *statement of activities* or *income statement*, which shows the income and expense activity in a given month. This statement should be reviewed on a monthly basis for management control purposes. The director may want this statement to show columns for the income and expenses for that month, and also for the year to date, the budgeted amount, and the actuals for the same month the previous year. This statement provides a checkpoint for the director (and board, if the camp has one) to adjust certain expense items if income is not meeting expectations, or if some expense accounts are running over expectations.

At the end of the year, the not-for-profit's statement of activities provides a summary of all income and expenses by accounts for the year and indicates a net gain or loss for the year. See Figure 16-2 for an example of a nonprofit's statement of activities. Since nonprofits often have restricted income accounts due to designated contributions, an additional statement showing the changes in net assets can be very helpful; an example is shown in Figure 16-3. For-profit organizations generally call their statement of activities an income statement; see Figure 16-4 for an example.

In addition to a statement of activities, the second important camp financial statement is a *balance sheet* or, under new nonprofit terminology, a *statement of financial position*.[3] This statement summarizes the net assets and liabilities of the camp, and it is a key to the long-range financial health of the camp. Figure 16-5 shows a sample nonprofit statement of financial position. Figure 16-6 provides a sample format for such a balance sheet statement for a for-profit. The annual operations either add to or detract from the positive side of this equation. For instance, a deficit in a year's operation uses any surplus funds that are on hand from previous years or causes obligations against property. The goal of every camp, even the nonprofit operation, is to provide a growth in the assets of the camp to ensure that persons will be served in the future.

In the case of the for-profit camp, this investment usually is a good portion of the owner's assets, which are to provide income or security at the time of retirement. Both statements identify the actual bottom line of the camp's assets or investments.

The third important financial statement is a *cash-flow statement*. Under the new rules of the Financial Accounting Standards Board, nonprofits are required to prepare a cash-flow statement as for-profits have done traditionally. These statements identify the changes in cash flow during the year. The cash-flow statement shows the difference between the beginning and ending operating accounts. The increases or decreases are shown in the various lines on the statement of financial position, ultimately showing a net change in cash position at year's end. Not-for-profits should seek the assistance of their own certified public accountant to work out the correct format and records. See Figure 16-7 for a list of elements to include in a cash-flow statement, as well as a sample chart in Figure 16-8.

Nonprofit Statement of Activities

	Prior Year to Date	Current Year to Date	Current Budget to Date	Percentage Budget to Date
Revenues				
Earned				
Program A: Summer				
Program B: Environmental education				
Program C: Rentals				
Income from investments				
Contributed				
Contributions				
Released from restrictions*				
Expired				
Equipment acquisition				
Program				
Total unrestricted revenue				
Expenses				
Program:				
Program A: Summer				
Program B: Environmental education				
Program C: Rentals				
Development (fund raising)				
Administrative				
Total expenses				
Net Unrestricted Income				
Released contributions				
Released to unrestricted				
Net Restricted Income				
Net All Activity				

* If preferred, the income released from restricted categories may be shown as a positive in the natural income category and a negative in the "released to unrestricted" line.

Figure 16-2. Nonprofit statement of activities

Nonprofit Statement of Activities

	Unrestricted	Temporarily Restricted	Permanently Restricted	Total
Revenues				
Earned				
Program A: Summer				
Program B: Environmental education				
Program C: Rentals				
Income from investments				
Development				
Contributions				
Grants				
Released from restrictions*				
Expired				
Equipment acquisition				
Program				
Total unrestricted revenue				
Expenses				
Program:				
Program A: Summer				
Program B: Environmental education				
Program C: Rentals				
Development (fund raising)				
Administrative				
Total expenses				
Net Unrestricted Income				
Released contributions				
Released to unrestricted				
Total Restricted Income				
Net All Activity				

* If preferred, the income released from restricted categories may be shown as a positive in the natural income category and a negative in the "released to unrestricted" line.

Figure 16-3. Nonprofit statement of changes in net assets

For-Profit Income Statement

	Monthly Actual	Monthly Actual	Last Year	Year to Date	Annual Budget
Revenues					
Camper fees					
Special fees					
Investment income					
Sales					
Miscellaneous					
Total revenues					
Expenses					
Salaries and benefits					
Food					
Utilities					
Equipment					
Taxes and insurance					
Repairs					
Depreciation and amortization					
Transportation expenses					
Program expenses					
Training expenses					
Office expenses					
Total expenses					
Net Income					

Figure 16-4. For-profit income statement

Nonprofit Statement of Financial Position

Assets

Cash and cash equivalents	Assets restricted to investment in land, buildings, and equipment
Account and interest receivable	Land, buildings, and equipment
Inventories and prepaid expenses	Contributions receivable
Short-term investments	Long-term investments
Total Assets	

Liabilities and Net Assets

Accounts payable and accrued expenses	Notes payable
Grants payable	Long-term debt
Total Liabilities	

Net Assets

Unrestricted
Temporarily restricted
Permanently restricted

Total Net Assets

Total Liabilities and Net Assets

Figure 16-5. Nonprofit statement of financial position

For-Profit Balance Sheet

Assets
Current assets
   Cash and cash equivalents (investments)
   Accounts receivable
   Inventories
   Prepaid expenses
Total current assets
Facilities
   Land
   Building
   Furniture
Subtotal facilities
Accumulated depreciation and amortization (minus)
Total facilities

Total Assets

Liabilities and Owner's Equity
Liabilities
   Accounts payable and accrued expenses
   Deferred income
Total current liabilities
Long-term liabilities
   Mortgage payable
Total long-term liabilities
Owner's equity
   Capital stock
   Retained earnings
Total owner's equity

Total Liabilities and Owner's Equity

Figure 16-6. For-profit balance sheet

Elements to Include in Cash-Flow Statements

Nonprofit

Cash flow from operating activities

Change in net assets

  Adjustment to reconcile change in net assets to net cash used by operating activities

  Depreciation

  Increase in accounts and interest receivable

  Decrease in inventories and prepaid expenses

  Increase in contributions receivable

  Increase in accounts payable

  Decrease in grants payable

  Contributions restricted for long-term investment

  Interest and dividends restricted for long-term investment

Total cash used by operating activities

Cash flow from investment activities

  Purchase of equipment

  Proceeds from sale of investments

  Purchase of investments

Net cash used by investment activities

Cash flow from financing activities

  Proceeds from contributions restricted for:

    Investment in endowment

    Investment in plant

  Other financing activities

  Interest and dividends restricted for reinvestment

  Payments of annuity obligations

  Payments on notes payable

  Payments on long-term debt

Net cash used by financing activities

Net decrease in cash and equivalents

Cash and cash equivalents at beginning of year

Cash and cash equivalents at end of year

For-Profit

Cash flow from operating activities

Net income

  Adjustments to reconcile net income to cash used by operating activities

  Depreciation expense

  Increase or decrease in accounts receivable

  Increase or decrease in inventories

  Increase or decrease in prepaid expense

  Increase or decrease in other current assets

  Increase or decrease in accounts payable

  Increase or decrease in accrued expenses

  Increase or decrease in taxes payable

  Increase or decrease in other current liabilities

Total cash flow from operating activities

Cash flow from investment activities

  Proceeds from sales of investments

  Purchase of investments

  Purchase of equipment

Total cash flow from investment activities

Cash flow from financing activities

  Short-term debt

  Long-term debt

  Capital stock

  Other equity

Total cash flow from financing activities

Net change in cash

Cash and cash equivalents beginning of year

Cash and cash equivalents end of year

Figure 16-7. Elements to include in cash-flow statements

Accounts	Annual Budget	January	February	March	April	May	June	July	August	September	October	November	December	Total
Income														
111 Camper fees	$250,000	$5,000	$2,000											
112 Environmental education fees	100,000	10,000	8,000											
121 Horseback	10,000													
122 Bus fees *(until all are listed)*	15,000													
Totals	$375,000	$15,000	$10,000											
Expenditures														
210 Full-time employees	$75,000	$6,250	$6,250											
220 Part-time employees	100,000	2,000	1,750											
230 FICA	10,500	490	470											
240 Unemployment compensation taxes	2,000	70	60											
250 Health insurance *(until all are listed)*	8,000	600	600											
Totals	$375,000	$20,200	$9,130											
Difference	$-0-	($5,200)	$870											

(Difference between income and expenses indicates cash excess or cash needed that month.)

Figure 16-8. Sample cash-flow planning chart

Budgeting

According to *Webster's* dictionary, a budget is "a statement of the financial position of an administration for a definite period of time based on estimates of expenditures during the period and proposals for financing them." The budget is also a reflection of the camp's philosophy, since where the camp secures and spends money indicates the priorities of the operation.

Most budgets cover a 12-month period, though not all budget cycles follow the calendar year. Some fiscal years or budget years are established differently to parallel the owner's financial and budgetary activity, which often follows program operation. Where a parent organization is involved, the budget will need approval by the operating committee, board, or agency. This step necessitates planning and adoption well in advance of the starting date of the fiscal year.

A budget is part of a planning process and reflects the camp's goals, such as the number of participants to be recruited, the number of staff to be employed, the number and type of program activities that can be operated, and the ultimate balance-sheet position the director desires. Since a budget reflects planning and goal setting, it has to be adjusted to actual experience as time progresses. If recruitment reports show that the camp is likely to have fewer campers or groups than budgeted, then not only is the income item for campers lessened, but reductions in expenses must be made to the same degree. Where budgets are approved by groups or persons other than the owner and camp director, a system should be established by which revisions are made and approved.

The Budget Process

The development of a list or chart of accounts, or categories of income and expenses, is the starting point in the budget process. In organizations, those accounts will be given to the camp, and the camp will have to fit its income and expenses into those existing descriptions. Where a camp has the opportunity to develop its own set of accounts, it is wise to list all the types of income sources and expenses, grouping them into logical account names. A sample list of accounts is shown in Figure 16-9. Many organizations—including most not-for-profits—desire or require that this list of accounts be grouped by different functions or areas of income and expense. This functional accounting is demonstrated in Figure 16-10.

Projecting Income and Expense

The safest method of budgeting is to project income conservatively and expenditures more liberally. Ideally, of course, the projections should be as realistic as possible; however, it is better to err on the side of over projecting expenses than income.

In budgeting, the director should not project income from any more campers or groups than were actually enrolled the previous year unless the

Sample List of Accounts

Income

Account	Account Explanation		
110	*Tuition Fees*	*140*	*Sales*
111	Camper	141	Camper store (supplies, shirts)
112	Environmental education	142	Meals to visitors
120	*Fees*	*150*	*Miscellaneous*
121	Horseback riding		
122	Bus transportation	*160*	*Contributions*
123	Arts/crafts	161	Individuals
130	*Rental of Facilities*	162	Government grants
131	Summer	163	United Way
132	Fall, winter, and spring	164	Other

Expenditures

Account	Account Explanation		
200	*Wages and Benefits*	*600*	*Program*
210	Full-time employees	610	Equipment
220	Part-time/seasonal employees	620	Supplies
230	FICA	*700*	*Training*
240	Unemployment compensation/taxes	710	Organization dues
250	Health/accident insurance	720	Books, films, materials
300	*Food Service*	730	Conferences, workshops
310	Kitchen food	740	Training travel
320	Supplies	*800*	*Office*
330	Campout/trail food	810	Postage/UPS
400	*Occupancy*	820	Printing (stationery, envelopes, etc.)
411	Gas	830	Office supplies
412	Electricity	840	Promotional printing
413	Telephone	850	Promotional advertising
414	Water	860	Promotional travel
415	Sewer	*900*	*Board/Committee Expense*
420	Maintenance supplies	910	Board meeting expense
430	Equipment repairs	920	Board training
450	Taxes	930	Director/officer insurance
460	Property/liability insurance	*1000*	*Designated Contributions*
470	Building repairs	1010	Campership grants
480	Building construction	1020	Special projects
500	*Transportation*		
510	Charters or rental/lease		
520	Insurance		
530	Gas/oil		
540	Repairs		
550	Licenses		

Figure 16-9. Sample list of accounts

Accounts by Various Functions
Expenses

Administration*

210	Full-time employees
220	Part-time/seasonal employees
230	FICA
240	Unemployment compensation
250	Insurance (health, workers' compensation)
420	Supplies
710	Organization dues
730	Conferences/workshops
810	Postage/UPS
820	Printing (stationery, envelopes, etc.)
830	Office supplies

Food Service

210	Full-time employees
220	Part-time/seasonal employees
230	FICA
240	Unemployment compensation
250	Insurance (health, workers' compensation)
310	Kitchen food
420	Supplies
320	Campout/trail food

Program

210	Full-time employees
220	Part-time/seasonal employees
230	FICA
240	Unemployment compensation
250	Insurance
420	Supplies
610	Equipment
700	Training

Promotion/Marketing

210	Full-time employees
220	Part-time/seasonal employees
230	FICA
240	Unemployment compensation
250	Insurance
413	Telephone: long distance
420	Supplies
810	Postage/UPS
820	Printing
850	Advertising
860	Travel

Fund-Raising**

210	Full-time employees
220	Part-time/seasonal employees
230	FICA
240	Unemployment compensation
250	Insurance (health, workers' compensation)
413	Telephone: long distance
420	Supplies
810	Postage/UPS
820	Printing
910	Campership grants
920	Allowance for uncollectible pledges

Occupancy

210	Full-time employees
220	Part-time/seasonal employees
230	FICA
240	Unemployment compensation
250	Insurance (health, workers' compensation)
411	Gas
412	Electricity
413	Telephone
414	Water
415	Sewer
420	Supplies
430	Equipment purchases
440	Equipment repairs
450	Taxes/licenses
460	Insurance (building, liability, etc.)
470	Building repairs
480	Building construction
510	Charters/rental/lease vehicles
520	Insurance: vehicles
530	Fuel: vehicles
540	Repairs: vehicles

Volunteer Leadership

910	Meeting expense
920	Training
930	Director/officer insurance

*Where it is not possible to differentiate functions for certain expenses, a section labeled "Administrative" can be added. Those expenses can then be totaled and divided among the other functions on the basis of a percentage based on income, facility, usage, or staff time.

Where camps have substantive operations other than summer camp or conferences (e.g., outdoor education, retreats, etc.), separate functional divisions may be established.

**Nonprofits only.

Figure 16-10. Accounts by various functions

director has strong reason to believe additional campers will come (e.g., other camps in the area are no longer offering the same programs, the camp has increased promotion efforts). When increasing fees, which affects budgeted income, consideration should be given to whether the increase will lead to any reduction in enrollment. Other income accounts should be compared to expenditures for those related activities or services (camp store, transportation to and from camp, special activities) to see if the fees are adequate to provide an acceptable margin of income beyond expenditures in each area. It is vital to include all of the related costs of such activity in this comparison; for example, the salary and related costs for the personnel to operate an activity should be added to the cost of materials and facilities when setting an activity's fees.

In projecting expenditures, one should identify the *fixed costs* of operation, or those that will not change as the number of campers or staff changes (e.g., property taxes, base utilities, office space, and salaries and benefits of full-time employees). Expenses that are not fixed are considered *variables* (e.g., food for 50 campers versus 100 campers). Several projections may be necessary with these expenses based upon various levels of camper enrollment. A point will occur when the fixed expenses plus the variable expenses will balance with or exceed the projected income. This figure becomes the minimum target for budgeting and marketing. The director should always consider the most disastrous thing that could happen, for example, price increases, need for extra staff, equipment breakdown and replacement. Large-expenditure items should be carefully documented. Salaries and food often account for as much as 50 to 60 percent of a camp budget and need to be carefully analyzed since a slight change in either item could substantially alter the budgeted expenditures.

Final Budget Development

Only when a director has viewed the realistic expectation of income and expenses is he in a position to work toward final budget development. It is critical that all of the expenses of camp operation be included in the budget. Particularly in the not-for-profit sector, certain expenses may have been covered in other budgets, or allowances may not have been made for depreciation; thus, the budget won't reflect the true cost of the camp. For example, in some organizations, the salary and related benefits of the year-round professional employee responsible for the camp and/or certain insurance or bookkeeping services may be carried in the overall organizational budget rather than the camp's budget. The accurate amount of any such costs based upon the percentage of time devoted to the camp should be carried in the camp's budget in order to give true costs. All of these issues are important in producing an accurate picture of the camp's state of being for management purposes, for presentation to committees and boards, and for the public.

Adjusting Expenses

If, at this point in the budget process, expenses exceed income, the director should review each expense account to see what can be pared down or eliminated without endangering the program objectives of the camp or the health and safety of the campers. Once the director has determined essential expenses, the camper income that can be expected based upon past experience, other self-generated income (such as from the camp store, program and transportation fees), and possible outside funding available (subsidies, foundation grants, camperships funds, contributions), a decision can be made whether any remaining difference should come from increased fees or from reduced expenditures—which may mean decreased program or personnel. Since camper fees need to be set early in the promotional year, decisions related to fees should be completed by early fall.

In determining income from campers' fees in a camp where some campers pay the full fee and others pay a reduced fee or no fee, it is important to show the source of income for the subsidy of camper fees in the income statement. The director must know the actual cost of the camp experience per camper, especially when he is seeking supplemental funds for campers who cannot pay the full fee. Donors often respond well to the concept of sending a less privileged camper to camp, but they may expect documentation of costs. Outside funding sources—including the United Way and most foundations—require such documentation as well.

Cash Flow

As important as whether a camp is meeting or exceeding budgetary plans is whether the cash received matches the cash needed to cover the expenses for the same time period. Developing a cash-flow planning chart prior to the beginning of the fiscal year will assist the director in planning for cash shortages or overages. A worksheet should be completed with the income accounts and descriptions in a vertical column to the left, followed by columns for an estimate of how much will be received or spent in each account for each month, plus a year-end total. See Figure 16-8 for an example of a cash-flow planning chart. The income and expense accounts are also totaled separately for a given month, providing a cash position. If the cash needs are higher than the income expected for several months in a row, then a plan must be developed to draw cash from reserves or from a bank loan. Similarly, if the camp will have cash excesses for several months in a row, plans should be made for short-term investments during that period to gain interest income. Where the camp has flexibility, the cash-flow planning chart also provides an opportunity to adjust the timetable for certain expenditures.

Internal Controls and Operational Systems

A document stating the internal controls should be developed by staff, accountant/auditor, and treasurer and approved by the board or operator. The purpose of this document is not only to confirm instructions to staff, but also to help prevent any embezzlement, theft, or questions of inappropriate actions on the part of staff and board.

This document should include statements relating to the following questions:

- Who is the person responsible for day-to-day operations?
- Who may assume that responsibility in absence of responsible person?
- When does a board or body responsible for camp meet, will each agenda include a financial report, and who will present it?
- Will the board or appropriate body adopt an annual budget?
- Will an annual audit be performed?
- Is a personnel policies and procedures manual current?

The internal controls policy should also include specific policies relating to the following:

- Day-to-day recording of accounting transactions
- Cash receipts (receipts, banking)
- Bank accounts (various type funds, deposits, signatories, reconciliation)
- Accounts receivable
- Restricted funds
- Purchases (authorization, limits in amounts)
- Accounts payable disbursements
- Credit cards (acceptance, use by staff)
- Petty cash
- Payroll
- Assets and liabilities (how valued, depreciation/capitalization)
- Information technology
- Records retention

In addition, the document should state clearly that employees can be assured that reporting any inappropriate activity with the camp's financial management may be provided to the camp director and/or any individual committee/board member in an anonymous and confidential manner under the Sarbanes-Oxley Act (Pub.L. 107-204, 116 Stat. 745, enacted July 30, 2002). Such a report may be made orally or in writing, without fear of retribution, including firing, demotion, suspension, harassment, and failure to consider the staff member for future promotion or any other kind of discrimination. It should be stated that failure to report such inappropriate financial activity may be considered as an act of complicity.

Receipts and Documentation

Careful accounting of all funds received is essential for accurate records, for good public relations, and for the protection of all concerned. A written or digital record should be kept of each payment received. It is wise to be able to provide a receipt to each payee, although many individuals may accept their canceled check as a receipt. The camp's record of the receipt is used for two purposes: crediting the payee's account and designating the deposit of that payment to the proper budget account. Receipt records should be maintained for seven years.

Receipts should be deposited with the bank or organizational office at regularly scheduled times. A daily deposit of such funds is preferable; but, in many camps, payments come in cycles (at the beginning of the period, for example). This situation may necessitate a daily deposit at the beginning of a session, but only a weekly deposit during the balance of the period. By promptly depositing checks and cash, the director can avoid having substantial amounts of money in camp.

Accounts Receivable

Most camps ask for payment of the entire camper fee in advance or upon arrival at camp. A billing system is usually necessary either to secure the advance payments or to follow up on delinquent payments. Bills should specify the amount to be paid, the person served, the dates covered, the services rendered, any amounts already paid, service fees for late payments, and the balance due. Many camps secure authorization at the time of payment of the deposit by credit card to charge the balance of the fee to the card at a specific later date. A plan should be put in to place that identifies how delinquent payments are reminded and collected.

Restricted Funds

Camps may receive contributions for specific projects such as a new building, equipment, education tuitions, or paying camp fees for needy youngsters. Such funds should be placed in an account separate from fees and operating income. If such gifts are occasional and not large in size, one restricted account with a record of the designation of each gift may be kept. If many gifts are to be received or the designated use is to extend over several years, a restricted account should be named for each project. As a project comes into being, funds may be expended out of the reserved account for specific purposes. For instance, if a scholarship fund is established, as a youngster qualifies and comes to camp, the amount of the camp fee is withdrawn and deposited in the fee account. Not only should the contributor receive an acknowledgement letter expressing appreciation, but at the time the project is complete, the donor should be notified.

Purchasing

Once a budget is approved, a plan of purchasing should be adopted, which will give the director control over what is spent against each budgeted account. A purchase order system is the most common approach to purchasing. See Figure 16-11 for one type of purchase order form. The basic principle of a purchase-order plan is that a written order (typically in multiple copies) for each purchase is filled out and approved in advance of the purchase: one copy to the vendor from whom merchandise is being purchased, one copy for the bookkeeper (to compare to the invoice when it arrives), and one copy for the person making the purchase. Often, purchase orders are prenumbered, providing a means of tracking for the purchaser and the vendor. If the purchase order is not given to or mailed to the vendor, the purchase order number is

Purchase Order Form

Camp Everyone
234 Same Street, Everyplace, NY 12345-6789
123-456-7890 • everyone@camp.com

Purchase Order No.: _____ Date: _____

To: _____

Ship: ❏ Parcel Post   ❏ UPS   ❏ Motor Freight   ❏ Best Way

Quantity	Item Number	Description	Unit Cost

To arrive by: _____ Date: _____
Signature:_____

Figure 16-11. Purchase order form

usually given when the purchase is authorized by telephone or confirmed via e-mail. The principle of purchase orders can be followed, with some shortcuts, even in a small operation. However this system is implemented, it is vital that the following steps be taken:

• Purchasing should be limited to as few people as is possible.
• Purchase orders should be approved in advance of ordering.
• Copies of the purchase orders should be written for the vendor and the purchaser.
• A secure, agreed-upon price should be obtained and included on the purchase order.

A policy relating to the size of purchase a staff member may make without prior authorization should be established. Policies should include the maximum purchase amount before bids of some nature are required, and how bids are requested and evaluated for approval. If applicable, a camp should have a process to develop requests for proposal.

Purchasing should begin early in the year, and ample time should be given to investigate sources and compare prices and quality for value. The best discounts are secured through advance planning and purchasing. Use of the camp's cash-flow planning chart will be invaluable in maximizing potential discounts from suppliers. It is important to order early to ensure delivery of items on time or in advance of the opening date of camp.

Accounts Payable Disbursements

A system of payment should also be worked out in advance. Most vendors expect payment within 30 days, although some will require payment in advance or on actual delivery. The method of payment should be understood at the time the order is placed and specified on the purchase order. A disbursement system or payment-for-goods system for a camp should include provisions for the following points:

- The time at which the person placing the order, or someone designated by that person, checks to make sure the merchandise or service has been delivered. When the merchandise arrives, each item should be checked as to quantity, type, and condition, and all items should be checked against those appearing on the purchase order.
- A careful check of the invoice for mathematical errors and inclusion or exclusion of proper tax and discounts, as well as a check to see that the bill includes only the items received.
- Payment upon receipt of approved invoice, which either matches a purchase order already on file or has been approved by an appropriate staff member.
- Payment by check or credit card.
- If necessary to pay in cash, a receipt including all pertinent information and marked "paid" should be secured.
- Checks should have at least two authorized signatories; checks larger than a predetermined amount should be signed by both persons.
- Blank checks should be stored in a safe or locked cabinet.

If the camp has company credit cards, policies should be developed that relate to:
- Storage of those cards when not in use
- Who is authorized to use the cards
- Return of receipts with an invoice and the card after purchases are made

Petty Cash

Due to their rural locations and variety of day-to-day immediate needs, camps generally have more frequent cash payments than do many organizations. A careful procedure for cash expenditures should be worked out. Persons who have custody of cash should be bonded (insured).

A petty cash fund is the most common method of dealing with cash expenditures. A check for a set sum is issued at the beginning of the year, season, or period, and it is cashed. The cash is kept in a locked box in the safe, if the camp has one, and handled by only one or two authorized and bonded persons. Staff members may make authorized purchases and be reimbursed in cash from the fund upon presentation of a signed receipt, or cash may be advanced for purchases and an accounting made after the purchase. In the case of advances, the amount of cash advanced and the date should be recorded on a slip of paper, which is signed by the person taking the cash. See Figure 16-12 for a sample petty-cash advance slip. Upon the return of a receipt for the amount spent and the proper change, the advance cash slip is discarded and the change and receipt returned to the cash box.

Petty Cash Advance Slip

Date: _____

Received: $ _____ for: _____

_____

Account no.: _____ By: _____

Signature: _____

Figure 16-12. Petty-cash advance slip

The receipts and cash should be balanced regularly, depending on the volume of use: daily during periods of heavy cash receipts, weekly during less busy times. When the receipts become significant and available cash is dwindling, receipts should be attached to a written summary, assigned account numbers, and a check written to the cash box caretaker for the total amount, bringing the cash fund back up to the original amount. At the end of the fiscal year or season, any remaining cash should be deposited in the main camp account.

Payroll

In today's society, the simplest way to pay employees and keep accurate trip of the various deductions for taxes and benefits is by computer. Since deductions for taxes and benefits often amount to 26 to 30 percent of total payroll, it is critical that accurate records and timely reports are made.

Depreciating Buildings and Equipment

Many camps have been slow to include a budget line for appropriate depreciation of camp buildings and equipment. A policy should be in place that establishes a depreciation schedule in the capitalization policy. Each building and every piece of major equipment should be depreciated, or have its value reduced, on an agreed-upon schedule, after consultation with the camp's accountant and/or board. In an ideal situation, the amount depreciated in a given year is placed in a reserve account for the eventual replacement of the building or equipment. Nonprofit camps have often avoided this issue by relying upon campaigns for charitable contributions to replace major structures. However, it is increasingly difficult for many sponsoring organizations to obtain major capital funds. With increasing financial pressures upon nonprofit organizations, camps may have to be aggressive to get the attention of the organization's board for needed capital expenditures and ask the board to choose between setting up replacement reserves or committing to securing capital funds from other sources. In any case, each camp needs to develop a plan for replacement of buildings and equipment over appropriate time periods.

Information Technology

The computerization of the camp has changed the way in which many functions are handled. Computer programs are available that allow the entire registration process of individuals or groups to be recorded on the computer, creating not only a registration record, but an accounts receivable, a billing mechanism, labels for mailings, a living-group assignment preference, and program group sign-ups. Standard programs are available in the marketplace that can provide accounting, e-mailing, word processing, mailing list maintenance, mail merge, spreadsheets, and desktop publishing. At the same time, several companies have developed special software for camps that provide the program group and living-group assignment process, as well as the camp registration format. Christine Howe identifies a variety of applications available as shown in Figure 16-13.[4]

Computers with Internet access now allow even more convenient information transfer across the country and around the world. The camp may receive camper mail or allow registration via e-mail or the camp website, or staff may be part of the Camp Professional Discussion Group or other groups that discuss current issues. This development provides new opportunities to communicate with families and campers, with other directors, and with other businesses.

Since computers will often be used by a variety of staff for a variety of functions, an information security policy may need to be put into place. Each authorized user should have his own individual sign-on. Since passwords can be programmed to give a person access only to functions appropriate to that position, under no circumstances should any staff member share a computer sign-on with another staff member. Similarly, when leaving a workstation, a staff member should lock his computer or sign off. Any staff member who leaves the employment of the camp should immediately have his computer sign-on deactivated.

With privacy laws as they exist, this factor becomes particularly important as it relates to personal and health information of campers and staff being available only to the appropriate people. From the viewpoint of security of the financial records, the careful use of such security policies protect the camp and individual staff members from the problems of theft and embezzlement.

It is important that a system is designed to regularly back up all files on the computer systems daily. It is recommended that back-up of important information occur in three different areas, with one located off site. Online systems are available to back up files in a secure location.

Selected Applications for Personal Computers

Administration
Financial
Accounting
General ledger
Investments
Forecasting and decision support
Work-load cost tracking
Utility management
Invoices and billing
Budget and revenue and expenditures

Personnel
Recordkeeping and employee rosters
Recordkeeping and volunteer rosters
Recordkeeping and client rosters
Payroll
Insurance
Performance standards and job descriptions

Word Processing/General
Permits and licenses
Mailing labels
Bulk mailing
Manuals and training materials
Printing
Graphics and mapping
Aggregate client data-participation and demographics
Monthly reports

Research
Accident studies
Marketing
Long-range planning
Demand studies
Survey tabulation

Maintenance
Custodial cost tracking
Vandalism monitoring
Horticultural and irrigation management
Aquatics scheduling and management

Service Delivery
Recordkeeping
Activity registration
Attendance reporting
Facility and site usage
Activity scheduling

Program Planning and Evaluation
Advertising and publicity
Activity master planning
Activity analysis
Activity tracking

Activities
Games (electronic and simulation)
Arts and crafts
Music forms
Interactive stories and reading

Leisure Counseling and Education
Counseling
Recreational needs assessment
Interest inventories
Problem solving
Values awareness and clarification
Individual demographics
Communication and expression of thoughts and
  feelings

Education
Development of positive self-concept through
  mastery referral/leisure matching systems

Figure 16-13. Selected applications for personal computers

Whether investing in a computer for the first time or simply adding new software, it is wise to investigate carefully the variety of options. Technology changes so rapidly and varies so much in applicability to different camp settings that it is wise to examine several hardware and/or software options and compare notes with other camp directors on problems and successes. New software should be implemented program by program, because unforeseen problems will slow the process and frustrate office personnel. For example, it is best to implement the new accounting system or the word processing system first and get the office staff familiar with the new system rather than to install all programs at once. Henderson and Bialeschki outline several steps to be taken in getting started with computers:

- *Review the present operation for sizing. Determine how large your camp enrollments, budgets, and inventories are so you can more accurately decide which computer system you will need and what the benefits might be for its use.*
- *Set goals and objectives and criteria for what a computer can do for you ... . Do not buy a computer ... and then try to decide how to use it. The applications must be determined first.*
- *Find a vendor and locate software sources. It may be necessary to consult with more than one vendor to determine what the best buy is and who will provide the most support services.*
- *Design an implementation schedule to determine how you will begin to use the computer and its software. It is impossible to do everything at once, so you must decide systematically how you will begin to use the equipment.*
- *Begin implementing applications with a continual approach for evaluating and adding potential software.*[5]

However, it is without question that, even in the smallest operation, the right computer system can provide a long-term solution to many traditional problems and time-consuming functions in the camp setting. It is critical to have either a very knowledgeable person on the staff or a convenient and helpful supplier who can troubleshoot and makes a commitment to stick with the camp through the conversion process. In any case, the question of the type of supplier support is critical; the firm's reputation, references, maintenance contract fees, and troubleshooting response should be checked thoroughly.

The most effective systems are those that work together seamlessly. For example, a camp might seek a registration program that automatically prints a letter and sends customers an e-mail when someone registers online. The same program could also generate letters and e-mails of information at the appropriate times (send out a supply list four weeks before camp). Further, this program could automatically download online payments into a financial management software package and could be programmed to automatically generate the aforementioned reports on a monthly basis. The more the various computer applications work together, the more efficient and effective the camp's financial recordkeeping can be.

Maintaining Records

The checkbook and bank deposit slips should be reconciled with the monthly bank statement upon receipt. If multiple staff members are in the finance office, the appropriate checks and balances between employees need to be established and followed.

For instance, the reconciliation of the checking account and back statement should be done by a different staff member than the person who writes the checks.

Records should be kept in a fireproof container and should be retained by the camp or organization for at least five years. Backup computer records can help to reconstruct financial histories, but they should not be considered equal to or replacements for the primary paper documents.

Record-retention requirements vary from state to state; but, in general, records should be kept for the minimum time shown in Figure 16-14.[6] The director should give careful thought to minimum record retention and should obtain legal counsel.

Gerald G. Newborg suggests four values to be considered in retention:

- Administrative value relates to the need of the office or agency in carrying out its work.
- Legal value adheres to essentially any record which provides documentation for a legally enforceable right or obligation. These values may be embodied in state or federal law, state or federal regulations, or in local ordinances.
- Fiscal value … records which document financial transactions.
- Archival value … is permanence … [and] enduring.[7] (Each camp will determine its own records of historical and enduring value.)

The written policy of the organization or camp on recordkeeping and record retention should be developed on the basis of law, the rule of reason, and the risk involved. Such a policy should be in writing and available to the people who file and maintain these records. In developing a retention policy, the period for retention should be clearly defined by typing the specified retention period to the beginning or end of a calendar or fiscal year.

Taxes

Although an accountant or an attorney is of great assistance for most financial matters, it is in the area of taxes that such expertise becomes essential. The type of taxes applying to a specific camp will vary not only in the locality of the office and camp location, but also in whether the camp is a for-profit or nonprofit organization. Specific tax areas to be examined are payroll, real estate, personal property, and sales. Always get advice from the camp's CPA. A good financial-management software package can greatly assist a tax consultant come tax time.

Recommendations for Record Retention

Type of Record	Minimum Retention
Accident/incident reports	Adults, 7 years
	Minors, 2 years beyond age of majority
Accident/incident reports/claims	30 years
Accounts payable ledgers/schedules	7 years
Accounts receivable ledgers/schedules	7 years
Affirmative action records	180 days after selection
Annual reports*	Indefinitely
Applications (employment)—not hired	3 years
Applications (employment)—hired	3 years after employment ends
Audit reports	Indefinitely
Bank reconciliations	1 year
Bid records	5 years after award
Blueprints/surveys/plans	Indefinitely
Camper registration forms*	Adults, 6 years
	Minors, 2 years beyond age of majority
Camper health records (including treatments)*	Adults, 6 years
	Minors, 2 years beyond age of majority
Cash books	Indefinitely
Charters, constitution, bylaws, incorporation records	Indefinitely
Charts of accounts	Indefinitely
Checks (canceled)	4 years
Checks (exceptions: payments such as taxes, property purchases, special contracts, etc.)	Indefinitely
Complaints	1 year after resolution
Contracts and leases (expired)	7 years
(current)	Indefinitely
Correspondence (routine)	1 year
(general)	3 years
(legal and important matters)	Indefinitely
Deeds, mortgages, and bills of sale	Indefinitely
Depreciation schedules	Indefinitely
Duplicate deposit slips	1 year
Employee health records (including treatments)*	30 years
Employee I-9 forms	3 years after date of hire
Employee pay records	4 years from date of execution
Employee personnel records**	3 years after termination
Employee W-4 forms	Indefinitely
Employment applications (not hired)	3 years
Equal employment opportunity compliance records	3 years after final action/audits resolved
Expense analyses/expense schedules	7 years
Financial statements (end-of-year)	Indefinitely
Fire inspection reports*	6 years
Forms used, dated file copies*	Indefinitely
General and private ledgers with end-of-year trial balances	Indefinitely
Grant files	5 years after project completion
Insurance policies (expired)	3 years
Insurance records (current accident reports, claims, policies, etc.)	Indefinitely

Figure 16-14. Recommendations for record retention

Internal audit reports*	Depends
Internal reports	3 years
Inventories of products, materials, supplies	7 years
Invoices to customers	7 years
Invoices from vendors	7 years
Licenses (federal, state, local)*	Dispose of after receiving new license
Journals	Indefinitely
Minutes of directors', stockholders' meetings	Indefinitely
Notes receivable ledgers/schedules	7 years
Occupational injury/illness records	5 years
Operational statistical reports	Until obsolete
Payroll records and summaries	3 years
Personnel records	5 years after termination
Personnel records disciplinary files	5 years after final action
Petty cash vouchers	3 years
Physical inventory tags	3 years
Position description records	2 years after superseded or obsolete
Property appraisals	Indefinitely
Property records including costs, depreciation reserves, blueprints, and plans	Indefinitely
Purchase orders (except primary copy)*	1 year
(primary copy)*	7 years
Safety inspection reports*	8 years
Securities transactions	3 years
Stock and bond certifications (canceled)	6 years
Stock and bond records	Indefinitely
Subsidiary ledgers	7 years
Tax returns and worksheets	Indefinitely
Time books/records	7 years
Training material records	Until campers in that session are 2 years beyond age of majority
Travel expense reports*	3 years
Unemployment compensation records	3 years
Unemployment compensation records	3 years Vouchers for payments 7 years
Withholding tax statements*	4 years
Workers' compensation records	5 years

Source: American Society of Association Executives.

*These record-retention timelines are not from the American Society of Association Executives, but from miscellaneous other sources. In many cases, American Society of Association Executives did not offer a suggested retention policy on these items.

**When a minor is involved, records should be kept at least four years beyond the year when the age of majority is reached. This requirement, along with other record-retention requirements, should be checked with your state requirements.

Figure 16-14. Recommendations for record retention (cont.)

Nonprofit camps should understand the federal tax laws as they relate to "unrelated business income." Though nonprofits are allowed to have income that is not directly related to the stated mission of the camp/organization, such income is taxable. This complex issue should be examined with the camp's accountant at the time of the annual audit.

Camp Store and Camper Bank

In most camp situations, campers will need certain supplies (e.g., toothpaste, toothbrushes, stationery, stamps) other than those that the camp supplies as part of the fee. Campers are also anxious to have souvenirs or reminders of their camp experience (e.g., t-shirts, patches, pennants, postcards). The director should consider how such items may be sold to campers in a way that is consistent with the camp's philosophy.

Campers will arrive at camp with varying amounts of cash, whether or not the camp has items for sale. Most camps do not wish to have the camper go to commercial establishments off site. The presence of cash in a camper's duffel or clothing may lead to losses and disputes. A plan to safeguard this cash as well as to disburse it, if items are to be sold to campers, should be developed and announced in advance of camp. Most camps have a plan for campers to deposit funds on arrival, allowing the camper to draw against those funds for necessary expenditures on personal items or for additional activity fees. The following processes should be considered in development of such a plan:

- Suggest to parents and campers in advance the maximum and minimum amount of cash needed during the camper period.
- Indicate what essential items the campers may need to purchase.
- List programs that may require additional expenditures, depending on the camper's interests and skill (e.g., craft supplies, trips, horseback riding, ammunition for riflery). If possible, it is best if these expenses can be included initially in the camper fee or identified as an option in the payment of the fee plus extras.
- Identify what items the camp may wish to make available to campers for purchase.
- Provide the camper with a receipt for cash deposited.
- Set up a simple plan of accounting; that is, charge against an individual's account for purchases, enter deposits, and provide a refund (if necessary) at the end of the period. Two sample systems are shown in Figure 16-15. The first is a checkbook, which the camper uses to write a check for each purchase (providing the camper with a record of expenditures and the experience of keeping his own record). The second is a card held by the camp on which deposits and expenditures are recorded at the time the purchase and deposits are made.

Where camps serve groups, the problem of dealing with the individual's cash does not arise. However, a system for selling the various supplies should be established and the group leader given information in advance about what is available at camp during the group's stay.

In developing a camp store, careful accounting practices should be established. The store operation should provide income to the camp over and above the cost of merchandise, the cost of labor, and related overhead. It is unrealistic to expect to cover only the cost of the merchandise. Many camps have found a camp store to be a significant source of income. The sale of items with the camp name and logo is also another method of public relations.

Expenditure/Deposit Record: Checkbook Type

Balance forward: $ _____

Deposited: $ _____

Less check no.: _____

For: $ _____

Balance: $ _____

_____20_____ Check No.: _____

Pay to Camp: $ _____ . _____

$ _____

For: _____

Signed: _____ Cabin: _____

Expenditure/Deposit Record: File Card Type

Name: _____ Cabin: _____

Date	Item Purchased	Cost	Department	Balance

Figure 16-15. Expenditure/deposit record

It advertises the camp wherever that individual goes, and name recognition is important. It can also stimulate others to ask the individual about the camp and his experience there.

The camp's philosophy and parental desires will determine whether to have snacks for sale (e.g., ice cream, candy, chips). Selling drinks and snacks is often a lucrative form of income for camps. However, the camp may want to limit the number of snacks and drinks a camper can buy each day, or the camp's philosophy may lead the camp to provide snacks at given hours.

An appropriate location that will provide security, accessibility, and appropriate storage should be selected. The display of items with clearly marked prices will stimulate sales and save time when campers come to the store. Camp stores are usually open only at certain times that coincide with the program schedule. While one person should have the ongoing responsibility for the store, including the inventory of stock, ordering of additional supplies, and supervising of sales, additional persons may be needed at busy times.

A camp might also wish to provide an online store. Again, selling items with the camp name and logo is a good method of public relations. The product advertises the camp wherever the purchaser goes. It can also stimulate others to ask the individual about the camp and his experience there. Further, an online camp store can provide families the opportunity to purchase camp related paraphernalia. Most website packages contain the option of establishing online payment options, so that element of establishing an online store is rather easy. The difficult aspects of creating an online store include updating the products offered in the store to match inventory and shipping the items. Careful consideration should be given to making sure the online store would be profitable, and that it is a viable option in the camp's area.

Camp Office

Many camps will have two offices: one in a home or city, and another at camp. The camp office should be in a location that is easy to find when arriving at camp, yet be located where noisy activities will not be distracting to those who work or visit there. Though the office should be the center of efficiency and accuracy in terms of records and administration, it should have a relaxed, congenial atmosphere. It often provides the first impression of the camp, and serves as the reception area for visitors, vendors, and often the families of campers.

The telephone may serve a similar function of greeting people. Since many of the inquiries and questions from prospective campers and their parents come by telephone, it is important that the person answering the phone reveal a pleasant personality and have many immediate answers to questions. Those employees who answer e-mail queries should follow similar etiquette.

Staff

The size of the office staff will vary with the size of the camp, with larger camps having a receptionist/telephone operator, a bookkeeper, a secretary, and a business manager. Smaller camps may have only one person in addition to the camp director in the office. At times, any camp office may be overly busy and harried, but it is important that people be willing to stop and deal graciously with the public—whether in person or on the phone.

Arrangement of the Office

Several factors should be considered in the construction or arrangement of the office. Sufficient storage for supplies and records is essential (going "digital" can help free up space). A room that provides privacy for the camp director, other administrators, and program personnel is also necessary since conferences with individual staff or campers may be of a confidential nature. A second door with direct access to the outside may provide more privacy. An area near the front door should have some chairs where people may wait. A counter here may assist in separating visitors from the work area and also give a space where it is convenient for a staff member to write or stand and provide information. A more-than-average number of electrical outlets with adequate power supply will be needed because of the variety and quantity of office equipment and desk lighting. Consideration of controlled access areas should also be made for the security of cash, computer equipment, and records. Any desk with computers or wireless routers that need to access the Internet should have a phone line or cable outlet nearby.

Fundraising

Most nonprofit camps rely on some contribution income to operate the camp. Many independent camps have moved to nonprofit foundations to ensure the continued operation after the present owners are gone. Other independent camps have utilized an arrangement with the American Camp Association by which friends and parents make contributions to that Association, a 501(c)(3) organization, in the name of a particular camp, and the gifts are used to fund campers who cannot afford their full camp fee. In other words, almost every camp director is faced with the prospect of mastering another skill: that of fundraising.

Each state has developed regulations which affect fundraising. Therefore, it is important to consult with the camp's attorney and accountant to understand the applicable laws and regulations.

Determining the Use of Funds

If funds are to be raised for the camp, their overall use should be carefully evaluated before collecting them. These funds might be used in the following ways:

- To help alleviate the cost of the camp experience for *every* camper, thus lowering the fee for all
- To lower the cost of the camp experience for particular campers who cannot pay the usual fee
- To cover capital expenditures, such as land development, building facilities, purchasing computer systems, making extensive large equipment purchases, or undertaking major renovation
- To experiment with new programs which might eventually offer a year round program or diversification
- To improve the wage and benefit package for staff, thus enabling the director to recruit and/or retain more qualified staff

In other words, the camp director and board (if the camp has one) must consider carefully the purpose of the fundraising, for the camp must have a clearly felt need resulting in a clearly stated purpose for those funds. It may be that the camp has varying needs, ranging from keeping the fees lower than average to replacing buildings or equipment. Before lumping all of the needs together, consideration should be given to the types of fundraising. It may be helpful at this stage to consider an outside consultant to assist in the creation of a financial development strategy, which provides a foundation and pattern for fundraising over a period of time.

Basic Principles

Some basic principles should be followed in fundraising, regardless of the type of fund-raising activity:

- Establish a clearly stated purpose for the funds.
- Seek professional fundraising counsel to conduct a feasibility study and conduct the campaign or train the camp director.

- Develop a carefully scripted plan for the fundraising activity or effort with target dates.
- Recruit capable volunteers to raise the funds.
- Provide a training program for the volunteers.
- Develop attractive, succinct, and clear descriptive materials.
- Acknowledge every gift, and recognize the giver in some fashion.
- Use the funds for the purpose for which they are raised, and report their use to the giver.
- Maintain careful accounting of all gifts, including pledges. Under new accounting rules, pledges are considered to be income in the year they are made, not the year they are paid.

David Schaeffer suggests:

> A fund-raising plan usually covers three to five years and provides direction and clarity around how your organization approaches sources of funding for support. A typical fundraising plan establishes objectives, includes an action plan for achieving each objective as well as a time line for completing the action plan.[8]

No fundraising effort is too small or too large to ignore these basic principles and establish a planning process.

Annual Giving

Annual giving is one type of fundraising in which an approach is made yearly to the camp's constituency. In this type of fundraising activity, a specific period is set aside each year for the effort, and volunteer leadership secured either from the board, committee, or alumni group. An organization with subchairs and workers is developed similar to the diagram in Figure 16-16. A list of prospective givers is developed from the records of the camp: parents and grandparents of campers, former campers and staff, foundations, board or committee personnel, and vendors.

The annual giving campaign or event lends itself best to providing funds for the ongoing operating budget of the camp through direct subsidy or the provision of camperships for needy youth. Some camps have used funds from a campaign to replace budgeting depreciation reserves. Once a person has committed to the camp with a charitable gift, it becomes easier to go back to that donor each year, as long as a sound acknowledgment and information program is in place.

A variety of methods may be used to approach potential annual givers:
- *Direct mail*: A letter and material describing the needs with an addressed and, possibly, stamped envelope for returning a contribution is sent.
- *Telethon*: A group of trained volunteers come together in a location where there are multiple telephone lines, call prospective givers, and take pledges by telephone. A confirmation letter and a return envelope are then sent to those pledging.

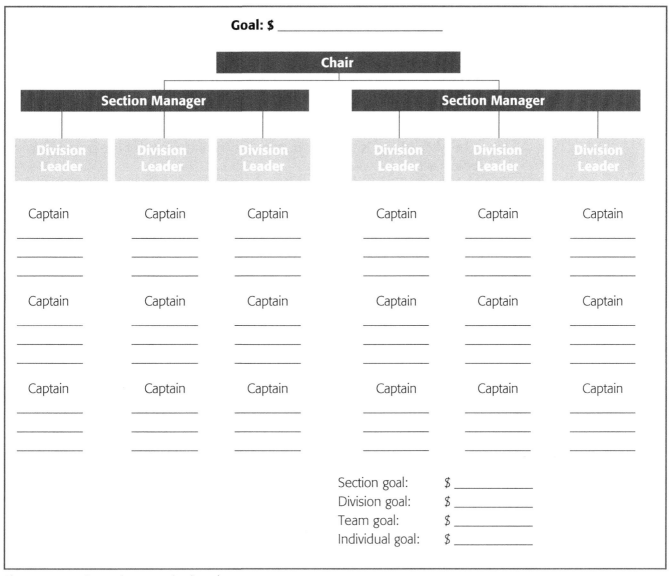

Figure 16-16. Campaign organization chart

- *Personal approach*: A volunteer approaches a prospective giver, explaining the needs and asking for a contribution. This method is always the most effective.
- *Public gathering*: A presentation is made at some type of special event sponsored by the camp, and return envelopes and pledge cards are distributed after a public appeal.
- *Fundraiser*: An activity is developed which will render its profits to the cause by the tickets sold or money collected through other activities.
- *Camp website*: A section of the website is devoted to asking donors to contribute to the camp through an online payment.

Capital Campaigns

Capital campaigns are another type of fundraising. In contrast to annual giving, this approach is undertaken less frequently, generally every 5 to 10 years, depending on the size of each campaign. The constituency to be approached is the same as for annual giving, but also can be extended to businesses in the area and certain foundations that consider capital projects. Again, a volunteer organization is developed, not dissimilar to that of the annual campaign. This type of campaign is dependent upon having individual volunteers approaching potential donors individually.

In capital campaigns, professional counsel is especially important. It is not wise to embark on such a campaign without some certainty that the goal can be reached. A professional consultant may complete a feasibility study, which will examine the willingness of potential large givers to contribute to the campaign, uncover persons who are willing to serve in leadership roles, and assess the potential capability of the camp to raise funds. A capital campaign is especially dependent upon securing one or two large gifts equal to 20 percent of the goal and 60 to 70 percent of the goal from large givers. Therefore, the identification, cultivation, and assessment of potentially large givers are a vital part of this type of fundraising. In addition, professional counsel should lay out the steps and give advice in a smaller campaign, or be a resident consultant for the period of a major campaign.

Endowment Development

Endowment development is another type of fundraising, and requires a quite different approach from the capital or annual support campaigns. Though onetime campaigns, similar in organization to the capital campaign, can be run for endowment purposes, they are not as customary for camps as for universities, hospitals, and other organizations. Encouraging supporters to remember the camp in their wills, insurance, or through trusts requires a program of cultivation and education that may not show immediate results.

While it is possible to approach prospects who have not given to the camp and interest them in planned giving, those persons who have given to the camp through annual support efforts or capital campaigns are usually the best prospects for the endowment effort. Since these donors are known to the camp, and the camp reports to them through mailings somewhat regularly, it is possible to begin to develop an awareness of the various instruments used in planned giving without initially asking for a gift. The use of planned-giving instruments affects the estate of a person, and in many cases has beneficial tax implications. Therefore, any decision usually requires more consideration, consultation, and often the advice of an attorney, trust officer, or accountant.

A program of endowment development should be carefully charted, with the strong commitment of the committee or board related to the camp. Professional guidance from a person knowledgeable about endowment development efforts should be sought initially. Only nonprofit 501(c)(3) organizations can provide the tax benefits that make this method of fundraising attractive to many people.

Fundraising Personnel

To develop effective fundraising efforts takes considerable time, training, and expertise. The camp director should carefully evaluate the willingness to allot the amount of time from his schedule, or that of another staff member, for this purpose. Even when an outside consultant is brought in to help with fundraising, it will still require time from the camp director. Fundraising cannot be done effectively if done half-heartedly, poorly, or without professional planning. On the other hand, most nonprofit organizations cannot survive without an effective program of fundraising.

It may be helpful to seek outside fundraising counsel to help develop a plan for the total financial development and to actually assist in the fundraising efforts. The experience and competence of the fundraising counsel should be explored carefully by checking references with previous or present clients.

Checkpoints

- Outline the budgeting process for the camp.
- What are internal control policies?
- Describe the three basic types of fundraising and the principles that affect all good fundraising.
- Who may purchase for the camp? By what methods? Who checks the order when it is received and approves payment?
- Who handles cash at camp? Are they bonded? What check is in place on the cash received?
- What security controls need to be placed on computer usage?
- Have the expenses and income related to the camp store been examined to show what margin of income over expenses is being achieved?
- Describe how a seamless computer system could benefit the camp.
- When was the camp's record retention policy last reviewed?

Related Standards

American Camp Association's Accreditation Standards for Camp Programs and Services Additional Professional Practices: Operational Management

Endnotes

1. John A. Ledlie. 1961. *Managing the YMCA Camp*. New York: Association Press (YMCA of the USA). p. 125.

2. Financial Accounting Standards Board, P.O. Box 5116, Norwalk, CT 06856-5116.

3. Kathy J. Tyson. 1994. "Accounting Alert." *Camping Magazine*. Vol. 66, No. 5, May/June, p. 44.

4. Christine Z. Howe. 1984. "Change, Computers, and the Camp Administration." *Camping Magazine*. Vol. 57, No. 1, September/October, p. 17.

5. Karla Henderson and M. Deborah Bialeschki. 1983. "Computer Consciousness." *Camping Magazine*. Vol. 55, No. 7, May, p. 16.

6. American Society of Association Executives. 1992. *Association Management*. Vol. 44, No. 9, September, pp. 50–51.

7. Gerald G. Newborg. 1989. "Records Retention and Disposition Schedules." *Technical Leaflet 107*. Nashville, TN: American Association for State and Local History.

8. David Schaeffer. 2005. "Twin Lakes Strategic Fund Raising." *Camping Magazine*. Vol. 78, No. 4, July/August, p. 28.

VOLUNTEERS

Camp Echo (Burlingham, NY)

Chapter Seventeen

It seems to me that the first and foremost reason that volunteers dedicate so much of their personal lives to chosen projects ... is that they believe in the organization's mission. In leadership training we call this "alignment" with the mission and vision of the organization.[1]

—George Burns

Few camps operate without some volunteer assistance—whether volunteers are on the staff, on a board or committee, or come from referrals from former staff, parents, or campers. A volunteer is any person who gives services to the camp without any compensation. The growth and nurturing of volunteers is an art that every camp director needs to develop. Volunteers spread and enhance the mission of a camp and stimulate an enthusiasm unmatched by staff.

The director's first reaction is that volunteers should be cultivated because they save the camp money if they serve as staff members, work at camp in other capacities, or take on roles that are ordinarily performed by employees. Another reaction is that volunteers bring in money because they become fundraisers or recruiters of campers. Either or both may be true, but first and foremost, volunteers should be cultivated because they are an outgrowth of the spirit and philosophy of the camp. It is a tribute to a camp that former campers or staff and parents of either may wish to share the experience of the camp with others. However, to be most effective and to gain the greatest personal satisfaction from the experience, volunteers also need professional leadership to provide some structure for the task to be done.

Principles of Volunteer Service

Some principles of any volunteer service should be kept in mind. A volunteer should feel needed. The need may be stimulated or sold by the professional, but it must challenge the volunteer or rekindle earlier positive experiences or perceived needs. That need must parallel the individual's motivation, which varies from person to person. As Clary, Snyder, and Ridge state, "people volunteer to satisfy personal and social needs and goals ... . The first step toward successful recruitment is considering the audience from which recruiting will take place so that the relevant motivations of potential volunteers can be identified."[2]

Volunteers should be guided to the type of activity in which they can be most effective. Success is important in any task, particularly when someone is giving energy, time, and money to accomplish the task. It is not wise to randomly assign or recruit volunteers.

A written job description should be prepared for the task and shared with the volunteer. In a face-to-face interview, the volunteer should be asked if he has a problem with any of the functions, as it may be useful to adjust some portions of the description. Along with the job description should be the hours to be worked or a targeted time for accomplishment and the evaluation procedure.

The volunteer should be informed of the ground rules: personnel policies, limits of authority, budget limitations, or whatever limits may exist. The volunteer should also be given adequate assistance in accomplishing the task—whether it be funds, tools, manpower, or the director's consultation. Supervision should be provided as needed and should include observation by the supervisor and regular conferences to gain insights into the assigned task. The performance of the volunteer should be appraised upon completion of the task.

Public recognition of the volunteer should occur before his peers and could take the form of a meal, a plaque, a printed communication, or other tangible recognition. However, this recognition cannot substitute for the regular personal expression of appreciation by the supervisor of the volunteer.

Legal Ramifications

Several court cases have centered around the legal definition of volunteerism. *Corpus Juris 2d*, a legal encyclopedia, defines a volunteer as:

> One who does or undertakes to do that which one is not legally or morally bound to do, and which is not in pursuance or protection of any interest … one who enters into service of his own free will; one who gives his service without any express or implied promise of remuneration … ; one who has no interest in his work, but nevertheless undertakes to assist therein … .[3]

The definition of a *pure* volunteer is very narrow and somewhat different from a *gratuitous* volunteer. Volunteers may be differentiated by a two-part test concerning whether the person is subject to the control of the organization and whether the person receives any benefit from the job performed. The pure volunteer performs a task when and how he prefers and for no benefit whatever. The gratuitous volunteer performs the task at a time or in a manner prescribed by the organization and/or receives some benefit from the organization. The pure volunteer may not be able to expect the same sort of legal safeguards that a gratuitous volunteer may expect, where the organization takes on some control or responsibility for the volunteer. Since camps may use both types of volunteers, it is important to understand this difference.

Occasionally, persons provide leadership for an activity that takes place at a given time for campers, such as a nature hike or canoe trip. If that person controls the manner and method of the activity and is responsible for its occurrence, then that person may be considered an independent contractor. This type of volunteer role requires many of the same safeguards an employee requires such as a written agreement, training, and issues such as insurance, liability, and written policies.

A number of court cases illustrate some of the problems for the organization in *gratuitous* volunteer service. For example, in *Bond v. Cartwright Little League, Inc.*,[4] the Little League solicited help from volunteers to remove some large lights it had purchased from a municipal baseball field. A volunteer started up one of the 100-foot poles and fell 40 feet, injuring himself. The Arizona Supreme Court reasoned that the volunteer was not a *pure* volunteer because the Little League set the time and place as well as the manner in which the lights were to be removed and had control over the volunteer.

In the North Dakota Supreme Court case *Olson v. Kem Temple, Ancient Arabic Order of the Mystic Shrine*, a volunteer was denied financial recovery when he fell off a small stepladder and was injured, because the stepladder is considered a "simple tool."[5] The court reasoned, "Where the tool or appliance is simple in construction and a defect therein is discernible without special skill or knowledge, and the employee is as well qualified as the employer to detect the defect and appraise the danger resulting there from," no recovery is required.

In the Washington Court of Appeals case *Baxter v. Morningside, Inc.*,[6] a volunteer driver for a charitable organization was in an accident, negligently causing injury to several persons. The court held that the organization was liable for the volunteer driver's actions because it "controlled or could have controlled the physical conduct and performance of the volunteer driver."[7]

In 1985 the Supreme Court decided in *Tony and Susan Alamo Foundation v. Secretary of Labor*[8] that workers for the foundation who received room and board were not true volunteers because "they were working with the expectancy of some remuneration." Therefore, the court held that volunteer workers were subject to the provisions of the Fair Labor Standards Act (FLSA), which included the minimum wage. It has been suggested that this decision has "created a new category which might be called the 'quasi-volunteer' who, though functioning like a volunteer, is afforded the 'protection' of the Act, because there is some identifiable expectation of compensation." The *Alamo* case involved two elements relevant to the non-profit foundation: a commercial activity and the payment of room and board, both unrelated to its exempt purpose. Consequently, Grange and LeSourd point out that in a camp setting, the room and board are provided as conditions of employment; that is, because of their job in working with campers and being in the camp setting, it is to the benefit of the camp to provide the meals and lodging.[9] This factor has yet to be tested in court.

Several principles arise from these cases that should be taken into consideration by camp directors:
- No remuneration should be given that is not for the convenience of the camp. For example, lodging is provided a camp counselor as a convenience to the camp because the person could not effectively do the job without living at the camp. Therefore, it is for the convenience of the employer.
- No remuneration should be given that is not a part of the responsibility undertaken. For example, to provide meals and lodging to a person whose home is a mile down the road from camp and the person only instructs an activity one or two hours a day is beyond the responsibility undertaken.
- If the camp asks that a specific task be undertaken at a given place and time, the camp should provide safeguards and give supervision to the activity. It is also helpful to have the volunteers discuss risks in their training

period, and identify individually or as a group the sorts of risks they expect to encounter in their time in camp.

- The same care and training should be required of volunteers as with employees who undertake potentially liable services, such as driving.
- Volunteers should be urged to carefully inspect equipment before using it, though that in no way relieves the camp of ordinary care and upkeep of that equipment.
- Volunteers are generally held to same duty of care as a staff member in the same situation, and they are responsible for the acting as any prudent person would act.

Volunteers as Staff

Many nonprofit organizations utilize volunteers either as the majority or total of the camp staff. A volunteer director is recruited for a one- or two-week period and then recruits staff to work during that session or sessions. In other camps, the core program staff is employed, and volunteers recruited as counselors or assistants in other functions. Throughout this book, no differentiation has been made between the volunteer and employed staff member. Generally speaking, the principles involved in the selection, retention, orientation, training, and supervision of employed staff should also apply to volunteer staff. It means that the camp director or organization should:

- Select volunteer staff carefully, following the same type of screening methods discussed earlier, including an application, references, and fingerprint and/or criminal-record check.
- Where certifications are needed, they should be required of volunteer staff and kept on file.
- Have a *written* agreement with each volunteer staff member that states:
  - ✓ The person is a volunteer and not a paid employee.
  - ✓ Room and board is provided as a convenience of the employer.
  - ✓ The camp assigns sleeping space and duties to the volunteer.
  - ✓ No fringe benefits provided a regular employee are provided the volunteer.
  - ✓ Volunteer services can be terminated by either party at any time.
  - ✓ A training period, before the campers arrive, will be provided.
  - ✓ Supervision will be provided during the camp periods.
  - ✓ An evaluation and recognition of their service will be conducted at the end of the period.

The camp director needs to carefully assess the differences between volunteer-staffed camps and camps with paid staff. For example, training may have to occur on several weekends during the spring or early summer because the volunteers cannot give another week prior to the camp period. Online training might be another viable option for training volunteers since they can accomplish this training anytime, anywhere, and they can progress at their own pace. In addition to specialized training, more supervision may be needed in certain program areas because of the limited time for training and orientation of volunteers. Therefore, care should be given to ensure that training and supervision is thorough and volunteers know how to act responsibly in their positions.

It should be pointed out that the practice of giving honorariums or scholarships rather than wages to someone considered a volunteer, and exempting that person from minimum wage or FICA provisions, would probably not hold up under the court definitions of a "pure volunteer" or "gratuitous employee."

The law of the operator's state, and the camp's if different, should be reviewed carefully. The camp's attorney should be able to provide the degree to which volunteers or a camp using volunteers has immunity from liability. Some such immunity exists under the Federal Volunteer Protection Act (42 USC 14501, et seq), and some states have provided limited immunity in certain circumstances. The camp should review the use of volunteers with the insurance carrier as it pertains to workers' compensation and liability policies. Gregg and Hansen-Stamp suggest: "Workers' compensation can provide a valuable benefit to employer camps, should their employees be injured within the scope of their employment. The employee is entitle to 'no fault' insurance coverage and is generally not entitled to bring a civil lawsuit against the camp— that is, the camp is provided some limited immunity from civil liability."[10]

Volunteer Committees and Boards

In not-for-profit camps, a governing board or committee of the organization's board works with the employed or volunteer camp director. The relationship between the committee or board and the director can be a most creative and exciting experience, or it can deteriorate into a struggle for power. Peter Drucker suggests that the potential for friction between the board and the executive "has forced an increasing number of non-profits to realize that neither board nor CEO is 'the boss.' They are colleagues, working for the same goal but each having a different task."[11]

Early in employment, the camp director should try to understand the structure of the particular organization for which he works. The director should seek answers to the following questions:
- Who is the chief elected officer of the organization?
- What is the elected governing body and its policy function?
- What is the body to which the camp committee or board reports, if any?
- What are the types of policies the camp committee or board has under its jurisdiction?
- What is the organization's staff role as it relates to these committees or boards?
- What is the stated purpose of the organization, especially its "exempt purpose," that is, the purpose for which it is granted exemption from certain taxes?
- What are the job descriptions of board members and officers?

Obviously, no two organizations operate in exactly the same way. Therefore, generalizations made in this chapter must be adapted to the specific camp's situation. Figure 17-1 presents an overview of the roles often assumed by committees or boards and by the director of a camp.

Responsibilities Within the Volunteer Organization

Operator Responsibilities

- See that the camp is operated in harmony with the organization's overall mission and goals.
- Set policy for the camp.
- Recruit a capable administrator for the camp, and provide adequate support services.
- Provide resources (site, capital, community support).
- Approve an annual operating budget with overall financial policies and direction.
- Be responsible for meeting the applicable local, state, and federal laws.
- Set admission requirements (age, membership, sex).
- Develop overall program goals and direction.
- Be responsible to the community.
- Supervise the administrator.

Shared Responsibilities

- Keep minutes of decisions and meetings.
- Assist in site development and maintenance.
- Raise capital funds.
- Raise supplemental (contributed) funds.
- Be responsible for meeting the applicable local, state, and federal laws.
- Promote the camp and recruit campers.
- Monitor good standards of operation in health, safety, and personnel.
- Evaluate.

Camp Director Responsibilities

- Recommend and implement policy.
- Recruit and train the staff of the camp (full-time, part-time, and volunteer).
- See that the camp site is maintained in good condition, and alert the board or committee to needs.
- Develop a budget, and provide a careful and honest accounting of income and expenditures.
- Be responsible for meeting the applicable local, state, and federal laws.
- Recruit campers.
- Develop, implement, and evaluate camp program.
- Ensure good standards of operation in health, safety, and personnel.

Figure 17-1. Responsibilities in volunteer organizations

A set of bylaws should govern the actions of the board and its subcommittees. This legal document outlines the way in which the organization elects officers and members, and the manner in which meetings of the board and organization must be held. It is an important document to understand, and the employed director has a legal responsibility to help ensure that the elected officials adhere to the bylaws of the organization. Bylaws may be changed, and the method of change is usually specified in the bylaws.

The volunteer support system should never be viewed as an unnecessary step in administration since it can be the greatest advantage the non-profit organization has. The volunteer committee member can be a vital checkpoint of community or organizational reaction, as well as an additional staff member. However, few volunteers are simply interested in another committee position or in having their names listed. If they commit themselves to membership on a committee or board, they expect to perform useful and meaningful services. To simply be figureheads is degrading and demoralizing, and in the ultimate analysis, counterproductive to a camp and its sponsoring organization.

John Pearson, former executive director of Christian Camping International/ USA, suggests:

> The care and feeding of a board member will be much easier if the director can participate in the board member selection process. Camp boards are selected through a variety of election procedures. The alert camp director, however, will request that the nominating committee consult with him before the nominees are recruited.[12]

After the recruitment process is completed, each new board member should be involved in a group or individual orientation session and given a copy of the bylaws, the policy manual, and a job description. When a meeting of the camp committee or board is scheduled, the camp director should make certain that:

- The agenda is developed with the chairperson in advance of the meeting.
- The written reports on subjects to be discussed are clear, concise, and, when possible, have been circulated in advance of the meeting.
- The decisions or actions to be considered are outlined clearly.
- The members who are expected to report have the data or information they need.
- The room and setting are ready for a comfortable and informal meeting.

The director's next step is to involve the volunteer in a task over and above attendance at the committee or board meeting. The assignment of a task by the chairperson to a subgroup often moves that subgroup to action; at this point the camp director should be an aide to that group, helping them outline the steps to be taken and assisting as needed. It is of particular value to have the committee members visit the camp, especially during sessions, so that the program and objectives can be personalized. Workdays, weekends, and special program events will also provide opportunities for volunteer leadership and contribution.

A careful and accurate record of committee proceedings, with particular attention to actions taken, should be maintained in the office or headquarters of the camp. Though the position of secretary may be elected or appointed, the camp director has responsibility for assisting and making sure minutes of all meetings are circulated to appropriate persons and kept in a permanent file in the office, preferably bound. The policies adopted by the committee or board should be pulled from minutes and placed in some appropriate sequence or order in a notebook, which is then given each member of the committee or board. Orientation of new committee or board members should be a part of the ongoing procedures of the committee or board. A regular set of materials— including the policy manual of the group, as well as past minutes—should be given each new member, along with a verbal orientation to the way in which the group works.

A plan of volunteer recognition should be established early in the year. The material aspect of the recognition is not as important as the sincerity and public expression of appreciation. If an award or symbol of recognition is presented, it should be chosen on the basis of its appropriateness to the task and service given, and should be of a permanent nature. Ordinarily, volunteers should take the public leadership in recognizing other volunteers.

Legal ramifications also exist for those volunteers who agree to serve on a managing committee or board of a non-profit organization. Generally, a board member is not held liable individually for either the directives of the board or the negligence of an employee. If legal action against directors does occur, it is on the basis that the board or an individual failed to take action or that some action taken was inadequate or irresponsible. Although the specific laws in each state may differ, the three major categories of violations of a board's fiduciary responsibility are: mismanagement, or failure to follow fundamental management principles; non-management, or failure to use existing opportunities for good management; and self-dealing, or personally benefiting from the decisions of the board (not disclosing conflicts of interest). The basic principle is that the board must make sure that its decisions are informed and reasonable.

For the director working with a board, George Webster suggests six guidelines as the result of *Smith v. Van Gordkum* in the Delaware Supreme Court:

- *Make decisions deliberately and without undue haste or pressure.*
- *Be as thoroughly and completely prepared as possible before making a decision. Make sure the board receives and reviews, in advance, materials pertaining to any major decision.*
- *Become actively involved in deliberations during the board meeting. Comment as appropriate on written materials presented to the board.*
- *Keep written records of board preparation and deliberation. It is necessary to create a paper trail showing compliance with procedural requirements.*
- *In the case of any major transaction, review all basic legal documents and all analyses by experts.*
- *Ensure that at minimum, in-house experts, and at best, accountants and lawyers, prepare independent evaluations of important issues.*[13]

Other Roles

One function that camp committees and boards in today's climate must expect to undertake is that of fundraising. Fundraising is a volunteer function, even though it deserves professional leadership and assistance. The actual fundraising should be done by a volunteer and recognized by the board or committee.

Many camps are fortunate in having volunteers who are also able and willing to be involved directly in program or work events. These volunteers will often organize and lead groups to camp for work or activity weekends, implement much of the promotion of camp and recruitment of campers, and come to camp for a specific work project. In certain activities, the camp may be wiser to utilize independent contractors to undertake portions of work projects or activities for which the camp or its volunteers have no documented expertise.

The relationship between the volunteer and staff member can be most creative and satisfying when they share a common purpose and both feel a sense of contribution and worth. As the staff member is an extension of the policy-making group, so may the volunteer become an extension or arm of the staff member.

Checkpoints

- Does the camp have a written agreement with volunteers?
- Has the camp consulted an attorney concerning liability in terms of using volunteers in the state in question?
- Does the camp have a regular program orientation and training for all volunteers—both at the staff and the committee/board level?
- How could online training be used in conjunction with face-to-face training to train the camp's volunteers?
- Is a diagram or outline of the volunteer structure in place? If not, develop one for the director's understanding and use.
- Who is the volunteer person responsible for overall organization direction?
- What are the specific responsibilities of the camp committee/board and its subgroups?
- In what ways not currently in place could the camp use volunteers?

Related Standards

Many of the standards and additional professional practices refer to policies, and to the degree that a volunteer board or committee may be responsible for setting policy, those standards would need to be considered. *American Camp Association's Accreditation Standards for Camp Programs and Services*: HR.1–21

Additional Professional Practices: Human Resources

ACA e-Institute Online Course

Volunteer Management 101

Endnotes

1. George Burns. 1989. "How to Keep Volunteers Coming Back." *Journal of Christian Camping*. Vol. 21, No. 5, September, p. 6. Reprinted with permission from CCI/USA.

2. E. Gil Clary, Mark Snyder, and Robert Ridge. 1992. "Volunteers' Motivations: A Functional Strategy for the Recruitment, Placement, and Retention of Volunteers." *Non-Profit Management & Leadership*. Vol. 2, No. 4, Summer, p. 341.

3. Robert A. Christenson. 1982. "What You Should Know About the Legal Definition of a Volunteer." *Voluntary Action Leadership*. Fall, p. 17.

4. (536 p. 2d 697, 1975) Citations made using this format may be used to look up the complete text of the legal cases mentioned in this chapter. Take the citation to a law library, and ask for assistance; law firms and local bar associations often have law libraries.

5. (43 N.W.2d 385, 1950)

6. (521 p. 2d 948, 1974)

7. Christenson, p. 17.

8. (105 S.Ct.1953, 1985)

9. George (Chip) R. Grange II and Nancy Oliver LeSourd. 1989. "Volunteers: Court Decisions vs. Cost Effective Help." *Journal of Christian Camping*. Vol. 21, No. 5, September/October, p. 8. Reprinted with permission from CCI/USA.

10. Charles R. Gregg and Catherine Hansen Stamp. 2009. "Using Volunteer Staff Members: Look Before You Leap: Legal Ramifications." The *CampLine*. Fall, p. 8.

11. Peter F. Drucker. 1989. "What Business Can Learn from Non-Profits." *Harvard Business Review*. July/August, p. 91.

12. John Pearson. n.d. *The Director and The Camp Board: A Creative Partnership*. Wheaton, IL: Christian Camping International, United States Division. p. 39. Reprinted with permission from CCI/USA.

13. George D. Webster and Hugh K. Webster. 1994. "Avoiding Personal Liability: How to Minimize the Risks of Board Service." *Association Management, Leadership*. p. L-57.

EVALUATION AND STRATEGIC PLANNING

Camp Wawenock (Raymond, ME)

Chapter Eighteen

Evaluation comes at the end of the relationships, training and program processes. It is also the beginning of new relationships, improved training, and more exciting and purposeful programming. Strategic planning is a circular process which begins and ends with evaluation.

—Armand Ball

Evaluation

In an era when the consumer is demanding more value for money spent, the competition for services in the recreation and education fields continues to grow. Parents are demanding that camps do more to meet expectations concerning their children's experiences. To meet the increasing competition, a camp director can improve quality by establishing a process of evaluation for every part of the camp operation. Dozens of questions need to be asked: Was this season successful? Did this year's staff do a better job than last year's? Can the food be improved without increasing costs? Which program was the most popular? Did the camp meet its financial budget this season? How did this season's enrollment compare to last season's? Which staff members should be hired for next season?

Evaluation can be regarded as the process of examining the camp operation to see that every part of the predetermined plan is functioning according to the performance standard necessary for accomplishing established goals. Henderson defines evaluation as "the systematic collection and analysis of data to address criteria and make judgments about the worth or improvement of something."[1]

Henderson and Bialeschki further suggest that "evaluation includes all strategies and technologies that are used to determine the value and worth of programs, facilities, administrative procedures, and staff within organizations .... The two major reasons for evaluation are accountability and decision making."[2]

The director does not wait for a problem to surface before considering an evaluation plan. The advantages of a plan of systematic evaluation of all segments of an operation can be numerous. A comprehensive plan of evaluation can help the director to determine:

- Whether desired outcomes and indicators have been met
- Whether campers enjoyed camp
- Any shortcomings in various segments of the operation
- The effectiveness of staff performance
- The financial efficiency of the business operation
- The value of various camp program activities
- The effectiveness of administrative staff as well as the director
- What is working and what is not working
- Quality control measures
- Areas to be considered in planning for the future

Determining Criteria

In order to evaluate objectively, the director must establish criteria against which to examine performance. The more precise or specific the criteria, the better are the chances for useful information at the end of the evaluation process. A variety of sources can be used for establishing the basic performance criteria:

- The mission desired outcomes and indicators of the organization and/or camp
- Governmental regulations
- Standards of an accrediting body
- Standards of the sponsoring organization, if any
- Expectations of families, campers, or customers
- A plan of work or strategic planning document

More than one set of criteria may need to be established. For example, to evaluate the camp food service on the basis of governmental regulations or standards and not take into consideration the expectations of families and campers cannot provide the full information needed.

If the evaluation effort is the result of identification of an existing problem, the focus for evaluation will be more quickly determined and the criteria more easily isolated. Taking the previous example further, if the existing problem is too much leftover food after meals, then examination of standards or regulations will be meaningless, whereas the examination of the expectations of campers and staff may reveal useful information.

If the director is following a comprehensive plan of evaluation, all or most of the listed sources may be considered in the development of the criteria. It is recognized that establishing objective criteria will be easier in some areas of operation, for example, a balanced budget, than in others, such as a camper making new friends.

Who administers the evaluation can also affect the outcomes and/or the credibility of the resulting report. Though more costly than internal evaluation, sometimes it is more important to have an impartial evaluation from an outside consultant concerning an operational area, where problems are creating significant internal or external concerns. The accreditation visit of the American Camp Association is one example of an external evaluation that carries with it an internal evaluation component. It provides a test against established industry standards and a public recognition of minimum compliance. A consultant may assist in analyzing areas not possible to be covered by standards or regulations, or may offer credibility to the evaluation process that is important only to the immediate camp community (e.g., board, staff, present or potential contributors). An ongoing plan of evaluation can be accomplished internally with staff and volunteers, as long as objective criteria are set and appropriate collection and analytic methods chosen and administered properly.

Gathering Data

Before beginning to gather data, a director needs to identify the principal areas to be considered in the evaluation process: site and facilities, program, personnel performance, administrative practices, marketing, and the camper. Some of these areas—such as personnel performance—require continuous data collection, while others—such as site and facilities—may require only an annual review.

Before selecting methods or instruments, the difference in quantitative and qualitative data should be considered. Quantitative data exists or is converted into numbers from answers such as yes or no. Such data is often most helpful in determining whether goals and desired outcomes have been met. Obviously financial records, enrollment statistics, maintenance records, and attendance reports can provide quantitative data by the use of a variety of instruments.

Quantitative data relies most often on:
- Questionnaires (self-administered, or administered in person or by telephone)
- Tests (self-administered or in group setting)
- Records (financial, maintenance, historical, etc.)
- Observations (from predetermined checklists)
- Physical evidence (leftovers, wear and tear, etc.)

Qualitative data deals most often with words and their meanings in a given context. Open-ended questions provide clues and new information not easily gained through yes-or-no answers. The use of qualitative data is most often helpful in looking at processes and describing what happens in given situations.

Qualitative data relies most often on:
- Interviews (open-ended questions, in person or by telephone)
- Questionnaires (with open-ended questions)
- Focus groups (trained leader asking open-ended questions)
- Observations (with field notes)
- Records (minutes, camper logs, narratives, testimonials, letters, publications, etc.)

Some expertise is required in the collection and use of both kinds of data, and in the selection and use of various instrument(s) available. It is wise to seek outside guidance in the development of instruments. The very wording of a question—whether open-ended or requiring a yes-or-no answer—can greatly affect the outcome.

Since quantitative data is most often reduced to yes/no/don't-know answers or numbers relative to degree of agreement (1-2-3-4-5, also known as a Likert Scale), computer statistical packages can be helpful in sorting and analyzing the various factors under consideration.[3]

At this point, the director must carefully analyze:

- How will the information desired be secured in statistical format—yes/no, numbers?
- How many individuals are available to collect data?
- What is the ease of tally?
- What is the cost?
- What degree of training is required?
- What type of sample—everyone, purposeful, random?
- How will the data collected be interpreted?
- Who is the audience for the information—public, staff, board, parents?
- Can data be secured without intruding?

Having considered these questions, the director is in a position to choose whether qualitative or quantitative data is needed and what instruments will best provide that information.

If for some reason it is not possible or practical to collect information from all parties, the type of sample to be used must be examined with a person knowledgeable in statistics and randomization.

To be sure that every part of the operation is included, the director should first develop a list of each component of the camp operation. One way to begin is to list these components, one to a line, on the left side of a sheet of lined paper or in a spreadsheet. To the right, draw columns, and label them: camper, program staff, counselors, administrative board, committee, and so on—incorporating whatever groups will participate in the evaluation process. Then, each of the components listed should be examined and the appropriate columns on the right checked to indicate the group or groups that participate in each phase of camp life. From this completed chart, the director can then consider the instruments most appropriate to each group and area. (See Figure 18-1.) Particular consideration should be given to the following areas of evaluation.

Staff Evaluation of Overall Operation

A questionnaire may provide the most objective information in this situation, but a dialogue with the staff can reveal concerns not easily identified through a questionnaire. A group dialogue by staff should be led by someone who is very objective and has the trust of the group. If the director can establish a reputation for openness to suggestions and ideas throughout the season, staff may be quite willing to respond to questions about the operation. Should this not be the case, a person with skills new to the group may be able to secure more objective responses. It would be quite natural to set aside an afternoon or a day after campers depart for a group evaluation. The director or discussion leader should give staff members an opportunity to react to each camp area and to make observations about the season and suggestions for the next season. If the director and other administrative staff can keep from being defensive and simply make notes as the discussion moves along, such a meeting may reveal attitudes as well as founded observations.

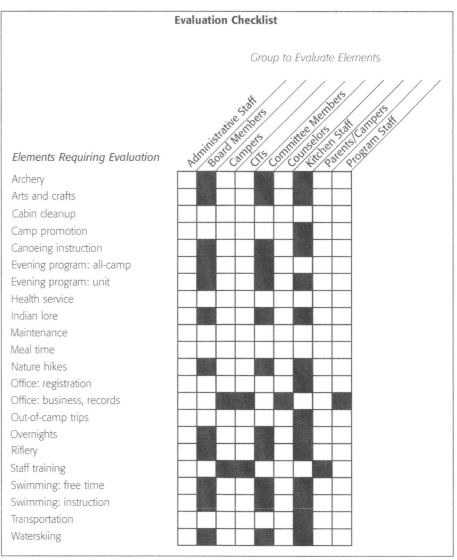

Figure 18-1. Evaluation checklist

It is not easy for a director to always remain objective as the various questionnaires, staff reports, and summaries of discussion sessions. Taking some time after the close of the camp session to relax and reflect on the season before tackling all of these documents is wise. After that time period, Chris Thurber suggests writing a one-page summary of principal themes of evaluations divided by departments or subjects such as program, personnel, policy, and the like.

At that point, he suggests circulating the document to key members of the camp staff and suggest a time for a meeting of the group in person, by telephone or webinar. The meeting agenda could be organized to include:

- Clarification of any areas of the report that are unclear or in question
- Discussing principal themes, getting suggestions of possible causes or consequences
- Identifying the camp's most notable strengths and weaknesses

- Brainstorming possible solutions or improvements for the next season
- Thanking the group for their candor and creativity[4]

The value of such a conversation will depend on the director's follow-through in taking into consideration the ideas and comments in planning for the next season.

If the size or departure schedule of the staff makes such an approach unfeasible, a questionnaire may be developed. To be most effective, such a form should use a simple method, allowing for quick answers, in which the person can check or circle a choice of answers for each question. It is also effective to include one or two open-ended questions near the end of the form, which will elicit more extended comments. If signing the form is optional, staff members can be honest without feeling that they might be jeopardizing their chance to return for another season. A password-protected area of the camp's website also could be made available for evaluative questionnaires and/or narrative comments.

Program Evaluation

Since the camp program is the channel through which desired outcomes are realized, it should be subjected to careful assessment to determine whether desired outcomes and indicators are being met and where changes should be made. Prior to camp, a method should be devised, and specific staff should be given the responsibility of how data on individual campers and programs will be gathered throughout the period. This data can be used for a mid-season evaluation or the end-of-season evaluation. The plan may include a carefully designed checklist for staff to record data on the program from their own observations and from discussions with counselors and campers who participate in a particular program.

Depending on the age and experience of the campers, securing a valid program evaluation from them may be more difficult. If a natural evaluation of an experience can occur informally (such as on an overnight, on a canoe trip, or in a group activity), it can provide qualitative information. A living-group counselor is often the most effective leader of any camper evaluation, except where it deals with the counselor's own performance. If a spontaneous evaluation occurs, a form or some other method of documentation should be available for the counselor to use to relay the information to the administration.

Use of video cameras or tape recorders in an evaluation session where campers participate can be a valuable tool. Certainly an agreement from the families of non-adult campers that they may be photographed and/or taped should be part of the registration form. However, it takes a very experienced leader to help the group to be relaxed and not become self-conscious when recording or taping.

Some camper experiences and situations lend themselves to a recounting in personal logs or journals. This activity helps the camper to reflect on his experiences daily, as well as aiding the camper in understanding the changes during the time frame covered by the experience. This process becomes an avenue of self-evaluation for the camper. Sometimes campers will share their journals with the counselor or director. Some camps have had the privilege of publishing excerpts from such journals, again with the consent of the camper and family.

An evaluation questionnaire may also be helpful. However, handing each camper a form to check off on the last day of camp may diminish the feelings of the moment. Use of a form by the counselor with the living group earlier in the day may be better. Another alternative is to mail the camper a form with a return envelope after the camper returns home or send a fun type e-mail. A camp director might also e-mail campers after they return home and ask them to fill out an online evaluation.

Alternatively, the director can request evaluations from parents after the camper has returned home. Parents may be able to more effectively voice the camper's feelings as well as evaluate any changes. To encourage responses, the questionnaire needs to be carefully designed and as brief as is consistent with securing the necessary information. Providing a stamped, self-addressed envelope and making a signature on the form optional will probably increase the percentage of return. Providing an online questionnaire for parents will probably increase response rates, since they don't have to bother with mailing the form or hunt for it later.

Where particular program activities are run or supervised by particular staff members, these staffers should be provided with an opportunity to evaluate their effectiveness—either orally or by a questionnaire. An opportunity to make recommendations for future changes in the program should be included. Obviously, staff members most closely associated with a particular activity should have the best viewpoint for appraising the procedures and methods used.

Some general questions about programs or activities will help staff think about effectiveness. Determine to what extent the program or activity accomplish the following:
- Were the needs, developmental stage, and interests of campers considered?
- Did the program provide for individual differences in skill and maturity?
- Did the activity leader stress the values of participation: group loyalty, tolerance, and concern for others?
- Did the activity allow for self-expression or creativity?
- Were campers enabled to realize a sense of achievement through participation?
- Did the activity promote the development of leadership skills?
- Was a progression to higher skill levels involved?
- Were the relative indicators met in terms of expected outcomes?

In considering the framework of a particular program or activity, some organizational factors should be assessed. Was consideration given to the optimal size and makeup of the program group? Was the area where the activity took place adequate? Was the equipment adequate, in good repair, and available in sufficient numbers for the group size? Was the activity conducted within safe guidelines?

Administrative Services Evaluation

All administrative services should be appraised throughout the season and reviewed not only by those responsible for the operation, but by other staff outside each operation.

Camp property, facilities, and equipment need to be reviewed not only for purposes of safety and good maintenance, but with an eye to possible improvements. The suggestions of participants, parents, and staff regarding changes should be considered.

The food-service operation should be examined regarding factors such as food quality and quantity, cost per meal, sanitation, efficiency of management and organization, and the maintenance of happy relationships with campers and staff as they move in and out of the dining area during mealtimes.

The health and safety and risk management program should be measured. Can the daily routine for treating persons at the health center be improved? Do some activities have a high accident rate? How can injuries be reduced? On out of- camp trips, are all health and safety precautions taken? Can the procedures at the waterfront be improved to offer a better check on swimmers?

Hospitality Services Evaluation

In a conference/retreat center or where a camp rents facilities to others, questionnaires should be devised to enable guests, group leaders, and staff to comment on housing, equipment, food, staff, hospitality, service, health and safety concerns, grounds, and facilities. Different questions should be asked of the secondary customers (i.e., guests) from those asked the primary customer (i.e., organizations or leaders). Responses can prove to be a valuable tool in marketing, as well as in improving services.

Staff Performance Appraisal

A major part of the evaluation process is the appraisal, at all levels, of employed and volunteer camp staff. This process is discussed in full in Chapter 8.

Evaluation of the Director

Often, the camp director has the most difficult time getting a direct critique of his job performance. A method should be devised for staff and volunteers to share reactions to the director's performance. Sometimes, direct verbal feedback is a possibility, but most often, a questionnaire—which does not have to be signed—is given to staff and volunteers to be returned anonymously. Open-ended questions usually elicit the most helpful comments. A sample form is provided in Figure 18-2. The use of such a form may be helpful to

Director Evaluation Form

Director's name _____ Date _____

Scale

5 = Superior performance; consistently goes beyond expectations; demonstrates appreciable growth

4 = Consistently meets expectations; shows personal initiative; shows progress in personal growth and competency

3 = Meets minimal expectations most of time; little personal initiative or personal growth; performs to level of abilities

2 = Achieves at a level lower than abilities; occasionally meets minimal expectations; shows no growth

1 = Fails to meet expectations; performs below level of ability; no discernible growth; performance unacceptable

0 = No knowledge

	0	1	2	3	4	5
• Demonstrates vision regarding camp's objectives and long-range plans						
• Sets high standards for the committee, staff, and campers						
• Sees that high standards are met in:						
✓ Maintenance and improvement of site						
✓ Selection and training of staff						
✓ Health and safety of campers and staff						
• Has good physical health and stamina						
• Demonstrates personal interest in:						
✓ Each staff member						
✓ Campers						
✓ Committee members and volunteers						
• Communicates well with:						
✓ Staff						
✓ Campers						
✓ Committee members and volunteers						
✓ Public						
• Demonstrates fairness in working with people						
• Keeps well informed on all aspects of operation						
• Effectively delegates responsibility and related authority						
• Maintains effective program of evaluation:						
✓ Of program						
✓ Of staff						
✓ By campers and parents						
• Maintains a team-building approach						
• Inspires confidence and trust						
• Has pleasant personality and gets along well with people						
• Is effective in marketing approach						

Other comments:

Signed _____

Figure 18-2. Director evaluation form

the director's supervisor which could be an agency executive director, camp administrator, owner, or personnel committee of an operating board, since such an annual evaluation and feedback is beneficial to a director.

Evaluation of Boards or Committees

In camps that have governing committees or boards, it is important both to the director/administrator and the chief elected officer to have regular times to check the effectiveness of their work with that body. It is also important for the volunteer governing body to evaluate its own operation. Sometimes, this evaluation can be done in an informal dialogue in a retreat setting, where time is not as pressed as in regular meetings, and methods can be used to secure qualitative input. Where such an approach is not possible, a checklist, such as that shown in Figure 18-3, may provide a more objective evaluation. Similarly, volunteers need feedback as to their performance and participation. Performance appraisal of volunteer staff members is covered in Chapter 9.

Evaluation of Campers

The evaluation of campers varies greatly from camp to camp. Many camps keep careful records of each child's program participation and relationship to peers. This information is often helpful in placing the camper in a living group another year and may be useful in planning activities at the beginning of the next season.

Ideally, the evaluation of campers should go back to the developmental goals of the age group served and the desired outcomes directed to those developmental goals. At the end of the season the degree to which the camp experience has met the indicators for those outcomes is one true test of the camp experience. Having focused staff on those developmental goals during staff training and referred staff back to them during supervisory conferences, it is logical that the level of achievement of those outcomes be measured. These results can be most helpful in responding to parents and also in assessing changes needed in program operations for the next season.

Two nationwide research projects (Nationwide Camp Evaluation Project, 1993–96 and the National Inclusive Camp Practices, 1997–2000) used qualitative data and comparative case studies to reveal camper growth. "A summative analysis of all interview comments received from campers and parents revealed that increased independence (self-reliance) was the predominant growth outcome for the case-study campers."[5]

Between 2001 and 2004, the American Camp Association conducted research with over 5000 families from 80 ACA-accredited camps to determine the outcomes of the camp experience as expressed by parents and children. Parents, camp staff, and children reported significant growth in: self-esteem, independence, leadership, friendship skills, social comfort, peer relationships, adventure, environmental awareness, spirituality, values, and decisions. The research not only examined youth development outcomes, but also targeted program improvement.[6]

Volunteer Committees and Boards Evaluation Form

This document is designed to obtain your evaluation of our board's (committee) effectiveness. Circle the number on the rating scale that corresponds to your evaluation of the board in each category. Number 1 indicates poor performance and number 5 excellent performance, as illustrated by the statements

Clarity of Role and Function
Lacks. We're fuzzy about our responsibilities.
1 2 3 4 5
Present. We distinguish clearly between policy determination and management functions. We know what we are about.

Leadership
Dominated by one or a few persons. Other resources within the board are never used.
1 2 3 4 5
Shared among members according to abilities and insights. All resources are used.

Important Issues
Not addressed, but "swept under the rug" or dealt with outside of the board.
1 2 3 4 5
Consistently on the agenda for open consideration, debate, and decision.

Preparation
Lacks. We're consistently caught off guard without adequate information, facts, and documentation.
1 2 3 4 5
Outstanding. Committees and staff do excellent preliminary work. Members are well informed and understand the pros and cons of all decisions.

Communication of Ideas
Poor. We don't listen. Ideas are ignored.
1 2 3 4 5
Good. We listen and try to understand one another's ideas. Ideas are well presented and acknowledged.

Responsible Participation
Lacks. We reflect our own biases. We "grind our own axes" and watch from the "outside."
1 2 3 4 5
Present. We're sensitive to the need to reflect for our camp and its clientele. Everyone is "on the inside participating."

Freedom of Persons
Stifled. Conformity is explicitly or implicitly fostered. Members are often manipulated.
1 2 3 4 5
Enhanced and encouraged. Creativity of persons and their individuality is respected.

Climate of Relationships
One of hostility, suspicion, indulgent politeness, fear or anxiety.
1 2 3 4 5
One of mutual trust and genuineness. Atmosphere is relaxed and friendly.

Decision-Making
Superficial. We're a "rubber-stamp" body. Decisions are crammed down our throats.
1 2 3 4 5
Participative. All data is available and all opinions are aired, with resultant ownership of decisions that are made.

Action Agreements
Not reached. We don't set target dates or plan for follow through.
1 2 3 4 5
Reached. We agree on next steps and set target dates for review.

Fiscal Accountability
Lacks. We don't consider the cost of an action before it is taken.
1 2 3 4 5
Present. We carefully consider financial implications of proposals before approval.

Continuity
Lacks. Each meeting seems to "start from scratch."
1 2 3 4 5
Present. We build on previous work in an efficient manner.

Productivity
Low. We're proud and happy, just coasting along. Meetings are irrelevant and a waste of time and money.
1 2 3 4 5
High. We are digging hard and earnestly at work in important tasks. We create and achieve at each meeting.

Please list any additional suggestions or ideas you have for increasing the effectiveness of this board. Particular attention to items you rated 1 or 2 is greatly appreciated.

Figure 18-3. Evaluation for boards and committees

Such research programs require involving a professor or staff person skilled in program evaluation techniques to help design the instrument and plan for evaluation in addition to clarifying program desired outcomes and involving the approval of the governing organization, if there is one.

In keeping families in touch with the camper's progress, some camps use a regular report form for families at the end of the season, while others require counselors to write progress reports to parents at regular intervals. Some families can even keep track of their camper's progress by reading blogs or viewing pictures of camp activities placed daily or weekly on the camp's website. Camps with shorter sessions may require the progress reports at the end of the session the camper attended. Whatever the form or time frame, the evaluation should be approached with concern for objectivity and balance. Counselors need to understand that they see the camper in isolation from his familiar environment, which means that their observations may be one sided or limited in scope. In addition, these records are sometimes necessary for reports to an agency that referred the camper or that has an ongoing relationship to the camper.

In many instances, the most effective form of evaluation is that done in one-on-one conversation with the camper. Helping a camper see himself through the eyes of others is an important desired outcome for many camps. If that is a goal, then it can only be reached in an open and trusting living situation. Counselors need careful training and sensitivity in order to give campers a positive experience of self-evaluation. The process should begin with discussing with each individual camper, as well as with the group, individual goals for the camp period. Their conversations with campers should begin on a positive note and emphasize positive achievements toward that camper's goals, but the areas in which a camper can improve should also be pointed out and discussed honestly.

The best evaluation of a camper happens when the camper can be led into a realistic self-evaluation. If the focus of conversations and observations can be on how the camper perceives his achievement, skill level, behavior, or response to others, it is more likely to become a part of his ongoing life experience.

Accreditation

The program of accreditation pioneered by the American Camp Association is designed to measure the performance of a particular camp or conference center against a list of standards of operation in many areas. The accreditation program features a visit by trained professionals. Preparation for the visit may extend over a period of months. The ACA standards, developed over a period of more than 70 years and now accepted nationally as industry standards, can also be used as a tool for self-evaluation across all areas of camp operation. Involvement of administrative staff, as well as any operating committee or board, can also be most useful, as long as staff is helped to understand that the process is not an "inspection" but rather a self-evaluation process. This may require a review of the rationale for certain standards and/or paperwork in a preparation meeting.

Finances

Though monthly financial reports give a clue to the financial operation, the yearend report provides an opportunity for a variety of evaluations. These reports will be of the greatest interest to the camp director, business manager, and a governing board. The reports should include: cost per meal served, cost per camper day, cost-effectiveness analysis, cost-benefit analysis by specific services or program activities, and a comparison of income and expenditures by category over a five-year period.

Figure 18-4 provides a chart showing the instruments most applicable to the various areas of evaluation covered previously. Though other instruments are available, these are the most commonly used in the camp operation.

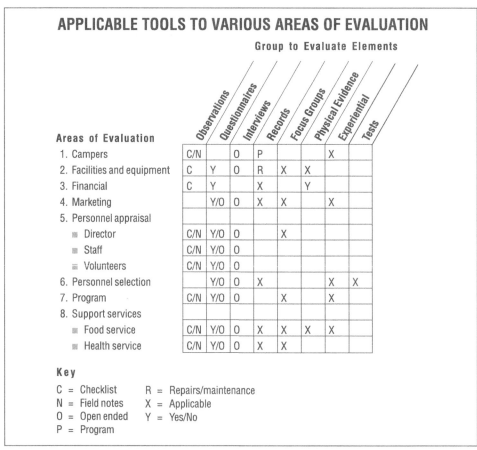

APPLICABLE TOOLS TO VARIOUS AREAS OF EVALUATION

Group to Evaluate Elements

Areas of Evaluation	Observations	Questionnaires	Interviews	Records	Focus Groups	Physical Evidence	Experiential	Tests
1. Campers	C/N		O	P			X	
2. Facilities and equipment	C	Y	O	R	X	X		
3. Financial	C	Y		X		Y		
4. Marketing		Y/O	O	X	X		X	
5. Personnel appraisal								
Director	C/N	Y/O	O		X			
Staff	C/N	Y/O	O					
Volunteers	C/N	Y/O	O					
6. Personnel selection		Y/O	O	X			X	X
7. Program	C/N	Y/O	O		X		X	
8. Support services								
Food service	C/N	Y/O	O	X	X	X	X	
Health service	C/N	Y/O	O	X	X			

Key

C = Checklist   R = Repairs/maintenance
N = Field notes   X = Applicable
O = Open ended   Y = Yes/No
P = Program

Figure 18-4. Applicable tools to various areas of evaluation

Reporting: The Judgment Phase

The final step—once the criteria has been determined and the data gathered— is to make judgments about the meaning of the data in relationship to the camp operation. In a single proprietorship, the data gathered lands on one desk, and the judgments are made there. In most cases, however, multiple persons are involved in the judgment process, which will require reports describing the data and conclusions.

In interpreting quantitative data, the director must not be too quick to simply assume that the highest numerical sums necessarily provide the proper judgment. Rather, the frequencies must be examined to see if particular portions of the data skew the results in some fashion. Establishing a mean (or average) and a median (the position at which an equal number is distributed above and below that figure) in the data will help the director discover if the two are relatively close. If a substantial difference is found, the data may need to be examined more closely for anything unusual that is skewing the results. If the quantitative data becomes this complex, many camp directors may wish to consult with someone who has training in statistical analysis for assistance in interpreting the data.

In interpreting qualitative data, Henderson suggests that early in the organization of data, the director should "continually reexamine the data. 'Negative evidence,' which means you will be trying to make sure everything fits your categories, will be sought." In this instance, the evaluator looks to see whether any evidence does not fit the interpretations emanating from the data.

Further, she suggests the director look "for multiple sources of evidence to draw conclusions … that interpretations come from being intimately familiar with the data. Therefore, the evaluator … read[s] the data over and over."[7]

The director must carefully examine the data for information that he did not necessarily seek since there are often unexpected insights that arise from evaluation. This information may be more valuable than much of the data deliberately sought. Look for negative impacts as well as positive experiences.

Once the data has been examined repeatedly and basic conclusions and inconclusive areas identified, the director writes the report, outlining the areas studied, criteria identified, the sample used, the instruments chosen, the data collected, and resulting conclusions and recommendations for action. The use of this report will vary with the audience to whom it is addressed, with considerably more detail offered to the decision makers than to parents or campers. Each audience requires a different approach.

Reporting to the Corporate Board

Most camps have a governing group, which expects reports at the conclusion of the camp season. These reports can take many forms but are most often directed to the camp director's supervisor or a governing committee or board. This report should certainly highlight the events of the summer, giving the group a sense of the program and values derived from the experience. The use of comments from camper logs or parental letters can be helpful in sharing this feeling.

In addition to communicating the programmatic aspects of camp, it is vital that the results of the evaluation process be shared with the governing group. Summaries of the data with comparative data from previous summers will provide perspective to the facts. Furthermore, the director may wish to make recommendations for improvements and steps for the next season growing out of the evaluation process. This approach helps the governing body focus discussion on the major concerns and alternatives to the recommendations.

Such a report should summarize the research criteria, the methods used to collect the data, any instrument used in the process, and the resulting data. Following this narrative, a list of conclusions and resulting recommendations may be presented. If the report is quite long, an executive summary plus the conclusions and recommendations may be used for wider distribution. These reports should be retained in the camp's files, along with the raw data collected in the process.

Reporting to Families and Participants

The report to the families and participants often emphasizes the overview of the season with comments on camper activities and projects. Pictures and stories will make such reports more interesting and readable. It should be kept in mind that the report parents receive is an important tool in developing loyalty and interest in camp for another season, and many times developing a case for future contributions of money or services.

Many camps publish a yearbook, newsletter, e-mail newsletter, or annual calendar, which tells the season's story in pictures and words for the campers and staff. The emphasis in these publications is given to the good times had by all, with pictures of as many different campers and staff as possible. Not only is this instrument helpful for next year's recruitment, but it also provides a tool that might be shared with friends.

The size and layout of the camp's report will depend partially on the funds available. In any case, the report should be designed to be an attractive, interpretative tool. The Internet is one cost-effective method of distributing the results of evaluation efforts.

Reporting to Alumni

Developing an updated list of camper and staff alumni is valuable for sharing information about the camp. Certainly, a report of each season should be shared with the alumni group. This report goes beyond the sort of communication sent to families and is not as detailed as the report to the governing body. The report for alumni might be a summary of the major events of the camp season with an enclosure concerning the major decisions the camp is facing in the near future.

This report is designed to maintain the interest of the alumni, assuring them of the continuing allegiance to the philosophy of the camp and stimulating interest in ways the alumni can further serve the camp through contributions of money and services. Again, providing this report in digital format can be a cost effective approach to disseminating this information.

Strategic Planning

Evaluation leads one to consider *change*, and in today's society, a camp that does not confront change is likely to flounder in light of constantly changing societal needs. Strategic planning is a process and involves not only the director or owner, but all of the stakeholders in the life of the camp: staff, board, parents, and campers. In even considering strategic planning, the question must be asked: "Why are we even considering planning?" "Are we willing to change." This is step number *one* and listing those reasons will help provide a focus for the process. There must be a readiness for the planning process from the outset.

Step *two* is to identify and involve the stakeholders in the camp and what representatives of those groups need to be included in the process. These persons may form the planning group. Pulling these persons together to discuss the need of a strategic plan will lead to many questions and concerns being expressed. This discussion may lead to a revision of the reasons originally listed.

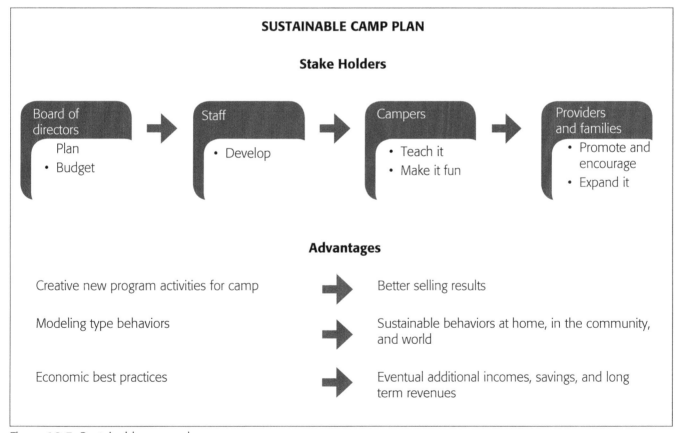

Figure 18-5. Sustainable camp plan

As each of the reasons will raise questions and questions will help develop a list of the pieces of information that will be needed to have an intelligent discussion. Listing those pieces of information will guide the process of where and who can gather it. Some of this information will need to be gathered before another step can be taken, and other pieces may take longer and be more important later in the process.

Step number *three* is for the group to be called together for longer meeting, usually overnight. This provides time to look at the present mission or purpose of the camp. Is that written mission the one all members of the group felt was the mission? Is the mission relevant to the current population served, the current geographic community, and the operator's mission, especially of the operator is an organization rather than an individual?

The evaluation of that mission and the actual development of an adjusted or new mission may be agonizing for the group. Having an overnight meeting also provides time for reflection between some of the sessions. It is often at this stage that having the need an outside objective person or consultant to help the group becomes apparent. Such a person or group should be chosen carefully based upon the types of groups with whom that person has worked, his background, and compatibility with the working group. In most cases, retaining such a person will mean a cost (fee, travel, etc.). That expenditure will be worth it, as a director looks back at the process.

Once a written mission has been agreed upon, the leader can guide the group through the following steps:
- Review the information gathered, and assess whether the existing operation expresses that mission.
- Test the mission on internal and external stakeholder groups, and identify the issues or questions that arise. How will the stakeholders be affected?
- List those issues, and identify other critical issues that need response or more information for consideration.
- Evaluate the strengths, weaknesses, threats, and opportunities presented by the present operation, including the programming and site/facilities.
- Review these in light of the proposed mission.
- Agree upon the criteria for dealing with any key issues and for setting priorities.
- Select future key strategies that cover the areas of camp activity: site/facilities, clientele, programming, governance, and staff. Develop goals/objectives for each strategy.
- Test the mission/goals/objectives that have been developed with key stakeholders.
- Evaluate responses and any revisions that are needed.
- Develop financial projections for the years covered in the plan.
- Analyze whether the camp can accomplish the financial projections, and if any revisions need to be made in goals/objectives.
- Put all of this into a written plan; review and finalize for adoption by the operating body.

- Divide the plan to annual segments, with specific outcomes for each year, identifying who is responsible for them.
- Evaluate annually, adjusting goals and outcomes as needed.

This brief description of a sample strategic planning process can only point the group in the direction of planning that needs to be considered. They may encounter blocks at any point in the process, causing the group to pause. However, pausing too long can be detrimental to the group process and necessitate back tracking to repeat earlier steps.

As Allison and Kaye suggest, "strategic planning is both a creative and participatory process that engenders new insights and helps an organization pursue its mission. A tool's effectiveness, though, ultimately depends on how well it is wielded."[8] It is the responsibility of the camp director to stimulate interest and commitment to the principle of strategic planning, and search out effective leaders to make it happen. As mentioned earlier, it will be essential to involve an objective, outside trained person to assist in the process as it moves along.

Throughout the planning process, consideration should be given to sustainability in terms of environmental practices, economic outlook, and the social/cultural aspects. Much attention has been voiced in terms of the sustainability of current lifestyles unless changes are made in the stewardship of natural resources around the world. Therefore, any plan should evaluate the current environmental practices of the camp in terms of facility, day-to-day operations, and program. Evaluation of each of these areas should be conducted on the basis of best environmental practices. Similarly, any economic outlooks should be considered on the basis of sustainability over the longer period. Development of program in terms of activities, equipment, and desired outcomes should be tested against sound environmental practices.

Camp is a miniature community and, in a sense, a miniature world. The plan for the future of any camp should reflect practices that will improve the quality of that community, and in turn, the world—in hopes that those practices will become the normal behaviors in the home environment. Sustainable actions have impact across all areas of life (Figure 18-6).

SUSTAINABLE PRACTICES

Sustainability Actions

Environment	Social and Cultural	Economic
• Power electricity	• Folklore and traditions in camp	• Local people as a main part in camp operations and jobs
• Trash management	• Local people as a main part in camp operations and jobs	• Business development
• Construction materials	• Reinforce local basic daily uses	• Provide business opportunities to local organizations
• Wild animals and species preservation	• Others	• Entrepreneur spirit encouraged through local investors
• Chemical waste		• Others
• Others		

Figure 18-6. Sustainable practices[9]

Checkpoints

- Were evaluations conducted in previous seasons? If so, are copies retained in the files?
- What type of evaluations would have been helpful to a new camp director to begin planning for the first season?
- Using Figure 18-1 as a basis, develop a chart listing the areas of the camp program and the people who should be involved in the evaluation of each area.
- Develop an overall evaluation plan that will provide desired information (refer to the second checkpoint).
- What information would the camp's governing committee or board prefer to have at the end of the season?
- Review the camp's evaluation plan to see if it will provide the information the board wants (refer to previous checkpoint).
- What sort of evaluation from the staff will be most helpful?
- How does the camp help campers begin the process of self-evaluation?
- Is a system in place to evaluate the camp program against the developmental goals of the each age group? If not, how does evaluation occur?
- Develop a plan for disseminating this research to all interested parties.
- Has strategic planning been any consideration?

Related Standards

American Camp Association's Accreditation Standards for Camp Programs and Services: OM.3, OM.10

Endnotes

1. Karla A. Henderson with M. Deborah Bialeschki. 1995. *Evaluating Leisure Services: Making Enlightened Decisions*. State College, PA: Venture Publishing, Inc. p. 3.
2. Karla A. Henderson and M. Deborah Bialeschki. 1993. "Camp Was Great, But the Water Was Too Cold." *Camping Magazine*. Vol. 65, No. 5, May/June, pp. 31–32.
3. Henderson with Bialeschki. Evaluating Leisure Services. pp. 225–226.
4. Christopher Thurber. 2010. "They've Done Their Jobs…Now What Will You Tell Them?" *Camping Magazine*. Vol. 83, No. 5, September/October, p. 46.
5. Steve Brannan and Ann Fullerton. 1999. "Case Studies Reveal Camper Growth." Camping Magazine. Vol. 72, No. 1, January/February, pp. 22–25.
6. American Camp Association. 2005. Directions: Youth Development Outcomes of the Camp Experience. www.acacamps.org/research/ydo.pdf.
7. Henderson with Bialeschki, pp. 268–269.
8. Michael Allison and Judie Kaye. 1997. *Strategic Planning for Nonprofit Organizations: A Practical Guide and Workbook*. New York: John Wiley & Sons, p. xvii.
9. Juan Mario Gutierrez. 2011. International Camp Director Course Curriculum. Huntsville, Ontario, Canada: International Camping Fellowship.

PROFESSIONAL DEVELOPMENT

Camp Mah-Kee-Nac (Lenox, MA)

Chapter Nineteen

> *The impetus for an educational experience naturally should come from camp directors. This would not only be the best guarantee of its productiveness, but would also reflect a high degree of genuinely professional consciousness on the part of camp directors.*[1]
> —Hedley S. Dimock

All the answers are not in this volume because no one can provide all those answers. Many answers will have to be found by the camp director on his own—through experience, peer relationships, research, study, and workshops and conferences. The quotation from Hedley Dimock at the beginning of this chapter is as true today as it was when it was written over 60 years ago.

Camping as a Profession

The subject of the camp director as a professional has been an issue since the early part of this century, but has intensified during the past four decades. In our society, the term *professional* has been so greatly overused that, at times, the only commonality among its many uses is that it differentiates between a paid and an unpaid person—one exception being the expression "professional volunteers." Originally, the word was used to talk about law, medicine, and religious vocations, but it has been broadened in modern times.

It is recognized that many persons come into the camping and conference/retreat center field for a few years only, before taking other positions in human-service organizations. Many individuals in other professions, such as education, spend their summers as well as part of the school year involved in the camp field. However, a significant number of directors are individuals who spend their lives in the camp field—as camp directors, administrators, consultants, and teachers. These people often have a strong feeling that being a camp or conference/retreat center director is a profession worthy of note.

A workgroup at the ninth Character Education in Camping Seminar at George Williams College identified the following seven marks of a profession:[2]

- A profession rests upon "a social function, distinct from other functions, that is basic, important and relatively permanent." This aspect is most obvious in medicine, ministries, engineering, and law. Camp administration is so young, as compared to these professions, that it is a bit premature to espouse our social function, much less equate 130-plus years as permanency.
- A profession has a "distinctive or specialized body of knowledge," a theory that ties together many disciplines that represent a unique body apart from other fields. As identified in this text, many disciplines have to be mastered in this field, but what makes that body of knowledge unique from education, perhaps the closest profession to camping?
- A profession "demands a specialized or professional preparation, in addition to general education, for its practitioners." In other words, the body of knowledge is so complex and large that it cannot be mastered on the job as in a craft. It is one of the differences between a carpenter and an architect.

Standards for specialized education are set, and only those individuals who meet them are eligible for admission to that profession. An effort was made, in this regard, through an American Camp Association Certified Professional program, but after a number of years of granting certification, it became apparent that the public was far from accepting this certification as an eligibility requirement to practice in the field. Consequently, the program was discontinued.

- A profession functions collectively through people "joining together for mutual betterment and growth and to provide a service to the public."

- These were once called guilds or societies, but today they are known as associations. The functions include:

  ✓ Formulating the conditions for entrance into the profession.

  ✓ Developing a code governing ethical practices of those in the field, as it relates to the "relationships between the practitioner and the other practitioners, and the practitioner and the public."

  ✓ Stimulating the "discovery of new knowledge and practice pertinent to the profession." Researching and publishing articles on various aspects of the field's practice is a recognized way of advancing the body of knowledge in a field and one's professional contribution. Betty van der Smissen and Judy Brookhiser developed a bibliography of research in the field in 1982.[3] A great deal of other research has occurred since then. Much of this research is included in the ACA Knowledge Center online. The center is organized by 13 core competency areas. ACA maintains a Committee for the Advancement of Research and Evaluation (CARE) which advises and supports the research function of the association as it serves to develop and enhance knowledge generation and dissemination within ACA. Current research efforts can be viewed on the ACA website.

  ✓ "Facilitating the interchange and dissemination of" knowledge in the field throughout the entire profession. This function is the obligation and effort to continually update the field and provide new input into the body of knowledge. This initiative is advanced today by camp directors who write for such publications as *Camping Magazine, Insite*, and the *Journal of Experiential Education*, and who author books in the field. Such interchange and dissemination of knowledge has happened in the Christian Camp and Conference Association, the American Camp Association, and the International Association of Conference Center Administrators. It follows that when the camp director becomes part of one or all of those bodies, he/she moves toward being a professional.

- A profession "formulates and applies standards that govern the practice of the profession in the community." This goal has been met in our field through the standards of the American Camp Association, which have been developed over more than 60 years and are now the accepted standards for the industry in the United States. However, the industry is still some distance from having all camps or conference/retreat centers meet those standards, or having all states recognize accreditation as essential for licensing.

- A profession is "motivated by a social spirit and purpose. Social values presumably transcend individual and economic values in a profession." In other words, the reason for camps to exist is to serve the public, and that becomes an essential ingredient of any professional organization or association that brings camp directors together. The challenge, therefore, is to keep individual directors and their associations focused on the growth of the camp director and service to the public, rather than mutual protection societies. Pressures will always be present to move toward the mutual protection society rather than toward the protection of the public, and the voices of professionals in the field will have to keep their associations on course.

- A profession "implies a personal standard of workmanship characterized by both sincerity and intellectual integrity. The professional person seeks to maintain high standards of competence, to keep abreast of changing conditions and of new knowledge and techniques, and to embody the new learnings in his practice." This requirement means that a professional has an obligation to continually update his knowledge in the field. A professional is a person who is up to date on the current and best practices in the field. Herein, the director has to move beyond his own camp or organization to exchange information and to converse with fellow professionals about key issues and development.

An examination of the seven marks of a profession gives us evidence that some requirements have been fulfilled in the field, while others have not. Therein is the challenge for the future. Hedley S. Dimock, in speaking to this issue, wrote:

> A professional ... will submit himself to the rigid discipline of straight thinking, to a constant search for new knowledge and better techniques that should be embodied in practice. In this quest for higher standards of workmanship, he will ally himself with other camp directors and personnel through camping associations or similar organizations. He will accept his share of collective responsibility to discover and disseminate knowledge through research and publications, to raise the standards of camping generally, and to interpret to the public the objectives and standards of the modern camp. He will work within the planning structure of the community to make camping experience available for the larger number of persons who need this experience.[4]

Expanding the Camp Director's Education

At least six areas of educational endeavor will enable a camp director to gain additional knowledge and keep current with developments in the field. For camp directors, the American Camp Association has come up with the following 13 core competencies for professional development:

- Youth/Adult Growth and Development
- Learning Environment and Curricula
- Program Planning
- Observation, Assessment, Evaluation
- Professional Development and Leadership
- Health and Wellness
- Risk Management
- Cultural Competence
- Families and Community Connection
- Nature and Environment
- Business Management and Practices
- Human Resources Management
- Site/Facilities Management

The American Camp Association offers a Basic Camp Director's Course (BCDC), which is the best comprehensive introduction to the management of camps and covers the core competencies of directing a camp. These core competencies are a framework to help guide carrier development. Primarily designed for camp directors with less than six years of experience, the course is offered in conjunction with American Camp Association national, regional, and local conferences. A schedule of upcoming courses may be viewed on the ACA website. A similar course tuned to international camping is offered as the International Camp Director's Course and upcoming courses can be viewed on the International Camping Fellowship website (www.campingfellowship.org).

The American Camp Association has developed a Certificate of Added Qualifications (CAQ) opportunities available under its Professional Development Center on its website. It is possible to pursue certificates for different camp-related competencies for targeted audiences. For example, some are specifically designed for the professional development of entry-level frontline staff, middle managers, camp directors, and so on. All are available online.

Participation in the ACA Standards Program Course is a significant educational experience, whether a director is seeking accreditation or not. The Christian Camp and Conference Association offers a professional training program in certain areas, entitled the Cairns Series®.

The American Camp Association, the Christian Camp and Conference Association, and the International Association of Conference Center Directors offer a variety of workshops, courses, and conferences that will assist the camp director in areas in which he/she feels deficient and will help the director keep abreast of current practices. The annual and regional conferences of the organizations provide a wealth of such information. A variety of other organizations offer courses, workshops, and conferences that will benefit camp directors in certain areas. Many of these organizations are listed in Appendix C. In addition, a number of colleges and universities offer courses in camp administration or related subjects through physical education or recreation and leisure studies departments or programs.

Participation in the American Camp Association and/or the Christian Camp and Conference Association provides an opportunity to meet fellow camp directors and to develop relationships that will allow sharing and problem solving together. The American Camp Association's website (www.ACAcamps.org/education) provides details regarding local educational opportunities and opportunities for taking online courses. ACA has a full online course catalog.

Continuing education credits (CECs) can now be received through ACA for any courses offered by ACA as well as for a set of courses that ACA has endorsed. These CECs can be found online. By earning CECs, camp and youth development professionals are building their professional resumes. Some related organizations require a certain number of hours of continuing education, which these CECs often fulfill.

Participation in the accreditation process of the American Camp Association is one of the best educational tools available. The Basic Standards Course and a study of the American Camp Association *Accreditation Process Guide* is an ideal way to start, whether or not the camp is seeking accreditation. Of course, actual participation in the accreditation of the camp is an exciting and grueling educational experience, and it is well worth the time, effort, and money. Further, completion of the course for standards visitors and participating in accreditation visits to other camps is a way to expand your professional horizons, understand the broader field of camping, and provide a valuable service to the profession.

Personal reading and study cannot be dismissed as any less important than the items listed previously. The professional publications in the field should be read regularly, and journals in related fields should be perused as occasion allows. The American Camp Association bookstore (acabookstore.org) offers the most comprehensive selection of print publications and DVDs in the field. Christian Camp and Conference Association (ccca.org) also offers a variety of publications. While some individuals are distant from conferences and workshops and able to make them only every few years, books and DVDs are as close as the bedside table or television.

All of the costs for the activities mentioned are business-related and should be borne by the camp, where possible. However, where not covered by the camp, they may be itemized for personal tax deductions.

A professional portfolio is a career-planning tool to help analyze competencies and document professional development experiences. It should contain information commonly included in a resume, including such items as:
- Career goals
- Previous job experience
- Completed degree programs
- Courses, seminars, and workshops completed, specific to the camping industry
- Participation in other educational events
- Self-study experiences
- Regularly updated needs assessment

- ACA leadership and volunteer experiences
- Other experiences relevant to the profession

Finally, every camp director has an opportunity to add to the body of knowledge of the field of camping. Among the exciting aspects of the camping field are opportunities to experiment and explore more efficient ways of operating camps and conference/retreat centers, as well as developing new methods of helping children and adults grow through interaction within the camp environment. As a director, study, experiment, document, and add to that body of knowledge. Whatever the director does, his work in the camping field should aid not only those participants and staff in the program, but also ensure that future generations will continue to benefit from this unique human experience called camp.

Checkpoints

- Which of the seven marks of a profession accurately reflects the camping profession?
- How does the Code of Ethics apply to an individual's work at camp or the camp experience?
- Is a professional development plan in place? If not, develop a plan for professional development.

Related Standards

American Camp Association's Accreditation Standards for Camp Programs and Services: HR.1

Endnotes

1. Hedley S. Dimock. 1948. "Camping and the Future." IX in a series, *Character Education in the Summer Camp*. New York: Association Press. p. 59.
2. Ibid., pp. 24–26.
3. Betty van der Smissen and Judy Brookhiser, Eds. 1982. *Bibliography of Research in Organized Camping, Environmental Education, Adventure Education, and Interpretative Services*. Martinsville, IN: American Camping Association.
4. Hedley S. Dimock. 1948. *Administration of the Modern Camp*. New York: Association Press (YMCA of the USA). p. 269.

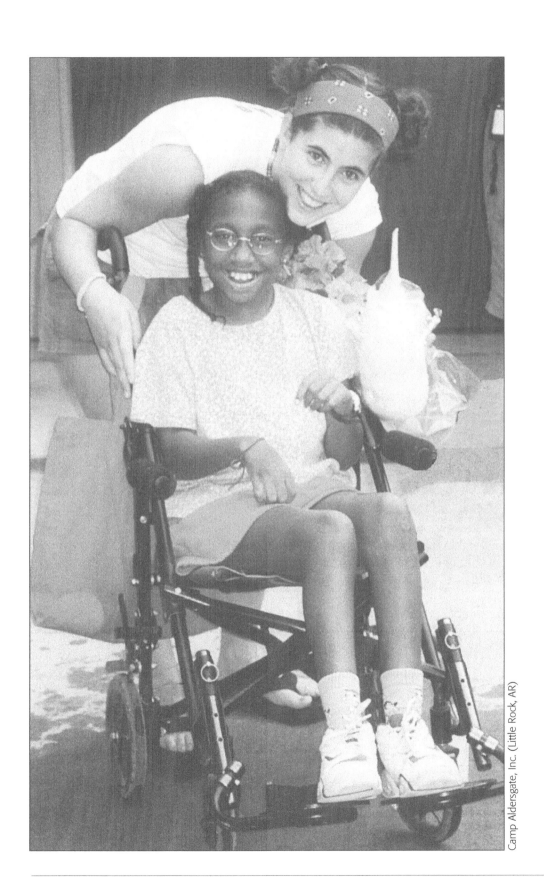

Camp Aldersgate, Inc. (Little Rock, AR)

Appendices

Appendix A: Sample Job Descriptions

Position Title: **Program Director**

Responsible to: Camp Director

General Responsibility: To be responsible for the camp program and to assist in staff training

Qualifications:
- At least 21 years of age, preferably at least 25 years of age
- At least two years of college, preferably a graduate
- Extensive experience as a group counselor or staff member in camp setting; experience at programming in a camp setting preferred
- Emotionally mature and willing to accept responsibility
- Belief in the individual worth of the camper
- Ability to work with a minimum of supervision

Specific Responsibilities:
- Assist the camp director in planning and carrying out precamp and inservice staff training.
- Be responsible for all camp programs provided for the camper.
- Directly supervise and appraise the unit counselors, nature specialist, arts and crafts specialist, aquatics specialist, equine specialist, and tripping specialist.
- Maintain proper records as required by the camp director.
- Coordinate, with assistant director and maintenance supervisor, matters of interest in areas of overlapping responsibility, while always seeking the best solution for campers and the camp.
- Review program budget, and search for ways to increase services offered within budgetary constraints; be prepared to defend proposed programming budget changes.
- Be responsible for the health and welfare of campers.

Essential Functions:
- Be able to train the staff.
- Visually observe the assigned staff in performance of their duties, as well as the behavior of campers in their care, and be able to provide guidance as needed.
- Visually identify hazards in the camp operation, and respond appropriately.
- Be able to work and communicate well with a variety of age groups.
- Be physically able to navigate the campsite to observe programs, facilities, and staff.

Position Title: Site Manager

Responsible to: Camp Director

General Responsibility: To oversee and maintain all properties of the camp

Qualifications:
- High school diploma required, with some college or technical school work beyond high school preferred
- Experience in carpentry, plumbing, electrical, and general maintenance repairs
- Experience in supervising work of others
- Ability to get along well with people

Specific Responsibilities:
- Oversee and maintain all properties according to annual work plans and schedules.
- Live on the camp site, and act as site manager of camp property.
- Hire occasional helpers and subcontractors for projects and ongoing maintenance.
- Supervise any employee assigned to maintenance area of camp.
- Make recommendations for budgeted repairs and maintenance during budget preparation period; outline costs and details.
- Recommend maintenance and improvements that are beyond budgeted amounts; develop cost figures and details.
- Direct volunteer groups who come to camp for work weekends and projects.
- See that all major equipment and vehicles are maintained and housed appropriately.
- Order maintenance supplies and check delivery; forward approved invoices to the camp director.
- Welcome rental groups when asked by camp director, and check them out at time of departure; check facilities for damage or unusual disarray.
- See that all repair requests are completed or responded to within 18 hours.
- Be responsible for the health and welfare of campers.

Essential Functions:
- Be able to drive all camp owned vehicles.
- Have the necessary physical strength to carry out maintenance and repairs (e.g., to lift heavy objects, to dig, to load and unload trucks, to carry out assigned repairs).
- Visually identify hazards throughout the camp property, and respond appropriately.
- Visually identify repairs and cleaning that need to be accomplished throughout the camp property.
- Be able to make the appropriate repairs.

Position Title: Food-Service Supervisor

Responsible to: Camp Director

General Responsibility: To oversee the food service and dining area of the Camp

Qualifications:
- A minimum of two years documented experience and training in foodservice management; previous camp experience preferable
- Emotionally mature
- Ability to manage and supervise subordinates
- Ability to relate well to children and other adults

Specific Responsibilities:
- Supervise all kitchen activities.
- Enforce all health standards and regulations established by the Department of Health, plus those deemed necessary by the camp director.
- Supervise the serving of all meals.
- Plan all menus according to healthful nutrition standards two weeks in advance for review by the camp director.
- Order all food and kitchen supplies; maintain costs within the prescribed budget.
- Provide for special food needs, such as cookouts, snacks, and special events, as well as for persons with special needs.
- Participate in the total camp program when appropriate, and as long as primary duties are not neglected.
- Be responsible for the health and welfare of campers.

Essential Functions:
- Have ability to operate gas, electrical, and mechanical equipment in the food-service area.
- Maintain accurate records (e.g., menus, food orders, inventories).
- Have visual ability to determine the cleanliness of the entire kitchen and dining room, and ability to supervise corrective action as needed.
- Possess physical strength to lift heavy pots and pans and to move food and supplies.
- Have ability to assess the condition of food upon preparation and in storage.
- Have ability to provide supervision to kitchen staff.

Appendix B:
Risk-Management Checklist
for Camp Personnel

Staff Recruitment

- Clear organizational chart showing who supervises whom
- Established ratios (in writing) for
  - ✓ Supervisor to supervisee
  - ✓ Counselor to campers
  - ✓ Program leaders to campers (may vary due to risks)
- Job description in writing
  - ✓ General responsibilities
  - ✓ Specific responsibilities
  - ✓ Essential functions
  - ✓ Qualifications
  - ✓ Revised (in writing) any time duties change or at least annually
- Written policies on remuneration
  - ✓ Time off
  - ✓ Insurance coverage
  - ✓ Meals/lodging credit toward minimum wage, if any
  - ✓ Minimum wage
  - ✓ Wages
  - ✓ Written job performance and appraisal processes

Screening

- Application
  - ✓ No gender questions, unless required for a specific job (e.g., cabin counselor)
  - ✓ No marital-status questions (may ask about housing needs for family in resident camp)
  - ✓ No race or national-origin questions
  - ✓ No religion questions, unless required for a specific job (e.g., religious education)
  - ✓ No disability questions, unless basis of essential functions of job
  - ✓ No specific age questions (may ask if over a specific age)
  - ✓ References (at least three)
    - ⇨ Specific to position skills
    - ⇨ Volunteer supervisors
    - ⇨ Specific to work with children
    - ⇨ Employers
  - ✓ Criminal background check and/or volunteer disclosure statement
  - ✓ Application updated by returning staff

- References checked
  - ✓ Form includes reference to work with children (if applicable)
  - ✓ Form includes reference to child abuse
  - ✓ Form includes reference to specific skill required for position
  - ✓ Mailed to each reference
  - ✓ Telephone call to references not received or questionable with written notes on call
- Interviews
  - ✓ Face-to-face
  - ✓ Telephone or second-hand, when face-to-face not possible
  - ✓ Questions outlined for interview in advance
  - ✓ Notes taken during interview
  - ✓ Specific questions around child abuse
  - ✓ Specific questions around drug use
  - ✓ Specific questions around discipline
- Employment agreement
  - ✓ Reviewed by legal counsel

Training

- Staff or employee manual
  - ✓ Statement of philosophy, mission, goals
  - ✓ Personnel policies
  - ✓ Sexual-harassment policy
- Precamp training
  - ✓ Written schedule
  - ✓ Specific sessions on
    - ⇨ Human development relative to age groups
    - ⇨ Risk management
    - ⇨ Disciplinary policy and practice
    - ⇨ Rules and regulations
    - ⇨ Training specific to each job's functions
  - ✓ Hazards and known risks
  - ✓ Abuse identification
  - ✓ Abuse of camper to camper, staff to camper
  - ✓ Abuse prevention
- Abuse allegations report requirements
- Documented
  - ✓ As to who led sessions
  - ✓ Content of sessions
  - ✓ Length of sessions
  - ✓ Who attended (sign-up sheet)

- Training provided for late hires or late arrivals (documented)
- Tools required by job
  - ✓ Provided
  - ✓ Training given in use and care
  - ✓ Protective devices, with training given in use of
- In-service training
  - ✓ Documented
    - ⇨ Dates
    - ⇨ Who led
    - ⇨ Material covered
    - ⇨ Who attended (sign-up sheet)
    - ⇨ Length of sessions

Supervision

- Each employee given information as to supervisor
- Plan for supervision
  - ✓ Observation
  - ✓ Written reprimands signed by supervisor
  - ✓ Formal conferences
  - ✓ Performance-appraisal system
  - ✓ Informal conferences
- Training provided supervisors
  - ✓ Uniform performance-appraisal system
  - ✓ Observation methods and recording
  - ✓ Appropriate/inappropriate staff behavior and consequences
  - ✓ Conference formats, recording, and techniques
- Plan for termination
  - ✓ Documented
  - ✓ Exit interview

Other

- OSHA
  - ✓ OSHA 101 form
  - ✓ OSHA poster
  - ✓ OSHA 200 form
  - ✓ MSDS sheets
- Personnel files
  - ✓ Application
  - ✓ Interview notes
  - ✓ Notes on references contacted by telephone
  - ✓ Voluntary disclosure statement or criminal background check
  - ✓ Exit interview, if terminated

- ✓ Job description, plus any documented changes
- ✓ Employment agreement
- ✓ Time cards, if applicable
- ✓ Attendance record
- ✓ References
- ✓ Supervisory notes
- ✓ Any written reprimands
- Master file for each year of
  - ✓ Staff/employee manual
  - ✓ Staff training outline/documentation
  - ✓ Supplemental training
  - ✓ List of staff by positions
  - ✓ Counselor/camper housing assignments
  - ✓ Health records
  - ✓ Incident reports
  - ✓ Health and safety bulletins
  - ✓ Emergency plans
  - ✓ Completed OSHA forms
- Staff health and accident records kept separate from personnel files

Appendix C: Organizational Resources

Adventure Programs/Challenge Courses

American Mountain Guides Association
P.O. Box 1739
Boulder, CO 80302
303-271-0984
303-271-1377 (fax)
www.amga.com

Association for Challenge Course Technology
P.O. Box 47
Deerfield, IL 60015
847-685-0670
847-325-5864 (fax)
acct@net-link.net
www.acctinfo.org

Association for Experiential Education
3775 Iris Avenue Ste. #4
Boulder, CO 80301
866-522-8337
303-440-9581 (fax)
info@aee.org
www.aee.org
www.princeton-edu/-curtis/aee
(journal, conferences, publications, accreditation program, and manual)

Experience Based Learning (EBL)
3634 Laura Lane
Rockford, IL 61114
815-637-2969
815-637-2964 (fax)
www.ebl.org

National Outdoor Leadership School (NOLS)
284 Lincoln Street
Lander, WY 82520
800-710-NOLS (6657)
307-332-1220 (fax)
www.nols.edu
(training programs)

Outward Bound National Office
100 Mystery Point Road
Garrison, NY 10524
866-467-4121
info@obusa.org
www.outwardbound.org

Project Adventure
701 Cabot Street
Beverly, MA 01915
978-524-4501
978-524-4505 (fax)
info@pa.org
www.pa.org
www.adventurebusiness.com
(publications, training, ropes courses)

Wilderness Education Association
900 East 7th Street
Bloomington, IN 47405
812-855-4095
812-855-8697 (fax)
wea@indiana.org
www.weainfo.org
(training, certification)

Aquatics

American Canoe Association
7432 Alban Station Boulevard,
Suite B232
Springfield, VA 22150-2311
800-929-5162
703-451-0141
703-451-2245 (fax)
www.aca-net.org
(journal, newsletter, books, maps, certification programs)

American Red Cross
2025 E Street NW
Washington, DC 20006
800-797-8022
202-303-4498
202-303-0044 (fax)
www.redcross.org
(certification, publications in swimming, boating, and first aid)

American Whitewater
P.O. Box 1540
Cullowhee, NC 28723
866-BOAT4AW
info@amwhitewater.org
www.whitewater.org

Aquatics International
Hanley-Wood, LLC
6222 Wilshire Boulevard, Suite 600
Los Angeles, CA 90048-5123
866-269-8410
www.aquaticsintl.com

Boy Scouts of America
(National Office)
1325 Walnut Hill Lane
P.O. Box 152079
Irving, TX 75015-2079
972-580-2000
www.scouting.org

Canadian Red Cross
170 Metcalfe Street, Suite 300
Ottawa, Ontario, K2P 2P2 Canada
613-740-1900
613-740-1911 (fax)
feedback@redcross.ca
www.redcross.ca

Ellis and Associates, Inc.
508 Goldenmoss Loop
Ocoee, FL 34761
800-742-8720
407-654-1723 (fax)
www.jellis.com
(safety inspections, lifeguard training, design
and safety consultation for new aquatic facilities)

Lifesaving Society—Canada
322 Consumers Road
Toronto, Ontario M2J 1P8
Canada
416-490-8840
416-490-8766 (fax)
experts@lifeguarding.com

National Association of Underwater Instructors
(NAUI)
P. O. Box 89789
Tampa, FL 33689-0413
800-553-6284
813-628-6284
813-628-8253 (fax)
nauihq@nauiww.org
www.naui.org
(training programs, certification)

National Organization for Rivers
212 West Cheyenne Mountain Blvd.
Colorado Springs, CO 80906
www.nationalrivers.org
719-579-8759
719-576-6238 (fax)
(publications)

PADI Americas (Scuba Diving Instructors)
30151 Tomas
Rancho Santa Margarita, CA 92688
949-858-7234
800-729-7234
webmaster@padi.com
www.padi.com
(training programs, certification)

Royal Life Saving Society (RLSS)—Australia
National Branch
P.O. Box 528
Broadway NSW 2007
Australia
61-02-8217-3111
61-02-8217-3199
info@rlssa.org.au
www.rlssa.org.au
(water-safety education, instructor manuals)

Lifesavers Royal Life Saving Society (RLSS)—
United Kingdom
River House, High Street
Broom, Warwickshire B50 4HN United Kingdom
44-1-789-773994
44-1-789-773995 (fax)
membership@rlss.org.uk
www.rlss.org.uk
(water-safety education, instructor manuals)

Scuba Schools International
2619 Canton Court
Ft. Collins, CO 80525-4498
970-482-0883
970-482-6157 (fax)
admin@ssiusa.com
www.ssiusa.com

U.S. Coast Guard
2100 Second Street SW
Washington, DC 20593-0001
202-267-2229
www.uscg.mil

U.S. Coast Guard
Office of Boating Safety
800-368-5647
800-689-0816 (TTY)
uscginfoline@gcrm.com
www.uscgboating.org
(magazine, publications)

U.S. Sailing Association
15 Maritime Drive
P.O. Box 1260
Portsmouth, RI 02871-0907
800-USSAIL1 (Ext. 1)
401-683-0800
401-683-0840 (fax)
info@ussailing.org
www.ussailing.org

U.S.A. Water Ski
1251 Holy Cow Road
Polk City, FL 33868
863-324-4341
863-325-8259 (fax)
usawaterski@uswaterski.org
www.usawaterski.org
(coaching clinics, nationwide clubs, water ski
kids' club, certification)

YMCA of the USA
101 North Wacker Drive, 14th Floor
Chicago, IL 60606
800-872-9622
312-9987-0031
312-977-1134 (fax)
fulfillment@ymca.net
www.ymca.net

Health, Wellness and Safety, Including First Aid/CPR

American Academy of Pediatrics
141 Northwest Point Boulevard
Elk Grove Village, IL 60007-1098
847-434-4000
847-434-8000 (fax)
kidsdocs@aap.org
www.aap.org
(professional association, advocacy,
research, publications)

*American Association for Leisure and Recreation Council
on Outdoor Adventure, Education and Recreation*
1900 Association Drive
Reston, VA 20191
703-476-3471
800-213-7193
703-476-9527 (fax)
www.aahperd.org/aalr
(journal, publications, conferences)

American Heart Association
7272 Greenville Avenue
Dallas, TX 75231-4596
877-AHA-4CPR (242-4277)
www.americanheart.org/cpr
(publications, research, courses)

American Red Cross
2025 E Street NW
Washington, DC 20006
800-797-8022
202-303-0044 (fax)
www.redcross.org
(certification, publications in swimming, boating,
and first aid)

American Safety and Health Institute
4670 Richmond Road
Warrensville Heights, OH 44128
800-246-5101
www.ashinstitute.com
(certification, first aid)

Association of Camp Nurses
8504 Thorsonveien NE
Bemidji, MN 56601
218-586-2633
218-586-8771 (fax)
acn@campnurse.org
www.campnurse.org
(workshops, conferences, publications, research,
consulting)

Centers for Disease Control (CDC)
1600 Clifton Road NE
Atlanta, GA 30333
888-246-2675
www.cdc.gov
(publications, research, statistics, training)

Medic First Aid International
1450 Westec Drive
Eugene, OR 97402
541-344-7099
800-800-7099
541-344-7429 (fax)
response@medicfirstaid.com
(first aid/CPR, certification)

National Fire Protection Association
P.O. Box 9101
Quincy, MA 02269-9101
617-770-3000
617-770-0700 (fax)
library@nfpa.org
www.nfpa.org
(publications)

National Safety Council
1121 Spring Lake Drive
Itasca, IL 60143-3201
800-621-7619
630-285-1315 (fax)
info@nsc.org
www.nsc.org
(publications)

NSF International
P.O. Box 130140
Ann Arbor, MI 48113-0140
877-867-3435
info@nsf.org
www.nsfconsumer.org
(information on food and drinking water safety, including
food service equipment, plumbing products, and water
treatment)

President's Council on Physical Fitness and Sports
HHH Building, Room 738H
200 Independence Avenue SW
Washington, DC 20201
202-690-9000
202-690-5211 (fax)
www.fitness.gov
(awards)

SOLO
P.O. Box 3150
Conway, NH 03818
603-447-6711
603-447-2310 (fax)
info@soloschools.com
www.soloschools.com
(wilderness-med certification)

Wilderness Medicine Associates
400 Riverside Drive
Suite A-6
Portland, ME 04103
207-297-6005
888-945-3633
207-797-6007 (fax)
office@wildmed.com
www.wildmed.com
(education, search and rescue, outdoor leadership, pre-
hospital medicine)

Wilderness Medicine Institute
National Outdoor Leadership School (NOLS)
284 Lincoln Street
Lander, WY 82520
800-710-NOLS (6657)
307-332-1220 (fax)
www.nols.edu
(training programs)

Horseback Riding

American Association for Horsemanship Safety
Headquarters and Training Center
4125 Fish Creek Road
Estes Park, CO 80510
865-485-6800
512-488-2319 (fax)
mail@horsemanshipsafety.com
www.horsemanshipsafety.com
(certification, seminars, workshops)

Certified Horsemanship Association
4037 Iron Works Parkway, Suite 18
Lexington, KY 40511
800-399-0138
859-355-0726 (fax)
pberger@cha-ahse.org
www.cha-ahse.org
(certification, job placement, insurance program, group
buying program, camp riding program guidelines)

National American Riding for the Handicapped
Association (NARHA)
P.O. Box 33150
Denver, CO 80233
800-369-7433
303-452-1212
303-252-4610 (fax)
www.narha.org

U.S. Pony Clubs, Inc.
Kentucky Horse Park
4041 Iron Works Pike
Lexington, KY 40511-8462
859-254-7669
859-233-4652 (fax)
uspc@ponyclub.org
www.uspc.org
(newsletter, publications, clinics)

Target Sports

Civilian Marksmanship Program
P.O. Box 576
Port Clinton, OH 43452
419-635-2141
888-267-0796
419-635-2573 (fax)
www.odcmp.com
(camp riflery programs)

National Field Archery Association
31407 Outer I-10
Redlands, CA 92373
800-811-2331
909-794-8512 (fax)
nfaa-archery@aol.com
www.NFAArchery.com
(magazine, youth archery program)

National Rifle Association of America
11250 Waples Mill Road
Fairfax, VA 22030
800-672-3888
membership@nrahq.org
www.nrahq.org
(range operations, safety standards, teaching marksmanship, activities)

USA Archery (National Archery Association)
1 Olympic Plaza
Colorado Springs, CO 80909
719-866-4576
719-632-4733 (fax)
info@usaarchery.org
www.usaarchery.org
(certification, training)

Youth Organizations

4-H
National Headquarters
CCREES/USDA
1400 Independence Avenue SW
Stop 2225
Washington, DC 20250-2225
202-720-2908
202-720-0366 (fax)
4hhq@csrees.usda.gov
www.4h-usa.org

Boys and Girls Clubs of America
1273 West Peachtree Street NW
Atlanta, GA 30309
404-815-5700
404-815-5727 (fax)
info@bgca.org
www.bgca.org

Boy Scouts of America
(National Office)
1325 Walnut Hill Lane
P.O. Box 152079
Irving, TX 75015-2079
972-580-2000
www.scouting.org
(educational programs, character building)

Camp Fire USA
1100 Walnut Street, Suite 1900
Kansas City, MO 64106-2197
816-825-2010
816-285-9444 (fax)
info@campfireusa.org
www.campfireusa.org

Child Welfare League of America
2345 Crystal Drive, Suite 250
Arlington, VA 22202
703-472-8400
703-472-2401 (fax)

Girl Scouts of the USA
420 Fifth Avenue
New York, NY 10018-2798
800-478-7248
www.girlscouts.org

JCC Association
520 Eighth Avenue
New York, NY 10018
212-532-4949
info@jcca.org
www.jcca.org

Pioneer Ministries
220 Hofstra University
Hampstead, NY 11549
516-463-5808
516-463-6275 (fax)
hprneh@hofstra.edu
www.hofstra.edu

YMCA of the USA
101 North Wacker Drive
Chicago, IL 60606
800-872-9622
312-977-1134 (fax)
www.ymca.net

YWCA of the USA
1015 18th Street NW, Suite 1100
Washington, D.C. 20036
202-467-0801
202-467-0802
www.ywca.org

Other Professional Organizations

American Camp Association, Inc.
5000 State Road 67 North
Martinsville, IN 46151-7902
765-342-8456
765-342-2065 (fax)
888-229-5745 (bookstore)
pr@acacamps.org
www.ACAcamps.org
(Camping Magazine, catalog of publications, accreditation, conferences)

Canadian Camping Association
2494 Route 124 Sud Street
Donat, QC J0T 2C0, Canada
877-427-6958
819-424-2662
819-424-4145 (fax)
info@ccamping.org
www.ccamping.org
(journal, provincial conferences, accreditation)

Christian Camp and Conference Association
P.O. Box 62189
Colorado Springs, CO 80962-2189
719-260-9400
719-260-6398 (fax)
info@ccca.org
www.ccca.org
(journal, newsletter, conferences, publications)

International Association of Conference Center Administrators
5976 20th Street, Suite 80
Vero Beach FL 32966
772-562-4017
jabegley@aol.com
www.iacca.org
(magazine, directory, workshops, conference)

National Association of Therapeutic Wilderness Camps
264 Brown Hill Road
Marklesburg, PA 15459
724-329-1098
natwc@qcot.net
www.natwc.org

National Recreation and Parks Association
22377 Belmont Ridge Road
Ashburn, VA 20148
703-858-0784
703-858-0794 (fax)
info@nrpa.org
www.nrpa.org
(journal, conventions, publications)

Other Program Resources

Adventure Cycling Association
P.O. Box 5308
Missoula, MT 58907
800-755-2453
406-721-8754 (fax/phone)
info@adventurecycling.org
www.adv-cycling.org

American Bicycle Association
P.O. Box 718
Chandler, AZ 85244
www.ababmx.com

American Hiking Society
1422 Fenwick Lane
Silver Spring, MD 20910
301-565-6704
301-565-6714 (fax)
ahs-webmaster@c-t-g.com
www.americanhiking.org

Bicycle Helmet Safety Institute
4611 Seventh Street South
Arlington, VA 22204-1419
703-486-0100
info@helmets.org
www.helmets.org

Environmental Protection Agency
Ariel Riso Building
1200 Pennsylvania Avenue NW
Washington, D.C. 20640
202-272-0167
www.epa.gov
(President's Environmental Youth Awards—PEYA;
Environmental Explorer's Club)

National Association of Rocketry
P.O. Box 407
Marion, IA 52302
800-262-4872
nar-hq@nar.org
www.nar.org

National Audubon Society
700 Broadway
New York, NY 10003
212-979-3000
212-979-3188 (fax)
education@audubon.org
www.audubon.org
(magazine)

National Speleological Society, Inc.
1813 Cave Avenue
Huntsville, AL 35810-4413
205-852-1300
nss@caves.org
www.caves.org

National Wildlife Federation
8925 Leesburg Pike
Vienna, VA 22184-0001
800-822-9919
www.nwf.org
(magazines, publications)

USA Gymnastics
Pan American Plaza
201 S. Capitol Avenue, #300
Indianapolis, IN 46255
800-345-4719
317-237-5069 (fax)
admin@usa-gymnatics.org
www.usa-gymnastics.org

U. S. Golf Association
P.O. Box 708
Far Hills, NJ 07931
908-234-2300
908-234-0000 (fax)
www.usga.org

Target Populations—Accessibility

American Association of People With Disabilities
18 Harvard Drive
Milford, MA 01757
866-241-3200
mail@aapd.com
www.aapd.com

Americans With Disabilities Act (ADA)
U. S. Department of Justice
950 Pennsylvania Avenue NW
Washington, D. C. 20530
800-514-0301 (technical info line)
800-514-0383 (TTY)
202-307-1198 (fax)
www.usdoj.gov/crt/drssec.htm

National Center for Accessibility
501 N. Morton Street, Suite 109
Bloomington, IN 47404
812-856-4422
812-856-4480 (fax)
nca@indiana.edu
www.nca.org

U. S. Access Board
1331 F Street NW, #1000
Washington, DC 20004-1111
800-USA-ABLE (872-2253)
800-993-2822 (TTY)
800-272-0081 (fax)
202-272-5447 (fax)
www.access-board.gov

Appendix D: International Resources

Many camps are interested in adding an element of cultural exchange to their programs. Often this includes recruiting international cultural-exchange visitors to serve on the camp's staff. The U.S. Department of State (USDS) offers a special visa for internationals to come to the United States and participate as camp counselors and in other support positions at camp. This J-1 visa is only granted through organizations that have been identified by the USDS as "sponsors" of the program. Camps work with these organizations to implement the cultural exchange program and recruit these international visitors.

The American Camp Association has developed best practices for camps that utilize international exchange visitors. These best practices focus on compliance with the USDS rules, supporting the international exchange visitor, and providing a meaningful cultural exchange program for your campers, your visitors, and your American staff. The best practices (as of August 2011) are included in this appendix. Updated as the regulations change, the best practices can also be found online at: www.acacamps.org/international/practices.

Sponsors of the J-1 visa program are identified by the USDS and can be found on the USDS Web site at: http://j1visa.state.gov/participants/how-to-apply/sponsor-search/?program=Camp Counselor. Many of these organizations are business affiliates of the American Camp Association, and as such, work closely with ACA to develop educational resources for camps interested in utilizing cultural exchange visitors. ACA's business affiliates are listed in our Buyer's Guide online at: www.acacamps.org/buyers-guide. We encourage camps to work with these organizations as they have a commitment to supporting and following the best practices.

Best Practices for International Staff in American Camp Association Camps

Updated August 2011

The availability of international staff for job placement in the United States is made possible by a number of organizations that are formally designated as cultural exchange program sponsors by the U.S. Department of State's Bureau of Educational and Cultural Affairs. Over the last several decades, the employment of international staff has evolved from a value-added opportunity into a vital cultural resource for many American summer camps. As this trend continues, we must take care not to lose sight of the cultural exchange dimension of these programs. It is also important to remember that these governmental programs carry with them a number of regulatory obligations that all parties involved, including international staff, camps, and sponsoring agencies, must meet. Compliance with these regulations will help to ensure that the delicate balance between concerns for homeland security and support for cultural exchange is maintained.

American Camp Association (ACA) volunteers and staff meet regularly with the leaders of the international cultural exchange organizations that work with the camp community. This relationship has allowed ACA to promote the benefits of cultural exchange programs while monitoring public policy issues that affect these programs. Taking a unified approach with the agencies that recruit and screen young people from other countries for work at American camps also allows ACA to address emerging issues and trends and better understand the needs and expectations of participating camps. In addition, we have enumerated exemplary practices (i.e., those that display a higher degree of commitment to the education and welfare of international staff and to the tenets of cultural exchange). This document provides the best practices as either "expected practices" or "exemplary practices."

As camp professionals, we unite to address a wide array of environmental, educational, legal, and financial issues. We set standards to which we hold ourselves accountable, and we understand the moral and ethical aspects of conducting an enterprise that is essentially human in nature. It is reasonable, therefore, that we identify and engage in best practice as we employ counselors and support staff from other countries. Moreover, following such practices is consistent with ACA's mission of "… enriching the lives of children, youth, and adults through the camp experience."

We are proud of the fact that many camp programs already make extensive use of these practices. Whether you currently employ international staff, or plan to do so in the future, we hope that this guide serves as a useful tool for benchmarking current methods and procedures. We look forward to ongoing cooperation with camps and international staffing agencies as we maximize and enhance our use of this highly important human resource and celebrate the youth development opportunities that these programs provide.

For the most current information about the U.S. Department of State's J-1 visa program, visit: http://j1visa.state.gov/basics/. For a list of the international cultural exchange organizations that are ACA Business Affiliates, visit: www.acacamps.org/buyers-guide.

The following "best practices" have been identified as those that directly contribute to the success of the cultural exchange experience for camps, staff, and the campers they serve. They also support the legal and regulatory obligations of the exchange visa program.

THE CAMP

Administrative Practices

Expected practices of directors:

- Understand that the purpose of the J-1 visa program is cultural exchange, and implement that philosophy.
- Understand and comply with the regulatory opportunities and limitations of the J-1 visa program.
- Establish a strong relationship with the sponsoring agency (or agencies) you have selected.

- Complete SEVIS validation for arriving staff promptly in accordance with sponsoring agency procedures.
- Assist international staff in obtaining a Social Security card.
- Provide appropriate wages and access to money owed. (Be aware that checks may be hard for international staff to cash. Offer help with that process!)
- Provide worker's compensation insurance in accordance with state laws and regulations.
- Develop and implement a crisis plan for dealing with the injury, arrest, or death of an international staff member.
- Develop and implement policies that include providing immediate notification to the sponsoring agency of any personnel action, including changes to location/site within the organization, or any emergency situation involving an international staff member.

Exemplary practices of directors:

- Feature cultural programming at camp.
- Showcase international programs and staff in camp marketing materials.

Hiring Process

Expected practices of directors:

- Define and articulate why your camp wants to include international staff (other than to fill vacancies).
- Interview international applicants on the phone prior to hiring.
- Be thorough in evaluating candidates and selecting staff.
- Spend as much time on the hiring process as you would with American staff.
- Be forthright in matching candidates' skills and interests with the camp's staffing needs.
- Provide clear expectations of staff while at camp.

Exemplary practices of directors:

- Define and articulate how inclusion of international staff fits into your camp philosophy.
- Avoid stereotyping nationalities by demonstrating a willingness to hire international staff from all countries and use them in all positions.

After Hiring—Prior to Camp

Expected practices of directors:

- Communicate with the staff member by phone or e-mail before they arrive at camp.
- Through regular post or e-mail, provide information such as policies, handbooks, organizational charts, maps, weather reports, lists of what

to bring, camp website information, orientation/training schedules, job descriptions, camper profiles, rules and regulations, camp mission statement, time-off policies, transportation-to-town options, e-mail address of a mentor/buddy, local attractions/local community info, etc.

- Present a realistic picture of the camp and establish expectations (i.e., help with understanding life in the community, sleeping accommodations, typical menus).

Exemplary practices of directors:

- Provide opportunities for networking with former international staff from their home country (e.g., share e-mail addresses of former camp staff).

Arrival and Precamp

Expected practices of directors:

- Provide comfortable and efficient transportation to camp from the orientation site.
- Welcome international staff upon arrival.
- Show sensitivity to time and cultural adjustments.
- Provide adequate housing that is welcoming and clean, including fresh linens and bedding.
- Provide additional orientation/training for international staff to help them with cultural adjustments.
- Make an active effort to integrate the entire staff into one group.
- Show sensitivity to language issues.
- Demonstrate in training an understanding of cultural differences (i.e., differences in hygiene, fashions, customs).
- Provide responsible education/orientation and training for understanding and competence.
- Show sensitivity to food issues, health/stamina issues, allergies, and cultural and religious practices (e.g., lactose intolerance, halal, or kosher diet).

Exemplary practices of directors:

- Demonstrate an attitude of: "I care about you and want you to have a successful summer."
- Provide training to American staff on the purpose of the J-1 visa program and how to create a successful international team.
- Utilize a contact/liaison on the camp staff who understands international issues.
- Develop a buddy/mentor system.

During the Summer

Expected practices of directors:

- Provide positive feedback and reinforcement.

- Continue to acknowledge and work with language differences.
- Help arrange transportation on time off.
- Continue to partner with the sponsoring agency on any problems or issues that arise.
- Show sensitivity to financial issues (e.g., cashing checks).
- Provide a secure place for storing important documents and other valuable items.
- Provide access to the Internet, e-mail, and a telephone.
- Treat all staff as adults; treat support staff the same as program staff.
- Have trained/competent supervisors.
- Create open lines of communication between the director and international staff.
- Demonstrate a commitment to working with international staff and an understanding of cultural differences.
- Provide ongoing training and support.
- Provide cultural programming as a part of the camp's activities.
- Show sensitivity to health issues (i.e., access to doctors, dentists, medications).
- Encourage staff to obey the rules of the program and to return to their home country after the summer.
- Support the rules governing the J-1 visa program, which restricts switching staff between support and counseling roles.
- Develop a program of training and support to solve problems, using a fair termination policy as a last resort and after consultation with the sponsoring agency.
- Provide opportunities for out-of-camp recreational and/or touristic experiences.
- Make provisions for international staff to do their laundry.
- Provide equal access to camp activities and facilities to all staff members.
- Treat American and international staff equally, especially in number of hours required to work and adequate time off.

Exemplary practices of directors:

- Provide outstanding cultural programming.
- Provide international staff with access to food, drinks, and newspapers from their home country.
- Provide opportunities to show multi-national diversity at camp.
- Feature international staff and programming in camp media and marketing materials.
- Identify and work with local families or alumni to help integrate international staff into the local community.
- Provide international staff with equal access to key positions and leadership opportunities.
- Help with arranging transportation postcamp.

THE SPONSORING AGENCY

Expected practices of agencies:

- Understand, monitor, and comply with all issues, regulations, and requirements of the J-1 cultural exchange Camp Counselor and Summer Work Travel programs.
- Conduct thorough in-person interviews with every applicant using a suitable and qualified interviewer.
- Recruit applicants with a good level of English proficiency.
- Conduct thorough and in-depth pre-departure and/or arrival orientation.
- Provide twenty-four hour emergency support for applicants during their J-1 visa term.
- Provide camps with as much information as possible on applicants.
- Provide applicants with information about American culture as well as different types of camps, the nature of camp life, and working with children.
- Check references to ensure quality applicants are being accepted.
- Require participants to provide a criminal background check and provide help for this when necessary.
- Place participants at camps and in positions best suited to their skills, interests, background, and experience.

Exemplary practices of agencies:

- Ensure that staff placed as camp counselors understand they will be working with children and are suitable candidates to do so.
- Encourage camps to hire participants from a variety of countries.
- Provide camps with information about participants' countries of origin and cultural background.
- Educate camps on the best way to host international staff.
- Provide readily accessible and quality ongoing care, advice, and support for participants and camps during the summer, including camp visiting, monitoring, and collecting of feedback.
- Monitor and evaluate the quality of the experience provided to international staff by each camp and work with camps and participants to improve the overall program experience and level of agency service.

THE AMERICAN CAMP ASSOCIATION

Expected practices of ACA:

- Monitor public policy issues related to the J-1 visa exchange program and keep camp professionals informed of these policies.
- Maintain J-1 visa regulatory and legislative issues as a priority focus of ACA's public policy work.
- Facilitate communication with and among sponsoring agencies.

- Promote the benefits of cultural exchange programs to camps as well as to the general public.
- Develop and track statistical information that is of value to camps, the agencies, and ACA.

Exemplary practices of ACA:

- Provide educational resources to help camp professionals address international staff issues.

Appendix E: Government Resources

Essential Area	Federal Government Agency	State Agency/Department *(if applicable)*
Business and Finance		
Business Development	Small Business Administration (SBA) www.sba.gov Minority Business Development Agency www.mbda.gov	
Foreign Funds	Export-Import Bank of the United States www.exim.gov	
Government Grants	Federal Grants www.grants.gov	
Loans	Small Business Administration (SBA) www.sba.gov	
Taxes	Internal Revenue Service (IRS) www.irs.gov	Revenue (Taxation, Assessor)
Licenses/Permits		
Varies by state, for each state, visit: www.acacamps.org/publicpolicy/regulations		
Food Services		
Food Safety	United States Department of Agriculture (USDA) www.usda.gov USDA Food Safety and Inspection Service www.fsis.usda.gov	Local Health Department
Summer Food Service Program	United States Department of Agriculture (USDA) www.usda.gov	State Child Nutrition Programs: http://www.fns.usda.gov/cnd/Contacts/StateDirectory.htm
Health and Wellness		
Health	Department of Health and Human Services (DHHS) www.hhs.gov Centers For Disease Control (CDC) www.cdc.gov , and Let's Move: www.letsmove.gov	Health (Environmental Resources, Environmental Health, Health and Sanitation)
Medication Management	Food and Drug Administration (FDA) www.fda.gov	Local Health Department
Septic Tanks Water Systems	Centers For Disease Control (CDC) www.cdc.gov	Health (Environmental Resources, Environmental Health, Health and Sanitation)
Human Resources		
Labor Regulations, Work Permit	Department of Labor (DOL) www.dol.gov	Labor
Employment Practices	Equal Opportunity Employment Commission (EEOC) www.eeoc.gov	
Employment Services	Department of Labor (DOL) www.dol.gov	Labor

Essential Area	Federal Government Agency	State Agency/Department (if applicable)
FICA	Social Security Administration www.ssa.gov	Labor
International Staff	Department of State, J-1 Visa Program www.state.gov	
Minimum Wage, Overtime	Department of Labor www.dol.gov	Labor
Unemployment Compensation (FUTA/SUTA)	Department of Labor www.dol.gov	Labor
Workers' Compensation	Department of Labor www.dol.gov	Labor
Leadership		
Small Business Administration www.sba.gov		
Marketing		
Small Business Administration www.sba.gov		
Mission and Outcomes		
Small Business Administration www.sba.gov		
Participant Development and Behavior		
Department of Health and Human Services www.hhs.gov		
Program Design and Activities		
Boating	Coast Guard (if in the USCG jurisdiction) www.uscg.mil	Department of Natural Resources
Conservation and Environmental Education	Environmental Protection Agency www.epa.gov	
Firearms	Bureau of Alcohol, Tobacco, Firearms, and Explosives www.atf.gov	
Fishing	Department of Interior: Fish and Wildlife Services www.doi.gov	Department of Natural Resources: Fish and Game/Environmental Protection
Aviation Programs	Federal Aviation Administration (FAA) www.faa.gov	
Hunting	Department of Interior: Fish and Wildlife Services www.fws.gov	Department of Natural Resources: Fish and Game/Environmental Protection
Radio	Federal Communications Commission (FCC) www.fcc.gov	
Sports and Fitness	President's Council on Physical Fitness and Sports www.fitness.gov Let's Move www.letsmove.gov	
Risk Management		
Occupational Safety	Occupational Safety and Health Administration (OSHA) www.osha.gov	Labor

Essential Area	Federal Government Agency	State Agency/Department *(if applicable)*
Site and Facilities		

Accommodations (ADA)
  Dining Facility
  Housing
  Restrooms
	Department of Justice: Civil Rights Division www.usdoj.gov
	Office of American Disabilities Act www.ada.gov
	Department of Transportation www.dot.gov
	Federal Communications Commission www.fcc.gov
	Architectural and Transportation Barriers Compliance Board www.access-board.gov	

Building
  Codes
  Electrical
  Inspections
  Plumbing
		City/County/State Building Departments

Environment (Pollution, Spills, etc.)	Environmental Protection Agency www.epa.gov	Environmental Protection
Soil Conservation/Erosion	Department of Agriculture: Forest Service www.fs.fed.us	Department of Natural Resources
Water	Environmental Protection Agency www.epa.gov	Health
Strategic Planning		
Small Business Administration www.sba.gov		
Target Population and Diversity		
Camper Assistance Funds	Department of Health and Human Services (DHHS) www.hhs.gov	Public Welfare
Persons With Disabilities	Department of Justice, Office of American Disabilities Act www.ada.gov	Civil Rights
Transportation		

Vehicles
  Registration
  Licenses Operator's
  Licenses
  Inspections
	Department of Transportation www.dot.gov
	National Highway Traffic Safety Administration www.nhtsa.dot.gov
		Department of Motor Vehicles

Appendix F: Precamp Training Topics

The codes following each topic refer to specific ACA Standards for Accreditation. Some of the topics will vary from camp to camp, depending on the philosophy and program of the camp.

Site and Food Service

- Proper handling of flammable or poisonous materials (e.g., kerosene, cleaning agents) (SF.2)
- Required general maintenance routines (e.g., cleaning, reporting maintenance problems) (SF.7)
- Proper handling and use of power tools (SF.8)
- Food preparation, storage, and handling procedures (SF.19 through SF.23)

Transportation

- Procedures in case of accident during transportation (TR.1, TR.7)
- Safety procedures for traffic control, orderly arrival and departure, and for loading and unloading of vehicles (TR.4)
- Transportation of persons in non-passenger vehicles (TR.2)
- Transportation policies that specify supervision ratios of staff to campers, availability and location of health information, and permission-to-treat forms
- (TR.6)
- Orientation of safety regulations and procedures in vehicles provided for passengers (TR.8 through TR.9)
- Safety check procedures and mechanical evaluation (TR.12, TR.13)
- Training for vehicle drivers (TR.15)

Health and Wellness (HW.13)

- Procedures for informing staff of special needs of campers (HW.13)
- Responsibilities of staff for camper health care (HW.4)
- Providing health care and emergency treatment when out of camp and appropriate recordkeeping (HW.3, HW.22)
- Availability and use of AED (HW.17)
- Storage of prescription and nonprescription drugs at camp (HW.18)

Operational Management

- Procedures for dealing with possible intruders (OM.7)
- Emergency and safety procedures (OM.6, OM.8 through OM.12)
- Policy and procedures covering personal property (OM.4)
- Smoking policy
- Completing incident and accident reports (OM.17)

- Missing persons procedures (OM.10)
- Camper release procedures (OM.13)

Human Resources (HR.11 through HR.13)

- Staff training in diversity (HR.11)
- Training for their particular job (HR.10)
- Personnel policies (HR.7, HR.21)
- Camper-staff ratios (HR.8)
- Supervision of general camp activities (HR.15)
- Staff-camper interaction (HR.16)
- Behavior management (HR.17)
- Sensitive issue policy (HR.18)
- Supervision of staff (HR.19)
- Supervisor training (HR.19)

Program Design and Activities

- Procedures for overnights and trips (PD.9)
- Environmental policies, practices, and program (PD.14, PD.1, PD.7)
- Program equipment availability and care (PD.8, PD.38)
- Use of program equipment (PD.8)
- Program goals and outcomes (PD.1, PD.5)
- Emergency information (PD.10)
- Procedures for out-of-camp activities (PD.11, PD.38, PD.39)
- Operating procedures for each specialized activity (PD.13, PD.15, PD.16, PD.20, PD.25 through PD.29, PD.31 as well as the following standards when the following activities are operated: Adventure/Challenge— PD.8, PD.12, PD.13, PD.15, PD.16, PD.18 through PD.21, PD.24, PD.29, PD.38, PD.39; Horseback Riding—PD.8, PD.15 through PD.18, PD.20, PD.22, PD.29 through PD.39; and the entire sections of Aquatics—PA and Trip and Travel—PT)
- Procedures for controlled access of activity areas (PD.12)
- Safety orientation for participants (PD.18)
- Competency demonstration (PD.19)

Appendix G: Sample Personnel Hiring Log

Sample Personnel Hiring Log

Applicant's name: _____

Position sought: _____

Application Information

Date application received: _____

Certifications received: _____ Date _____

_____   _____

_____   _____

_____   _____

_____   _____

_____   _____

Criminal Background Checks

Date criminal background records check requested from:
Local: _____ State: _____ Federal: _____

Date criminal background information received from:
Local: _____ State: _____ Federal: _____

and/or Volunteer Disclosure Form received: _____

References and Employment

Date requests for references sent: _____ Dates references received: _____

Reference #1: _____

Reference #2: _____

Reference #3: _____

	Date Past Employment Requested	Verification Received
Employer #1	_____	_____
Employer #2	_____	_____
Employer #3	_____	_____
Employer #4	_____	_____

Personal Interview

Person doing interview: _____

Date interview completed: _____

Job Offer

Date employment agreement sent: _____

Date signed agreement received: _____

Other Information Requested After Hire

Date health records received: _____

Date I-9 received: _____

Date W-2 received: _____

Reasonable accommodations requested: _____

Other Notes

_____

_____

_____

_____

_____

_____

_____

_____

Index

About the Authors

Armand Ball, a native of Louisiana, has spent most of his adult life in organized camping as director of faith-based and YMCA camps in Florida, Tennessee, Texas, and Minnesota, and then as chief executive of the American Camp Association. Currently, a resident of Sanibel Island, Florida, he has been active in the local conservation foundation, the city's below-market-rate housing foundation board, the city's park and recreation committee, and the board of the Center for Environmental and Sustainability Education of Florida Gulf Coast University. Listed in Who's Who in America since 1980.

Armand was one of the founders of the International Camping Fellowship, and he served on its steering committee and as editor of their newsletter for a decade. He is now an emeritus member of the steering committee.

Beverly Ball, a native of Mississippi, has served in various positions in faith-based and YMCA camps in Tennessee and Minnesota, as well as a trainer for Girl Scouts of the USA at the local and national level. Her professional career has included work as a high school teacher, church youth director, director of college faith-related student activities, and publications director for the American Camp Association. She has been active as a volunteer in conservation and wildlife organizations, including the J. N. "Ding" Darling National Wildlife Refuge on Sanibel Island.

From 1988 to 2009, Armand and Beverly have worked as Alpha Beta consultants with camps and organizations, as well as teaching training courses for camp directors across the United States and in Australia, Bermuda, Canada, Japan, Malaysia, Mexico, Russia, and Venezuela. Their text, *Basic Camp Management* is available in English, Japanese, Portuguese, and Russian, with an edition pending in Georgian and Spanish.